PERSPECTIVES
ON CRIME AND JUSTICE

Joseph A. Schafer,
Series Editor

DEMYSTIFYING THE
BIG HOUSE

EXPLORING PRISON EXPERIENCE AND MEDIA REPRESENTATIONS

WITHDRAWN
UTSA LIBRARIES

Edited by KATHERINE A. FOSS

Southern Illinois University Press
Carbondale

Southern Illinois University Press
www.siupress.com

Publication of this book has been underwritten by the Elmer H. Johnson and
Carol Holmes Johnson criminology fund.

Cover illustrations: camera (image altered) by Kaique Rocha, from Pexels;
prison (cropped and altered) by Andrea Cappiello, from Unsplash.

Cover design by Nick Pellman

Library of Congress Cataloging-in-Publication Data
Names: Foss, Katherine A., 1980–
Title: Demystifying the big house : exploring prison experience and media
representations / edited by Katherine A. Foss.
Description: Carbondale : Southern Illinois University Press, [2018] | Series:
Perspectives on crime and justice | Includes bibliographical references and
index.
Identifiers: LCCN 2017042995 | ISBN 9780809336579 (pbk. : alk. paper) |
ISBN 9780809336586 (e-book)
Subjects: LCSH: Prisons in mass media. | Prisoners—United States. |
Reformatories for women.
Classification: LCC HV9471 .D395 2018 | DDC 791.45/6556—dc23 LC
record available at https://lccn.loc.gov/2017042995

Printed on recycled paper. ♲

To Eric, Nora, and Hazel

Thank you for giving me the time to write
and making me smile when it's time to play.

Contents

Preface

I love television. I am admittedly an avid fan of most genres, including reality shows and sitcoms. Even more so, I am hooked on fictional crime dramas—*CSI*, *Criminal Minds*, *Bones*, and others. My interest in prison representations stems from my research on victim portrayals, as the "next step" in the fictional justice system. I will confess that despite how theoretically problematic familiar archetypes and narratives are in prison films and TV programs, I enjoy the characters and story lines that they bring. I never tire of *The Shawshank Redemption* and silently cheer at other victorious escapes from the "big house." It has never bothered me that actual inmates likely do not routinely perform jazz numbers like "Cell Block Tango" or dream about "Big Rock Candy Mountain." So when *Orange Is the New Black* debuted on Netflix, I binge-watched the show, quickly becoming fascinated with the complex characters and fictionalized world of Piper Kerman's memoirs.

Of course, as a media studies professor, my interest led to research. In August 2015, three media scholars and I presented on a panel at the Association for Education in Journalism and Mass Communication's annual conference. In the session "*Orange Is the New Black*: Redefining Gender, Sexuality & Difference through Prison Representations," we each critiqued the media text from different perspectives, all the while sharing our mutual love of the popular show. At the same conference, I attended a session in another division, in which Kalen Churcher discussed her ethnographic work on media produced in prison. The competing discourses I encountered between our session and Churcher's study sparked the idea for this edited volume—a chance to bring together scholars across disciplines, unified by an interest in cultural studies approaches to prison research.

I am grateful to all of the contributors to this book, not only for their diligent work but also for sharing their unique experiences. At Middle Tennessee State University, I have appreciated discussion and support from students, colleagues, and administrators, including Dean Ken Paulson, Associate Dean Zeny Panol, and the School of Journalism director, Dr. Greg Pitts. I would also like to thank Dr. Tanya Peres for providing feedback, encouragement, and understanding. Finally, I need to acknowledge my family for their direct and indirect support (Eric), their willingness to discuss this project with me (Kristi), and the many pleasant distractions they provided (Nora and Hazel).

Demystifying the Big House

Introduction: Uniting Media, Prison, and Experience

Katherine A. Foss

In 1955 Johnny Cash wrote and recorded "Folsom Prison Blues," a song that became immensely popular, especially with incarcerated audiences.[1] Despite his reputation as a lawbreaker, Johnny Cash never served a prison sentence but wrote his famous lyrics after watching a fictional film on penitentiary life.[2] From a critical view, then, Cash's song epitomizes media's dominant carceral representation, as it is voiced through a Caucasian male, written without actual experience, and fiercely anecdotal, removing the prisoner from the institution.

When most people think of prison, they imagine popular culture's stereotypes of "Folsom Prison Blues" and archetypes depicted in other songs, literature, film, and television: picturing the crooked warden, or a sadistic guard thumping his nightstick into a sweaty palm, eager to deliver off-the-books "justice" to some "new fish." One might think of inmates, stereotyped as a "snitch," the thong-wearing femme, Mafia king, skinhead gang member, or the "butch dyke" ruling the roost as she lures an unsuspecting mousy virgin under her wing. Through the fictional lens, prison meals consist of maggot-filled gruel served on clanging metal trays. Days are spent on the chain gang, where inmates use short-handled shovels to dig continuously at a Ford-modeled labor of futility—broken up with time in solitary, a bleak hole of despair. Riots break out regularly between rival gangs, shutting out guards to leave prisoners fending for themselves, as inmates secretly dig tunnels or orchestrate other means of breaking out.

Or people may imagine the comic spin on the incarcerated life: "Prison Mike" of *The Office* describing "the Dementors," episodic sitcom story lines of protagonists briefly spending time in holding cells (e.g., Sheldon's arrest for questioning a judge in *The Big Bang Theory*), or the town drunk "sleeping it

off" in the local jail, like Otis in *The Andy Griffith Show*. Even children's popular culture products play on the "jail" theme, as illustrated by Lego's "Prison
Island," a 754-plastic-brick masterpiece complete with all the "tools" need
for an Alcatraz-level escape, including a tiny crowbar and a hot air balloon.

In real life, most inmates' experiences are far more mundane, with bore-
dom punctuated by meals and meager-paying jobs. More than 1.5 million
inmates are currently housed in state and federal correctional facilities in
the United States, with an additional 4.7 million under "community supervision."[3] Even more disturbing, 57,190 children and adolescents are serving
sentences in juvenile facilities—a number that has declined but remains
high.[4] A disproportionate number are people of color, with 59 percent of
male prisoners identified as African American or Hispanic.[5] In female correctional facilities, Caucasian women outnumber the combined population
of Hispanic and African American female offenders.[6]

Criminals themselves are less exciting. News and entertainment media
profoundly overestimate the rates of violent offenders, when in real life,
inmates convicted of drug offenses far outnumber those convicted of violent crimes in the federal system. Contrary to popular culture's depictions,
significantly more people are serving time for drug offenses (50 percent of
the federal inmate population) than for violent crimes (only 7 percent).[7]
Moreover, media discourse emphasizes justice and punishment, largely ignoring prison rehabilitation and programs to reduce recidivism. The Prison
Communication, Activism, Research, and Education (PCARE) collective
highlights this impact: "The ubiquity of mass-mediated representations of
crime and criminals means that the consciousness of the nation is flooded
with images provided by and usually supporting the policies of the prison-industrial complex."[8] As a result, attention has been given to individual
crimes and prisoners, eschewing problems within the prison system itself.

Scholars have noted the extensive inaccuracies of these media texts, which
misrepresent prison life as they stereotype inmates, guards, wardens, and
others who work in the system, painting a false picture of incarceration.[9]
Unfortunately, these distorted messages are the general public's primary source
of information about the prison experience. As Michelle Brown articulated,
"Americans choose when and under what conditions they would prefer to see
prisons and, in the particularity of that engagement, invoke and reproduce
specific kinds of logics and explanatory frameworks . . . the majority of citizens
are much more likely to screen the prison rather than visit it."[10] Thus, for the
public, the prison experience is a constructed one, distant from the authentic

life behind bars. Positioned as a "penal spectator," a person can view prison life through an abstracted lens, firmly "secure in his or her place with sovereignty and the opportunity to exercise exclusionary judgment from afar."[11] Building on Brown's work, Ross labeled the consumption of carceral narratives "prison voyeurism," which, as he argued, "tends to reinforce the myths and stereotypes of correctional facilities, inmates, and correctional officers."[12] Media and other institutions perpetuate these myths, creating a false reality about crime, prisoners, correctional officers, and the prison system itself.[13]

Formulas and generic conventions of fictional drama may explain some of the exaggeration, as Hollywood has long attracted viewers by playing on preconceived notions of the incarcerated life.[14] At the same time, gatekeeping has also hindered journalists and other writers from attaining accurate understandings of the penitentiary experience. Sussman explained how prison restrictions have hindered journalists' access to, and therefore coverage of, incarceration.[15] Additionally, news media "have often indulged in distortion and self-censorship in their coverage of crime, prisons, and prisoners, sometimes in response to the presumed demands of the marketplace," according to Sussman.[16] This gatekeeping, then, has contributed to the narrow discourse in media that perpetuates outdated stereotypes and ignores more in-depth and complex investigation.

Academic work has primarily featured either media criticism or ethnography, with a general divide between communication studies and scholarship in the social sciences. In other words, those who study media's constructions of prison have worked separately from scholars conducting research in prisons, resulting in a lack of synthesis across media criticism and lived experience. This edited book addresses the gap in the literature by combining scholarly analysis of media portrayals of prison life with the authentic voices of those who have been incarcerated. Scholars from across disciplines share their research on varied texts and prison populations. The purpose, then, is to bring together media's depictions, studies on media produced in prison, and ethnographic research on the prison experience.

Literature Review

An overview of scholarship on past and present media constructions of prison helps to contextualize this book. In addition, ethnographic research conducted in prison and with former inmates provides a foundation for exploring its connection with media portrayals. The following section draws from film studies, women and gender studies, criminal justice, sociology, and other disciplines in reviewing the existing research.

Research on Prison Representations

The prison narrative has consistently been a part of popular culture, showcasing for public curiosity the life behind bars. Scholars and critics have agreed that fictional prison narratives offer distorted messages. Fiddler described the fictional prison as a "façade," or falsely constructed space, one that dilutes the chaos of the incarcerated life.[17] Broad perspectives on prison have pointed to particular myths about crime, criminal justice, and prison that permeate narratives in different media. Ross identified sixteen common myths about the correctional system based on an examination of representations, his experience working in corrections, and relevant evidence.[18] Among his findings, Ross stated that media presented living conditions as either "too harsh or too lavish" (with no in-between), correctional officers as apathetic or quick to use violence, and prisoners as "intimidating, overpowering, strong, and muscular, with bodies laden with tattoos."[19] Ross also argued that myths work against the rehabilitation of prisoners, instead highlighting punitive measures as effective. Media's focus on severe punishment for crime has also been noted in other studies.[20] On the whole, scholars have argued that media exaggerate prison violence, while criticizing administration for its lenience.[21] Furthermore, violent chaos conveyed on television ignores the fact that, as Britton explained, inmates "have at least some stake in the maintenance of prison order, if for no other reason than the preservation of their own lives."[22] Media also perpetuate racial and ethnic stereotypes about delinquency and crime, marginalizing and blaming certain "othered" groups.[23]

Most literature focuses on portrayals of inmates, staff, and the system of male correctional facilities. Wilson and O'Sullivan discussed how prison narratives provide a watered-down view of prison.[24] O'Sullivan argued that 1990s films about men's prisons offered generally negative and somewhat conflicting messages about prison, while limiting women to a few conventional roles.[25] In a case study of the HBO prison drama *Oz* (1997–2003), Yousman described how this show consistently showcases extreme violence leading to frequent character deaths, thus reinforcing prisoner stereotypes, especially for the African American criminal characters.[26] On the contrary, Wilson and O'Sullivan asserted that *Oz* humanized the male prisoners, even the violent ones, through the telling of multiple perspectives. Either way, both scholars emphasized the exaggerated violence of this program.[27]

While studies of male prison representations have focused on violence and power, research on women's fictional prisons have centered on gender and sexuality. Ciasullo reviewed stereotypes in the women-in-prison film genre, including the "prison lesbian," describing how the conventional narrative begins with a young, naïve, Caucasian woman's first time in prison.[28] The main character then meets a host of stereotypical characters and experiences the "prison themes" of temptation, the "shower scene," solitary confinement, a mud-covered "catfight," and a peripheral character's death. The heroine then has her redeeming moment when she is released into her husband's arms, back to "heterosexual bliss."[29] In these films Ciasullo explained how "lesbian" characters are expected to create "deviance" in the narrative as they threaten the protagonist's heterosexuality.

Offering a different perspective, Herman argued that this genre can be counterhegemonic, providing a space for homonormativity.[30] The British drama *Bad Girls* features lesbian heroines through complex lesbian central characters, thus normalizing lesbian identity and relationships.[31] Similarly, Weiss described how *Orange Is the New Black* (*OITNB*) portrays the fluidity and complexity of gender identification and sexuality, thus challenging stereotypes about both prison and lesbians.[32] Scholars have also noted how most prison narratives are channeled through a white, educated, privileged protagonist, who takes the audience into the prison.[33] Herman observed that even with the homonormative lens in *Bad Girls*, it is solely a Caucasian perspective.[34] And with *Oz*, a similarly privileged audience tuned in because of its titillation and distance from their own lives.[35] Regardless of interpretations of representation and audience, the prison-industrial complex presented in films and television shows like *The Shawshank Redemption*, *OITNB*, *Bad Girls*, and others paints a false picture of life behind bars.

Media in Prison and from Prison

Most people are unaware of the function and place of media within prison. In *Reading Prisoners*, Jodi Schorb documented the important roles that literacy and the consumption of literature have played for inmates.[36] As motion-picture media emerged, their products also entered the penitentiary. Alison Griffiths detailed how films have been shown in prisons since the early 1900s, serving as an outlet and an escape for inmates.[37] Prisoners also produce media, an area that has received little attention. Kalen Churcher outlined how the Louisiana State Penitentiary has produced radio shows, magazines, and other products, which together offer inmates voice and agency, help build community, and allow the incarcerated media producers to connect with and educate the general public outside the prison walls.[38] Given the presence of media consumed in prison and produced in prison, literature in this area is surprisingly sparse.

More attention has been given to popular biographical works of life behind bars, as former and current prisoners have written autobiographies of their incarcerated experience. Most notable in recent years is Piper Kerman's *Orange Is the New Black*, in which she described her experience serving time in an upstate New York penitentiary.[39] Yet, while this book and its television adaptation have certainly garnered mass interest (and praise from critics for expanding diverse roles in fiction), it is hardly the only experience, nor is it reflective of most inmates' stays in correctional facilities, as Kerman admittedly wrote from a position of privilege. Other works include *The Autobiography of Malcom X*, Rubin "Hurricane" Carter's *The Sixteenth Round*, Malcolm Braly's *On the Yard*, and lesser-known books like Michael Santos's *Inside: Life behind Bars in America*.[40] Published pieces by former and current inmates can act as advocacy pieces for prison reform. For example, Tina Reynolds wrote of the abuse and oppression she experienced while incarcerated, and she currently serves as the cofounder and chair of Women On the Rise Telling HerStory (WORTH), which works with other organizations to implement prison reform.[41] Experiences of guards, wardens, and others working and volunteering in the system have also been explored through books like *The Warden Wore Pink, American Prison: 10 Months as a Prison Guard, Newjack: Guarding Sing Sing*, and Sister Helen Prejean's *Dead Man Walking*.[42] Prison life and experience has also served as inspiration for theatrical performance, poetry, and other art forms.[43] Such works provide glimpses into prison life and expression. As anecdotal evidence, though, they typically focus on individuals, not on the prison system.

Ethnographic research allows for theorizing experience of the prison institution. According to Loïc Wacquant, up to the 1970s, groundbreaking prison ethnographies paralleled the expansion of the incarcerated population, demonstrating public and scholarly interest in (vicarious looks) at life behind bars.[44] This type of research greatly declined in the 1980s due to tighter restrictions on both writing within prison and writing about prison. Such obstacles continue, as ethnographers may face difficulty in obtaining approval to study prison life from their university's human subjects research committee, as well as trouble accessing correctional facilities.[45] Even with these challenges, in a call to action for prison ethnographers, Wacquant stressed the importance of such work: "It is essential to *investigate the varied linkages between the prison and its surrounding institutions on the ground*, as they actually exist and operate, rather than from afar and above, from a bird's-eye view unsuited to capturing process, nuance, and contradiction" (emphasis in original).[46]

Indeed, contemporary work has helped shed light on the diversity of experience in prison, from the racialization of the initial entry into prison,[47] to what it means to be transgender in prison,[48] to have a disability behind bars,[49] or to raise children in prison nurseries.[50] With this work and more, ethnography has given voices to those dehumanized and/or ignored in the media discourse on prison. For example, Juanita Diaz-Cotto interviewed Chicana women, examining how incarceration fit into their whole life experience, from their upbringing, through gang activity and juvenile court (when relevant), into adulthood.[51] In this work Diaz-Cotto contextualized their criminal activity as largely produced by a life of poverty, abuse, and instability, paired with stiff sentencing and discrimination from the criminal justice system.[52] Likewise, Murty, Owens, and Vyas conducted a comprehensive ethnography to explore the experiences of African American male prisoners.[53] Through a somewhat different approach, Philip Goodman observed prison reception areas to better understand and theorize racial segregation in California correctional facilities.[54] Scholars have also looked at the influence of prison visitation in regard to one's social capital and in connection to race and spatial distancing.[55] Moreover, scholars have studied the experiences of pregnant and postpartum incarcerated women.[56] Taken collectively, these ethnographic studies provide in-depth theory, voice, and context by situating experience within the prison institution.

Such work has also explored sports and physical exercise in prison,[57] along with reform and rehabilitation programs that have included writing instruction for prisoners,[58] parenting education for prison fathers,[59] sex offender treatment and its connection to the parole hearing experience,[60] and preparation for release into the workforce with *Dress for Success*.[61] Scholars have also looked at successful reentry programs, including those in which former inmates assisted those just released.[62] Additionally, some research has examined life after prison. LeBel surveyed formerly incarcerated men and women, and found that perceptions of personal stigma linked to offender status are conflicting and complex—tied as they are to race, neighborhoods, social networks, and other factors.[63] Similarly, Mbuba conducted interviews with former inmates, finding that many had experienced violence in prison, some of which was tied to race.[64] Moreover, participants expressed difficulty in adjusting to life after prison, particularly in regard to employment.[65] Such scholarship suggests opportunities for prisoner rehabilitation, rather than more punitive approaches to imprisonment.

Media's Influence on Society

Representations of prison in news and entertainment should not be simply dismissed as frivolous enjoyment. Rather, considering media's distortion of incarceration, it is profoundly problematic that most people draw their understanding of prison from such discourse. Media exaggerate the risk of crime and the "danger" of criminals, encourage "draconian punishment" over rehabilitation, and convey false information about citizens protecting themselves from victimization.[66] Moreover, media place blame for criminal deviance on individuals while ignoring the "deeper social problems that we do not have the will to confront," asserted Kappeler, Bloomberg, and Potter.[67]

It has been established that media can shape public perceptions of the world—a relationship known as cultivation. In the 1970s George Gerbner and colleagues first demonstrated cultivation effects, correlating a person's television consumption with perceptions and estimations of crime (i.e., "the mean world" syndrome).[68] Extensive research has corroborated these initial results, demonstrating connections between media consumption habits and perceptions. Heavy viewers of television tend to overestimate crime rates and favor imprisonment over rehabilitation for offenders.[69] In addition, heavy viewers of news are more likely to be afraid of crime and overestimate its risk than are light viewers.[70] Research has shown that women generally fear crime more than men.[71]

Cultivation effects are also demonstrated for crime and race. In other words, media consumption reinforces a fear of particular crimes and criminals, typically perpetuating racial stereotypes.[72] Heavy viewers of reality shows and news programming are more likely than other media consumers to believe, falsely, that an offender's race does not affect juvenile sentencing.[73] Moreover, a Dutch study found that persons exposed to newspapers that portray ethnic minorities negatively were more likely to view ethnic minorities as threatening compared with those who read other newspapers.[74] Similarly, in an experiment measuring the effect of news consumption on perceptions of race, participants were more likely to assume perpetrators described in a news story were African American.[75] Moreover, heavy news viewers tended to perceive unidentified police officers as Caucasian in comparison with light viewers.[76]

Cultivation has also been used to explain the pervasiveness of rape myth acceptance. Lonsway and Fitzgerald defined rape myths as *"attitudes and beliefs that are generally false but are widely and persistently held, and that serve to deny and justify male sexual aggression against women."*[77] Belief in these myths can influence public support for rape victims, have consequences for assailants, including prison sentencing, and affect restitution for victims.[78] As rape myths are especially prevalent in certain media products, viewers of specific genres, particularly soap operas, are more likely to overestimate sexual assault and buy in to rape myths.[79] This correlation is found not only among male viewers. In a survey of college women, Kahlor and Morrison discovered that heavy television viewers were more likely to accept rape myths and believe in the prevalence of false rape accusations than were light viewers.[80] These effects are mitigated by other factors, including direct experience with crime and the type/genre of television consumed.[81] Hust and colleagues noted a significance difference between the television program and its impact on rape myth acceptance, even within the crime drama genre.[82] While watching *Law & Order* resulted in lower rape myth acceptance, and greater intentions to acquire consent for sexual activity and to intervene to stop sexual assault, no correlation was identified between viewing the programs *CSI: Crime Scene Investigation* and *NCIS* and rape myth acceptance.[83] Overall, television consumption has also been correlated with a higher level of fear and greater perceived risk of sexual assault.[84] From this work in cultivation, it can be assumed that media affect viewers in other ways as well, including shaping public perception of prison and its inmates.

The prison system, as an institution, manifests and perpetuates the intersectionality of inequality that privileges the social categories of white, masculine, heterosexual, gender-conforming, educated, upper socioeconomic, and able-bodied. Indeed, it was from his prison experience that Antonio Gramsci first theorized hegemony—as the "common sense" that enables a dominant group in society to maintain power over others.[85] While Gramsci wrote primarily about socioeconomic class division, his term has been generalized to explain how and why certain groups have obtained and maintained control in society, through ideological consent and physical coercion.[86] In prison, the hegemonic systems that exist in the outside world are amplified, as both ideological consent and coercion come together to "maintain order," while reinforcing a racist, sexist, and classist hierarchy.[87] Media representations often reinforce hegemonic notions by perpetuating stereotypes that bolster inequality.[88] As Kappeler, Blumberg, and Potter explained in their discussion of crime myths, "The media tell us what criminals, crime fighters, and victims look like and whom we should be afraid of."[89] Such stereotypes set up dichotomies between a "deviant population" that commits crime, the "helpless victims," and the crime fighters that attempt to stop the criminals.[90] These groups falsely reinforce racial stereotyping. For example, depicting African American men as violent criminals presents them as the "Other," or a group to be feared, instead of a respected part of society.[91] This false perception has been linked to the negative police encounters reported by men of color.[92] Similarly, media's consistent use of male prison guards, even in female prison depictions, reinforces a false belief that women cannot serve as guards, even among women.[93] Such messages help explain why prison guards are disproportionately male.

With the ways that media impact public perception, it is important for us to understand how prisons have been and are constructed. Just as significant is awareness of media's distortions: the common tropes, themes, and clichés of prison films, and the one-dimensional characters in prison TV dramas and the inmates and ex-cons played for comedy in sitcoms. Additionally, we must identify whose voices are omitted from the story, whose perspectives go unheard. With this intention and my theoretical framework explicated, I aim to close this gap, highlighting historical and contemporary representations of incarceration, with special attention to race, gender, and socioeconomic class, as connected to real-life experiences.

The Implications of Prison Discourse

Media's consistent distortion of prison has had and can have very serious real-world implications. Because most people have little to no firsthand experience of incarceration, much of their information and many of their beliefs may stem from media exposure. News and entertainment narratives of prison can impact public perception of crime rates and the criminal justice system, from initial arrests through trials and sentencing. For example, not all racial groups are treated equally by police officers, as demonstrated by a string of murders of unarmed African Americans and other racially charged tragedies that have contributed to Black Lives Matter, an "ideological and political intervention" against racial and other injustices.[94] Studies have shown that white officers are more likely to target black drivers in traffic stops than white drivers, especially in predominately "white" neighborhoods.[95] Racial and gender bias can also influence what happens before the trial, during sentencing, and in later possibilities for rehabilitation. For example, Demuth and Steffensmeier found that female offenders were more likely to be released before the trial than were male offenders, as were Caucasians over Hispanic and African American men.[96] Furthermore, a study of 77,236 federal offender cases determined that those offenders who were male, black, and lower in socioeconomic class and education level had significantly longer sentences for the same crimes than their counterparts.[97] Furthermore, changing immigration laws have led to a significant increase in the number of inmates who are incarcerated, many of whom had no prior offenses.[98] Other populations also face additional discrimination. For example, people who are d/Deaf have experienced further obstacles during arrest, on trial, in prison, and even after parole.[99] The prison-industrial complex is deeply racialized, discriminating against people of color and intersecting with class at each step of the justice process.[100] As Wacquant articulated, "The caste regime, weakened on the outside, regains its full vigor inside the gaols of America."[101] Marginalized groups are disproportionately targeted and affected by the U.S. focus on punishment.[102]

Media messages about prison paint a different picture by ignoring individuals' struggles against a biased system; instead, they dehumanize the incarcerated as violent and overwhelmingly masculine—ignoring poverty, drug addiction, and other factors that make certain populations more likely to commit crime.[103] With this limited discourse, many people have little knowledge of why people go to prison or what the experience is actually like. Sussman laid out the implications of this disconnect: "The secretiveness that has come to characterize many of our country's prison systems hampers the public's ability to help shape government policy, to correct abuses, to understand crime, to evaluate prison programs and practice, and generally to reassess our costly and ineffectual system of criminal justice sanctions."[104] Recognizing the significant role that news and entertainment media play in shaping perceptions, PCARE's call to action listed media reform as the first step, with the understanding that negative representations "lead to distortions in public opinion and public policy."[105] Since life after incarceration is nearly invisible to the public eye, media reform could help encourage employers to hire ex-offenders. After release many former inmates face difficulty finding housing and employment. A lack of education, marketable skills, and appropriate social networks hinder their job search, not to mention media's stigma about the dangers of hiring ex-convicts.[106] And yet, finding a job after prison can reduce the likelihood of recidivism, especially when combined with strong family ties and assistance from prisoner reentry programs.[107] In addition, stronger connections between media and prison experience could improve public support for programs to help reduce the poverty and substance abuse that lead to crime. Finally, expanded media exposure of different populations could improve recognition of the need for stronger support of policy and funding reform, including more rehabilitation programs.

Methodology, Voice, and Experience

As contributors to an interdisciplinary collection, the scholars whose work is featured in this book apply multiple methodologies and approaches. For a cultural studies approach, media scholars in the book turn to the work of Michel Foucault, Laura Mulvey, Gramsci, Stuart Hall, and others to analyze representations of prison using critical discourse analysis, framing, thematic and historical analysis, and appropriate textual methodologies. Furthermore, feminist epistemology, grounded theory, and other theoretical positions underpin the interviews, surveys, and other forms of ethnographic work collected here. In every chapter authors explicate their specific theoretical framework and methodology, while situating their work within the book's central purpose of connecting representation to experience.

Structure of the Book

This book is divided into three sections. First, in chapters 1 to 6, scholars analyze representations of prison life, addressing the intersectionality of gender, race, sexuality, socioeconomic class, and other traits as depicted in film and television. Media scholars trace the history of the women's prison film genre, analyze the "gaze" and aesthetic elements in telling the incarcerated story, illuminate the role of religion and spirituality in the prison narrative, examine gender disparity through medical social control in prison dramas, discuss reality TV that features families of the incarcerated, and connect constructions of masculinity in prison dramas to contemporary racial tension.

Next, in chapters 7 to 10, the book moves to the presence of media in prison, as scholars discuss personal correspondence with death row inmates (and the television counterpart), the experience of prisoners writing for a prison magazine or hosting on a prison radio station, the lived experiences of women serving life sentences, and the reactions of women convicted of murder to the media coverage of their arrest and trial.

Chapters 11 through 14 give voice to prison populations and experiences that are marginalized or overlooked in media, using ethnographic research to convey firsthand stories of life behind bars. Authors explore lactation programs in women's prisons, the stories of those who are transgender and incarcerated in men's prisons, and the perspectives of African American men after incarceration. Chapter 14 combines ethnography with personal narrative as a researcher tells her story of volunteering in prison.

Across these chapters, authors and their subjects reflect on the gross misrepresentation of prison life in media discourse and the implications of its messages. The book concludes with an overall look at media and experience, acknowledging the voices that are missing from literature and scholarship.

Notes

1. Turner, *Man Called CASH*.

2. Cash, *Cash*; Turner, *Man Called CASH*.

3. Carson, "Prisoners in 2014 from the Bureau of Justice Statistics"; Bonczar, Kaeble, and Maruschak, "Bureau of Justice Statistics (BJS)—Probation and Parole in the United States, 2014."

4. Hockenberry, Sickmund, and Sladky, *Juvenile Residential Facility Census, 2012*.

5. Carson, "U.S. Prison Population Declined One Percent in 2014."

6. Ibid.

7. Ibid.

8. PCARE, "Fighting the Prison–Industrial Complex," 404.

9. Yousman, "Inside *Oz*"; Ciasullo, "Containing 'Deviant' Desire"; Fiddler, "Projecting the Prison"; Britton, *At Work in the Iron Cage*.

10. Brown, *Culture of Punishment*, 4, 14–15.

11. Ibid., 8.

12. Ross, "Varieties of Prison Voyeurism," 399.

13. Kappeler, Potter, and Blumberg, *Mythology of Crime and Criminal Justice*; Ross, "Debunking the Myths of American Corrections"; Ross, "Varieties of Prison Voyeurism."

14. Griffiths, *Carceral Fantasies*.

15. Sussman, "Media on Prisons."

16. Ibid., 258.

17. Fiddler, "Projecting the Prison."

18. Ross, "Debunking the Myths of American Corrections."

19. Ibid., 417.

20. Kappeler, Potter, and Blumberg, *Mythology of Crime and Criminal Justice*; Brown, *Culture of Punishment*.

21. Britton, *At Work in the Iron Cage*; Cheliotis, "Ambivalent Consequences of Visibility."

22. Britton, *At Work in the Iron Cage*, 1.

23. Cheliotis, "Ambivalent Consequences of Visibility."

24. Wilson and O'Sullivan, *Images of Incarceration*.

25. O'Sullivan, "Representations of Prison in Nineties Hollywood Cinema."

26. Yousman, "Inside *Oz*."

27. Wilson and O'Sullivan, *Images of Incarceration*.

28. Ciasullo, "Containing 'Deviant' Desire."

29. Ibid., 197.

30. Herman, "*Bad Girls* Changed My Life."

31. Ibid.

32. Weiss, "Lesbian, Bisexual, and Trans Identities."

33. Smith, "'Orange' Is the Same White"; Gutierrez, "Redeeming the Myth"; Ciasullo, "Containing 'Deviant' Desire."

34. Herman, "*Bad Girls* Changed My Life."

35. Yousman, "Inside *Oz*."

36. Schorb, *Reading Prisoners*.

37. Griffiths, "Portal to the Outside World."

38. Churcher, "Journalism behind Bars."

39. Kerman, *Orange Is the New Black*.

40. X [Malcolm] and Haley, *Autobiography*; Carter, *Sixteenth Round*; Braly, *On the Yard*; Santos, *Inside*.

41. Reynolds, "Formerly Incarcerated Woman Takes On Policy."

42. Miller, *Warden Wore Pink*; Westgate, *American Prison*; Conover, *Newjack*; Prejean, *Dead Man Walking*.

43. Shailor, *Performing New Lives*; Chevigny, *Doing Time*.

44. Wacquant, "Curious Eclipse of Prison Ethnography."

45. Ibid.

46. Ibid., 387–88.

47. Goodman, "It's Just Black, White, or Hispanic."

48. Jenness and Fenstermaker, "Agnes Goes to Prison."

49. Ben-Moshe, Chapman, and Carey, *Disability Incarcerated*; Miller, Vernon, and Capella, "Violent Offenders"; Vernon, "Horror of Being Deaf and in Prison."

50. Luther and Gregson, "Restricted Motherhood."

51. Diaz-Cotto, *Chicana Lives and Criminal Justice*.

52. Ibid.

53. Murty, Owens, and Vyas, *Voices from Prison*.

54. Goodman, "It's Just Black, White, or Hispanic."

55. Liu, Pickett, and Baker, "Inside the Black Box"; Cochran, "Breaches in the Wall"; Cochran, Mears, Bales, and Stewart, "Spatial Distance."

56. Williams and Schulte-Day, "Pregnant in Prison."

57. Meek, *Sport in Prison*.

58. Maher, "You Probably Don't Even Know I Exist."

59. Bushfield, "Fathers in Prison."

60. Lacombe, "Mr. S., You Do Have Sexual Fantasies?"

61. Black and van den Broek, "Tracksuit or Business Suit."

62. LeBel, Richie, and Maruna, "Helping Others."

63. LeBel, "Invisible Stripes?"

64. Mbuba, "Lethal Rejection."

65. Ibid.

66. Brown, *Culture of Punishment*; Ross, "Debunking the Myths of American Corrections"; Kappeler, Potter, and Blumberg, *Mythology of Crime and Criminal Justice*, 21.

67. Kappeler, Potter, and Blumberg, *Mythology of Crime and Criminal Justice*, 357.

68. Gerbner and Gross, "Living with Television."

69. Goidel, Freeman, and Procopio, "Impact of Television Viewing"; Romer, Jamieson, and Aday, "Television News and the Cultivation of Fear of Crime."

70. Custers and Van den Bulck, "Relationship of Dispositional and Situational Fear"; Romer, Jamieson, and Aday, "Television News and the Cultivation of Fear of Crime."

71. Custers and Van den Bulck, "Relationship of Dispositional and Situational Fear."

72. Kappeler, Potter, and Blumberg, *Mythology of Crime and Criminal Justice*.

73. Goidel, Freeman, and Procopio, "Impact of Television Viewing."

74. Lubbers, Schneepers, and Vergeer, "Exposure to Newspapers."

75. Dixon, "Black Criminals and White Officers."

76. Ibid.

77. Lonsway and Fitzgerald, "Rape Myths in Review," 134.

78. Karmen, *Crime Victims*.

79. Kahlor and Eastin, "Television's Role in the Culture of Violence."

80. Kahlor and Morrison, "Television Viewing and Rape Myth Acceptance."

81. Custers and Van den Bulck, "Relationship of Dispositional and Situational Fear"; Custers and Van den Bulck, "Cultivation of Fear of Sexual Violence"; Kahlor and Eastin, "Television's Role in the Culture of Violence"; Goidel, Freeman, and

Procopio, "Impact of Television Viewing on Perceptions of Juvenile Crime"; Bilandzic and Rössler, "Life according to Television."

82. Hust, Garrigues Marett, Lei, Ren, and Ran, *"Law & Order, CSI,* and *NCIS."*
83. Ibid.
84. Custers and Van den Bulck, "Cultivation of Fear of Sexual Violence."
85. Gramsci, *Selections from the Prison Notebooks.*
86. Ibid.
87. Britton, *At Work in the Iron Cage.*
88. Hall, Evans, and Nixon, *Representation.*
89. Kappeler, Potter, and Blumberg, *Mythology of Crime and Criminal Justice,* 20.
90. Ibid., 23.
91. Hall, Evans, and Nixon, *Representation.*
92. Brunson, "Police Don't Like Black People."
93. Britton, *At Work in the Iron Cage.*
94. Capehart, "From Trayvon Martin to 'Black Lives Matter'"; "Guiding Principles," Black Lives Matter.
95. Rojek, Rosenfeld, and Decker, "Policing Race."
96. Demuth and Steffensmeier, "Impact of Gender and Race-Ethnicity in Pretrial."
97. Mustard, "Racial, Ethnic, and Gender Disparities in Sentencing."
98. Kilgore, "Immigration and Mass Incarceration."
99. Vernon, "Horror of Being Deaf and in Prison."
100. PCARE, "Fighting the Prison–Industrial Complex."
101. Wacquant, "Curious Eclipse of Prison Ethnography," 374.
102. Ibid.
103. Sussman, "Media on Prisons"; Sickmund and Puzzanchera, *Juvenile Offenders and Victims: 2014*; Britton, *At Work in the Iron Cage.*
104. Sussman, "Media on Prisons," 258.
105. PCARE, "Fighting the Prison–Industrial Complex."
106. Schmitt and Warner, "Ex-offenders and the Labor Market."
107. Kim, Tripodi, and Bender, "Is Employment Associated with Reduced Recidivism?"; Raphael, "Incarceration and Prisoner Reentry."

Bibliography

Ben-Moshe, Liat, Chris Chapman, and Allison C. Carey, eds. *Disability Incarcerated: Imprisonment and Disability in the United States and Canada.* New York: Palgrave Macmillan, 2014.

Bilandzic, Helena, and Patrick Rössler. "Life according to Television. Implications of Genre-Specific Cultivation Effects: The Gratification/Cultivation Model." *Communications* 29, no. 3 (2004). doi:10.1515/comm.2004.020.

Black, Prudence, and Diane van den Broek. "Tracksuit or Business Suit: What Should a Woman Wear Coming out of Prison?" *Continuum* 28, no. 6 (2014): 787–96. doi:10.1080/10304312.2014.966405.

Bonczar, Thomas P., Danielle Kaeble, and Laura Maruschak. "Bureau of Justice Statistics (BJS)—Probation and Parole in the United States, 2014." Bureau of Justice Statistics. Office of Justice Programs, November 19, 2015. Accessed September 16, 2017. http://www.bjs.gov/index.cfm?ty=pbdetail&iid=5415.

Braly, Malcolm. *On the Yard.* 2nd ed. New York: New York Review of Books, 2002.

Britton, Dana. *At Work in the Iron Cage.* New York: New York University Press, 2003.

Brown, Michelle. *The Culture of Punishment: Prison, Society, and Spectacle.* New York: New York University Press, 2009.

Brunson, Rod K. "'Police Don't Like Black People': African-American Young Men's Accumulated Police Experiences." *Criminology & Public Policy* 6, no. 1 (2007): 71–101. doi:10.1111/j.1745–9133.2007.00423.x.

Bushfield, Suzanne. "Fathers in Prison: Impact of Parenting Education." *Journal of Correctional Education* 55, no. 2 (2004): 104–16.

Capehart, Jonathan. "From Trayvon Martin to 'Black Lives Matter.'" *PostPartisan* (blog), *Washington Post*, February 27, 2015. Accessed September 16, 2017. https://www.washingtonpost.com/blogs/post-partisan/.

Carson, E. Ann. "Prisoners in 2014 from the Bureau of Justice Statistics." U.S. Department of Justice, September 2015. Accessed September 16, 2017. https://www.bjs.gov/index.cfm?ty=pbdetail&iid=5387.

———. "U.S. Prison Population Declined One Percent in 2014." Press Release: Bureau of Justice Statistics. Office of Justice Programs, 2015. Accessed September 16, 2017. http://www.bjs.gov/content/pub/press/p14pr.cfm.

Carter, Rubin "Hurricane." *The Sixteenth Round.* 2nd ed. Chicago: Lawrence Hill Books, 2011.

Cash, Johnny. *Cash: The Autobiography.* New York: HarperCollins, 2003.

Cheliotis, Leonidas K. "The Ambivalent Consequences of Visibility." *Crime, Media, Culture: An International Journal* 6 (2010): 169–84.

Chevigny, Bell Gale, ed. *Doing Time: 25 Years of Prison Writing.* 2nd ed. New York: Arcade, 2011.

Churcher, Kalen M. A. "Journalism behind Bars: The Louisiana State Penitentiary's *Angolite* Magazine." *Communication, Culture & Critique* 4, no. 4 (2011): 382–400. doi:10.1111/j.1753–9137.2011.01113.x.

Ciasullo, Ann. "Containing 'Deviant' Desire: Lesbianism, Heterosexuality, and the Women-in-Prison Narrative." *Journal of Popular Culture* 41, no. 2 (2008): 195–223. doi:10.1111/j.1540–5931.2008.00499.x.

Cochran, Joshua C. "Breaches in the Wall: Imprisonment, Social Support, and Recidivism." *Journal of Research in Crime and Delinquency* 51, no. 2 (2014): 200–229. doi:10.1177/0022427813497963.

Cochran, Joshua C., Daniel P. Mears, William D. Bales, and Eric A. Stewart. "Spatial Distance, Community Disadvantage, and Racial and Ethnic Variation in Prison Inmate Access to Social Ties." *Journal of Research in Crime and Delinquency* 53, no. 2 (2016): 220–54. doi:10.1177/0022427815592675.

Conover, Ted. *Newjack: Guarding Sing Sing.* New York: Vintage Books, 2001.

Custers, Kathleen, and Jan Van den Bulck. "The Cultivation of Fear of Sexual Violence in Women: Processes and Moderators of the Relationship between Television and Fear." *Communication Research* 40, no. 1 (2013): 96–124. doi:10.1177/0093650212440444.

———. "The Relationship of Dispositional and Situational Fear of Crime with Television Viewing and Direct Experience with Crime." *Mass Communication and Society* 14, no. 5 (2011): 600–619. doi:10.1080/15205436.2010.530382.

Demuth, Stephen, and Darrell Steffensmeier. "The Impact of Gender and Race-Ethnicity in the Pretrial Release Process." *Social Problems* 51, no. 2 (2004): 222–42. doi:10.1525/sp.2004.51.2.222.

Diaz-Cotto, Juanita. *Chicana Lives and Criminal Justice.* Austin: University of Texas Press, 2006.

Dixon, Travis L. "Black Criminals and White Officers: The Effects of Racially Misrepresenting Law Breakers and Law Defenders on Television News." *Media Psychology* 10, no. 2 (2007): 270–91. doi:10.1080/15213260701375660.

Fiddler, Michael. "Projecting the Prison: The Depiction of the Uncanny in *The Shawshank Redemption*." *Crime, Media, Culture* 3, no. 2 (2007): 192–206. doi:10.1177/1741659007078546.

Gerbner, George, and Larry Gross. "Living with Television: The Violence Profile." *Journal of Communication* 26, no. 2 (1976): 172–94. doi:10.1111/j.1460–2466.1976.tb01397.x.

Goidel, Robert K., Craig M. Freeman, and Steven T. Procopio. "The Impact of Television Viewing on Perceptions of Juvenile Crime." *Journal of Broadcasting & Electronic Media* 50, no. 1 (2006): 119–39. doi:10.1207/s15506878jobem5001_7.

Goodman, Philip. "'It's Just Black, White, or Hispanic': An Observational Study of Racializing Moves in California's Segregated Prison Reception Centers." *Law & Society Review* 42, no. 4 (2008): 735–70. doi:10.1111/j.1540-5893.2008.00357.x.

Gramsci, Antonio. *Selections from the Prison Notebooks.* Edited and translated by Quintin Hoare and Geoffrey Nowell Smith. London: Lawrence & Wishart, 1971.

Griffiths, Alison. "A Portal to the Outside World: Motion Pictures in the Penitentiary." *Film History: An International Journal* 25, no. 4 (2013): 1–35.

———. *Carceral Fantasies: Cinema and Prison in Early Twentieth-Century America.* New York: Columbia University Press, 2016.

"Guiding Principles." Black Lives Matter, n.d. Accessed September 16, 2017. http://blacklivesmatter.com/guiding-principles/.

Gutierrez, Peter. "Redeeming the Myth of Upward Mobility: *The Shawshank Redemption*." *Screen Education* no. 70 (2013): 98–103.

Hall, Stuart, Jessica Evans, and Sean Nixon, eds. *Representation: Cultural Representations and Signifying Practices.* 2nd ed. London: Sage, 2013.

Herman, Didi. "'*Bad Girls* Changed My Life': Homonormativity in a Women's Prison Drama." *Critical Studies in Media Communication* 20, no. 2 (2003): 141–59. doi:10.1080/07393180302779.

Hockenberry, Sarah, Melissa Sickmund, and Anthony Sladky. *Juvenile Residential Facility Census, 2012: Selected Findings.* U.S. Department of Justice, March 2015. http://www.ojjdp.gov/pubs/247207.pdf.

Hust, Stacey J. T., Emily Garrigues Marett, Ming Lei, Chunbo Ren, and Weina Ran. "*Law & Order*, *CSI*, and *NCIS*: The Association between Exposure to Crime Drama Franchises, Rape Myth Acceptance, and Sexual Consent Negotiation among College Students." *Journal of Health Communication* 20, no. 12 (2015): 1369–81. doi:10.1080/10810730.2015.1018615.

Jenness, Valerie, and Sarah Fenstermaker. "Agnes Goes to Prison: Gender Authenticity, Transgender Inmates in Prisons for Men, and Pursuit of 'the Real Deal.'" *Gender & Society* 28, no. 1 (2014): 5–31. doi:10.1177/0891243213499446.

Kahlor, LeeAnn, and Matthew S. Eastin. "Television's Role in the Culture of Violence toward Women: A Study of Television Viewing and the Cultivation of Rape Myth Acceptance in the United States." *Journal of Broadcasting & Electronic Media* 55, no. 2 (2011): 215–31. doi:10.1080/08838151.2011.566085.

Kahlor, LeeAnn, and Dan Morrison. "Television Viewing and Rape Myth Acceptance among College Women." *Sex Roles* 56, nos. 11–12 (2007): 729–39. doi:10.1007/s11199-007-9232-2.

Kappeler, Victor E., Gary W. Potter, and Mark Blumberg. *The Mythology of Crime and Criminal Justice.* 4th ed. Prospect Heights, IL: Waveland, 2005.

Karmen, Andrew. *Crime Victims: An Introduction to Victimology.* 8th ed. Belmont, CA: Wadsworth, Cengage Learning, 2013.

Kerman, Piper. *Orange Is the New Black: My Year in a Women's Prison.* New York: Spiegel & Grau, 2010.

Kilgore, James. "Immigration and Mass Incarceration." *Race, Poverty & the Environment* 18, no. 2 (2011): 42–43.

Kim, Johnny S., Stephen Tripodi, and Kimberly Bender. "Is Employment Associated with Reduced Recidivism?" *International Journal of Offender Therapy and Comparative Criminology* 54, no. 5 (2010): 706–20.

Lacombe, Dany. "'Mr. S., You Do Have Sexual Fantasies?' The Parole Hearing and Prison Treatment of a Sex Offender at the Turn of the 21st Century." *Canadian Journal of Sociology* 38, no. 1 (2013): 33–63.

LeBel, Thomas P. "Invisible Stripes? Formerly Incarcerated Persons' Perceptions of Stigma." *Deviant Behavior* 33, no. 2 (2012): 89–107.

LeBel, Thomas P., Matt Richie, and Shadd Maruna. "Helping Others as a Response to Reconcile a Criminal Past: The Role of the Wounded Healer in Prisoner Reentry Programs." *Criminal Justice and Behavior* 42, no. 1 (2015): 108–20. doi:10.1177/0093854814550029.

Liu, Siyu, Justin T. Pickett, and Thomas Baker. "Inside the Black Box: Prison Visitation, the Costs of Offending, and Inmate Social Capital." *Criminal Justice Policy Review* 27, no. 8 (2016): 766–90.doi:10.1177/0887403414562421.

Lonsway, Kimberly A., and Louise F. Fitzgerald. "Rape Myths in Review. *Psychology of Women Quarterly* 18, no. 2 (1994): 133–64. doi:10.1111/j.1471-6402.1994.tb00448.x.

Lubbers, Marcel, Peer Schneepers, and Maurice Vergeer. "Exposure to Newspapers and Attitudes toward Ethnic Minorities: A Longitudinal Analysis." Howard Journal of Communications 11, no. 2 (2000): 127–43. doi:10.1080/106461700246661.

Luther, Kate, and Joanna Gregson. "Restricted Motherhood: Parenting in a Prison Nursery." *International Journal of Sociology of the Family* 37, no. 1 (2011): 85–103.

Maher, Jane. "'You Probably Don't Even Know I Exist': Notes from a College Prison Program." *Journal of Basic Writing* 23, no. 1 (2004): 82–100.

Mbuba, Jospeter M. "Lethal Rejection: Recounting Offenders' Experience in Prison and Societal Reaction Post Release." *Prison Journal,* 92, no. 2 (2012): 231–52. doi:10.1177/0032885512439009.

Meek, Rosie. *Sport in Prison: Exploring the Role of Physical Activity in Correctional Settings.* New York: Routledge, 2013.

Miller, Katrina R., McCay Vernon, and Michele E. Capella. "Violent Offenders in a Deaf Prison Population." *Journal of Deaf Studies and Deaf Education* 10, no. 4 (2005): 417–25. doi:10.1093/deafed/eni039.

Miller, Tekla Dennison. *The Warden Wore Pink.* Brunswick, ME: Biddle, 1996.

Murty, Komanduri S., Angela S. Owens, and Ashwin G. Vyas. *Voices from Prison: An Ethnographic Study of Black Male Prisoners.* Lanham, MD: University Press of America, 2004.

Mustard, David B. "Racial, Ethnic, and Gender Disparities in Sentencing: Evidence from the U.S. Federal Courts." *Journal of Law & Economics* 44, no. 1 (2001): 285–314. doi:10.1086/320276.

O'Sullivan, Sean. "Representations of Prison in Nineties Hollywood Cinema: From *Con Air* to *The Shawshank Redemption.*" *Howard Journal of Criminal Justice* 40, no. 4 (2001): 317–34. doi:10.1111/1468–2311.00212.

PCARE. "Fighting the Prison–Industrial Complex: A Call to Communication and Cultural Studies Scholars to Change the World." *Communication and Critical/Cultural Studies* 4, no. 4 (2007): 402–20. doi:10.1080/14791420701632956.

Prejean, Helen. *Dead Man Walking.* New York: Vintage Books, 1993.

Raphael, Steven. "Incarceration and Prisoner Reentry in the United States." *ANNALS of the American Academy of Political and Social Science* 635, no. 1 (2011): 192–215. doi:10.1177/0002716210393321.

Reynolds, Tina. "A Formerly Incarcerated Woman Takes On Policy." *Dialectical Anthropology* 34, no. 4 (2010): 453–57. doi:10.1007/s10624–010–9182-x.

Rojek, Jeff, Richard Rosenfeld, and Scott Decker. "Policing Race: The Racial Stratification of Searches in Police Traffic Stops." *Criminology* 50, no. 4 (2012): 993–1024. doi:10.1111/j.1745–9125.2012.00285.x.

Romer, Daniel, Kathleen Hall Jamieson, and Sean Aday. "Television News and the Cultivation of Fear of Crime." *Journal of Communication* 53, no. 1 (2003): 88–104. doi:10.1111/j.1460–2466.2003.tb03007.x.

Ross, Jeffrey Ian. "Debunking the Myths of American Corrections: An Exploratory Analysis." *Critical Criminology* 20, no. 4 (2012): 409–27. doi:10.1007/s10612–012–9158-z.

———. "Varieties of Prison Voyeurism An Analytic/Interpretive Framework." *Prison Journal* 95, no. 3 (2015): 397–417. doi:10.1177/0032885515587473.

Santos, Michael G. *Inside: Life behind Bars in America.* New York: St. Martin's, 2006.

Schmitt, John, and Kris Warner. "Ex-offenders and the Labor Market." Washington, D.C.: Center for Economic and Policy Research, November 2010.

Accessed September 16, 2017. http://cepr.net/documents/publications /ex-offenders-2010-11.pdf.

Schorb, Jodi. *Reading Prisoners: Literature, Literacy, and the Transformation of American Punishment, 1700–1845.* New Brunswick, NJ: Rutgers University Press, 2014.

Shailor, Jonathan. *Performing New Lives: Prison Theatre.* London and Philadelphia: Jessica Kingsley, 2011.

Sickmund, Melissa, and Charles Puzzanchera. *Juvenile Offenders and Victims: 2014 National Report.* National Center for Juvenile Justice, December 2014. Accessed September 16, 2017. http://www.ojjdp.gov/ojstatbb/nr2014 /downloads/NR2014.pdf.

Smith, Anna Marie. "'Orange' Is the Same White: Comments on *Orange Is the New Black.*" Social Science Research Network, July 2, 2014. doi:10.2139 /ssrn.2461799.

Sussman, Peter Y. "Media on Prisons: Censorships and Stereotypes." In *Invisible Punishment: The Collateral Consequences of Mass Imprisonment,* edited by Marc Mauer and Meda Chesney-Lind, 258–78. New York: New Press, 2002.

Turner, Steve. *The Man Called CASH.* Nashville: W. Publishing Group, 2004.

Vernon, McKay. "The Horror of Being Deaf and in Prison." *American Annals of the Deaf* 155, no. 3 (2009): 311–21.

Wacquant, Loïc. "The Curious Eclipse of Prison Ethnography in the Age of Mass Incarceration." *Ethnography* 3, no. 4 (2002): 371–97. doi:10.1177 /1466138102003004012.

Weiss, Michaela. "Lesbian, Bisexual, and Trans Identities in *Orange Is the New Black.*" *Moravian Journal of Literature & Film* 5, no. 1 (2014): 45–62.

Westgate, Adam. *American Prison: 10 Months as a Prison Guard.* CreateSpace Independent Publishing Platform, 2014.

Williams, Lori, and Sandy Schulte-Day. "Pregnant in Prison—the Incarcerated Woman's Experience: A Preliminary Descriptive Study." *Journal of Correctional Health Care* 12, no. 2 (2006): 78–88. doi:10.1177/1078345806288914.

Wilson, David, and Sean O'Sullivan. *Images of Incarceration: Representations of Prison in Film and Television Drama.* Hampshire, UK: Waterside, 2004.

X, Malcolm, and Alex Haley. *The Autobiography of Malcolm X: As Told to Alex Haley.* 2nd ed. New York: Random House, 1987.

Yousman, Bill. "Inside *Oz*: Hyperviolence, Race and Class Nightmares, and the Engrossing Spectacle of Terror." *Communication and Critical/Cultural Studies* 6, no. 3 (2009): 265–84. doi:10.1080/14791420903049728.

SECTION ONE

Media Representations of Prison

How do entertainment media construct the incarcerated life? Using a cultural studies lens, the chapters in this section offer new perspectives on fictional portrayals of prison and the prison myths identified in existing literature. Scholars discuss analyses of women-in-prison films, the "gaze" and religion in *Orange Is the New Black*, medicine as social control in male and female prison dramas, prison wives in reality television, and masculinity in *Oz*.

1. Bims, Babes, and Molls in the Big House: The Women-in-Prison Genre Film

L. Clare Bratten

Since the inception of the penal system, as Michel Foucault described in *Discipline and Punish*, public display of prisoners who were tortured, hanged, burned at the stake, or disgraced publicly was a routine part of the discipline administered by the sovereign state.[1] These public displays of torture, meant to instill fear of the power of the sovereign or state, were eventually replaced by more private ministrations of "justice," but public fascination with the lives of miscreants and their eventual fate as prisoners persisted. Women among them were particularly interesting subjects of public and media scrutiny. The Victorian ideal of women as the "angel of the house" was rudely contradicted by the guttersnipes, whores, and female miscreants in reports of women who fell from grace. The spectacle of punishment in the public square was replaced by accounts of punishment and discipline as fodder for the print media—and, indeed, all subsequent forms of media. Where public display was not possible, stern or breathless news reports titil-lated the public with stories of evildoers or innocent victims of "justice" and their punishments. As Lucy Williams traces in her dissertation research on "wayward women" of Victorian England, early newspaper reports reveled in the details of women prisoners who strangled their illegitimate newborns, women of ill repute or servants who stole from their employers, or jealous wives and girlfriends who violently attacked their rivals. One such report in the *Liverpool Echo* newspaper in 1882 warned of women as "A Growing Class of Offenders."[2] As the film medium became established, the appetite for stories of women who had transgressed social mores and legal boundaries led to the transformation of news reports into a visual subject for a film text offering voyeuristic pleasures even as early as the silent era.

According to film scholar Thomas Doherty, the prison film genre developed around narratives with the tensions and injustices of the criminal justice system as a main motivating factor around 1930. This is interesting from a film technology standpoint since the prison genre, despite its colorful and action-packed sequences, seemed to depend upon the arrival of film sound capabilities to convey the injustices and drama of the prison story adequately. Perhaps this was because the silent films did more *showing* via action sequences than *telling* via dialogue, whereas prison-based dramas took place within confined spaces—similar to a theatrical proscenium arch—and therefore depended more upon dialogue to make clear the psychological drama. Both gendered versions of the prison film soon developed recognizable themes, plot devices, and tropes that made it a genre. But investigation of the women-in-prison (hereafter WIP) form reveals that the genre was not stable; it responded to changes in social and cultural norms, the industrial and economic imperatives of the film industry, and the producers' perceptions of the taste of its audience. These changes are more apparent in the gender dynamics of the WIP film than in the men's prison film, as the form was transformed from a primarily melodramatic form in the first thirty years of commercial filmmaking into an "exploitation" film genre in the 1960s. By summarizing the metamorphosis of the WIP genre, this chapter provides a background for the genre in its more contemporary form such as the Netflix series *Orange Is the New Black*. It is hoped that an exploration of the degree to which the genre was transformed over time, as well as the social milieu and industrial pressures on film production, will offer a context for the more contemporary iteration of the genre.

The methodology for this analysis is to examine representative film texts from various "periods" of the WIP genre—as it evolved from the silent-film era, to the melodrama phase of the 1950s, and to the exploitation era of the 1960s to 1980s—and to place these texts in a social context and an industrial one. The films included are set in a variety of incarceration sites: reformatories, prisons, and even prisons outside the United States.

Early Days: 1929–35

The narratives of WIP/bad girls became part of the cinema as early as the silent era with films titled *The Godless Girl* (1929)[3] and *Acquitted* (1929),[4] two early pre-Code talkies. *Pre-Code* refers to the period, before enforcement of the so-called Hays Code, in which Hollywood films had glamorized criminal behavior and sexual indiscretions as part of their plots. The social context of the 1920s and early 1930s may have inspired such narratives. This was the era of Prohibition, with its massive public flouting of the Eighteenth Amendment and the Volstead Act, both of which prohibited the manufacture and sale of alcohol in the United States, and the well-publicized gangland activity of notorious criminals such as Joe Colosimo, Joe Torrio, Al Capone, and others operating in the Roaring Twenties.[5] Eventually, the Catholic Church and various groups concerned with morality, such as the Legion of Decency and local film censorship boards, agitated against films whose plots seemed to glamorize and reward bad behavior. Politician and Hollywood insider Will Hays and a committee produced the Motion Picture Production Code in 1930,[6] which aimed to clamp down on portrayals deemed as promoting licentiousness or as letting corrupt behavior go unpunished, in favor of morality tales that punished the wicked.[7] However, not until Joseph I. Breen became administrator of the Code in 1934 was it really enforced.[8] Before then Hollywood producers felt free to ignore the Code; hence pre-Code pictures are those released before 1934.

The WIP melodramatic film genre developed in parallel with the prison film genre for men. As Doherty writes, in his study of pre-Code Hollywood, several of these films, most notably Universal Studio's *Hell's Highway* (1932),[9] the Warner Brothers film *I Am a Fugitive from a Chain Gang* (1933),[10] and RKO's *Laughter in Hell* (1933),[11] had plots sensationalizing the violence and abuses of the prison system and became prison-reform cautionary tales.[12] Doherty identifies MGM's *The Big House* (1930) as what he calls the "first true prison film and genre prototype":

> The frightened perspective of Ken Marlowe (Robert Montgomery), a rabbity young man serving six years for manslaughter in a drunk driving case, serves as orientation to life inside the walls. After a lecture from the warden (Lewis Stone, MGM's in-house fount of patriarchal sagacity), the regimentation begins: fingerprinting, mug shot, the surrender of civilian clothes and personal tokens, and the issuing of an ill-fitting prison uniform, a ritualistic cleansing before immersion into the world behind bars.[13]

In this film and in most of the men's prison and WIP films, the introduction of the prisoner protagonist into the world of incarceration includes such tropes: arrival at the prison; meeting a cruel warden, overseer, or matron; physical transformation from citizen to prisoner through an abasing physical examination, haircut, cleansing, fingerprinting, and issuance of a uniform; and assignment to a cell and the wary introduction of the prisoner to a tough crowd, with identification of potential rivals and allies. To a great extent, the filmic journey of the hazing of the WIP protagonist in the world of the prison often assumes the point of view of a participant-observer character—often sympathetic and, at times, wrongly accused. This plot device allows the film text and the audience to vicariously explore the hidden prison culture in the same way an audience might follow a sympathetic ethnographer or anthropologist guide as she enters a strange and hostile foreign culture.

It is significant that despite the occasional "reform school" drama (such as the 1929 silent film *The Godless Girl*[14] and the 1950 film *So Young, So Bad*[15]), the WIP film genre almost always used women in penitentiary prisons—that is, those in which women are housed in one large facility, in close living quarters—perhaps because the cramped quarters incited tensions, bickering, and the abuses of the penitentiary system were better fodder for the violence, sexual transgression, and cruelty that propelled many a Hollywood film plot. This choice of setting may also have had production-oriented reasons as well as plot-driven motivations since the confined physical arrangement of the penitentiary made conflict among inmates easier to stage in scripted stories on sets and locations.

However, the social context in American society outside Hollywood, during the period between 1900 and 1935, was marked by a degree of prison reform—especially for women.[16] Reformers pushed for the introduction of the reformatory model for many women prisoners—unwalled campuses designed to provide some degree of domestic normalcy and to teach more socially acceptable behavior to women whose crimes were not as serious. According to Rafter, seventeen states had built women's reformatories by 1935.[17]

The philosophy of reform that guided women's reformatories emphasized living in cottages or smaller buildings and training in the domestic skills of cooking, cleaning, and waiting tables. Presumably women who served time in a reformatory could be sent to work as domestic help upon parole. As Rafter notes, however, the reformatories paradoxically may have resulted in longer incarcerations for women in order to reform them properly:

> And in the case of women's reformatories, these were mainly lawbreakers who, before the institutions were established, were liable to only brief terms in local jails. In the course of saving fallen women then, the founders of women's reformatories institutionalized a double standard, one that

made it possible to incarcerate women for minor offenses for which men were not subject to lengthy punishment by the state.[18]

Despite this transformation of penal justice, the WIP film genre seemed to concentrate more on the penitentiary model unless the inmates were teenagers. As noted, perhaps this was because the penitentiary model offered a confined and more brutal space to motivate the conflict of the plot. It may also have been because reformatories treated women as if they were children, and social moral standards of the time may have found the idea of juvenile justice a distinctively different problem requiring a gentler solution. Rafter writes, "During their early years, some reformatories had populations in which the majority of inmates were between sixteen and twenty-five years old. A few states went so far as to prevent reformatories from receiving women over thirty on the theory that older women were unlikely to reform."[19]

The Melodramatic Form: Redemption through Love

Although Doherty identified *The Big House* (1930)[20] as the first true prison film of the genre (making no distinction between films featuring male or female protagonists), the two silent films already mentioned, *Acquitted* and *The Godless Girl* (1929), might be considered the early form of the WIP film genre since both predated *The Big House* by one year. Doherty may have viewed these earliest WIP films as romance-centered melodramas, which introduced the plot device of a woman in prison who eventually forms a relationship with a "good man." Silent-film actor Margaret Livingston (known best perhaps for her role as the temptress, or the "woman from the city," in F. W. Murnau's 1927 film *Sunrise*) stars in *Acquitted*. The film explores the relationship between a wrongly convicted Dr. Bradford (Lloyd Hughes), who falls in love with Marian (Margaret Livingston), who is a prison inmate. When Marian is released from prison, she works to expose the truth of his wrongful conviction. In this case, although Dr. Bradford is a prisoner, he is good and completely innocent. After her release Marian can redeem herself through working to save his reputation by confronting her former lover Frank Egan (Sam Hardy), who is the true culprit.

In Cecil B. DeMille's silent film *The Godless Girl* (1929), an avowed atheist and schoolgirl, Judith Craig (Lina Basquette), inspires a riot between a group of atheists, of which she is a leader, and a group of Christian believers led by Bob, the romantic male lead (actor Tom Keen billed as George

Duryea). Although Judith and Bob are both clearly physically attracted to each other in the classroom, he learns she is an atheist seeking to "kill the Bible." This inspires the fury of the riot that ensues when Bob leads a group of Christians to attack the atheist meeting. The melee ultimately results in the death of a schoolmate when a stairway bannister collapses. Judith and Bob, as ringleaders, are sent to a reform school. This is an early story with a guilty female protagonist (as one of the leaders of the riot). Judith finds that the so-called reform school is actually a place of horrors that exceeds the punishment that might be expected for causing an accidental death or for a manslaughter charge. Hard labor, beatings, and nonlethal electrical shocks are part of this film's so-called reform school environment—illustrating how Hollywood would at times make no distinction between penitentiaries and reform schools. More importantly, by making both Judith and Bob culpable for the death of the student, the film maintains a focus on a sadistic reform school system (unlike the enlightened model of the reform movement) and avoids the distraction of a "wrongly accused" innocent victim story. The story evolves into a romance where the opposing leaders of the riot, (believer Bob and atheist Judith) finally unite in shared misery, communicating through a fence separating boys from girls. When a fire breaks out in the school, Bob heroically rescues Judith and the cruel guard (Noah Beery), an act that wins release for both of them, and, in an epilogue, Judith converts to Christianity.[21] So, despite the reform school model set up to rehabilitate youth, this film turns reform schools into vicious places more like penitentiaries.

This may be because the melodrama of many WIP films, like their Hollywood prison brethren, had overarching themes of the injustices and cruelty of the prison system set against an economic and social backdrop that disadvantaged a sympathetic and otherwise ordinary citizen who was driven or tempted to take desperate measures. As Doherty notes, the WIP drama of the early 1930s was often framed by the social context of the Depression era in which women and men were driven to crime, prostitution, and thievery:

> Women can be bought for the price of a meal, tempted no longer by jewelry and fancy clothes but by nourishment. Decent girls are forced to put themselves in compromising positions, going against their better judgment to satisfy a basic need. Picked up by a flush fellow with loose pockets, the female ingénue eats ravenously as the man looks on, the two trading urge for urge. . . . In *Blonde Venus* (1932), Marlene Dietrich

begins her descent into prostitution by trading her virtue to feed her child and herself. The price of the meal is 85 cents.[22]

In these early films emerges one of the tropes identified by Anne Morey in her analysis of WIP films of the 1950s—that of a good and decent man (usually outside the prison) who helps to reform the fallen woman, as the love of the woman prisoner for the wrongfully convicted physician in *Acquitted* demonstrates.[23]

Bad girls is a slang term for stock characters in WIP films—the woman (or women) who commit crime. *Ladies They Talk About* (1933)[24] stars Barbara Stanwyck as Nan Taylor, an unrepentant accomplice to bank robbers. This film appears to push the genre closer to the male prison film, as it features a malefactor who is unapologetic about her misdeeds, and away from the sympathetic and vulnerable protagonist. Perhaps because it was a pre-Code film (before the enforcement of the Hays Code of censorship requiring moral rectitude and reform or compensatory punishment), the character Nan, who is part of a bank-robbing gang, goes back to prison after she confesses her part to childhood acquaintance David Slade (Preston Foster), who is a radio preacher and pious man who loves her. However, following her initial release, he turns her in after her confession, and she gets two to five years in San Quentin.[25]

Stanwyck as Nan mimics jailbird bravado, sauntering with a swagger and chewing gum with a "tough cookie" performance, which becomes a model for future actors in bad-girl roles. She tricks Slade when he visits her in an attempt to reform her. She asks the unsuspecting Slade to deliver a message in a sealed envelope to her accomplice and former boyfriend, Lefty, with an impression of a jail key for a jailbreak, but the message is discovered and read by prison censors. Her bank robber companions are shot trying to break her out of the prison, and she blames Slade and swears revenge upon her release. In the end, she impulsively shoots Slade in the shoulder. She immediately expresses regret for her actions. He forgives her, and she is won over when he covers for her by announcing to police their intention to marry and says, "I'm going to take you home and find something suitable for you to do." Again, the love of a reforming good man becomes the neat trick used by Hollywood to redeem the heroine of this WIP film and provide a happy ending.

Although the ministrations and encouragement of a good man are often the way in which the imprisoned woman finds redemption, another trope the genre depicts quite clearly is that the women prisoners of the genre are often incarcerated because of an association with a bad man; they have been accomplices (at times unwittingly), have been set up by their criminal boy-friends, or willingly have taken the rap for their male partner. For example, in *Caged* (1950)[26] Marie Allen is a teenage bride in the car while her young husband desperately sticks up a gas station for forty dollars. The melodrama *Ladies of the Big House* (1931)[27] starred Sylvia Sidney as Kathleen Storm and Gene Raymond as Standish McNeil and depicts the capriciousness and crookedness of the criminal justice system with a star-crossed lovers motif. Kathleen falls in love with a good man, McNeil, but one day after their wedding her former (and criminal) suitor, Kid Athens (Earle Foxe), follows and kills a detective who was sent to the newlyweds' house to bring Kathleen in as a witness against Athens. Athens escapes, and the couple is held for the murder. Both Kathleen and her new husband are convicted and imprisoned.

The Hays Code–Era Melodrama

Women without Names (1940)[28] seems to be a remake of *Ladies of the Big House* with only slight plot deviations and slightly different character names. Divorcée Joyce King (Ellen Drew) meets Fred MacNeil (Robert Paige), a nice guy, but warns him that her ex-husband is a wanted criminal. The couple marry, but her ex-husband, Walter Ferris (John McGuire), breaks into their house and kills a police officer who follows him. Just as in the earlier film, the ex-husband leaves, and the couple is wrongly accused of the murder. MacNeil is sentenced to death, and Joyce is given life in prison, providing another example of a woman accused and imprisoned for having consorted with or been married to a criminal. The overarching theme is not only that women are often wrongly convicted but also that a conspiracy exists within the judicial system to allow innocent people to take the rap for powerfully connected criminal interests.

In addition, as scholars have indicated, women who were not outright wrongly convicted often were jailed for what might now be considered a low-level crime or misdemeanor—and some charges such as vagrancy, drunk-enness, being "idle and disorderly," or crimes of chastity noted in statistics from prisons in Massachusetts, Indiana, and New York in retrospect seem grossly unfair.[29] In the opening scenes of *So Young, So Bad* (1950)[30] girls are brought to the reformatory for crimes of vagrancy, mental illness, and stealing food. In *Women's Prison* (1955) Helene Jensen (Phyllis Thaxter) is convicted of vehicular homicide after she accidentally kills a child.[31]

Suzanne Bouclin argues that the melodramatic form of WIP films (typical of the 1930s and 1940s) could prompt audiences to think about the injustices of the criminal justice system and the women who were warehoused in its facilities.[32] It is not clear, however, that the WIP genre had reforming effects on prison practices for women, since the reformatory movement for the rehabilitation of women had begun about the time of the silent-film era, whereas the men's prison genre may have influenced reform: the Paul Muni role in the 1932 film *I Am a Fugitive from a Chain Gang* was based on the true story of Robert Burns, and the book and film reportedly helped lead to the curtailment of chain gangs.[33]

Intersection of Race and Imprisonment in WIP Films

U.S. prisons varied in the degree to which racial segregation was practiced. Southern prisons in particular segregated the prison population after the end of slavery. (Prior to the Civil War, the punishment of slaves occurred on plantations, and as a result, prisons in the South before the end of slavery had mostly White prison populations.) Parchman Farm in Mississippi was a notorious and prime example of post–Civil War segregation until it was reformed in 1970 to prohibit segregation of the prison population.[34] However, de facto segregation of prisoners was practiced in some US prisons as late as 2005 as demonstrated by a lawsuit brought against the segregation practices of the California Department of Corrections and Rehabilitation in that year.[35] The fact that the prisons in most WIP films had few Black women may have related to de facto segregation, but it probably also related to the marginalization of minority actors in Hollywood films. During the silent-film era, a separate Black cinema existed, but mainstream Hollywood films rarely had roles for Black actors, according to Patricia Hill Collins, except those stereotyped as butlers, mammies, maids, or entertainers.[36]

Few African American prisoners are featured in prominent roles in the early WIP films. When they do appear, they are background characters who rarely have a line of dialogue. One notable exception is *Ladies of the Big House* (1931). The protagonist Kathleen is befriended by the gentle Ivory (Louise Beavers)—an African American woman who is imprisoned for one hundred years for killing her "no-good" husband. Ivory is compassionate and kind, showing Kathleen the ropes and warning her of prisoners who are dangerous or hostile. Ivory also plays the piano and sings, acting as an entertainer for the prisoners and thus embodying two stereotypical roles for African American actors in Hollywood: the protective mammy and the entertainer. When Kathleen discovers that the assistant district attorney was shielding the killer Athens and that state and prison officials colluded to keep her jailed and to execute her husband, she plans to break out of jail. Ivory agrees to help. She conducts the prison orchestra, composed completely of African American women, which provides the sound track for silent-film screenings at the prison. Ivory decides to conduct the orchestra at a very loud volume to disguise any sounds of Kathleen's escape attempt. Although Kathleen is captured during her jailbreak, her escape is sensationalized by the media, which print her charges of corruption leveled at the assistant district attorney. This starts an investigation into the corruption of the penal system, halts the execution of her innocent husband, and justice is restored. Ivory exists only as a helper to Kathleen and plays the part Toni Morrison has identified as the "Africanist presence" used as a catalyst in so many American fictional stories, whereby an African American character (such as Jim in *Huckleberry Finn*) assists in the epiphany or safe passage of the White protagonist.[37]

Louise Beavers's sympathetic and more visible role as Ivory in *Ladies of the Big House* is instructive in that she is one of the few African American characters with a speaking supporting role (rather than a background extra). Despite there being a predominantly White prison population on-screen in WIP films, African American women and other minority women were disproportionately imprisoned throughout U.S. history. As Nicole Rafter notes, the population of women's reformatories (as opposed to prisons) tended to be White, whereas custodial prisons tended to have more Black women—reflecting a gender bias that Black women were more "masculine" and less womanly and therefore appropriately assigned to the more masculine custodial prison.[38]

Nancy Kurshan cites Estelle Freedman's finding that mostly White women were in reformatories in the early twentieth century (as opposed to custodial prisons) and were more commonly convicted for "public order offenses" such as fornication, adultery, and drunkenness, whereas Black women were not charged with public order offenses to the same extent. Freedman speculates that this perhaps resulted from a racist assumption that Black women were not expected to be "womanly." "This was especially true in the South," writes Freedman, "where these so-called morality offenses by Blacks were generally ignored, and where authorities were reluctant to imprison White women at all."[39]

Prior to her role in the film *Ladies of the Big House*, Beavers had appeared in thirty other film roles—many of them not credited and almost always in the role of "maid." It is possible that the WIP genre offered Beavers a chance at a speaking and credited role as a sympathetic inmate and perhaps helped to propel her to her most notable film role (with Claudette Colbert) in the 1934 film *Imitation of Life* in which she played the role of Delilah Johnson, a housekeeper whose pancake recipe brings success to her employer.[40] Symptomatic of the formulaic representation of African American characters and the paucity of African American actors, Beavers appears in both *Ladies of the Big House* and the derivative 1940 film *Women without Names* as the character of Ivory.

In an interesting parallel, Juanita Moore, the African American actor who played the updated role of Delilah Johnson (renamed Annie Johnson) in the 1957 remake of *Imitation of Life* (starring Lana Turner), also appeared in a 1955 WIP film *Women's Prison* as a warm and sympathetic prisoner character, Polyclinic "Polly" Jones. Moore's character is first seen scrubbing floors and crooning "Swing Low, Sweet Chariot" and welcomes back Brenda (Jan Sterling), a repeat offender. As Brenda shows a new inmate the way to her cell, Polly tells her, "I'm sure glad you come home" to the women's prison. She asks the new inmate Helene (Phyllis Thaxter) what she is doing in prison: "Did you get mixed up with some man?" That question reprises one of the common plot mechanisms of the melodramatic form of the genre as it evolved in the 1950s. As Anne Morey notes in her article on the WIP genre from the 1950s to early 1960s, the filmic texts explored the ability of a good man to help in the reformation of a woman in prison, presumably by rescuing her through the institution of marriage—since no other respectable employment options would be viable.[41]

Women Prisoners and Sexuality

Despite the heterosexual-normative story arcs for most protagonists in the genre, the spectre of alternative gender performance or sexualities is presented in many films as a threatening presence, often encoded through signifying traits. The coding of the presence of lesbians within prisons was present almost from the inception of WIP films. This is perhaps not surprising since lesbian homosexuality was considered deviant but was not really illegal.[42] However, lesbian or mannish characters in earlier films had to be signified through dress, gender performance, and implication rather than named explicitly since the

Hays Code forbade depictions of male or female homosexuality. For example, in the earlier prison film *Ladies They Talk About* (1933), Nan (Stanwyck) and fellow inmate Linda (Lillian Roth) find a woman in the women's lavatory with slicked-back short hair, smoking a cigar and wearing a bow tie. Linda tells Nan to be wary: "Watch out for her, she likes to wrestle."

The film *Caged* of 1950 is cited by scholars as a particularly interesting text in that it is a culmination of the women's melodrama and prison tropes in a powerful performance by Eleanor Parker. The film, however, also introduces some of the themes of lesbian desire and criminal circles operating within a women's prison that foretell a devolution of the genre toward a more exploitative type of film. Marie Allen (Eleanor Parker), a naïve woman, is charged as an accessory and lands in jail because her husband steals forty dollars from a gas station and she tries to come to his aid when he is shot. Agnes Moorehead stars as Ruth Benton, a compassionate reforming warden. Her attempts to help "good" women survive are undercut by the matron of the prison, a tall, imposing, and hostile woman, Evelyn Harper (Hope Emerson), who delights in setting strict limits for the women prisoners. Although Harper announces that she is going on a date at one point in the film, she lacks any traditional womanly grace (by 1950s heteronormative standards), and her sadistic personality may lead viewers to wonder about what possible liaison she might attract. Marie Allen begs the warden to release her (the crime for which she is an accessory would not be an offense deserving prison had her husband stolen five dollars less), but the warden cannot release her.

Marie Allen meets some of the tough characters, including Kitty (Betty Garde), the leader of a "doll racket" that trains women to become shoplifters. It is also implied that these women may work for pimps on the outside who funnel women prisoners into the only jobs they will likely be able to find when they are released—larceny or prostitution. Subsequently, the naïve Marie becomes the target of the prison matron, Evelyn Harper, when Marie finds a kitten in the prison and refuses to give it up. She tries to escape with the kitten, but, in the ensuing melee, the kitten is killed. Harper sadistically shaves off Marie Allen's hair as punishment, among other cruelties. At the end of the film when Marie Allen finally is released, the benevolent warden Ruth Benton watches out the window as Marie is picked up by men in a car (arranged by doll racket recruiter Kitty). As Marie slides into the backseat, the camera's medium-close-up shot angles downward to show one of the men placing his hand on her thigh. The warden watches, sighs, and says to an office worker, "you'd better keep the file open on that one."

Exploitation Genre: 1968 and Beyond

Whereas, in 1946, three-quarters of Hollywood's potential audience went to the movies, with many adults attending more than one film per week, post–World War II attendance dropped off dramatically as television made its way into homes and families moved farther away from city centers into new suburban housing developments. As television entered most suburban homes, many once-thriving downtown movie theaters struggled to maintain audiences. Hollywood discovered the importance of a teen audience. Post–World War II teen audiences started to come of age by the mid-1960s with access to cars and drive-in theaters, and for this audience the exploitation genre film appeared to be tailor made.

The term *exploitation film* describes an early variety of film that dealt in subjects deemed shocking or those considered forbidden, such as miscegenation, abortion, or venereal disease. The earliest exploitation films of the 1920s, 1930s, and 1940s were produced by disreputable types such as carnival owners who produced only a couple dozen prints and toured around screening them.[43] Over time the term began to be applied to low-budget films (even those produced by studios): "During the postwar years, the designation of exploitation film was gradually expanded to include almost any low-budget movie with a topical bent. During the 1960s and 1970s, the term was modified to indicate the subject that was being exploited, such as for 'sexploitation' or 'blaxploitation' movie."[44]

The exploitation films of this era featured tawdry topics and sensationalized violence, partial nudity, and implied and lurid sexual liaisons as well as tongue-in-cheek horror or sci-fi offerings such as *Attack of the 50 Foot Woman* (1958).[45] These films used advertising and promotional techniques designed to titillate audiences beyond traditional trailers and ads with come-ons such as "Horror! Shock! Frenzy!" or other inflated prose and hyperbole to excite interest in their target market.

The WIP genre became fertile ground for young filmmakers working for older director hacks like exploitation film director and producer Roger Corman. A cadre of young filmmakers in the 1970s and 1980s were often hired to direct low-budget exploitation films for this market, thereby enabling young directors (almost always male) to find work. Directors such as Martin Scorsese, Peter Bogdonavich, Francis Ford Coppola, and Jonathan Demme all got their start with Roger Corman productions.[46] As foreign films of the French New Wave and Italian Neorealist movement gained young audiences for their innovation and more frank depictions of sexuality, Hollywood filmmakers began to push for the abandonment of the Hays Code of censorship. In his history of the evolution of Hollywood's various censorship codes, Pollard notes that the Hays Code was replaced by the MPAA (Motion Picture Association of America) ratings system in 1968 under Jack Valenti.[47] The MPAA ratings system used designations of G, general; M, suggested for mature audiences; R, restricted to persons sixteen years or older unless accompanied by a parent or adult guardian; and X, for which no persons under sixteen years old were admitted.[48] In 1990 the X rating was replaced by NC-17, which restricted admission to persons seventeen years or older. Wilbur Miller, in *The Social History of Crime and Punishment in America*, writes that post-1950 WIP films featured wicked, highly sexual, and wild women.[49] This meant that previously inferred themes of lesbian sexuality became more explicit in the WIP films of this era, but scenes of lesbian appetites and nudity (shower scenes and catfights between inmates) appeared to be staged for the male gaze if the connotations of marketing and promotional materials are considered. For example, the trailer for *Black Mama, White Mama* promises, "A thousand nights without men! A thousand reasons to kill! From a hellhole of twisted passion! . . . Women in Chains!"[50] The names of the films themselves suggest this exploitative nature: *Caged Heat* (1973), *Caged Fury* (1984), *The Naked Cage* (1985), *Red Heat* (1985), *Reform School Girls* (1986), and *Slammer Girls* (1987).

Jack Hill, another director who started in the exploitation genre working for Roger Corman on films like *Blood Bath* (1966),[51] *Spider Baby* (1967),[52] and *Isle of the Snake People* (1971),[53] moved to the WIP genre with the film *The Big Doll House* (1971)[54] and *The Big Bird Cage* (1972).[55] He saw the potential of the actor Pamela Grier in *Bird Cage* and very soon also featured her as a star in his blaxploitation films *Coffy* (1973) and *Foxy Brown* (1974).[56] Jack Hill's WIP films and those directed by others such as *Black Mama, White Mama* (1973), which also starred Grier, were set and shot in a cheaper location such as the Philippines or some undisclosed tropical island. These narratives made the most of women fighting each other or being ravished or tortured by male guards. The spectacle of women in chains, hanging from ropes by their wrists, and being both physically and sexually attacked by men apparently appealed to the prurient interests of what producers likely expected to be a male audience. Although tension and fights erupt between women in almost all WIP films, in the earlier melodramatic structures of these films, fights or prison riots were a more organic part of the story line.

A fight in an earlier WIP film might be between opposing leaders or groups in competing factions of women within the prison, or the fight would be a rebellion against authorities, such as when the women in *Caged* overturned their bunk beds. The exploitation genre parlayed these tensions into gratuitous catfights between semiclad women prisoners.

The exploitation genre of WIP films abandoned most of the sympathetic innocent (or nearly innocent) women of past WIP films and ramped up the stakes. The women brought to prison were clearly lawbreakers, and the prison was set up to make a spectacle of the torture from sadistic prison matron, warden, or guards. Shower scenes with full rear nudity and waist-up frontal nudity of women were de rigueur. In *Black Mama, White Mama*, a lesbian-coded woman spies on the women through a peephole as they shower and begin to frolic with each other as they soap up. The exploitation genre seemingly was designed to feature thin plots as excuses for excess in the form of nudity, more explicit lesbian sexuality, and sadomasochistic themes.

For example, *The Big Bird Cage* features Karen McKevic as a towering prison "dyke," who at one point runs fully nude through the prison camp. Women wrestle with each other in fights in mud puddles (another trope favored by exploitation films). The sadistic elements in this particular film include hanging women by their wrists, putting them in chains, dropping them from a tower, and whippings and rapes. The women turn on each other as well. The audience for some of these foreign-location films was targeted with colorful titles such as *Bangkok Hilton* (1989), *Caged Heat II: Stripped of Freedom* (1994), *Deported Women of the SS Special Section* (1976), *Female Prisoner Scorpion #701* (1972), *Ilsa, She-Wolf of the SS* (1974), *Isla, the Wicked Warden* (1977), and *Women in Cages* (1971).[57]

The genre continued through the 1980s with its predictably thin plots, sadistic wardens, prison doctors, and prisoner rebellions and catfights with the nudity and ritualized violence of the form. Exploitation film *Chained Heat* (1983)[58] featured Linda Blair, the memorable child star of *The Exorcist* (1973), whose star "brand" from a string of horror genre films may have helped to advertise and sensationalize the film in its marketing. WIP films also began to migrate to television as "telefilms" with many of the tropes minus the nudity and overt lesbian scenes. Ida Lupino, a Hollywood star and director, played the part of a controlling and abusive prison warden in both the 1955 film *Women's Prison* and the telefilm *Women in Chains* (1972).[59] A woman director, Karen Arthur, directed the telefilm *Against Their Will: Women in Prison* (1994),[60] which emphasized the corruption of the prison system in which women exchange sex for favors and the fight of one prisoner against it. The film aired on October 30th, just before Halloween, on the Lifetime television network, which had a reputation for "women in jeopardy" films.

The genre as a theatrical release has persisted, although to a lesser degree in the 1990s and beyond. I speculate that, to some extent, the availability of pornography online may have made the nudity and abasement (which may have been, for certain audiences, part of the titillation of the form) seem tame by comparison, thereby diminishing the number of titles. A future area of study might examine the contemporary film form to determine the appeal to audiences now. One of the more contemporary films, *Stuck!* (2009) was reviewed by *Curve*—a journal that bills itself as "America's best-selling lesbian magazine." The reviewer characterized the film as an homage or tongue-in-cheek recasting of the earlier exploitation form. In an interview, actor Pleasant Gehman recounts, "[I was] fulfilling one of my life's dreams to be in a women's prison movie and acting with one of my earliest screen idols . . . Mink Stole, especially when I found out she was going to be my cell mate." Gehman continues, excitedly, "And playing a white trash hooker lesbian cop killer, how could I say no?"[61]

Like the film *Stuck!* and the evolution of the WIP form in the televisual sphere with the new serial *Orange Is the New Black*, we find some of the same tropes of the WIP film form. However, in its serial televisual form it now appears to have evolved yet again—perhaps appealing to a more feminine audience with fully developed characters (and extensive backstories), strong roles for women of color, frank explorations of lesbian sexuality, lesbian love, and, beyond that, critiques of the prison-for-profit model of incarceration so prevalent in the United States. With a staggering increase in the number of women imprisoned in the United States, a rise of 280 percent between 1980 and 1999,[62] the social context of the series and its exploration of the abuses and stigma of warehoused women seems even more relevant. The series seems to be returning the genre to its original melodramatic roots—and doubtless will be the subject of much impassioned scholarship.

Notes

1. Foucault, *Discipline and Punish*.
2. Williams, "Growing Class of Offenders."
3. "Godless Girl: Summary," *AFI Film Catalog*.
4. *Acquitted*, directed by Frank Strayer.

5. Binder and Lurigio, "Introduction to the Special Issue."

6. Sklar, *Movie-Made America*.

7. The Code also can be found online at ArtsReformation.com.

8. Sklar, *Movie-Made America*, 174.

9. *Hell's Highway*, directed by Rowland Brown.

10. *I Am a Fugitive from a Chain Gang*, directed by Mervyn LeRoy.

11. *Laughter in Hell*, directed by Edward L. Cahn.

12. Doherty, *Pre-Code Hollywood*, 162.

13. Ibid., 160.

14. *Godless Girl*, directed by Cecil B. DeMille.

15. *So Young, So Bad*, directed by Bernard Vorhaus.

16. Rathbone, "Locked In."

17. Rafter, *Partial Justice*, xxix.

18. Ibid., xxviii.

19. Rafter, "Prisons for Women," 158.

20. *Big House*, directed by George W. Hill.

21. "Full Synopsis: *The Godless Girl*," Turner Classic Movies.

22. Doherty, *Pre-Code Hollywood*, 56.

23. Morey, "Judge Called Me an Accessory."

24. *Ladies They Talk About*, directed by William Keighley; *New York Times*, "A Woman Bandit."

25. Rafter, "Prisons for Women," 148. According to Rafter, the script may have referred to the female department of San Quentin, a facility that housed female inmates until the opening in 1932 of the California Institution for Women at Tehachapi, which was modeled on a reformatory.

26. *Caged*, directed by John Cornwall.

27. *Ladies of the Big House*, directed by Marion Gering.

28. *Women without Names*, directed by Robert Florey.

29. Freedman, *Their Sisters' Keepers*, 81–82.

30. *So Young, So Bad*, directed by Bernard Vorhaus.

31. *Women's Prison*, directed by Lewis Seiler.

32. Bouclin, "Women in Prison Movies."

33. Rodimtseva, "On the Hollywood Chain Gang."

34. McPherson, "Parchman's Plantation."

35. Goodman, "It's Just Black, White, or Hispanic."

36. Collins, *Black Feminist Thought*.

37. Morrison, *Playing in the Dark*.

38. Rafter, "Gender, Prisons, and Prison History."

39. Freedman quoted in Kurshan, "Women and Imprisonment in the U.S.," 5. The quotation comes from Freedman, *Their Sisters' Keepers*.

40. *Imitation of Life*, directed by John M. Stahl. The film gave top billing to stars Claudette Colbert and Warren Williams. Louise Beavers played the role of housekeeper Delilah Johnson, whose pancake recipe is coopted and marketed by the Colbert character, turning Delilah into the equivalent of an Aunt Jemima character—a marketed image (enjoying only auxiliary success through the success of her employer) with no real ownership of or trademark rights to her recipe.

41. Morey, "Judge Called Me an Accessory."

42. Valentine, "(Re)negotiating the Heterosexual Street." Laws forbidding sodomy and homosexuality in the Victorian era did not include laws forbidding lesbian love, reportedly because Queen Victoria denied that lesbians existed. Apparently this legal aporia or blind spot was also present in the United States.

43. Schaefer, *Bold!*

44. Ibid., 4.

45. *Attack of the 50 Foot Woman*, directed by Nathan Juran.

46. Clark, *At a Theater or Drive-in near You*.

47. Pollard, *Sex and Violence*.

48. "Hollywood Rating System, 1968," *Hollywood's America*.

49. Miller, *Social History of Crime and Punishment in America*.

50. *Black Mama, White Mama*, directed by Eddie Romero.

51. *Blood Bath*, directed by Jack Hill.

52. *Spider Baby*, directed by Jack Hill.

53. *Isle of the Snake People*, directed by Juan Ibáñez and Jack Hill.

54. *Big Doll House*, directed by Jack Hill.

55. *Big Bird Cage*, directed by Jack Hill.

56. *Coffy*, directed by Jack Hill; *Foxy Brown*, directed by Jack Hill.

57. *Bangkok Hilton*, directed by Ken Cameron, was a 1989 Australian TV miniseries (one season starring Nicole Kidman); *Caged Heat II: Stripped of Freedom* was a 1994 production of New Horizons Picture Corporation directed by Cirio H. Santiago and shot in the Philippines. *Deported Women of the SS Special Section* (1976) was directed by Rino Di Silvestro and featured young women in a prison camp in a Nazi-occupied country. *Female Prisoner Scorpion #701* (1972), directed by Shunya Itô and produced in Tokyo by the Toei Company, brought a Japanese version of the genre to the screen. *Ilsa, She-Wolf of the SS* (1974), directed by Don Edmonds, was a dominatrix-style "doctor" who does medical experiments (highly sexualized) on prison camp inmates. This produced several spin-offs known as the "Ilsa series" including *Ilsa, Harem Keeper of the Oil Sheiks* (1976) and *Ilsa, the*

Wicked Warden (1977), directed by Jesús Franco and released in the United States as *Wanda, the Wicked Warden*. *Women in Cages* (1971) was directed by Gerardo de Leon for Balatbat Productions and New World Pictures; it featured a character named Carol "Jeff" Jeffries, a naïve American woman staying in the Philippines who is given ten years in prison.

58. *Chained Heat*, directed by Paul Nicholas. Linda Blair said the script was rewritten so many times during filming that the final product did not resemble the script she had signed on for. A boom microphone made several appearances in the film as well.

59. *Women in Chains*, directed by Bernard L. Kowalski.

60. *Against Their Will: Women in Prison*, directed by Karen Arthur. The film was released in 2006 on DVD with the title *Caged Seduction: The Shocking True Story*.

61. *Stuck!* Directed by Steve Balderson. In addition to Mink Stole (a John Waters film actor), the film also starred Karen Black, and the production company's name appears to be a pun on the lesbian-centered audience they expected to watch the film.

62. Austin, Marino, Carroll, McCall, and Richards, "Use of Incarceration."

Bibliography

Acquitted. Directed by Frank Strayer. Hollywood: Columbia Pictures, 1929. Film.

Against Their Will: Women in Prison. Directed by Karen Arthur. Toronto: ABC Films, 1994. Telefilm.

Attack of the 50 Foot Woman. Directed by Nathan Juran (as Nathan Hertz). New Orleans: Woolner Brothers Pictures, 1958. Film.

Austin, James, Bruce Marino, Leo Carroll, Patricia McCall, and Stephen Richards. "The Use of Incarceration in the United States." *Critical Criminology* 10 (2001): 16–41.

The Big Doll House. Directed by Jack Hill. Hollywood: New World Pictures, 1971. Film.

The Big House. Directed by George W. Hill. Culver City, CA: Metro-Goldwyn-Mayer Studios, 1930. Film.

Binder, John J., and Arthur Lurigio. "Introduction to the Special Issue—the Rise and Fall of Chicago's Organized Crime Family: A Brief History of the Outfit." *Journal of Contemporary Criminal Justice* 29, no. 2 (2013): 184–97.

The Bird Cage. Directed by Jack Hill. Hollywood: New World Pictures, 1972. Film.

Black Mama, White Mama. Directed by Eddie Romero. Hollywood: American International Pictures, 1973. Film.

Blood Bath. Directed by Jack Hill. Hollywood: Avala Films; Jack Hill Films, 1966. Film.

Bouclin, Suzanne. "Women in Prison Movies as Feminist Jurisprudence." *Canadian Journal of Women and the Law* 21, no. 1 (2009): 19–34.

Caged. Directed by John Cornwall. Hollywood: Warner Brothers, 1950. Film.

Caged Heat. Directed by Jonathan Demme. Hollywood: New World Pictures, 1974. Film.

Chained Heat. Directed by Paul Nicholas. U.S. and West Germany: Heat GBR; Intercontinental Productions, 1983. Film.

Clark, Randall. *At a Theater or Drive-in near You: The History, Culture, and Politics of the American Exploitation Film*. New York: Routledge, 1995.

Coffy. Directed by Jack Hill. Hollywood: New World Pictures, 1973. Film.

Collins, Patricia Hill. *Black Feminist Thought: Knowledge, Consciousness, and the Politics of Empowerment*. New York: Routledge, 2000.

"Crimes: 1882." *Liverpool Journal* (January 7, 1882). *Old Mersey Times* (blog), 2002. Accessed September 16, 2017. http://www.old-merseytimes.co.uk/crimes1882.html.

Dixon, Wheeler Winston. "Filmmaking 'for the Fun of It': An Interview with Jack Hill." *Film Criticism* 29, no. 3 (2005): 46–59.

Doherty, Thomas Patrick. *Pre-Code Hollywood: Sex, Immorality, and Insurrection in American Cinema*. New York: Columbia University Press, 1999.

Foucault, Michel. *Discipline and Punish: The Birth of the Prison*. New York: Vantage Books, 1979.

Foxy Brown. Directed by Jack Hill. Hollywood: New World Pictures, 1974. Film.

Freedman, Estelle B. "The Prison Lesbian: Race, Class, and the Construction of the Aggressive Female Homosexual, 1915–1965." *Feminist Studies* 22, no. 2 (1996): 397–423.

———. *Their Sisters' Keepers: Women's Prison Reform in America, 1830–1930*. Ann Arbor: University of Michigan Press, 1981.

"Full Synopsis: *The Godless Girl*." Turner Classic Movies. Accessed September 16, 2017. http://www.tcm.com.

The Godless Girl. Directed by Cecil B. DeMille, Culver City, CA: C. B. DeMille Productions, 1929. Film.

"The Godless Girl: Summary." *AFI Film Catalog*. Accessed September 16, 2017. www.afi.com/members/catalog.

Goodman, Philip. "'It's Just Black, White, or Hispanic': An Observational Study of Racializing Moves in California's Segregated Prison Reception Centers." *Law & Society Review* 42, no. 4 (2008): 735–70.

Griffiths, Alison. "A Portal to the Outside World: Motion Pictures in the Penitentiary." *Film History: An International Journal* 25, no. 4 (2013): 1–35.

Hell's Highway. Directed by Rowland Brown. Hollywood: RKO Pictures, 1932. Film.

"The Hollywood Rating System, 1968." In *Hollywood's America: Twentieth-Century America through Film*. 4th ed., edited by Steven Mintz and Randy W. Roberts, 301–3. Malden, MA: Wiley-Blackwell, 2010.

I Am a Fugitive from a Chain Gang. Directed by Mervyn LeRoy. Hollywood: Warner Brothers, 1933. Film.

Imitation of Life. Directed by John M. Stahl. Hollywood: Universal Pictures, 1934. Film.

"Incarcerated Women." The Sentencing Project: Research and Advocacy for Reform. Updated November 2015. Accessed September 16, 2017. http://www.sentencingproject.org.

Irwin, Amos. "How *Orange Is the New Black* Misrepresents Women's Federal Prison and Why It Matters." *Huffington Post*, June 11, 2015. Accessed September 16, 2017. http://www.huffingtonpost.com.

Isle of the Snake People. Directed by Juan Ibáñez and Jack Hill. Santa Monica, CA: Azteca Film Company; Columbia Pictures Corporation, 1971. Film.

Joyrich, Lynne. "All That Television Allows: TV Melodrama, Postmodernism and Consumer Culture." *Camera Obscura* 6 (1988): 128–53.

Kramer, Fritzi. "The Godless Girl (1929): A Silent Film Review." *Movies Silently: Celebrate Silent Film* (blog), January 18, 2015. Accessed September 16, 2017. http://moviessilently.com.

Kurshan, Nancy. "Women and Imprisonment in the U.S.: History and Current Reality," Prison Activist Resource Center. Accessed September 16, 2017. http://www.freedomarchives.org.

Ladies of the Big House. Directed by Marion Gering. Hollywood: Paramount, 1931. Film.

Ladies They Talk About. Directed by William Keighley. Hollywood: Warner Brothers, 1933. Film.

Laughter in Hell. Directed by Edward L. Cahn. Hollywood: Universal Pictures, 1933. Film.

McPherson, James M. "Parchman's Plantation." *New York Times*, April 28, 1996.

Miller, Wilbur R., ed. *The Social History of Crime and Punishment in America: An Encyclopedia*. Los Angeles: Sage Reference, 2012.

Morey, Anne. "'The Judge Called Me an Accessory': Women's Prison Films, 1950–1962." *Journal of Popular Film and Television* 23, no. 2 (1995): 80–87.

Morrison, Toni. *Playing in the Dark: Whiteness and the Literary Imagination.* New York: Vintage Books, 1992.

"The Motion Picture Production Code of 1930." In *Hollywood's America: Twentieth-Century American through Film.* 4th ed., edited by Steven Mintz and Randy W. Roberts, 119–28. Malden, MA: Wiley-Blackwell, 2010.

New York Times. "A Woman Bandit." Review of *Ladies They Talk About. New York Times,* February 25, 1933.

Pollard, Tom. *Sex and Violence: The Hollywood Censorship Wars.* New York: Routledge, 2009.

Rafter, Nicole Hahn. "Gender, Prisons, and Prison History." *Social Science History* 9, no. 3 (1985): 233–47.

———. *Partial Justice: Women Prisons and Social Control.* New Brunswick, NJ: Transaction, 1990.

———. "Prisons for Women: 1790–1980," *Crime and Justice* 5 (1983): 129–81.

Rathbone, Christina. "Locked In: Ever Since America's First Women's Prison Opened Nearly 200 Years Ago, Debate Has Raged over How to Treat Female Inmates." *Boston Globe,* May 29, 2005, D1.

Reed, Jennifer. "Reading Gender Politics on the L Word: The Moira/Max Transition." *Journal of Popular Film and Television* 37, no. 4 (2009): 169–78.

Rodimtseva, Irina V. "On the Hollywood Chain Gang: The Screen Version of Robert E. Burns' *I Am a Fugitive from a Georgia Chain Gang!* and Penal Reform of the 1930s–1940s." *Arizona Quarterly: A Journal of American Literature, Culture, and Theory* 66, no. 3 (2010): 123–46.

Ross, Steven Joseph. "The Seen, the Unseen, and the Obscene: Pre-Code Hollywood." *Reviews in American History* 28, no. 2 (2000): 270–77.

Schaefer, Eric. *Bold! Daring! Shocking! True! A History of Exploitation Film, 1919–1959.* Durham, NC: Duke University Press, 1999.

Shatto, Rachel. "This Women-in-Prison Film Pushes the Boundaries of the Genre." *Curve,* April 2010, 34–35. Accessed September 16, 2017. http://www.starinajohnson.com/uploads/1/3/1/5/13157856/curve_interview.pdf.

Sklar, Robert. *Movie-Made America: A Cultural History of American Movies.* New York: Vintage Books, 1994.

So Young, So Bad. Directed by Bernard Vorhaus. Hollywood: United Artists, 1950. Film.

Spider Baby. Directed by Jack Hill. Hollywood: Lasky Monka Films, 1967. Film.

Stuck! Directed by Steve Balderson. Wamego, KS: Dikenga Films, 2009.

Truesdale, Jeff. "*Orange Is the New Black*: The Real Alex Vause Separates Fact from Fiction." *People.com,* May 7, 2015.

Valentine, Gill. "(Re)negotiating the Heterosexual Street: Lesbian Productions of Space." In *Body Space: Destabilizing Geographies of Gender and Sexuality*, edited by Nancy Duncan, 143–54. London: Routledge, 1996.

Williams, Lucy. "A Growing Class of Offenders." *Wayward Women* (blog), April 18, 2012. Accessed September 16, 2017. https://waywardwomen .wordpress.com.

Willis, Andrew. "*Forced to Fight* (1991): American Martial Arts Movies and the Exploitation Film Tradition." *Scope*, July 2000. Accessed September 16, 2017. http://www.nottingham.ac.uk/scope/documents/2000/july-2000/willis.pdf.

Women in Chains. Directed by Bernard L. Kowalski. Hollywood: Paramount Television Studios, 1972. Telefilm.

Women without Names. Directed by Robert Florey. Hollywood: Paramount Pictures, 1940. Film.

Women's Prison. Directed by Lewis Seiler. Hollywood: Columbia Pictures, 1955. Film.

2. Forever Imprisoned? Challenging the Gaze in *Orange Is the New Black*

Rebecca Kern

Fictional media representations of women's sexuality often have historically played into the cultural fantasies of the straight male gaze.[1] To achieve this, women's bodies have been constructed into a series of archetypes and dichotomies: the goddess / the villainess, the virgin / the whore, the damsel in distress / the femme fatale, the perfect mother and wife / the neurotic, among others.[2] For decades, examples of these representations have been seen in movies and television. Women's bodies are templates for which their sexuality and femininity are either revered or punished. The problematic nature of these representations is often discussed within feminist and gender studies literature.[3] Representations of women in prison, whether they be in film or television, have also played on these dichotomies, often highlighting the darker side of the archetypal imagery. Such representations have offered up these women as sexual objects imprisoned not only as punishment for their wrongdoings but also (or perhaps more so) as titillation for audiences. Their stories, experiences, and lives had no real place in the overarching plot, or perhaps more importantly were irrelevant. They were props, and as such, their bodies became further devalued. The power dynamics imbued in socio-sexual institutions seek to manage the morality of the body, and of sexuality, particularly that of the female. Much of this is based on the productive value of the body in society.[4] If the body overcomes or resists the natural law(s) of sexual and gender norms, it will be reined in—hence never allowing for those with oppressed bodies to break free from normative sociosexual values, as there are always strategic forces working in opposition. Mass media have the ability to act as a moralizer, as one of many social institutions that both construct and reflect matrices of power.[5]

Orange Is the New Black (*OITNB*), a recent original series on Netflix and a contemporary program about women in prison, has the potential to challenge sociosexual norms of power and the body in a number of ways. Since it began in 2013, *OITNB* has garnered immense popular media attention with its four seasons.[6] The show differs from previous prison dramas in a number of ways. First, its protagonists are women. Second, it is based (loosely) on the memoir of Piper Kerman, one of the primary characters in the show. Third, it explores various forms of diversity—sexual, racial, gendered, and aged—within a women's prison. Most importantly, the show appears to challenge historical representations of female sexuality by incorporating new constructions of female sexual identity in prison. These constructions often still focus on sexuality and gender; however, the gaze of the audience shifts in and out of sexual titillation when confronting female sexual experiences, such as rape, sexual disempowerment, pregnancy, gender fluidity, and transformations. The show accomplishes this through plot windows that offer the audience an understanding of who these women are and where they came from. In addition, the camera and other characters on the show provide additional lenses of identity construction and confrontation of broader sociopolitical issues relating to the sexuality and gendered identities of women. *OITNB* requires that the audience gaze upon it all, in the end forcing viewers to negotiate cultural norms, stereotypes, and perhaps even their own cultural roles and identities.

This chapter addresses the ways in which female identities in prison have been presented to audiences historically and the ways in which *OITNB* has challenged those constructions, including how the gaze changes when the audience may not be primarily male, or straight. Focusing specifically on the characters of Pennsatucky and Dayanara, both inmates, this chapter questions whether the show, even with the ways in which it challenges how the audience gazes upon these women and addresses their issues, actually deviates from some of the same problematic historical representations.

The Female Body on Screen

Sociopolitical institutions of power regulate the body.[7] These institutions write power on the body by establishing normative modes of practice and institutionalizing gender norms through education, government, religion, and legal systems. As a result, binary oppositions of the male/female and masculine/feminine act as ways to establish structure for hegemonic gender norms and to maintain institutionalized power. As Scott articulated, "Oppositions rest on metaphors and cross-references, and often in patriarchal discourse, sexual difference (the contrast masculine/feminine) serves to encode or establish meanings that are literally unrelated to gender or body."[8] The dichotomy of the female is that which is not male; she is passive, cold, and irrational.[9] The female body is constricted, restricted, determined, and defined, regardless of race, class, or ethnicity.[10] Those women who defy normative restrictions by speaking their minds, talking too loudly, expressing their sexual desires, or taking up too much space with their bodies are immoral and deserve punishment.[11] Alternatively, hypersexualization of the body, while often a tactic of conforming within patriarchy, also incurs judgments of morality. Restraint in all forms—body, mind, voice, sexuality, and appearance—is more normative, more moral.

Regulation of female bodies on-screen is the same as in many other sociocultural environments. Bodies are spectacle, objectifiable.[12] Fictional story lines, such as those presented in film and television, suggest behaviors, bodily comportments, and other forms of sexualized appearance that adhere to normative or transgressive identities. As such, the same series of dichotomies is made present in media as a way to reiterate the normative and transgressive dualities, and exemplify those that are most socially compliant. There is the good and bad woman who engages in good and bad forms of sexual activity.[13] The mythical structure of the good/evil dichotomy appears in many representations of woman in film and television: the good—the virginal and sexually chaste, the perfect caregiver and wife, the damsel in distress; and the bad—the sexually deviant, the slut or whore, the villainess, the neurotic. The former follows a trajectory that is manageable, one that feminist scholars have noted as the feminine complement to the masculine hero. The latter cannot be managed as easily, and as a result her femininity is coupled with her sexuality. This latter representation is often discussed as the most powerful for women as she has the most agency. If a woman can be the heroine, or be the seductress, for example, then she is using her power. Women are given their due on-screen, but in the end, their bodies, femininity, and sexuality are usurped by the very story lines that gave them the power in the first place. As Butler noted, "gender is a performance with clearly punitive consequences," and "those who fail to do their gender right are regularly punished."[14] Such a woman is punished either by other characters on-screen or by the audience who has decided that she is an unworthy woman unless her sexuality and femininity are contained.

The gaze of the audience, however, makes the issue of women's bodies on-screen even more complicated. While narratives may provide closure and act as a moralizing agent, the audience also plays an important role as judge and jury for female on-screen bodies and social norms of women's sexuality. Social norms of morality, which are in themselves a form of institutional control, are enacted every time viewers connect with images of the body and sexuality on-screen. Viewers cast judgment, recognize social wrongs, and at times may see the theme or character as a reflection of their own lives. The audience is the Panopticon, as defined by Foucault: "A machine for dissociating the see/being seen dyad: in the peripheric ring, one is totally seen, without ever seeing; in the central tower, one sees everything without ever being seen."[15] One of the primary media characterizations for which the audience is asked, whether consciously or subconsciously, to act as surveyor is of images of women in prison. In prison narratives, particularly ones that focus on women's bodies and sexuality, the Panopticon takes on multiple meanings.

Women and Sexuality in Prison Scenes

Media images of women in prison have historically been highly sexualized depictions of woman-on-woman action.[16] The depictions, primarily in film, are best described as soft pornography, stereotypically presenting the women as objects of deviant flesh. As discussed in the chapter 1, *Caged Heat* (1974), *The Big Bird Cage* (1972), and *The Big Doll House* (1971) are three of the more recent examples of films that offered up these images of women. However, they are certainly not the first, as there were examples of films from the 1930s—*Ladies They Talk About* (1933); 1950s—*Girls in Prison* (1956), *Female Convict* (1952), and *Caged* (1950); and 1960s—*House of Women* (1962), *Reformatory Girls* (1960), and *Women in Prison* (1961), which Ciasullo argued are cinematic constructions of the women-in-prison pulp novel.[17] Cecil claimed that the "'babes-behind-bars' films are detrimental in that they negate the issues surrounding women in prison"; instead the imagery "still presents [women in prison] stereotypically and inaccurately."[18] The dichotomies of female innocent and transgressor are always made immediately known to the audience. Prison films, as Morey noted, "are sites of contradictions" because they "brutalize and masculinize both female inmates and female staff members."[19]

These films tend to feature a young woman newly brought into prison. Prior to prison she may have led a life as a loving wife and mother, at once the prude virgin, caregiver, and the more civilized of the sexes. Yet, somewhere along the way she committed a crime, and then the standard narrative arc begins. She is met by a series of matronly guards, usually with short hair and read as masculine and homosexual.[20] Her body is then searched, her possessions are removed, and the audience watches as she is stared at and/or objectified by a number of different female prison archetypes—the victimizer (warden or other prison administrator, the sexual predator), the victim (the innocent female or the sexual pawn), and the heroine seeking justice.[21] Alternatively, other characterizations of women in prison show representations of women in situational comedies or dramas.

Although to date there have been few programs on television that focus on women in prison, a few notable fictional programs include *Wentworth* (a current Australian drama), *Prisoner* (an Australian drama from the 1980s—also known as *Cell Block H* in the United States and Britain), *Bad Girls* (a popular British drama that ran for seven years), *Women in Prison* (an American sitcom from the 1980s), and the current American program *OITNB*. As Marsh suggested, these characterizations typically began as educational dramas and quickly declined into camp and stereotypical imagery.[22] The stereotypical imagery Marsh spoke of is the sexuality of the inmates rather than their lives and the crimes that they committed, which is not dissimilar to what appeared in earlier movies.[23] Cecil also noted in her study that documentaries, talk shows, and televised newsmagazines generate similar characterizations, and sexuality and sexual relations as seen in earlier movies were frequently discussed on newsmagazines.[24] The hardships women faced before going into prison, the types of actual rehabilitation programs available in prison, or what the women may face upon their release is primarily avoided, except in rare circumstances.[25] Hence, media "have not generally improved public understanding or stimulated reform [in the system]."[26] In the end, the seemingly civilized, motherly figure that society expects women to embody gets shifted inside the prison walls as they become even less the woman that society wants them to be (and more the masculinized version society has deemed undesirable) and become, ultimately, the woman that society with its social norms seeks to manage even further.

Images of women in prison directly conflict with depictions of men in prison, who are almost always shown in situations of conflict, such as fighting with their jailers or with other prisoners.[27] In these instances, men and male bodies are given the opportunity to fight back, despite also being in a contained environment. While male prisoners may not be considered productive members of society, their social use-value is not based solely on what their bodies can produce. Production is a form of power, inscribed through systematic social norms. Power also functions and is exercised in matrices of socioeconomic situations, and always with a strategic goal.[28] Power over the body happens through the body's ability to produce and through norms of sexuality written on the body. Foucault in *Discipline and Punish* discussed how unproductive people are considered problematic in society and thus disciplined in state institutions.[29] However, state institutions are merely a symbolic reference for a broader schema of social power dynamics. Current sociosexual norms and the subsequent sexual binaries were arguably born out of the psychiatricization or institutionalization of sexuality in the nineteenth and twentieth centuries,[30] and as such, control of the body and its sexual nature was/is a way to control morality. As Foucault stated, "You will have no sexuality except by subjecting yourself to the law."[31] The law includes social moralities as well as the institutions that influence jurisdiction over the body: religion, education, the penal system, and mass media. These institutions, which function as disciplinarians, are embroiled with and upheld by a society that continues to guarantee their existence. According to Foucault, "Discipline 'makes' individuals; it is the specific technique of a power that regards individuals both as objects and as instruments of its exercise."[32] Hence, the audience for media also functions as a part of the mechanism of surveillance, because media demand cooperation. Media require the audience to be the examiner of social norms. In Foucault's words,

> The examination combines the techniques of an observing hierarchy and those of a normalizing judgment. It is a normalizing gaze, a surveillance that makes it possible to qualify, to classify, and to punish. It establishes over individuals a visibility through which one differentiates them and judges them. That is why, in all the mechanisms of discipline, the examination is highly ritualized. [. . .] At the heart of the procedures of discipline, it manifests the subjection of those who are perceived as objects and the objectification of those who are subjected.[33]

OITNB is a show that constantly forces viewers to negotiate judgment. The show is constructed within the confines of the sociocultural norms of identity, even when it works to break free from totalizing narratives.

Sex, Sexuality, and *Orange Is the New Black*

In *OITNB*, a prison dramatic comedy on Netflix, women are portrayed in a series of dramatic story lines that switch between their current situations and lives within the prison and their lives before they were imprisoned. Created by Jenji Kohan (of *Weeds*), the four seasons of thirteen episodes each can be watched in succession on Netflix, rather than waiting for each episode to air weekly. Since the show began, numerous characters have been introduced, coming from various backgrounds and representing different races, ethnicities, ages, socioeconomic strata, and sexual orientations.

Popular media have rendered the show revolutionary for its portrayals of women in prison and for its inclusion of Latinas, lesbians (whether they be femme, butch, etc.), trans women, black women, women of different body types and ethnicities, women from different class backgrounds, and just because it is a show about women.[34] The show won a 2013 Peabody award for its "funny and perceptive exploration of race, class, power and the persistence of a ragged kind of hope."[35] *OITNB* and its actors also have to their credit six Golden Globe nominations, sixteen Primetime Emmy nominations, two Screen Actor Guild awards, and an international BAFTA award.[36] Other critics and journalists claim it to be an honest and intelligent look at life inside a women's prison.[37] Compared to earlier portrayals in film and television, it may have appeared to be less stereotypical on its face. However, some mention the stereotypes that the show presents up front. Writer Mike Hale, of the *New York Times*, noted that the show opens with a shower scene and that some of the women's stories "tend toward big-house clichés, right down to lines like 'You need to man up' and 'Hope is a dangerous thing.'"[38] While the show begins with and first focuses on the character of Piper, a blonde, feminine, upper-class, and bisexual woman—the show is loosely based on the real Piper Kerman's 2010 memoir, *Orange Is the New Black: My Year in a Women's Prison*—the show moves away from the memoir in later seasons.

Viewers learn about the characters of *OITNB* through a narrative structure that quickly draws them into the life of Piper and the women around her. Each hour-long episode focuses on life inside Litchfield Penitentiary, located somewhere north of New York City. It is a minimum-security prison, so the prison itself is enclosed by walls and barbed wire, and there is the typical surveillance tower associated with all Western prison complexes. The narrative, while primarily set in the present, has vignettes of characters' backstories—the stories of their childhoods and how they arrived at the prison.

In many ways the show starts as many prison narratives have before. The blonde, pretty, feminine, seemingly innocent woman (Piper) is thrust into the cutthroat environment of prison. She is first met by prison guards, almost all of whom are male, who proceed to strip her of her belongings. They then do a body-cavity search. Interestingly the assistant warden of the prison, Natalie "Fig" Figueroa, can be read as masculine in many ways. While she is presented as feminine in her dress and general appearance, she plays the role of cold villainess in her attitude toward others. However, she does use her sexuality as a way to get what she wants and to increase her role as victimizer.

Various forms of power are scripted onto these women's bodies and across these women's lives. The most obvious form is simply that these women are in prison. Additionally, the audience's gaze is established as a normative placeholder, one that is constructed to determine the value of each of these women's lives and wrongdoings. Another form is that the relationships between the guards and the inmates signify power dynamics, particularly when sex, gender roles, or sexuality is involved. These unequal power dynamics are further accentuated when the women are "othered" by more than just their sex and sexuality to include their race and ethnicity, class, and geographic upbringing. The primary characters that embody these ethnically "othered" identities include the Latinas—Gloria, Aleida, Flaca, and Dayanara; the black women—Sophia, Vee, Tastee, Poussey, and Suzanne; and even the Asian women—Brooke and Chang. Class is represented not only among the minority ethnicities of women but also the women who are Caucasian and come from rural locales, namely, Pennsatucky and Leanne. The women all come from different class upbringings and from different geographical places, all of which plays an important role in how the audience relates to and negotiates their stories. The judgmental gaze directed at these women is further strengthened by the audience, since women who embody the Other are those whom viewers expect to see in prison settings.

Two very important story lines related to power, sex, and gender are those of Dayanara, an urban working-poor Latina, and Pennsatucky, a rural, poor, white woman. These two primary characters are introduced in the first season, but we do not get their backstories until the third season. Both of these women have been taught that their bodies and femininity are connected to men and male appreciation. Their backstories help to illuminate the decisions they make while in prison, especially when negotiating power and their bodies. In addition, the audience is forced to cast judgment on these women—for their morality and even more so for their victimhood (or lack thereof).

Pennsatucky

The character called Pennsatucky, whose name is Tiffany Doggett, came to Litchfield after she murdered an abortion clinic nurse who offended her by commenting on how many abortions she had undergone. A self-proclaimed born-again Christian, Pennsatucky declares her own moral judgment against anyone who performs or grants abortions. She is portrayed as a Bible-preaching, Jesus-loving, self-righteous individual. She appears disheveled, with teeth missing from years of methamphetamine or crack cocaine abuse. All of this is made clear to the viewer in the first season, yet what is unknown is how she changed from someone having abortions to someone who murdered for them and then preached against them. The viewer also does not understand how many she has had or the circumstances under which they occurred. She is not well liked by the other inmates, except for her friends with an upbringing similar to hers. In addition, due to her teeth and long stringy hair, she is made fun of for being ugly. Pennsatucky does not outwardly show that she cares much, as she does not want the affections of the other girls. Her appearance does, however, place her in an important position of class. The viewer sees her as dirty, rural, and an addict.

A turning point for Pennsatucky comes in season 2 when she is given a new set of teeth, after losing her remaining teeth in a fight, and a new haircut. Pennsatucky is so proud that she keeps smiling at everyone, especially the male counselor, Sam Healy. For the viewer, Pennsatucky appears less damaged and more attractive. No longer is she just rural and pedestrian; she can now pass for someone more cosmopolitan and middle class. One commentator on the show wrote about the importance of Pennsatucky's teeth:

> For women, missing teeth also signifies being a victim of domestic abuse, and while we Americans pity victims, we also blame them for not being brave or strong or smart enough to get away from their abusers. More broadly, on one side of the class divide are those with normatively attractive bodies, respectable educational achievements and decent jobs. On the other side are those whose poor teeth and other "defects" are read as signs that they are incapable of managing their own lives.[39]

She becomes acceptable, despite being in prison, because she is attractive. The audience judges her appearance, once again showing the power in the gaze of the viewer. There is also a morality attached to this judgment. Although Pennsatucky has had abortions, the audience begins to feel pity, perhaps even empathy, because she is perceived differently due to her changed appearance. This attractiveness becomes even more important in season 3 when she is befriended by a new male guard.

In season 3, Pennsatucky undergoes a transformation. She begins to mourn the loss of her aborted fetuses by setting crosses into the earth and saying prayers over them, and she becomes less insolent and is given more privileges. She also makes friends with Big Boo, the butch lesbian. It is in this season that the audience receives her backstory. As a child, Pennsatucky was raised poor in rural Appalachia. Through flashbacks the audience learns that Pennsatucky's mother told her that men will want her for her body. In fact, her mother told her that, since she had started menstruating and so would begin "a tittin' and a hairin'," she should just lie back and take it from a man as it would go much faster. "Best thing is to go on and let them do their business," says her mama. "If you're real lucky, most of 'em will be quick, like your daddy. It's like a bee sting, in and out before you knew it was happening." The younger Pennsatucky replies that bee stings hurt.[40] Further into the same episode, another flashback shows her hanging out as a teen, finally finding love after a string of casual sexual encounters with men (as she was taught to do by her mother). Pennsatucky is portrayed as the stereotypical poor, rural woman who is promiscuous and deceitful,[41] behaviors passed down from her mother and so perhaps not her own fault. For the audience who may not be familiar with this environment, how she is defined in the viewers' eyes is paramount. While viewers may believe that no woman deserves to be raped, they may also not be able to navigate certain conditions. As such, her poor upbringing and her poor choices may make viewers less likely to feel empathy and more likely to dismiss what happened to her. After Pennsatucky's first successful relationship, another flashback shows her boyfriend leaving town, after which she is raped in a bathroom. The camera zeroes in on the confinement of the space. She resists her rapist at first but then stops fighting. She does not cry or yell for help. She just acquiesces, as if this is what she expects her life to be. Her face goes blank, suggesting to the audience that her life was constricted from an early age and that her body had been taken before she really had a choice.

The audience is confronted with a similar expression when Pennsatucky is raped for a second time in the same episode, in the present time of the story. This is particularly poignant, as Pennsatucky, in her newfound appearance and attitude, has also found some freedom as the prison van driver. She is accompanied by a male prison guard, who befriends her and also tells her that he likes her. Just as with the boyfriend from her youth, she appears to have someone she can trust, and even perhaps love. However, when they are late coming back from an appointment, the guard is reprimanded and takes it out on Pennsatucky. He inflicts violence on her body. She does not understand why he is mad and grabs his arm; he turns around, grabs both of her arms, and says, "What do you want from me? This? This is what you want from me? Huh? This?"[42] He pushes her onto the backseat of the van and rapes her from behind, in broad daylight in the parking lot behind the prison, all the while saying, "This is what you're asking for?! This is what you're begging for?! Isn't it? You just lay there. This is what you wanted. Isn't it, Doggett?"[43] While he rapes her, he says her name over and over again and tells her that he loves her. Once again she is reminded that men do not actually want her and that she is not (or should not be) worth any more than an object of sexual imprisonment. During the rape, the camera does not pull away to show the rape but instead tightly focuses on her face. Viewers can see only her face, framed by the edges of their screen. She has the same blank expression as before, except for one tear, and she does not resist. The freedom that she briefly experienced has been stripped from her, and again she is confined to a life predetermined. One critic remarked on the intent behind such a scene: "The reason—the only reason—to film a rape scene is to make the audience dig into that feeling of discomfort, to force us to be witnesses to the torture we are capable of inflicting on one another and come away with a deeper understanding of who we hurt and the depth of their pain."[44] For viewers, the camera forces their gaze into the confining space the camera frame provides. Everyone has to look, and look away.

Dayanara

Another prisoner at Litchfield, Dayanara also grew up seeing her mother and other women around her depend on men for emotional and financial support. Dayanara, a young urban Latina, grew up in the inner city. The oldest of five children, she was often neglected and was routinely forced to take care of siblings, as her mother was frequently out. The audience learns little of Dayanara's childhood until season 3, but we do know that she is in prison with her mother, Aleida, who had arrived there earlier on drug charges. Any understanding of Dayanara's circumstances until season 3 comes from understanding Aleida's crime, which involved taking the fall for her drug-dealing boyfriend, Cesar, who had set up a drug lab in their apartment. It is also understood that drugs were frequently in the home where Dayanara and her siblings lived.

Young Dayanara's relationship with her mother was volatile, as her mother fluctuated between needing her daughter and needing men. In the flashbacks to Dayanara's childhood, she is shown being taken to a summer camp by her mother. Dayanara does not want to go and would rather stay with her mother, but Aleida needs the break and tells her, "Wait a minute, you little brat. You think I got nothing better than to take care of you? This is my one month vacation and I got things planned starting tonight. Mommy's going out."[45] We then, however, see her sitting in her car, sad that she has left her daughter behind. Similar fluctuations of emotion occur when Dayanara returns ecstatic over her time at camp because Aleida is unhappy that Dayanara had such a good time without her. The push-and-pull dynamic the audience experiences with Dayanara and Aleida in the flashbacks helps to explain their mother-daughter dynamic as adults. Years later, after Aleida went to prison and Dayanara came to visit her with Aleida's children, Aleida's only concern was whether Dayanara had slept with Cesar. Aleida needed others in order to love herself, and attention from others allowed her to do that. Consequently Dayanara learned to behave similarly, which was then exploited by the prison's power dynamics.

In the first season Dayanara becomes involved in a prison romance with a white male guard called Bennett. They meet secretly on the yard or in utility closets in the prison. Since he cannot risk his job by showing her special treatment in front of other prisoners or staff, lest his feelings become known, he reprimands her along with the other women. Regardless of this behavior, Dayanara is still clearly enamored with him, and their sexual encounters eventually lead to a pregnancy. Viewers are party to all of these developments as voyeurs of a forbidden prison relationship: that of guard and inmate. Inmates, whether they consent to sex or not, are deemed unable to consent because of the unequal power dynamics. According to the Bureau of Justice Statistics, in 2011, 49 percent of all inmate allegations of sexual misdeeds "involved staff sexual misconduct (any sexual act directed toward an inmate by staff) or sexual harassment (demeaning verbal statements of a sexual nature) directed toward inmates."[46] However, in this instance, the audience is fooled into believing this is a love story. The morality becomes murky, but the way the narrative is presented, the audience does not see this as rape in the same way it would later perceive the rape of Pennsatucky. It is not violent and appears consensual, giving the false impression that power is shared.

As the series progresses into the second and third seasons, Bennett is no longer written as the "nice guy" and Dayanara's savior; rather he is someone

worried about what his "mistake" (the pregnancy) will do to his career. He meets
with Cesar, Dayanara's stepfather, to tell him he proposed. About raising kids
Cesar tells him, "This shit ain't easy,"[47] as he passes off his children to his new
girlfriend. He also tells Bennett to get "a little bacon on the side,"[48] meaning
to get a girlfriend. Bennett realizes his relationship is doomed and eventually
takes off, not telling Dayanara or anyone else. Even the popular press noted
that the relationship between Bennett and Dayanara is fraught with problems:

> We're meant to see their furtive glances and secret courtship as inappropri-
> ate and somewhat uncomfortable, but ultimately as a mutual, consensual
> love story—not what it legally is: rape. Even Bennett's outward signs of
> abusive control are played as romantic, as when the guard makes a big
> show of grabbing Daya and yelling that she needs to show "Less attitude!
> You're not in charge here, I am!" in a domineering manner, as cover to
> tuck a note in her pocket telling her where to meet him for a rendezvous.[49]

The narrative of Dayanara becomes even more problematic when her
mother, Aleida, suggests blaming the pregnancy on another guard (nicknamed
Pornstache for being sexually creepy) in order to save Bennett. Dayanara
publicly declares that Pornstache raped her, leading to his termination
and prison time for a crime he did not commit. This narrative poses three
issues. The first is that she was raped, but instead of the rapist (Bennett)
taking responsibility, it is pushed onto someone society has already deemed
a deviant. Second, if the audience decides that it was consensual in some
way and not a rape at all, she is lying about a violent encounter, which puts
other women in jeopardy who may actually be in danger and telling the truth
about rape and sexual assault. And third, as Tillet stated, "The show not
only reproduces stereotypes that women in prison are untrustworthy and lie
about sexual assault,"[50] but also that Dayanara is a Latina stereotype—fertile, passive, sexual, promiscuous, and in need of a man.[51] The narrative of
Dayanara neatly does what Molina-Guzman called "symbolic colonization,"
where "ethnic and racial differences are hegemonically tamed through the
media,"[52] and they function through disciplining the body and identity.
Having Dayanara enter into a forbidden relationship, couched as romance
but with unequal power dynamics, is symbolic colonization at the outset, as
her body is controlled through the romance and the subsequent pregnancy.
The colonization occurs again when the narrative turns her into a liar and a
Latin Lolita. Her body is further colonized by the audience who gazes upon
her body as something to be conquered.

As characters both Pennsatucky and Dayanara tell important stories. Their stories at times do engage the viewer in some uncomfortable moments, but the narratives also pose the characters as classic characters of ill repute. They are not virginal or innocent, despite the moments when they turn introspective. Due to the ways in which the characters are constructed, they are something to be managed—not just by a prison system but through narratives of socio-sexual norms based on their otherness in race and class. The audience plays an integral role in the disciplining of these women, because the audience decides if their fate is deserved through the act of watching.

Audience Negotiation

Power fluctuates, but only to a point. Control is not static but rather is a finely tuned set of strategies where those with more power or access use power against those in weaker positions. Female prisoners' bodies are disciplined through their daily routines—meals, sleep, exercise, work; however, control of their immediate selves (call it the corporeal body and its soul) is something important to each of these women, who look for ways to reassert it. In many ways, the body is all that these women have. It is theirs and it is personal. They own it. Everything else is communal or has been stripped away. To remove the body from the subject is to remove the last thing they own or control, whether it is taken by force or they willingly give it away to another in a position of power. In the process, the body is reduced to an object. Power for these women is in the negotiation of activity and passivity, and in subordination and liberation.

Foucault may have spoken from the position of a male voice, which has angered many feminist scholars,[53] but his position has merit. He discussed the cyclical nature of power, and nothing is more cyclical than the sociocultural structures of gendered control of the body. Its repetition begins from an early age, and it permeates class, race, and ethnic strata, among others. The ability for power to hold such an influence stems from the factors that make it commonplace and the players who make it an everyday practice. Within media, viewers are those players. They pass judgment, address social norms and wrongdoings, and see themselves reflected, however fictionalized, in what they watch. As Haugaard said about Foucault's concept of the Panopticon, "We do not come to know the 'truth' or our 'real interests' but come to recognize ourselves; and, in so doing, we are given the possibility of reflexively reconstituting ourselves, and the society which surrounds us, through social critique."[54] *OITNB* perhaps did not offer sexualized imagery through the characters of Pennsatucky and Dayanara in ways previously found in women's prison film or television. These women were not bound in chains, and at least with these two characters, the audience was not focused on the stereotypical girl-on-girl action notorious in earlier prison films. However, the narratives of these characters do force the audience to negotiate their transgressions as well as engage with the objectification of their bodies. To date, the fictional men who inflicted the bodily crimes against these women have not been punished, but societal practice would tell us that women who do not follow normative gendered behavior are managed. As both of these women are in prison, and are considered "othered" in society due to their race and class, they are not likely to receive story lines that reconcile what was done to them. The audience, as gazers, surveyors, and critics, may find that violence against women in any form is wrong, regardless of circumstance, and be angry that justice was not served. This may be the point where there is the most truth. While this show is fiction, it does reflect interesting and complex negotiations of power. For the audience watching, the real struggle is in how these power dynamics are a reflection of sociosexual norms. More importantly, the struggle is in deciding what to do with these power dynamics and in the ways that each audience member plays a role in a social machine that keeps the process going. The power of the gaze is more than what happens while watching; it is what viewers choose to do with the information after they finish.

Notes

1. Gledhill, "Pleasurable Negotiations"; Mulvey, "Visual Pleasure and Narrative Cinema."

2. Clowers, "Dykes, Gangs, and Danger"; Haskell, *From Reverence to Rape*; Morey, "Judge Called Me an Accessory."

3. Bartky, "Feminine Body"; Bartky, "Foucault, Femininity"; Bordo, *Unbearable Weight*; DeLaurentis, "Violence of Rhetoric"; Scott, "Deconstructing Equality-versus-Difference."

4. Foucault, *Discipline and Punish*.

5. Gramsci, "Hegemony, Intellectuals and the State."

6. McClelland, "'Orange Is the New Black': Caged Heat"; Matthews, "'Orange is the New Black' Is the Best TV Show"; Poniewozik, "Dead Tree Alert"; Sered, "What Pennsatucky's Teeth Tell Us"; Stuever, "Netflix's *Orange Is the New Black*: Brilliance behind Bars"; Thomas, "Yes, You Should Watch *Orange Is the New Black*"; Yuan, "'Orange Is the New Black' Is the Only TV Show That Understands Rape."

7. Althusser, "Ideology and Ideological State Apparatuses"; Gramsci, "Hegemony, Intellectuals and the State"; Foucault, *Discipline and Punish*; Foucault, *History of Sexuality*.

8. Scott, "Deconstructing Equality-versus-Difference," 760.

9. Juschka, *Political Bodies/Body Politic*.

10. Bartky, "Feminine Body"; Bartky, "Suffering to Be Beautiful"; Bordo, *Unbearable Weight*.

11. Bartky, "Feminine Body"; Bartky, "Suffering to Be Beautiful."

12. Bartky, "Foucault, Femininity."

13. Attwood, "Sex and the Media."

14. Butler, "Performative Acts and Gender Constitution," 404.

15. Foucault, *Discipline and Punish*, 201–2.

16. Cecil, "Looking beyond *Caged Heat*"; Ciasullo, "Containing 'Deviant' Desire"; Morey, "Judge Called Me an Accessory."

17. Ciasullo, "Containing 'Deviant' Desire."

18. Cecil, "Looking beyond *Caged Heat*," 306.

19. Morey, "Judge Called Me an Accessory," 80.

20. Ciasullo, "Containing 'Deviant' Desire."

21. Clowers, "Dykes, Gangs, and Danger"; Morey, "Judge Called Me an Accessory."

22. Marsh, "Media Representation of Prisons."

23. Clowers, "Dykes, Gangs, and Danger."

24. Cecil, "Looking beyond *Caged Heat*."

25. Ibid.

26. Bennett, "Good, the Bad, and the Ugly," 97.

27. Bennett, "Good, the Bad, and the Ugly"; Cheliotis, "Ambivalent Consequences of Visibility."

28. Foucault, *History of Sexuality*, 93.

29. Foucault, *Discipline and Punish*.

30. Foucault, *History of Sexuality*.

31. Ibid., 128.

32. Foucault, *Discipline and Punish*, 170.

33. Ibid., 184.

34. McClelland, "'Orange Is the New Black': Caged Heat"; Poniewozik, "Dead Tree Alert."

35. Peabody Awards, "Orange Is the New Black (Netflix)."

36. IMDb, "*Orange Is the New Black* Awards."

37. Matthews, "'Orange Is the New Black' Is the Best TV Show"; Stuever, "Netflix's *Orange Is the New Black*: Brilliance behind Bars"; Thomas, "Yes, You Should Watch *Orange Is the New Black*."

38. Hale, "Intrigue behind Bars," para. 8.

39. Sered, "What Pennsatucky's Teeth Tell Us," para. 7.

40. Kohan, Morelli, Kerman, and Harrison, "A Tittin' and a Hairin'."

41. Bullock, Fraser Wyche, and Williams, "Media Images of the Poor."

42. Kohan, Morelli, Kerman, and Harrison, "A Tittin' and a Hairin'."

43. Ibid.

44. Yuan, "'Orange Is the New Black' Is the Only TV Show That Understands Rape," para. 8.

45. Kohan, Morelli, Kerman, and Harrison, "Don't Make Me Come Back There."

46. Bureau of Justice Statistics, "Allegations of Sexual Victimization," para. 3.

47. Kohan, Morelli, Kerman, and Harrison, "Bed Bugs and Beyond."

48. Ibid.

49. Pozner, "TV Can Make America Better."

50. Tillet, "It's So Not *Oz*," para. 17.

51. Carstarphen and Rios, "Brown and Black Women"; Ramírez Berg, "Stereotyping in Films"; Rodríguez, *Latin Looks*.

52. Molina-Guzman, *Dangerous Curves*, 9.

53. Bordo, *Unbearable Weight*; Bartky, "Suffering to be Beautiful"; Bartky, "Foucault, Femininity"; Bartky, "Feminine Body"; DeLaurentis, "Violence of Rhetoric."

54. Haugaard, "Power, Ideology, and Legitimacy," 68.

Bibliography

Attwood, Feona. "Sex and the Media." In *The Handbook of Gender, Sex, and the Media*, edited by Karen Ross, 457–69. Oxford: Wiley-Blackwell, 2012.

Althusser, Louis. "Ideology and Ideological State Apparatuses." In *Cultural Theory and Popular Culture*, edited by John Storey, 15–164. New York: Pearson, 1998.

Bartky, Sandra. "The Feminine Body." In *Feminist Frameworks: Alternative Accounts of the Relations between Women and Men*, edited by Alison Jaggar and Paula S. Rothenberg, 454–61. New York: Routledge, 1993.

———. "Foucault, Femininity, and the Modernization of Patriarchal Power." In *Feminist Social Thought: A Reader*, edited by Diana Tietjens Meyers, 93–111. London: Routledge, 1997.

———. "Suffering to Be Beautiful." In *Gender Struggles: Practical Approaches to Contemporary Feminism*, edited by Constance Mui and Julien Murphy, 241–56. Lanham, MD: Rowan and Littlefield, 2002.

Bennett, Jamie. "The Good, the Bad, and the Ugly: The Media in Prison Films." *Howard Journal of Crime and Justice* 45, no. 2 (2006): 97–115.

Bordo, Susan. *Unbearable Weight: Feminism, Western Culture, and the Body.* Berkeley: University of California Press, 1993.

Bullock, Heather, Karen Fraser Wyche, and Wendy Williams. "Media Images of the Poor." *Journal of Social Issues* 57, no. 2 (2001): 229–56.

Bureau of Justice Statistics. "Allegations of Sexual Victimization in Prisons and Jails Rose from 2009 to 2011; Substantiated Incidents Remained Stable." Accessed September 16, 2017. http://www.bjs.gov/content/pub/press /svraca0911pr.cfm.

Butler Judith. "Performative Acts and Gender Constitution: An Essay in Phenomenology and Feminist Theory." In *Writing on the Body: Female Embodiment and Feminist Theory,* edited by Katie Conboy, Nadia Medina, and Sarah Stanbury, 401–17. New York: Columbia University Press, 1997.

Carstarphen, Meta, and Diana I. Rios. "Brown and Black Women in Nancy Savoca's *The 24-Hour Woman*: A Critical Analysis of Multicultural Imagery." In *Brown and Black Communication: Latino and African American Conflict and Convergence in Mass Media,* edited by Diana I. Rios and A. N. Mohamed, 27–41. Westport, CT: Praeger, 2003.

Cecil, Dawn. "Looking beyond *Caged Heat*: Media Images of Women in Prison." *Feminist Criminology* 2, no. 4 (2007): 304–26.

Cheliotis, Leonidas. "The Ambivalent Consequences of Visibility: Crime and Prisons in the Mass Media." *Crime, Media, and Culture* 6, no. 2 (2010): 169–84.

Ciasullo, Ann. "Containing 'Deviant' Desire: Lesbianism, Heterosexuality, and the Woman-in-Prison Narrative." *Journal of Popular Culture* 41, no. 2 (2008): 195–223.

Clowers, Marsha. "Dykes, Gangs, and Danger: Debunking Popular Myths about Maximum Security Life." *Journal of Criminal Justice and Popular Culture* 9, no. 1 (2001): 22–30.

DeLaurentis, Teresa. "The Violence of Rhetoric: On Representation and Gender." In *The Gender/Sexuality Reader,* edited by Roger N. Lancaster and Micaela di Leonardo, 265–78. New York: Routledge, 1997.

Foucault, Michel. *Discipline and Punish.* New York: Vintage Books, 1977.

———. *The History of Sexuality.* Volume 1. *An Introduction.* New York: Vintage Books, 1978.

Gledhill, Christine. "Pleasurable Negotiations." In *Cultural Theory and Popular Culture,* edited by John Storey, 236–47. New York: Pearson, 1998.

Gramsci, Antonio. "Hegemony, Intellectuals and the State." In *Cultural Theory and Popular Culture,* edited by John Storey, 210–16. New York: Pearson, 1998.

Hale, Mike. "Intrigue behind Bars: More 'Gossip Girl' Than 'Oz.'" *New York Times*, July 11, 2013.

Haskell, Mollie. *From Reverence to Rape: The Treatment of Women in the Movies.* Chicago: Chicago University Press, 1973.

Haugaard, Mark. "Power, Ideology, and Legitimacy." In *Power in Contemporary Politics: Theories, Practices, Globalizations*, edited by Henri Goverde, Philip Cerny, Mark Haugaard, and Howard Leetner, 59–76. London: Sage, 2000.

IMDb. "*Orange Is the New Black* Awards." Accessed September 16, 2017. http://www.imdb.com/title/tt2372162/awards.

Juschka, Darlene. *Political Bodies/Body Politic: The Semiotics of Gender.* London: Equinox, 2009.

Kohan, Jenji, Lauren Morelli, Piper Kerman, and Jordan Harrison, writers. *Orange Is the New Black.* "A Tittin' and a Hairin'." Season 3, episode 10. Directed by Jesse Peretz. Produced by Jenji Kohan. Los Gatos, CA: Netflix, 2015.

Kohan, Jenji, Lauren Morelli, Piper Kerman, and Jordan Harrison, writers. *Orange Is the New Black.* "Bed Bugs and Beyond." Season 3, episode 2. Directed by Jesse Peretz. Produced by Jenji Kohan. Los Gatos, CA: Netflix, 2015.

Kohan, Jenji, Lauren Morelli, Piper Kerman, and Jordan Harrison, writers. *Orange Is the New Black.* "Don't Make Me Come Back There." Season 3, episode 12. Directed by Jesse Peretz. Produced by Jenji Kohan. Los Gatos, CA: Netflix, 2015.

Marsh, Ian. "The Media Representation of Prisons: Boot Camps or Holiday Camps?" *Law, Crime, and History* 2 (2013): 162–72.

Matthews, Dylan. "'Orange is the New Black' Is the Best TV Show about Prison Ever Made." *Washington Post*, July 17, 2013.

McClelland, Mac. "'Orange is the New Black': Caged Heat; How Did the Unlikely Stars of 'OITNB' Revolutionize TV?" *Rolling Stone*, June 12, 2015.

Molina-Guzman, Isabel. *Dangerous Curves: Latina Bodies in the Media.* New York: New York University Press, 2010.

Morey, Anne. "'The Judge Called Me an Accessory': Women's Prison Films, 1950–1962." *Journal of Popular Film and Television* 23, no. 2 (1995): 80–87.

Mulvey, Laura. "Visual Pleasure and Narrative Cinema." *Screen* 16, no. 3 (1975): 6–19.

Peabody Awards. "Orange Is the New Black (Netflix)." Accessed September 16, 2017. http://www.peabodyawards.com/award-profile/orange-is-the-new-black-netflix.

Poniewozik, James. "Dead Tree Alert: *Orange Is the New Black* Is the New Way of Talking about TV." *Time*, July 25, 2013.

Pozner, Jennifer. "TV Can Make America Better." *Salon*, August 29, 2013.

Ramírez Berg, Charles. "Stereotyping in Films in General and of the Hispanic in Particular." In *Latin Looks: Images of Latinas and Latinos in the U.S. Media*, edited by Clara Rodríguez, 104–20. Boulder, CO: Westview, 1997.

Rodríguez, Clara, ed. *Latin Looks: Images of Latinas and Latinos in the U.S. Media*. Boulder, CO: Westview, 1997.

Scott, Joan. "Deconstructing Equality-versus-Difference: Or, the Uses of Post-structuralist Theory for Feminism." In *Feminist Social Thought: A Reader*, edited by Diana Tietjens Meyers, 757–70. London: Routledge, 1997.

Sered, Susan. "What Pennsatucky's Teeth Tell Us about Class in America." *BitchMedia*, July 1, 2014. Accessed September 16, 2017. https://bitchmedia .org.

Stuever, Hank. "Netflix's *Orange Is the New Black*: Brilliance behind Bars." *Washington Post*, July 11, 2013.

Thomas, June. "Yes, You Should Watch *Orange Is The New Black* This Weekend." *Slate*, June 13, 2013.

Tillet, Salamishah. "It's So Not *Oz*: Netflix's *Orange Is the New Black*." *Nation*, July 23, 2013.

Yuan, Jada. "'Orange Is the New Black' Is the Only TV Show That Understands Rape." *Vulture.com*, July 6, 2015.

3. Feminized Faith: The Intersectionality of Religion and Gender in *Orange Is the New Black*

Joy Jenkins and J. David Wolfgang

A s discussed in the previous chapters, *Orange Is the New Black* has been praised for its diverse depictions of race, gender, sexuality, and religion. Furthermore, television critics have applauded Netflix's original series for its faith-focused story lines.[1] The third season of the show included a speechless character's inspirational "miracles" and an African American inmate's conversion to Judaism. Season 4 introduced an African American Muslim inmate wearing a hijab. TV critic Arthur Chu articulated that through exploring a variety of approaches to faith, the series demonstrates how "institutions arise within institutions and the events of this season suggest that humans are simply not meant to be institutionalized—not under a prison system, or under a belief system," and the series might contribute to presenting a new potential for how religion is portrayed on television.[2]

Religion on television is increasingly secularized and reappropriated as religious symbolism.[3] Depictions of religion on television can present realistic portrayals of religious life, but they might also open organized religion to criticism, an approach used frequently in *Orange Is the New Black*. Similarly, because media portrayals of women tend to reflect dominant societal values,[4] depictions of gender may reflect outdated understandings. The continuing feminization of television, however, which is evident in this show, provides opportunities to assess how media content caters to female fantasy, produces collective memories, and spurs myths,[5] drawing clear implications for the role of religious practices and spiritual beliefs in women's lives.

Women's religious and faith practices and their connections to feminism have largely been understudied.[6] For some women, religion may be associated with patriarchy, oppression, and intolerance, but for others, faith may serve as a source of values and empowerment.[7] A feminist approach to studying religion considers women's sexually specific and distinctive expressions of faith.[8] Whether TV shows such as *Orange Is the New Black* accurately represent these complexities is worth considering.

This study assesses which religions, faiths, or spiritual practices are depicted in *Orange Is the New Black*, the tone of the depictions, and how the depictions intersect with the show's presentation of gender. Ultimately, we seek to understand whether *Orange Is the New Black*, through its portrayal of life within a women's prison, presents a more multifaceted view of religion and religious practice than has been offered in other TV programming, as well as what those depictions might reveal about how society views the ways that women practice religion.

Literature Review

Media spaces, particularly platforms such as blogs, message boards, commenting forums, and social media, represent sites for individuals to create their religious selves, practice religion, and publicly discuss religion.[9] For his study of religion and media, Mahan defines religion as a "human activity of practice and belief through which we connect the everyday to something we hold to be ineffable, transcendent, or sacred,"[10] which can encompass practices and beliefs that may not be religious but can be understood better by considering how they are like religion. Religion can also be defined as traditional: the study of symbols, practices, traditions, or meanings linked to religious culture; or as official: the study of belief practices tied to a religious institution or faith community.[11] Faith communities are groups that share common ideology, theology, patterns, and narratives that "support and justify their experience of the sacred and the everyday."[12]

Individuals are also increasingly considering religion to be an individual practice and are developing religious identities from multiple sources.[13] Traditional religious language may also be connected to behaviors and symbols not previously considered religious.[14] Religion, however, is helpful to people in situations of disruption, and they may rely on rituals and beliefs that are viewed as spiritual and sacred but do not rely on traditional institutions or on "lived" religion.[15]

Media can serve as forums where culture is debated and constituted, creating a natural connection with religious practices, as well as with religious leaders, institutions, practitioners, symbols, values, and ideas.[16] However, television shows are criticized for offering inadequate religious depictions.[17] An analysis of religion on popular television in 2002 found that 60 percent of characters that identified a religious affiliation were Protestant Christians, while the other 40 percent affiliated with Buddhism, Judaism, religious cults, and the occult.[18] Religion is rarely a central theme of television programming but is frequently portrayed as a personal and private act, rather than as part of an institution.[19] Television depictions of religion have become more secular, sexualized, and comedic.[20] Religious depictions are also frequently used as social critique and to ridicule religion.[21]

However, portrayals of religion on television can show that religion is intertwined with other cultural elements of daily life.[22] Religious institutions, such as Catholicism as depicted on the CW show *Supernatural*, may be portrayed as hegemonic to demean other religions and individuals who are agnostic or atheist.[23] However, some shows attempt to subvert hegemony by showing more accurate depictions of minority religions, although these shows typically suffer from poor ratings and are canceled.[24] Critic Mohammed considered depictions of Islam on the show *All-American Muslim* and found that depictions that challenged tropes helped to subvert negative stereotypes, but the show also suffered from low ratings and negative reviews.[25] As for depictions of religion and prison, *Dead Man Walking* featured a nun, Sister Helen, who assisted a death row inmate in his last week before his execution. Sister Helen's attempts to reform Matthew Poncelet through love and redemption led some to liken her to a Christlike figure in the film.[26] Sister Helen's depiction as a Christlike female character with power was praised for affording her agency via her ability to share Christ through her love and her representation of his message.[27] Released amid a population boom in U.S. prisons, HBO's *Oz*, which debuted in 1997, was the first U.S. television series to focus on prison life.[28] Like *Orange Is the New Black*, the show featured a Catholic nun, Sister Peter Marie Reimondo, who served as the maximum-security prison's psychologist and drug counselor. However, the series was also criticized for its "regressive articulation of violence, race, and class."[29]

Feminist Studies of Media and Religion

Television must please large audiences and maintain the status quo, resulting in programs that conceal women's work or reinforce conventional gender roles.[30] The way gender roles are portrayed in media carries social, political, and economic significance, as outdated representations might prepare young people, particularly women, for a reality that does not exist.[31] Media studies should consider gender as an analytical category through which individuals organize their social activity, and media are central sites through which meanings and values materialize.[32]

Feminist scholars examine how images and cultural constructions within media texts are connected to patterns of inequality, domination, and oppression.[33] Media might also serve as tools for resistance for women, and feminist critiques can consider specific genres of media content in particular social contexts.[34] For example, analyses have tended to generalize about the stereotypical nature of content, ignoring the differences among genres, media, and audience experiences, as well as the overall feminization of TV.[35] Other factors, including relationships between characters, their contributions to the narrative, their visual representation, and their status in a genre, are worthy of investigation.[36]

Analyses should also deconstruct how dominant and alternative meanings of gender are encoded in media texts and how they connect to other discourses, such as ethnicity, class, and sexuality.[37] This study considers how *Orange Is the New Black* represents the ideals of feminized television through its diverse cast and representative story lines. It also assesses how characters are presented in the show, including the narratives associated with them; their prominence in story lines; and the ways the show challenges stereotypical presentations of gender, class, sexuality, ethnicity, and other characteristics.

Empirical research into and theological assessments of women's religiosity and its connection to feminism have been limited.[38] Feminists might avoid incorporating religion into their agendas because of perceptions of religious communities as male dominated and suggestions that secularization has resulted in a decline in religion.[39] Arguments have tended to emphasize the dominant Christian realist form of monotheism, which privileges paternal and male figures of authority and excludes the material content of bodily life, desire, and sexual difference.[40] However, a feminist focus on the role of gender in religious communities can shed light on the institutionalized nature of gender inequality and allow women to critique their place in religion.[41]

For some women, religion may represent patriarchy, oppression, and intolerance; for others, embracing strong religious values can serve as a source of empowerment.[42] Associating religion with disempowerment may also limit full understandings of the role that feminism plays in the lives of deeply religious women.[43] Liberal feminists have focused on achieving inclusion within the current social order, which has translated to the "Women-Church" movement, or on seeking the right to ordination.[44] Ordained clergywomen's presence in some religions, as well as their actions in positions of power, is involved in changing the nature of work within and for the church and may be changing some fundamental religious understandings.[45] More radical feminists have argued for a "Goddess Religion" that "helps to break the hold of male control so that women no longer look to males for the divine and the savior."[46] Ultimately, Anderson argues that feminist scholars should consider the material content of women's religious beliefs, including women's sexually specific and distinctive expressions of desire, devotion, and death.[47]

Method

Although other television programs have focused on prison populations, *Orange Is the New Black* has been praised as "the best TV show about prison ever made" for its realistic portrayals of racial breakdowns, sexuality, work environments, and punishment in women's prisons.[48] Critics have also heralded the show for its diverse representations of race, gender, sexuality, and religion.[49] We sought both to document the representations of gender and religion on the show and to consider how these representations align with traditional depictions of gender and religion on television in the United States. The show's use of a women's federal prison as its setting also offered a valuable case study for considering how gender and religion interact within a diverse but highly regulated space.

We used critical discourse analysis to assess representations of religion and gender in the show by considering dialogue, visual representations, and symbols. Critical discourse analysis allowed us to investigate how power, dominance, and inequality are created, reinforced, and reproduced through talk and text.[50] Specifically, a feminist approach to critical discourse analysis assesses "how power and dominance are discursively produced and/or (counter-)resisted in a variety of ways through textual representations of gendered social practices, and through interactional strategies of talk."[51]

We developed a set of descriptive codes representing major religion and gender concepts from previous literature on religion and feminist interpretations of popular television. We took notes on the depictions present in specific episodes and scenes based on these codes while also considering overarching themes and concepts that emerged. In total, we analyzed seventeen episodes from three seasons of the show in which religion was a major theme.

The analysis was guided by the following open codes: diversity of religious practices and experiences, the oppressive or liberating tone of the depictions, the private and personal or public practice of religion, the critique of religion and religious institutions, the secularization of religion, the forms of empowerment or disempowerment that came from religion, how religion was used as a means of resistance, how gender roles and feminism were present in religion and leadership, and how religion represented patriarchal or feminist understandings of community.

After watching the episodes, we met to compare notes and emerging themes. We identified the most prominent themes for our findings. We selected specific scenes to represent certain themes, and we wrote the findings based on a mixture of broad themes and specific instances and representations of those themes.

Findings

Religious themes appear frequently in *Orange Is the New Black*, with religion taking on a particularly salient purpose in season 3. Religion presents itself in episode 5 of the first season, when a voice over the loudspeaker quotes Michael Jackson: "In a world filled with hate, we must still dare to hope. In a world filled with despair, we must still dare to dream." The announcer then reminds inmates that the chapel opens at 8 A.M. for Christian, evangelical, Wiccan, Baptist, Muslim, and other services. The chapel is a key symbolic space on the show, serving as a site for religious services, meetings of new spiritual groups, and even sexual rendezvous for inmates. This convergence of influences signifies the diversity of religious themes present on the show, including religion serving as a source of empowerment and disempowerment for the inmates, critiques of institutional forms of religion as oppressive or liberating, the use of religion as a form of resistance to the conditions of the prison, and an overall feminization of religion emphasizing female religious leaders and diverse approaches to religious organizing.

Characters in *Orange Is the New Black* frequently find empowerment through personal expressions of religion. When inmate Norma Romano, who does not speak because of a severe stutter, steps forward to sing in the prison Christmas pageant, her experience is shown as a significant step in her path to liberation, as she had never previously spoken on the show. For inmate Leanne Taylor, who grew up in the Amish faith, personal empowerment comes from her belonging to a faith community.

In her past she felt empowered through choosing her faith, which later materializes through her actions in the "Church of Norma," a religious movement stemming from Norma's perceived spiritual powers for which Leanne creates rules to institutionalize its practices. In other circumstances characters seek a personal experience with faith to feel empowered. Sister Jane Ingalls, a former nun and political activist, feels oppressed by the rules of the Catholic Church and has struggled to engage in advocacy efforts in alignment with Church rules, including a hunger strike during her time in prison to protest poor conditions for inmates. Instead she feels compelled to act on God's behalf herself and eschews institutional support, especially when a group of nuns arrives at the prison to support her hunger strike.

Seeking Empowerment through Religion

Characters express diverse reasons for seeking empowerment through religion. Poussey Washington, an African American former "army brat," and Alex Vause, the ex-girlfriend of lead character Piper, two characters who often critique religion, seek to connect with their deceased mothers, and faith expressions help them fill those voids. Characters also seek empowerment through pursuing religious leadership roles. For Norma this meant serving herself and her followers by using her "powers" for good. However, Norma recognizes that she has no real power and seems, ironically, to be following the same dangerous path of Guru Mack, a leader of a cultlike organization of which Norma was part.

Adapting Religion for Empowerment

Many characters desire a more inclusive form of religion and either eschew or adapt institutionalized forms of religion to fit their needs. Tiffany Doggett, an evangelical Christian who was imprisoned for murdering an abortion nurse, uses religion to combat the "gay agenda," but, through a discussion with her corrections-officer counselor, Sam Healy, she discovers that her real enemy is patriarchy, and she works to connect her religious beliefs with a more inclusive philosophy. In one of the most interesting cases of adapting religion, the "Church of Norma" looks for ways to institutionalize, thanks to the actions of characters like Leanne. She adopts rules, order, and structure for the group—to the frustration and exclusion of others—to make the group's experience more communal.

Symbolism as a Form of Empowerment

For the most devout practitioners, religious symbols can act as catalysts of empowerment. When the Church of Norma begins to lose followers, Leanne uses a piece of toast that she believes looks like Norma as a "sign" to reinvigorate the group. Unseen symbols can also empower individuals, such as several inmates who embark on a quest to find a chicken that Piper spotted on the prison yard. Shortly after Piper arrived at the prison, she saw the chicken and told some fellow inmates, who told her that the chicken was an urban legend. Others believed her and spent their recreation time searching the yard for the chicken. Counselor Sam Healy calls the chicken "popular fiction" and says that Piper should not scare the other inmates with "boastful claims." Eventually, the guards announce, "There is no chicken. There never was a chicken. The chicken was an urban myth. A grand illusion. Something to give your life meaning, but which is in fact not there. We will make a poster." This statement, while challenging what seems like a secular vision, also legitimizes the chicken as a source of hope and demonstrates the prison's institutional suppression of religious beliefs and communities.

Religion as a Means of Disempowerment

Some characters feel disempowered by religious practices and symbols. In one case, Tiffany accosts Piper while Piper is in the shower. Tiffany uses a cross in an attempt to stab Piper and then draws her own blood and smears it on Piper's body. In another case, Galina "Red" Reznikov critiques Norma's church as harmful to the women who follow her because it provides false hope. The show operates with an implicit understanding that hope is a dangerous concept in prison, where few dare to anticipate a positive outcome. Religion is also used to disempower characters through guilt. Sophia Burset, who is transgender, attempts to construct religious beliefs around her complex personal feelings about gender and sexual identity. However, Sister Jane suggests that personal guilt prevents Sophia from having a legitimate religious experience.

Institutional Religion as Oppressive or Liberating

Besides attempts to express faith and spirituality through personalized forms of religion, many characters hold attachments to institutionalized faith and seek liberation despite the oppressive nature of organized religion depicted in the show. These depictions appear to show differing approaches to how characters understand the role, philosophy, and purpose of institutionalized forms of religion and how they recognize the onerous nature of institutionalized religion as an oppressive imposition on the little freedom they have in prison.

Institutions and Oppressive Rules

Many characters suffer from the restrictions of institutionalized religion or did so in the past, whether it was Leanne being banished from her Amish family, Janae Watson being told she could not pursue a track scholarship by her Muslim father, or Cindy Hayes being scolded for eating before a dinner prayer by her hard-line Christian father. The characters attempt to overcome past oppression from an institution they want to see as liberating. For Leanne, institutional rules are still a part of the religious experience, so she attempts to build them into the Church of Norma, while others threaten to leave the group. The most troubling forms of oppression are evident in religious institutional rules that oppress those expressing diverse sexual norms. For example, Tiffany reports Piper and Alex to counselor Sam Healy after she sees them dancing together at a party. A Christian church leader who financially supports Tiffany praises Carrie "Big Boo" Black for overcoming her lesbian identity, prompting Boo eventually to make a passionate case against religious critiques of homosexuality.

Institutions of Religion Can Oppress in Diverse Ways

Religious institutions demonstrate many ways of oppressing individuals. In prison, membership in a religious group also provides benefits. Those who practice Judaism can receive a kosher meal, which tastes better than the regular prison meals. A number of prisoners imitate the Jewish faith to receive the meals. Tiffany also imitates a religious practice to receive benefits. She is in prison for shooting a nurse at an abortion clinic and takes on the persona of a violent pro-life activist, which is not true. She receives assistance from a church and uses the extra money to buy goods from the commissary. However, this radical Christian identity means having to meet with the minister when he visits and having to meet with her Christian attorney. Norma feels pressure to heal others because some believe she has this power, although she is certain she does not. If she denies it, however, she will lose the leadership role and "voice" that others have created for her.

Liberation through Religious Experience

Ultimately, liberation through religious experience is difficult for characters to achieve. For instance, in season 3, Cindy, who initially claimed Judaism to receive kosher meals, must be oppressed before being liberated. She is frustrated by the rabbi's refusal to admit her to the Jewish faith, so she studies and develops a personal religious philosophy, which she expresses as follows:

> Honestly, I think I found my people. I was raised in a church where I was told to believe and to pray and if I was bad, I'd go to hell and if I was good, I'd go to heaven. And if I asked Jesus, he'd forgive me and that was that. And here you all saying, there ain't no hell, ain't sure about heaven and if you do something wrong you've got to figure it out yourself. And as far as God is concerned it's your job to keep asking questions, and to keep arguing, and to keep learning. It's like a verb. It's like you do God.

After this speech the rabbi agrees to admit her into the Jewish faith but only after she is baptized. In this case Cindy finds liberation through traditional practices and acts.

Liberation can also be found within the escape narrative. In the final scene of season 3, Norma spots a hole in the fence and begins to run toward "Freedom Lake." Many inmates see this opportunity as a sign of liberation but connect it to a religious theme because "Norma Christ" is the first one to see the "miracle." During these few minutes of freedom, characters experience religious catharsis in different ways, with some making amends with former rivals and enemies and others reinforcing new beliefs and relationships.

Religion as a Form of Resistance

Characters often use religion to resist institutions, whether through responding to their imprisonment or to past experiences. Institutional leaders attempt to control religious expression because it presents opportunities for inmates to question authority. Through these scenarios, *Orange Is the New Black* allows viewers to consider the ways that religion serves as a socializing force through which certain ideas, values, and behaviors are presented, interpreted, and reinforced. However, some characters resist institutional control, developing their own understandings of and approaches to religion and aligning themselves with patriarchal religious leaders and ideas to achieve personal goals. The show, then, presents religion as a form of resistance and an oppressive force.

Institutional Control of Religion

For the prison officials on the show, religion represents a suspect institution because, despite their efforts to control or manipulate religious expression, they often face resistance from the inmates. In the first season, Tiffany Doggett talks with the prison chaplain about hanging a large wooden cross in the chapel. The chaplain tells Tiffany, "Nothing goes on the walls that can't be taken down before the next service" because "this chapel is not just for Christians." Tiffany eventually takes down the cross, although she accuses the chaplain of violating her religious freedom. Tiffany also becomes convinced she can heal other inmates through prayer, which leads to her being administered full-time psychiatric care. Tiffany tells her psychiatrist, "I'm not crazy. I'm chosen. There's a difference." The scene juxtaposes science and reason with passion and emotion. In season 3, Norma's followers stand in a circle on the prison yard and yell out why they believe in and follow Norma, which leads the prison guards to break up the gathering, subverting an opportunity for liberation. The prison consistently thwarts individual agency and empowerment in an effort to maintain consistency and control.

Religious Ceremonies as Resistance

These efforts to control inmates' practices suggest that religion is linked with patriarchy; as a result, assumptions about religion and how it should be enacted are frequently challenged. The show presents multiple situations in which inmates use faith practices to actively resist the prison and patriarchy. They also reimagine traditionally patriarchal religions and religious practices in ways that are liberating. In season 1, after the prison does not organize a formal funeral for Tricia Miller, her friends gather near her bunk to commemorate her life. In this scene the inmates decide to celebrate Tricia's life in a way that defies the institutional response—and avoids the institutional space, the chapel—but that proves to be cathartic. In season 3, during a prison-wide Mother's Day celebration, Tiffany holds a funeral for the babies she aborted. She prays, "I ask that the souls of my unborn babies be considered to enter the holy kingdom even though they never had a chance to get baptized 'cause I was wicked and I got 'em sucked out." Boo comforts Tiffany, telling her she was a good mother because she spared the babies a miserable upbringing.

Faith and Individual Empowerment

Individuals also use their beliefs to challenge institutions, authority, and injustice. Sister Jane is shown in flashbacks resisting the rules of a convent to attend protests against the Vietnam War and later other causes. After she writes a book about her experiences, a priest tells her, "It's not about service to God; it's about you. You're a narcissist." She refutes this by saying, "I love being a nun. If I seem prideful, it's only because I love the work I do and because I'm really good at it." Janae follows Norma's religion, and a flashback shows her arguing with her Muslim dad about accepting a college track scholarship. He says, "Money is not my god," and Janae answers, "Maybe Allah ain't my God. Maybe I don't want to be a proud daughter in the nation of Islam." These scenes show the inmates' complex interactions with religious authority and suggest that they seek out other approaches to faith as a response to their past experiences.

The Feminization of Religion

Religion and religious practices often take on feminine qualities and presentations in the show. When religious organizing occurs, it takes a different tone from patriarchal approaches, welcoming members from diverse backgrounds and elevating women to leadership positions, but the groups might also become exclusionary. The show represents different types of religious practices, with some characters, particularly men, challenging these expressions and others accepting and legitimizing them. These representations explore the experiences of deeply religious women, as well as religious communities in both female- and male-dominated sacred spaces where women can lead their own faiths or react to challenges associated with male-dominated religion. They also consider how femininity is constructed in reference to religion, including relationships between characters; women's roles in religious-oriented narratives; power structures; and how discourses of religion connect to ethnicity, class, and sexuality.

Connecting through Religion

Although religion has served as a divisive element on the show, it has also united characters from diverse backgrounds and belief systems who overcome barriers that have historically separated many people of faith. In season 1,

Sophia initially reaches out to Sister Jane to ask for her estrogen pills, but Jane recognizes that Sophia is actually struggling with being away from her wife and son. Eventually the two form a friendship, with Jane serving as a spiritual confidante for Sophia. They discuss scripture; joke together; and connect through uniquely female experiences such as menopause, motherhood, and relationships, despite their differences in age, race, and background. In season 2, Norma and Gloria Mendoza, a Catholic Latina who oversees the prison kitchen, work together to conduct a Santeria ceremony in hopes of ridding the prison of the "evil" of inmate Yvonne "Vee" Parker, who has manipulated and abused many inmates. These examples demonstrate how characters seek out religion to fulfill personal goals but develop connections with other women as a result.

Women as Religious Leaders

Through these efforts at religious organizing, women often serve as leaders. In some cases, religious leadership appears to be rooted in self-aggrandizement, as individuals work to maintain their leadership roles, silence or alienate critics, and gain personal legitimization. In season 1, Tiffany is vocal about her evangelical Christian beliefs and is nearly always surrounded by supporters. As her following grows, however, Tiffany condemns those who question her abilities. Alex is a particular target, and Tiffany tells her, "You're not invited because they don't allow gay people on the rapture bus." Tiffany also points to Sophia and says, "I don't want 'it' here," and orders that she be removed from the chapel because she is making God angry. Ultimately Tiffany remains at the mercy of male leaders, who have the overriding power to determine how and whether she can exert her religious authority.

In contrast, it is unclear whether Norma sought out a leadership role or it merely emerged around her because inmates desired a source of hope. Norma is willing to help the inmates but seems conflicted about her status as a leader, with other inmates, particularly Leanne, serving as the voices of the group. This hesitation may stem from Norma's past, when she was a follower of "Guru Mack," who promised to help her find confidence and peace despite her lack of voice. She eventually recognized Mack, whom she later married, as an oppressive leader who took power away from her, rather than empowering her through faith, and she ultimately pushed him off a cliff to his death. Norma is also questioned by inmates, such as Red, who are skeptical of her powers. Norma initially accepts this criticism, but later she is shown in the chapel blessing the women there with touches and kisses. Norma walks up on stage and smiles, seemingly recognizing that she is achieving guru-like status. In this, faith has become a way for formerly disempowered inmates to find personal fulfillment. However, because institutions and leaders influence them, they occasionally succumb to patriarchal approaches, such as excluding those who question them.

Diverse Expressions of Religion

The show often presents diverse religions and dedicates story lines to exploring characters' religious backgrounds, revealing how beliefs are shaped by class, ethnicity, race, and culture. Characters also often defend their religious experiences rather than rely on religious leaders to speak on their behalf, such as Leanne discussing her belief in Norma as a contrast to her espousing her Amish beliefs in a flashback; Cindy addressing her conversion to Judaism, in contrast to her father dictating her beliefs; and Tiffany exploring contradictions and challenges to her Christianity, rather than a male Christian lawyer telling her what to believe. Additionally, Piper emphasizes a belief in science over religion, which is evident in a speech she gives in season 1 after Tiffany attempted to baptize her:

> I believe in science. I believe in evolution. [. . .] I cannot get behind some supreme being who weighs in on the Tony Awards while a million people get whacked with machetes. I don't believe a billion Indians are going to hell, I don't think we get cancer to learn life lessons, and I don't believe that people die young because God needs another angel. I think it's just bullshit, and on some level I think we all know that. I mean, don't you?

In this, Piper addresses many criticisms of religion evident in secular society, such as condemning Muslims, justifying disease and tragedy through "God's will," and using prayer to achieve personal goals.

The movements that develop on the show, such as Norma's followers, also include women from an array of class, ethnic, and racial backgrounds, subverting the distinctions that tend to separate the women in the prison. The show also challenges traditional understandings of who is allowed to participate in religious practices, such as Cindy, who is black and grew up Christian, converting to Judaism. Even characters from similar religious backgrounds are presented in diverse ways. For example, in season 1, Tiffany is shown using her Christian beliefs to demonize and threaten others, while Sister Jane cites scripture to teach and empower women of various backgrounds, even those whom her religion might not typically accept.

Conclusion

Orange Is the New Black depicts not only traditional religion, or meanings linked to religious culture, but also official religious institutions.[52] The show also offers diverse depictions of faith communities.[53] Although some of these communities reflect traditional understandings of religion, others create faith practices and beliefs that do not rely on institutions. The show provides a more diverse and inclusive depiction of religion than is typical for U.S. television,[54] including uniquely personal forms of faith. The show also subverts the norm that American television only promotes Protestant Christian forms of religion,[55] by depicting characters as practitioners of other religions.

Orange Is the New Black supports previous literature exploring religion on television by depicting faith as a personal form of religion rather than one practiced through institutions.[56] This is especially true for characters Sister Jane Ingalls, Sophia Burset, and Norma Romano. The show also fits current trends with religion on television by featuring faith as a part of daily life.[57] For many prisoners, religious traditions, practices, and beliefs make up a substantial part of their lives, and the show depicts them as active practitioners who allow religion to guide them. *Orange Is the New Black* also uses religion as a comedic trope. However, the comedic depictions often shift into more serious story lines. For instance, when Cindy begins her conversion to Judaism, her initial motivation is kosher meals, but this goal turns into the serious pursuit of a faith that fits her view of God. In another case, the Church of Norma begins as a comedic attempt to lift up Norma as a faith healer, but the group takes on a serious tone for characters like Poussey Washington and Leanne Taylor, who acknowledge authentic feelings of acceptance.

Religious depictions are also used for social critique and to ridicule religion.[58] In *Orange Is the New Black*, some characters challenge Protestant Christian critiques of homosexuality, and evangelical Christian Tiffany Doggett eventually adopts a more inclusive understanding of homosexuality. However, Piper also critiques religion more broadly as irrational and antiscience. The show subverts traditional depictions of faith by resisting putting hegemonic forms of religion in a place of prominence.[59] Instead, the show portrays nonhegemonic faiths, such as Judaism, the Amish sect, and Islam, alongside religions like Protestant Christianity. By depicting minority religions, the show avoids othering people of nondominant faiths, a technique other shows have used to make minority religions seem threatening.[60]

Through its religious depictions, the show also challenges conventional representations of women on television. Its female characters outnumber male characters and drive the show's core narratives. Female characters are also frequently presented in positions of power, challenging male and other authority figures, subverting institutional norms, and leading efforts at collective resistance. These story lines show women, many of whom were victimized by religion and religious leaders in the past, achieving empowerment through religious organizing. In doing so, the show reinforces the value of media as sites where meanings and values about womanhood materialize and are contested.[61] It also demonstrates how the rise of feminized television[62] can challenge patterns of inequality, domination, and oppression[63] and become a tool for resistance.[64]

The show presents feminized understandings of religion and its role in women's lives. Religious communities have traditionally been considered male-dominated spaces[65] that privilege paternal and male authority figures.[66] *Orange Is the New Black*, however, critiques this norm and, as Page described,[67] allows women to question the role they play in religion. The show provides multiple examples of women preaching, leading religious rituals, legitimizing religious practices and beliefs, and defining religion.

Through these narratives, the show offers a feminist critique of the ways that religion represents patriarchy, oppression, and intolerance, but it also demonstrates how embracing strong religious values can serve as a source of empowerment.[68] For example, just as liberal feminists have focused on elevating women to leadership positions within institutionalized religions,[69] Tiffany and Sister Jane lead their own religious movements. The show, however, also presents more radical feminist understandings of religion by suggesting a woman-centered "Goddess Religion"[70] in the Church of Norma. Characters such as Sister Jane, Tiffany, and Cindy present their own interpretations of religious texts and rituals as well. *Orange Is the New Black*, while exploring how religion manifests itself in different cultures and settings, also does not limit religious practices to certain races, classes, sexualities, or ages, showing that belief systems can cross boundaries and relate to women's sexually specific and distinctive expressions.[71]

Thanks to alternative distribution platforms such as Netflix, shows like *Orange Is the New Black* can subvert traditional narratives and stereotypes of religion and offer more representative depictions of women's experiences than have been presented in prime-time television. Although shows marketed to mass audiences have tended to rely on stereotypes related to gender, race/ethnicity, sexuality, and religion, *Orange Is the New Black* challenges this approach by using a prison setting to represent a microcosm of society—a place where men and women of diverse backgrounds converge and compete. In doing so, the show provides a rich, complex, and nuanced commentary on religion while also addressing questions that challenge society more broadly.

Notes

1. Gelt, "*Orange Is the New Black* is Netflix's Most Watched."
2. Chu, "How *Orange Is the New Black* Found God."
3. Mallia, "From the Sacred to the Profane."
4. Tuchman, "Symbolic Annihilation of Women."
5. Van Zoonen, *Feminist Media Studies.*
6. Ali, Mahmood, Moel, Hudson, and Leathers, "Qualitative Investigation of Muslim and Christian Women's Views."
7. Ibid.
8. Anderson, *Feminist Philosophy of Religion.*
9. Mahan, *Media, Religion and Culture.*
10. Ibid., 11.
11. Campbell, *When Religion Meets New Media.*
12. Ibid., 9.
13. Mahan, *Media, Religion and Culture.*
14. Campbell, *When Religion Meets New Media.*
15. Davidman, "Studying Close to Home."
16. Hoover, *Religion in the Media Age.*
17. Head, "Content Analysis of Television Drama Programs"; Skill, Robinson, Lyons, and Larson, "Portrayal of Religion and Spirituality."
18. Clarke, "Created in Whose Images?"
19. Skill, Robinson, Lyons, and Larson, "Portrayal of Religion and Spirituality."
20. Lewis, "Religious Rhetoric and the Comic Frame"; Mallia, "From the Sacred to the Profane."
21. Lewis, "Religious Rhetoric and the Comic Frame."
22. Ibid.
23. Engstrom and Valenzano, "Demon Hunters and Hegemony."
24. Mohammed, "Muslims Next Door."
25. Ibid.
26. Guðmundsdóttir, "Female Christ-Figures in Films."
27. Ibid.
28. Yousman, "Inside *Oz*."

29. Ibid., 277.

30. Mattelart, "Women and Cultural Industries."

31. Tuchman, "Symbolic Annihilation."

32. Van Zoonen, "Feminist Perspectives on the Media"; Van Zoonen, *Feminist Media Studies.*

33. Gill, *Gender and the Media.*

34. Van Zoonen, "Feminist Perspectives on the Media."

35. Van Zoonen, *Feminist Media Studies.*

36. Ibid.

37. Ibid.

38. Ali, Mahmood, Moel, Hudson, and Leathers, "Qualitative Investigation of Muslim and Christian Women's Views."

39. Page, "Feminism and the Third Wave."

40. Anderson, *Feminist Philosophy of Religion.*

41. Page, "Feminism and the Third Wave."

42. Ali, Mahmood, Moel, Hudson, and Leathers, "Qualitative Investigation of Muslim and Christian Women's Views."

43. Ibid.

44. Shih, "Women, Religions, and Feminisms."

45. Charlton, "Women and Clergywomen."

46. Shih, "Women, Religions, and Feminisms," 227.

47. Anderson, *Feminist Philosophy of Religion.*

48. Matthews, "*Orange Is the New Black* is the Best TV Show about Prison."

49. Abad-Santos, "*Orange Is the New Black*'s Latina Characters"; Houston, "God Is a Verb."

50. van Dijk, "Critical Discourse Analysis."

51. Lazar, "Feminist Critical Discourse Analysis."

52. Campbell, *When Religion Meets New Media.*

53. Ibid.

54. Skill, Robinson, Lyons, and Larson, "Portrayal of Religion and Spirituality."

55. Clarke, "Created in Whose Images?"

56. Skill, Robinson, Lyons, and Larson, "Portrayal of Religion and Spirituality."

57. Lewis, "Religious Rhetoric and the Comic Frame."

58. Ibid.

59. Engstrom and Valenzano, "Demon Hunters and Hegemony."

60. Mohammed, "Muslims Next Door."

61. Van Zoonen, "Feminist Perspectives on the Media."

62. Van Zoonen, *Feminist Media Studies.*

63. Gill, *Gender and the Media.*
64. Van Zoonen, "Feminist Perspectives on the Media."
65. Page, "Feminism and the Third Wave."
66. Anderson, *Feminist Philosophy of Religion.*
67. Page, "Feminism and the Third Wave."
68. Ali, Mahmood, Moel, Hudson, and Leathers, "Qualitative Investigation of Muslim and Christian Women's Views."
69. Shih, "Women, Religions, and Feminisms."
70. Ibid.
71. Anderson, *Feminist Philosophy of Religion.*

Bibliography

Abad-Santos, Alex. "*Orange Is the New Black*'s Latina Characters Are Women We Hardly Ever See on Television." *Vox*, June 12, 2015. Accessed September 16, 2017. http://www.vox.com.

Ali, Saba R., Amina Mahmood, Joy Moel, Carolyn Hudson, and Leslie Leathers. "A Qualitative Investigation of Muslim and Christian Women's Views of Religion and Feminism in Their Lives." *Cultural Diversity and Ethnic Minority Psychology* 14, no. 1 (2008): 38–46.

Anderson, Pamela S. *A Feminist Philosophy of Religion: The Rationality and Myths of Religious Belief.* Oxford: Blackwell, 1998.

Campbell, Heidi. *When Religion Meets New Media.* New York: Routledge, 2010.

Charlton, Joy. "Women and Clergywomen." In *Feminist Narratives and the Sociology of Religion*, edited by Nancy Nason-Clark and Mary Jo Neitz, 53–58. Walnut Creek, CA: AltaMira, 2001.

Chu, Arthur. "How *Orange Is the New Black* Found God." *Daily Beast*, June 28, 2015. Accessed September 16, 2017. http://www.thedailybeast.com.

Clarke, Scott H. "Created in Whose Images? Religious Characters on Network Television." *Journal of Media and Religion* 4, no. 3 (2005): 137–53.

Davidman, Lynn. "Studying Close to Home: The Intersection of Life and Work." *Sociology of Religion* 61, no. 4 (2000): 425–32.

Engstrom, Erika, and Joseph M. Valenzano III. "Demon Hunters and Hegemony: Portrayal of Religion on the CW's *Supernatural.*" *Journal of Media and Religion* 9, no. 2 (2010): 67–83.

Gelt, Jessica. "*Orange Is the New Black* Is Netflix's Most Watched Original Series." *Los Angeles Times*, October 21, 2013.

Gill, Rosalind. *Gender and the Media*. Malden, MA: Polity, 2007.

Guðmundsdóttir, Arnfríður. "Female Christ-Figures in Films: A Feminist-Critical Analysis of *Breaking the Waves* and *Dead Man Walking.*" *Studia Theologica* 56 (2002): 27–43.

Head, Sydney W. "Content Analysis of Television Drama Programs." *Quarterly of Film, Radio, and Television* 9, no. 2 (1954): 175–94.

Hoover, Stewart M. *Religion in the Media Age*. New York: Routledge, 2006.

Houston, Shannon M. "God Is a Verb: 'Orange Is the New Black' Dares to Show Faith in a Positive Light." *Salon*, July 18, 2015. Accessed September 16, 2017. http://www.salon.com.

Lazar, Michelle M. "Feminist Critical Discourse Analysis: Articulating a Feminist Discourse Praxis." *Critical Discourse Studies* 4, no. 2 (2007): 141–64.

Lewis, Todd V. "Religious Rhetoric and the Comic Frame in *The Simpsons.*" *Journal of Media and Religion* 1, no. 3 (2002): 153–65.

Mahan, Jeffrey H. *Media, Religion and Culture: An Introduction*. New York: Routledge, 2014.

Mallia, Karen L. "From the Sacred to the Profane: A Critical Analysis of the Changing Nature of Religious Imagery in Advertising." *Journal of Media and Religion* 8, no. 3 (2009): 172–90.

Mattelart, Michèle. "Women and Cultural Industries." In *Approaches to Media: A Reader*, edited by Oliver Boyd-Barrett and Chris Newbold, 411–19. New York: St. Martin's, 1995.

Matthews, Dylan. "*Orange Is the New Black* Is the Best TV Show about Prison Ever Made." *Washington Post*, July 17, 2013.

Mohammed, Shaheed N. "The Muslims Next Door: Transgressive Hybridity in TLC's *All-American Muslim.*" *Mass Communication and Society* 18, no. 1 (2015): 97–118.

Page, Sarah. "Feminism and the Third Wave: Politicising the Sociology of Religion?" Presentation at the Thinking Gender: The NEXT Generation, UK Postgraduate Conference in Gender Studies, University of Leeds, UK, June 21–22, 2006.

Shih, Fang-Long. "Women, Religions, and Feminisms." In *The Blackwell Companion to Sociology of Religion*, edited by Bryan S. Turner, 221–43. Malden, MA: Blackwell, 2010.

Skill, Thomas, James D. Robinson, John S. Lyons, and David Larson. "The Portrayal of Religion and Spirituality on Fictional Network Television." *Review of Religious Research* 35, no. 3 (1994): 251–67.

Tuchman, Gaye. "The Symbolic Annihilation of Women by the Mass Media."
    In *Approaches to Media: A Reader*, edited by Oliver Boyd-Barrett and Chris
    Newbold, 411–19. New York: St. Martin's, 1995.
van Dijk, Teun A. "Critical Discourse Analysis." In *The Handbook of Discourse
    Analysis*, edited by Deborah Schiffrin, Deborah Tannen, and Heidi E.
    Hamilton, 352–71. Malden, MA: Blackwell, 2001.
Van Zoonen, Liesbet. "Feminist Perspectives on the Media." In *Mass Media
    and Society*. 2nd ed., edited by James Curran and Michael Gurevitch,
    33–54. London: Arnold, 1991.
———. *Feminist Media Studies*. Vol. 9. London: Sage, 1994.
Yousman, Bill. "Inside *Oz*: Hyperviolence, Race and Class Nightmares, and
    the Engrossing Spectacle of Terror." *Communication and Critical/Cultural
    Studies* 6, no. 3 (2009): 265–84.

4. Dominating the (Female) Incarcerated Body: Gender and Medical Control in Prison Dramas

Katherine A. Foss

"**D**antés crossed the formidable threshold, and the door closed behind him with a loud bang. He now breathed a different air, a thick and mephitic air. He was in prison." With these lines in *The Count of Monte Cristo*, Alexandre Dumas describes the all-encompassing despondency of the newly imprisoned Dantés, thus capturing the suffocating bleakness of the incarcerated life.[1] Foucault theorized this experience of the condemned as being sentenced to a system of control nearly hidden from the general public in his famous work *Discipline and Punish: The Birth of the Prison*.[2] Prison, Foucault wrote, "gives almost total power over the prisoners; it has internal mechanisms of repression and punishment: a despotic discipline."[3] This control extends not just to physical imprisonment of the body but to the mind and soul as well, for, as Foucault emphasized, control is "uninterrupted," never ceasing to exercise its "exhaustive disciplinary apparatus."[4] As part of this authority, prison, as an institution, holds medical control over the body, thus exhibiting a secondary system of social control until the prisoner is either executed or released.[5]

Certainly with Dumas, and for most of *Discipline and Punish*, the "condemned body" is a masculine one—a narrowed focus unfortunately representative of most theoretical, mediated, and experiential examinations of incarceration. Therefore, women's place in these institutions of control has been largely overlooked, despite the 106,200 women who were incarcerated in the United States in 2014—a number that is on the rise.[6] Fictional narratives have primarily featured men's prisons (for example, *The Shawshank Redemption*, *Oz*, and *Prison Break*), with the incarcerated female experience historically limited to the women-in-prison stereotypes of *Caged Heat* and other such films.[7] *Orange Is the New Black* (*OITNB*) has attempted to challenge these stereotypes through its diverse and complex characters and story lines. With its focus on a women's correctional facility, it provides viewers a mediated look into the (fictional) lives of incarcerated women.

Extensive research has analyzed prison representations in popular culture,[8] yet few studies have addressed gender constructions. The popularity of *OITNB* enables such a comparative study between male and female prison dramas. Furthermore, the frequent story arcs involving health and medical issues allow for an exploration into the construction of medicine as a mechanism of gendered social control in fictional prisons. This chapter uses three texts: *OITNB*; *Prison Break* (2005–2009), which features two male correctional facilities; and the 2009 made-for-TV movie *Prison Break: The Final Break*, set in a women's correctional facility. These texts provide an opportunity to better understand the role and power of medical social control in what Conrad called "total institutions," in which prison physicians serve as powerful intermediaries between the prison system and the inmate patients.[9]

Invisible Issues: Health in Prison

Popular culture downplays and overlooks issues of contagious disease, chronic illness, injury, and other health issues. Yousman discussed how characters frequently die from violence in the program *Oz*, but the show contains only one AIDS-related fatality, thus painting a false picture of the frequent causes of death in prison.[10] In fact, the most prevalent real-life health problems are nearly absent from film and television, and these problems differ greatly by sex. Compared to men, female prisoners have greater and more diverse health challenges.[11] Research found that over 60 percent of female prisoners reported having chronic medical problems, while only 50 percent of male prisoners did.[12] Female prisoners also exhibit a higher prevalence of mental health issues.[13] And, of course, female prison populations require medical attention for pregnancy and childbirth. Approximately one in twenty-five women in state prisons and one in thirty-three in federal prisons are pregnant when they enter the system.[14]

Theoretical Framework: The Gendered Medical Lens

This research draws from several theoretical areas. As defined in the introduction to this book, Gerbner's cultivation theory guides this study, which posits that heavier viewers of television will hold a more mediated perception of reality than light viewers.[15] Scholarship in this area confirms that media consumption negatively shapes public perception of many facets of race and gender, including rape myth acceptance.[16] Additionally, heavy viewers tend to overestimate crime rates and favor harsh prison sentences over rehabilitation.[17] Here, cultivation theory demonstrates the importance of the current study as it assumes that viewers of prison dramas will perceive prisoners and the prison system in real life as it is conveyed on television. This mediated "reality" includes misperceptions about gender inequality as it pertains the prison body, sexual assault (including rape myths), and other disparities presented in this genre.

In addition to cultivation theory, this study uses the theory of gendered organizations to explain gender inequality in prison and its representations. Acker proposed that institutions and organizations are not gender neutral, but in fact, "gender is present in the processes, practices, images and ideologies, and distributions of power in the various sectors of social life."[18] Moreover, because American institutions have been historically created, controlled, and dominated by men, gendered processes within these organizations reinforce a patriarchal hegemonic structure.[19] Building on Acker's work, Britton explicated how the prison system embodies and reinforces gender inequality at three levels:[20]

- The *structural* level—referring to divisions of labor, wage disparities, and conceptions of the public sphere versus the private sphere that have prevented equal opportunities for female employment in the prison system, especially at men's correctional facilities.
- The *cultural* level—the repetition and dissemination of language, images, and ideologies that legitimize gender inequality, including commonsense notions about work (prison as "a masculine place," for instance). Media discourse typically reinforces and perpetuates these gender constructions, yet this hegemonic structure can be challenged with counterideologies.[21]
- The *agency* level—the microlevel interactions "in which workers are involved that, intentionally or not, invoke gender or reproduce gender inequality, as well as processes of identity construction."[22]

Together, these levels produce and embody gender. Britton pointed out that in the prison system and for inmates, these processes are exacerbated in that people spend all of their time under supervision and control.[23]

Moreover, a secondary institution of control within the prison exists: medicine, which exerts its power through the regulation and care of inmates' bodies and minds.[24] Conrad and Schneider articulated this process, stating, "The greatest social control power comes from having the authority to define certain behaviors, persons, and things."[25] As applied to the control of deviance, Conrad explained how medical control has and can be used to curb and control deviance, referring to "the ways in which medicine functions (wittingly or unwittingly) to secure adherence to social norms: specifically, by using medical means to minimize, eliminate, or normalize deviant behavior."[26] In addition, medicine also works as a form of social control in excusing "deviant" behavior, particularly to excuse charges under a "diminished capacity" defense.[27]

Since inmates' lives are controlled by the prison system, they experience the medicalization of otherwise nonmedical activities, like eating, drinking, and bathing. According to Conrad, "*Medicalization* describes a process by which nonmedical problems become defined and treated as medical problems, usually in terms of illnesses or disorders."[28] Medicalization extends the jurisdiction of the health professional to regular or routine parts of life and can become problematic when society becomes dependent on conceptualizations of, as Zola articulated, what is defined as "'healthy' and 'ill.'"[29] This medical gaze has been applied to other previously nonmedical conditions and stages in life.[30] Conrad explained how medicalization has been and is gendered, stating, "It is abundantly clear that women's natural life processes (especially concerning reproduction) are much more likely to be medicalized than men's, and that gender is an important factor in understanding medicalization."[31] This medicalization has been used to grant permission to (male) doctors to make decisions about women's bodies, stripping them of consent and agency.[32] Thus, medicalization can be especially problematic in allowing "experts" (usually physicians) to dominate and control the bodies of the oppressed.[33]

Method

To explore gender constructions in the medicalization of fictional prison life, the following questions guided the study:

> What are the medical discourses identified in television prison dramas?
> How is gender constructed in medical discourses?

Methodology

Critical discourse analysis was used to examine medical discourses in prison dramas. According to van Dijk, this approach "studies the way social power abuse, dominance, and inequality are enacted, reproduced, and resisted by text and talk in the social and political context."[34] This method perceives text not as a fixed entity but as open and fluid, drawing from the dominant (and sometimes counter) ideologies in a society, which change over time.[35] In other words, discourses emerge from context and can reproduce and reinforce dominance, which van Dijk defined as "the exercise of social power by elites, institutions or groups that results in social inequality, including political, cultural, class, ethnic, racial and gender inequality.[36] Therefore, to study prison dramas is to better understand the intersection of gender, prison discourse, and social control at this cultural moment, as reflected and perpetuated in these programs, as it relates to power inequality structured by institutional authority. As a feminist study, this research particularly centers on "the construction of gender as a process and a product of social interaction and power relations."[37] The methodology, sample, and design reflect this focus.

The Sample

This research aimed to explore how contemporary dramas portray prison life. Therefore, older dramas that have been heavily studied, particularly the program *Oz*, were excluded. Three contemporary dramas were selected. As one of the first TV programs to explore women in prison, the first three seasons (forty episodes) of the Netflix series *Orange Is the New Black* (2013–) were examined. Second, the Fox network program *Prison Break* (2005–2009), which aired eighty-one episodes over four seasons, was studied. In this show, a man named Michael Scofield deliberately gets himself incarcerated so that he can break his brother out of prison. This program depicts Scofield's experiences at two fictional correctional facilities: Fox River State Penitentiary in Chicago, Illinois, and the Penitenciaría Federal de Sona, a prison in Panama. Third, I studied the made-for-TV movie *Prison Break: The Final Break* (2009), featuring the same characters of *Prison Break*, but it focuses on the daily experiences and escape from a women's prison.

Conducting the Study

An initial analysis was done of all episodes of *OITNB*, *Prison Break*, and *Final Break* (the TV movie). Of the 121 episodes and TV movie, only seasons set at an American prison were then further examined, which included all three seasons of *OITNB* (set at Litchfield Penitentiary, a fictional minimum-security prison), the TV movie *Final Break* (set at Miami-Dade State Penitentiary), and the first season of *Prison Break* (set at the fictional Fox River). The third season of *Prison Break*, set at a Panamanian prison, was excluded from this study, as the prison system scarcely exists aside from the external guards, as inmates must fend for themselves against other inmates because administration and structure have been abandoned.

To examine the medical discourses in the fictional TV programs, the narrative structures, characters, and relationships were studied using the following questions: What are the representations of health professionals and patients in these shows? Who serves as a gatekeeper to medical care? What aspects of prison life are medically controlled and medically overlooked? What medical issues do prisoners face and how are they treated? Is mental illness addressed? How do inmates compensate for inadequacies in the prison health care system? And, overall, gender constructions in regard to medical social control were identified.

Findings

To explore medical discourses in prison dramas, sixty-two episodes and one TV movie were analyzed. The need for medical intervention frequently arose in the two programs and TV movie studied, even if it was not always given. "Medical" representations included story lines about medication, violence requiring treatment, other injuries, illness, pregnancy and childbirth, signs of mental illness, and feigning illness or injury. In *OITNB* and *Final Break*, no medical staff appear regularly. On the other hand, in *Prison Break*, access to health care is easily and regularly gained, with the infirmary as a key set of the show, in which Dr. Sara Tancredi (the same character in *Final Break*) repeatedly advocates for Scofield and other patients. Overall, three discourses emerge from the analysis of medical depictions: 1) medicine as institutional control, 2) manipulation of the system, and 3) compensation by inmates in the absence of medical help. Combined, these discourses illuminate the vast gender inequality presented in the programs.

Medicine as Institutional Control

In *OITNB*, *Prison Break*, and *Final Break*, the prisoners' health depends on the willingness of the prison system to treat or prevent illness or injury, as the prison employees determined which prisoners had access to medical care and what treatment they received. In many representations, the prison system's total control over medical care not only serves as a constant reminder of captivity, but it also has very real implications for the prisoners' overall health. In addition, as this control dominates in the women's prison dramas far more than in the men's prison, it reifies existing notions of gender inequality.

Regulating access as a means of social control.—For the women's prison dramas, access to health care professionals is limited to emergencies or prison-sanctioned chronic issues. The inmates in *OITNB* largely rely on their assigned counselors for advice and access to further medical care. In season 3, inmate Brook Soso repeatedly tells counselor Sam Healy that she needs some professional help for her depression. Finally, Soso is granted a visit with a psychiatrist, who dismisses her concerns and merely offers medication. His negligence is nearly fatal for Soso, as she intentionally overdoses on antidepressants. *Final Break* also presents prison medical care as impersonal, limited, and protective of the institution. Inmate Sara Tancredi nearly dies from a guard's refusal to allow her medical intervention. During lunch Tancredi gasps for air and grabs her throat as she begs the guard for help, explaining that she has been poisoned. Finally, after minutes pass, Tancredi exclaims, "If I don't get to the hospital in the next 15 minutes, I will die and my baby will die! Please." At this pleading, the guard obliges, and the doctor saves Tancredi, just in time. As with the guard, the doctor is apathetic and impersonal, with no follow-ups or questions about her well-being.

The denial of care.—Social control is also exerted through the absence or denial of care. In *OITNB* inmate Rosa has ovarian cancer, for which she receives chemotherapy during the first two seasons. Toward the end of the second season, in the episode "Appropriately-Sized Pots," counselor Healy informs Rosa that the state will not pay for life-saving surgery, stating, "The, uh, DOC has set certain limits on invasive [pauses] It's not gonna happen. You're not out of options. We'll stick with the chemo." Rosa becomes angry and calls him a liar. Healy responds, "I wish I could help you." The scene concludes with Rosa replying, "But it's out of your hands. It's always out of your hands. You're all the same. Useless." Here, the prison's withholding of life-saving treatment has fatal effects.

Prisoners are also denied medication. In "Lesbian Request Denied," the pharmacist tells inmate Sophia (who is transgender) that her estrogen dosage has been reduced and refuses to listen to Sophia's objections. Sophia turns to counselor Healy for help in attaining the medication, explaining, "If I don't get my medication, I'm going through withdrawal. Hot flashes, night sweats. My face will sag, my body hair will start to grow back." She then demands, "I wanna see a doctor." Healy refuses her request, saying, "You can't go to the clinic unless it's an emergency." Sophia affirms, "This is an emergency." Healy quickly declares, "Yeah, well, we don't see it that way." In desperation Sophia swallows a bobble-head doll, warranting a visit to the clinic. Yet, the prison doctor further restricts the medication, causing more problems. As the prison administration becomes involved, Sophia's struggle for her medication is perceived as an unnecessary burden and expense. Healy approaches Natalie Figueroa, the executive assistant to the warden, about Sophia. She responds harshly, "He [Sophia] can suck it up. She. Jesus . . . We are only required to give her enough to maintain. This is a federal system. If he wanted to keep his girlish figure he should've stayed out of jail. Why would anyone ever give up being a man? It's like winning the lottery and giving the ticket back."

Figueroa's response demonstrates not only the control of the prison and an unsympathetic view of Sophia's well-being but also the prison system's cruel perceptions and treatments of people who are transgender. While Sophia struggles to obtain her medication, the prison staff is quick to distribute psychiatric drugs, including sedatives. With inmate Soso, Healy offers drugs at the first mention of depression. Likewise, in *Prison Break*, all prisoners on the psych ward are required to take medication. This requirement highlights the medical control of staff, who deem what is "necessary" and what is not.

Reaction, not prevention.—One prevalent discourse is that the prison system responds to, not prevents, illness and injury. Reflecting existing literature, violence is a consistent problem in the three texts studied. When threatened, the fictional female inmates beg for guards to intervene. However, the prison staff generally ignores conflict until it escalates to violence. In *OITNB* season 1, the character Pennsatucky becomes increasingly hostile toward Piper. This tension culminates to the season's final moments when Pennsatucky corners Piper alone outside and threatens her with a cross sharpened to a point. At this point Healy steps outside and sees the pair. Piper calls out, "Mr. Healy, she's trying to kill me!" He looks at her, then ignores her cries and walks inside. Pennsatucky slashes Piper's hand, and Piper then retaliates, knocking her to the ground and pummeling her to unconsciousness. Other inmates experience a similar pattern, in which they receive threats, but nothing is done until the warnings escalate into violence, as evidenced by Vee's assault on Red, Gloria's attack on Sophia, and the incident in *Final Break* when an unnamed inmate begins aggressively beating Tancredi. For these female victims, prison staff do not intervene until after the violence has ended.

Prison administration acts similarly in *Prison Break*, deliberately over-looking conflict. In the episodes "Cell Test" and "Allen," corrections officer

Brad Bellick intentionally leaves Scofield alone, allowing Mafia boss John Abruzzi and his crew to pin Scofield to a table and demand information about a Mafia informant. When Scofield refuses, they slice off his pinky toe with garden shears. He cries out but maintains his silence about the informant. The men move to the next toe, amputating it with a quick snip. At this point the incarcerated mob boss, John Abruzzi, orders them to stop. A guard then enters, discovers Scofield bleeding profusely, and calls for medical attention.

Although guard negligence is consistent across the programs, the aftermath of the violence and its lasting effects differ greatly between the female and male prisoners. Piper is taken to solitary confinement and undergoes a frightening transfer, later revealed to be unrelated to the crime. Red's attack causes a concussion so severe that she is hospitalized. Her scars last for episodes—marks that symbolize her weakness and vulnerability. Likewise, after Sophia's assault, with no makeup or wig, covered in bruises, she appears broken, a stark contrast to the playful and fiercely confident character of the previous two seasons. For these female inmates, their attacks and scars represent weakness, vulnerability, and a fall from power.

On the other hand, Scofield's assault and resulting amputated toes earn the trust and confidence of Abruzzi by showcasing his loyalty, even under threat. He limps for an episode, but his missing toes are never shown, nor are they mentioned again. Since Abruzzi becomes Scofield's partner in the escape plan, the amputation is regarded as just another necessary step in the path to freedom.

Sexual assault is also conveyed as a persistent problem in these programs about prison. In *OITNB* the guard known as "Pornstache" repeatedly blackmails inmates into performing sexual favors on him and visibly molests the female prisoners during pat downs. Because of Pornstache and other correctional officers, the female inmates constantly experience the threat of sexual assault in the power inequality between the (mostly male) guards and themselves. This disparity comes to fruition when a new guard, Charlie Coates, sexually assaults inmate Pennsatucky. In the third season, Pennsatucky is assigned the task of driving Coates around town. Their relationship begins playfully, as they stop for donuts and feed ducks at a nearby pond. Increasingly Coates's lighthearted teasing turns to stern orders, in which he forces her to get down in the mud. And then, in the episode "A Tittin' and a Hairin'," Coates rapes Pennsatucky in the van. This heartbreaking scene features close-up shots of Pennsatucky's pained face as she is violently attacked. In the aftermath Pennsatucky does not report the rape, fearing that she will be punished, not him. Instead she feigns a seizure while driving and crashes, ensuring that she will not be victimized again. And yet, as Coates continues to work as an officer, he remains a threat to all of the female inmates.

Sexual assault also occurs in *Prison Break* but not done by the guards. Two inmates, T-Bag and Avocado, prey on other male prisoners whom they perceive as weak, young, and vulnerable. When T-Bag gets a new cell mate, Seth, he presumably begins sexually assaulting him—violence that is not shown. Seth does not report the attack, but he begs for help from Scofield, whom he views as strong, masculine, and good hearted. When Scofield refuses to intervene, Seth hangs himself with a bedsheet, as the whole cellblock watches. Like T-Bag, Avocado is known for raping his cell mates. Aware of this crime, corrections officer Bellick uses this knowledge to punish another inmate, Tweener, by assigning him to Avocado's cell. As with Seth, the abuse is not shown or reported, except to Scofield, who once again declines to help. Tweener takes it upon himself to stop Avocado by brutally castrating him with a razor. Even this crime goes unreported, as Avocado decides to get his own revenge—not out of fear, but rage.

Ideological power as control: The trivialization of mental illness.—By consistently treating mental illness and other issues as unimportant or humorous, these dramas dismiss and delegitimize the conditions and the people who exemplify them. Across the prison depictions, mental illness is trivialized, used for comic relief, and treated only with sedating medication. The *OITNB* character Suzanne "Crazy Eyes" clearly has some mental illness issues. She appears childlike and hits herself when upset. She frequently provides the comedy of the show, with lines like "I threw my pie for you!" and scenes in which she talks to a mop. In "Lesbian Request Denied," Suzanne becomes upset with Piper. Instead of directly confronting her, Suzanne urinates on the floor next to Piper's bed. Suzanne's issues are usually dismissed, even though she is prone to violence. In seasons 1 and 2, Suzanne's frustration escalates into rage, leading to violent attacks on her fellow inmates. Apart from these incidents, which result in time in the psychiatric ward, Suzanne's mental health is overlooked and dismissed, with no discussion of additional therapy. Similarly, prison staff overlook the mental instability of a minor character, Lolly, in season 3. She is paranoid about possible government conspiracy and begins stalking inmate Alex Vause. Even after Lolly chokes her, Lolly remains in the minimum-security prison.

The prison staff also fail to provide services for Jimmy, an older woman with progressively worsening dementia. Even though she is clearly confused and needs help, the prison doctors and others do nothing until Jimmy's dementia becomes so severe that she believes she is on a diving board (while standing on the church altar) and jumps off, breaking her arm. The prison administration's solution is to give Jimmy a "compassionate release" onto the street, with a meager amount of money, no place to go, and little awareness of who or where she is.

In *Prison Break* and *Final Break*, characters with severe mental illness are one-dimensional, only serving as convenient plot devices. The third episode of *Prison Break* introduces a new cell mate, Haywire, a murderer with schizoaffective disorder. His buggy eyes, inappropriate conversation, and awkward mannerisms strongly contrast with Scofield's "normal" roommate, the confident and trustworthy Sucre. Fearing his plan will be jeopardized, Scofield punches himself, claiming that Haywire is hurting him. Because of Haywire's history, guards immediately take Haywire to the psychiatric ward. Later, Scofield uses Haywire to uncover destroyed parts of his tattoo map, which Haywire can recall only because of his mental differences. Likewise, in *Final Break*, inmates warn others about the temper of a large, silent woman nicknamed "Skittlez" when this character's anger issues become convenient to the plot. During a struggle between Tancredi and the prison bullies, one woman accidentally bumps Skittlez, who goes berserk, thus allowing Tancredi to escape without serious injury. Through these limited and narrow representations, the prison dramas delegitimize mental illness—placing it outside the bounds of what is deemed necessary to treat.

The medicalization of everyday life.—In prison, routine activities become regulated and even medicalized, or are under the systematic medical jurisdiction of the staff and administration. This process is especially evident with inmate pregnancy and the control of food in the prison. Pregnancy, labor, and birth are extensively regulated in the prison dramas. When inmates are in labor, prison staff refuse to intervene until the contractions reach a predetermined interval. In the "Moscow Mule" episode of *OITNB*, Maria goes into labor. The prison staff watches idly, as fellow prisoners offer Maria pineapple and other home remedies to help with contractions until she finally reaches the "acceptable" contraction spacing and the guards call an ambulance. Similarly, in the aptly named episode "Don't Make Me Come Back There," the guards watch as Dayanara labors in agony. It is only when she begins bleeding heavily and her mother (also an inmate) screams for help that they call for medical attention earlier than scheduled. The intentional lack of support and intervention (even for laboring mothers) exemplifies a medicalization of the birth process—with institutional control over the woman's body and her treatment. Although the actual birth is not shown, the mothers' first moments with their babies are also regulated. Maria and Dayanara receive only brief periods of time with their newborns before the babies are taken away. In *Final Break*, pregnant inmate Tancredi is told of a similar plan:

> DOCTOR: The day we induce, we'll secure you in an ambulance. We'll take you to St. Lucia down the road.
>> We'll cordon off a room. There'll be three armed guards in there with me, when you give birth.
> SARA: Do I get to see my baby?
> DOCTOR: You'll have 30 minutes before we take it away. I've seen this process a dozen times. After the mothers come back here, the depression's almost unbearable. My advice, it's a lot less messy, if you'd just think of yourself as a surrogate.

Here, the institutional control of these women extends to labor, delivery, and, ultimately, their relationships with their babies.

In prison, eating is also a medicalized process. The warden controls what food and how much is distributed in the prison. Food is used as incentives for inmates to serve as informants to the prison staff, as counselor Healy bribes Pennsatucky and other prisoners with donuts for information and corrections officer Bellick offers inmate Tweener a cheeseburger to snitch on his fellow prisoners. The kitchen staff (also inmates) ration food as a means of control. In the *OITNB* pilot, Piper offends Red, the cook, who retaliates by withholding food from her. For a week Piper starves until she figures out how to appease Red, prompting her to lift the ban. In *Final Break*, inmates attempt to poison Tancredi by tainting her lunch.

When prisoners withhold or taint food, the prison staff do not intervene. On the contrary, when inmates starve themselves, guards, counselors, and even the prison hospital personnel involve themselves to end the hunger strike. In *OITNB* the prison administration orders the force-feeding of Sister Jane Ingalls to end her hunger strike, thus suppressing her agency to protest and coercing her to conform so as to avoid bad publicity.

Manipulation of the System

While women are at the mercy of the prison system for health care, for both access and response, the fictional male prisoners do not face the same troubles. Prisoners easily and regularly visit the prison infirmary for treatment of injuries and illness. In fact, gaining entry to the prison physician, Dr. Sara Tancredi (the same character that is later featured in the *Prison Break* movie), is so easy that Scofield and other inmates frequently manipulate the prison health care system for their benefit. When Scofield enters the penitentiary, his medical file states that he has type 1 diabetes and requires regular insulin injections. In fact, Scofield is not a diabetic but is faking the condition to access the infirmary. When the injections begin to affect Scofield's health, causing him to shake, Tancredi questions the diagnosis. Before his next blood test, Scofield is able to acquire insulin-blocking medication on the black market from other prisoners, thus protecting his secret.

Similarly, Scofield feigns what is called a "mental break" to get himself admitted to the psych ward by punching a wall and then acting unresponsive to Tancredi's examination. As opposed to *OITNB*, the psych ward, here, is not a feared destination but one that is easily accessed and minimally supervised. Once admitted to psych, Scofield has enough freedom to acquire missing escape plans. He also easily outsmarts the medical staff, bypassing the "mandatory" medication. As soon as Scofield has what he needs, he simply tells Dr. Tancredi, "I think we both know I don't belong here." Without question, she releases him back into the general population, demonstrating the ease and fluidity of accessing and then leaving the psych ward.

Other inmates also feign illness as part of the escape plan. In "And Then There Were Seven," the character Tweener fakes a seizure and is rushed to the infirmary. As the guard and medical staff hurry to "save" him, Tweener is able to steal a watch from the guard (the purpose of the faked seizure). Tancredi never questions the authenticity of Tweener's problem. Likewise, Scofield is able to get a pill to the death row solitary cells for his brother, Lincoln. The medication causes temporary stomach problems, severe enough that Lincoln is brought to the infirmary in time for Scofield's escape plan. Again, Tancredi and the medical staff never question the authenticity of Lincoln's illness, instead offering compassion and intravenous fluids.

In the male correctional facility of *Prison Break*, negative health occurs, not because of negligence, but because of personal choice not to involve prison authority. Inmates typically choose not to report violence to the guards, as exemplified by the sexual assault victims Seth and Tweener, as well as by the amputation of Scofield's toes. In these cases the male inmates' responses seem empowering, allowing Scofield an "in" with the Mafia boss and enabling Tweener to escape his abuser.

Compensation by Inmates

In *OITNB* the inmates frequently rely on home remedies and superstition to make up for inadequate medical care in the prison, using maxi pads as makeshift face masks during a flu outbreak, as well as herbs and Lysol to protect against bedbugs. Prisoners also use home remedies and other means to compensate for the lack of treatment for chronic conditions. To help Red with her back pain, other inmates offer her a wooden board for sleeping, massage, and a salve made of hot peppers. Inmates also deal with the helplessness of prison life through faith and religion. In the third season, inmates believe that Norma, a woman who does not speak, is a faith healer and so divulge their secrets to her and even worship a piece of toast that they believe bears a resemblance to Norma's face. Those who follow Norma are portrayed as misguided and foolish, particularly in the scenes with the toast Norma.

Male prisoners also compensate for the lack of intervention, as demonstrated with Tweener's retaliation on his cell mate, Avocado, for sexual assault. This "eye for an eye" approach to justice is also evident in a struggle between T-Bag and Abruzzi, resulting in a near-fatal slash across Abruzzi's neck, and other moments of violence within the prison. As opposed to the women's prison dramas, compensation comes across here as empowerment and agency. Because it is primarily characters introduced as weak, and therefore feminized, who commit these violent acts, compensation creates equilibrium for the character, particularly for Tweener, by redefining him not as a peripheral character to be dismissed but as one "masculine enough" to become a protagonist. Britton articulated these preconceived notions about violence and masculinity, stating, "Violence is so closely tied to hegemonic forms of masculinity that to be a 'real man' is, by definition, to know how to use violence and to be willing to do so under appropriate circumstances."[38] Here, male characters' "justified" violence in a way restores their masculinity, enough to be accepted as a protagonist.

Discussion

In the prison dramas, viewers are brought into the incarcerated world through a white-privileged lens, in which the "fish out of water" learns about prison life. And while the inmate ensemble offers at least token diversity, those in power, including the medical staff and gatekeepers to health care, are predominately white and middle-upper class. Such stereotypical depictions are unfortunately aligned with existing research and commentary on the genre, which highlight the (white, privileged) viewer's identification with the primary protagonist.[39] Prisoners of color, then, experience multiple layers of oppression in this system, from the mostly white guards, administration, and prison medical staff, as well as from the protagonist's central role in the story line, which shifts other characters to the periphery.

Applying the theory of gendered organizations to these representations highlights the vast disparity and demonstrates how medicine works as a means of social control primarily for women, not for men. Even in these fictional worlds, the three levels of institutional gendering are apparent, creating a much harsher and far less healthy experience for female inmates—even when the story lines are scripted by essentially the same writers (as with *Prison Break* and *Final Break*). At the structural level,[40] the prison is a predominantly masculine system. In *OITNB*, although it is a women's correctional facility, the main counselor and many of the guards and administrators are white men, who have total control over the female prisoners. Likewise, *Prison Break* is an entirely masculine system with male correctional officers and a male warden. Only Dr. Tancredi and another medical staff person are female. Their femininity could explain why this show has more sympathetic health discourse. At the same time, Tancredi nearly becomes a victim to the inmates because she is a woman, thereby reinforcing discriminatory misperceptions that women "do not belong" in a men's prison, regardless of qualifications.[41] In addition, these programs ignore positive structural changes to help protect the welfare of inmates, including the standard procedure of regular well-being checkups for inmates.[42] The latest Bureau of Justice Statistics survey indicated that most inmates are content with their quality of health care in prison—a far cry from fictional television.[43]

These media constructions further gender the prison institution at the cultural level.[44] Beyond the problematic demographics, the extent to which female inmates are medically controlled by the prison system through their limited access to and denial of care, the narrative treatment of mental illness for multiple female characters, and the medicalization of the women's bodies in these dramas reinforce unequal gender dynamics in which men dominate women. This control is contrasted with the male prisoners in *Prison Break*, who appear to be too smart and too strong to be "taken" by the prison system, including its medical authority. The gender disparity is further emphasized through scenes of violence against women, in which the female inmates are portrayed as helpless and vulnerable, even if they have been established as hardened criminals. Moreover, the constant fear of sexual assault from the staff extends the prison's control into these inmates' minds and emotions: as long as they are incarcerated, they live under threat of rape, especially because (as Pennsatucky's case exemplifies) no one will believe them. Such messages characterize rape myths, conveying the horrifying message that rape is predetermined, unavoidable, and justified.[45] These representations also fail to portray staff sexual assaults on male prisoners, which statistically occur more often than assaults on female prisoners, thus reinforcing the invisibility of male sexual victimization and male rape myths.[46] At the cultural level, such discourse has been correlated with an increase in women's fear of rape and with public acceptance of rape myths, along with further gendering of both penal and medical institutions.[47]

Finally, at the agency level,[48] the interactions of characters on these programs construct and reflect gender inequality. Conrad wrote about the complicated role of the prison physician, who is torn between serving the system or the patient.[49] This tension, however, is largely absent from the programs studied. Characters either serve the institution or the patient—with the medical staff of *OITNB* and *Final Break* focused on institutional restrictions on access, budget, and time, thereby denying agency to the inmates over their own bodies, except for home remedies and superstitious practices. Their minds and their bodies are at the mercy of prison and medical institutional control, which is even more severe for Sophia, the transgender woman, who is dismissed and degraded for her gender identity. Unfortunately, this representation is reflective of the ill treatment and discrimination that trans people have faced in both the health care system and in incarceration.[50]

On the contrary, Scofield and most of the other male inmates retain control, not just with access to the infirmary and psych ward, but in scenes with prison staff. Even the tough and morally corrupt guards are no match for Scofield, as he (with the help of others) is able to manipulate the system so that they are no longer a problem. In the infirmary Dr. Tancredi, in *Prison Break*, is wholeheartedly a patient advocate, almost at the cost of her own demise. And in scenes with Scofield and Tancredi, they act as equals. He is not shackled or sedated, and he and his escape team are easily able to fool Dr. Tancredi into believing their feigned illnesses (diabetes, seizures, and stomach problems). The difference in agency between female and male inmates represents, not just divergences in these programs, but an inequality indicative of a hegemonic patriarchal society.

Conclusion

Consistently, these prison dramas construct and deepen inequality, and not just that between male and female inmates; they highlight, further, a gendered system that can easily control and oppress women but that can, in turn, easily be controlled by male inmates. Even with the same pool of writers for *Prison Break* and *Final Break*, the messages about social control differ vastly from the men's prison to the women's correctional facility—a disparity suggesting that the ideologies at the root of these representations extend far beyond individual writers, producers, and programs.

While the gender disparities here could be written off as fiction, as entertainment, they reflect and perpetuate a patriarchal system in which male dominance of women continues to be embraced. Thus the messages here, about mental illness, about sexual assault, about control of the body, reinforce existing inequality in power, relations, and social structures. At the same time, these dramas present a distorted perspective of prison life. As Foucault outlined in his writings on prison, without executions in the public square, most people have very little knowledge of and experience with punishment in the judicial system.[51] Therefore, it is likely that what is conveyed in popular culture about prison is largely what influences public perception of this experience, including its gendered connotations that encourage medical social control over women.

Notes

1. Dumas, *Count of Monte Cristo.*
2. Foucault, *Discipline and Punish.*
3. Ibid., 236.
4. Ibid., 235.
5. Conrad, "Types of Medical Social Control."
6. Carson, "Prisoners in 2014."
7. Ciasullo, "Containing 'Deviant' Desire."
8. Gutierrez, "Redeeming the Myth"; Mason, *Captured by the Media*; Yousman, "Inside *Oz*"; Wilson and O'Sullivan, *Images of Incarceration*; O'Sullivan, "Representations of Prison in Nineties Hollywood."
9. Conrad, "Types of Medical Social Control," 5.
10. Yousman, "Inside *Oz*."
11. Binswanger, Merrill, Krueger, White, Booth, and Elmore, "Gender Differences in Chronic Medical."
12. Maruschak, *Medical Problems of State and Federal Prisoners.*

13. Binswanger, Merrill, Krueger, White, Booth, and Elmore, "Gender Differences in Chronic Medical."

14. Maruschak, "Medical Problems of Prisoners."

15. Gerbner and Gross, "Living with Television."

16. Goidel, Freeman, and Procopio, "Impact of Television Viewing"; Lubbers, Schneepers, and Vergeer, "Exposure to Newspapers and Attitudes"; Dixon, "Black Criminals and White Officers"; Kahlor and Morrison, "Television Viewing and Rape Myth Acceptance."

17. Goidel, Freeman, and Procopio, "Impact of Television Viewing."

18. Acker, "From Sex Roles to Gendered Institutions," 567.

19. Ibid.

20. Britton, *At Work in the Iron Cage*.

21. Ibid.; Acker, "From Sex Roles to Gendered Institutions."

22. Britton, *At Work in the Iron Cage*, 15.

23. Ibid.

24. Zola, "Medicine as an Institution of Social Control."

25. Conrad and Schneider, *Deviance and Medicalization*, 8.

26. Conrad, "Types of Medical Social Control," 1.

27. Ibid.

28. Conrad, "Medicalization and Social Control," 209.

29. Zola, "Medicine as an Institution of Social Control," 470.

30. Conrad, "Medicalization and Social Control."

31. Ibid., 222.

32. Ehrenreich and English, *For Her Own Good*.

33. Ehrenreich and Ehrenreich, "Health Care and Social Control"; Ehrenreich and English, *For Her Own Good*.

34. van Dijk, "Critical Discourse Analysis," 352.

35. Jensen, "Introduction: The Qualitative Turn"; Larsen, "Textual Analysis of Fictional Media Content."

36. van Dijk, "Principles of Critical Discourse Analysis," 249–50.

37. van Zoonen, *Feminist Media Studies*, 131.

38. Britton, *At Work in the Iron Cage*, 2.

39. Smith, "'Orange' Is the Same White"; Herman, "*Bad Girls* Changed My Life."

40. Britton, *At Work in the Iron Cage*; Acker, "From Sex Roles to Gendered Institutions."

41. Britton, *At Work in the Iron Cage*.

42. Maruschak, *Medical Problems of State and Federal Prisoners*; Mukasey, Sedgwick, and Hagy, "Strategies to Prevent Prison Rape."

43. Maruschak, *Medical Problems of State and Federal Prisoners.*

44. Britton, *At Work in the Iron Cage*; Acker, "From Sex Roles to Gendered Institutions."

45. Lonsway and Fitzgerald, "Rape Myths in Review."

46. Turchik and Edwards, "Myths about Male Rape"; Beck, Berzofsky, Caspar, and Krebs, *Sexual Victimization in Prisons and Jails.*

47. Custers and Bulck, "Cultivation of Fear of Sexual Violence"; Kahlor and Eastin, "Television's Role in the Culture of Violence"; Kahlor and Morrison, "Television Viewing and Rape Myth Acceptance"; Britton, *At Work in the Iron Cage.*

48. Britton, *At Work in the Iron Cage*; Acker, "From Sex Roles to Gendered Institutions."

49. Conrad, "Types of Medical Social Control."

50. Jenness and Fenstermaker, "Agnes Goes to Prison Gender"; Routh, Abess, Makin, and Stohr, "Transgender Inmates in Prisons"; Kenagy, "Transgender Health."

51. Foucault, *Discipline and Punish.*

Bibliography

Acker, Joan. "From Sex Roles to Gendered Institutions." *Contemporary Sociology* 21, no. 5 (1992): 565–69. doi:10.2307/2075528.

Beck, Allen, Marcus Berzofsky, Rachel Caspar, and Christopher Krebs. *Sexual Victimization in Prisons and Jails Reported by Inmates, 2011–12.* Washington, D.C.: U.S. Department of Justice, Bureau of Justice Statistics, 2013.

Binswanger, Ingrid A., Joseph O. Merrill, Patrick M. Krueger, Mary C. White, Robert E. Booth, and Joann G. Elmore. "Gender Differences in Chronic Medical, Psychiatric, and Substance-Dependence Disorders among Jail Inmates." *American Journal of Public Health* 100, no. 3 (2010): 476–82. doi:10.2105/AJPH.2008.149591.

Britton, Dana. *At Work in the Iron Cage.* New York: New York University Press, 2003.

Carson, E. Ann. "Prisoners in 2014." Bureau of Justice Statistics, 2015. Accessed September 17, 2017. http://www.bjs.gov/index.cfm?ty=pbdetail&iid=5387.

Ciasullo, Ann. "Containing 'Deviant' Desire: Lesbianism, Heterosexuality, and the Women-in-Prison Narrative." *Journal of Popular Culture* 41, no. 2 (2008): 195–223. doi:10.1111/j.1540–5931.2008.00499.x.

Conrad, Peter. "Medicalization and Social Control." *Annual Review of Sociology* 18 (1992): 209–32.

———. "Types of Medical Social Control." *Sociology of Health & Illness* 1, no. 1 (1979): 1–11. doi:10.1111/j.1467–9566.1979.tb00175.x.

Conrad, Peter, and J. W. Schneider. *Deviance and Medicalization: From Badness to Sickness*. Philadelphia: Temple University Press, 2010.

Custers, Kathleen, and Jan Van den Bulck. "The Cultivation of Fear of Sexual Violence in Women: Processes and Moderators of the Relationship between Television and Fear." *Communication Research* 40, no. 1 (2013): 96–124. doi:10.1177/0093650212440444.

Dixon, Travis L. "Black Criminals and White Officers: The Effects of Racially Misrepresenting Law Breakers and Law Defenders on Television News." *Media Psychology* 10, no. 2 (2007): 270–91. doi:10.1080/15213260701375660.

Dumas, Alexander. *The Count of Monte Cristo*. New York: Penguin Books, 2008.

Ehrenreich, Barbara, and John Ehrenreich. "Health Care and Social Control." *Social Policy* 5, no. 1 (1974): 26–40.

Ehrenreich, Barbara, and Deirdre English. *For Her Own Good: 150 Years of the Experts' Advice to Women*. New York: Anchor Books, 1978.

Foucault, Michel. *Discipline and Punish: The Birth of the Prison*. 2nd ed. New York: Vintage Books, 1995.

Gerbner, George, and Larry Gross. "Living with Television: The Violence Profile." *Journal of Communication* 26, no. 2 (1976): 172–94. doi:10.1111/j.1460-2466.1976.tb01397.x.

Goidel, Robert K., Craig M. Freeman, and Steven T. Procopio. "The Impact of Television Viewing on Perceptions of Juvenile Crime." *Journal of Broadcasting & Electronic Media* 50, no. 1 (2006): 119–39. doi:10.1207/s15506878jobem5001_7.

Gutierrez, Peter. "Redeeming the Myth of Upward Mobility: *The Shawshank Redemption*." *Screen Education*, no. 70 (2013): 98–103.

Herman, Didi. "'*Bad Girls* Changed My Life': Homonormativity in a Women's Prison Drama." *Critical Studies in Media Communication* 20, no. 2 (2003): 141–59. doi:10.1080/07393180302779.

Jenness, Valerie, and Sarah Fenstermaker. "Agnes Goes to Prison: Gender Authenticity, Transgender Inmates in Prisons for Men, and Pursuit of 'the Real Deal.'" *Gender & Society* 28, no. 1 (2014): 5–31. doi:10.1177/0891243213499446.

Jensen, Klaus Braun. "Introduction: The Qualitative Turn." In *A Handbook of Qualitative Methodologies for Mass Communication Research*, edited by Klaus Braun Jensen and Nicholas W. Jankowski, 1–12. London: Routledge, 1991.

Kahlor, LeeAnn, and Matthew S. Eastin. "Television's Role in the Culture of Violence toward Women: A Study of Television Viewing and the Cultivation of Rape Myth Acceptance in the United States." *Journal of Broadcasting & Electronic Media* 55, no. 2 (2011): 215–31. doi:10.1080/08838151.2011 .566085.

Kahlor, LeeAnn, and Dan Morrison. "Television Viewing and Rape Myth Acceptance among College Women." *Sex Roles* 56, nos. 11–12 (2007): 729–39. doi:10.1007/s11199–007–9232–2.

Kenagy, Gretchen P. "Transgender Health: Findings from Two Needs Assessment Studies in Philadelphia." *Health & Social Work* 30, no. 1 (2005): 19–26. doi:10.1093/hsw/30.1.19.

Larsen, Peter. "Textual Analysis of Fictional Media Content." In *A Handbook of Qualitative Methodologies for Mass Communication Research*, edited by Klaus Braun Jensen and Nicholas W. Jankowski, 121–34. London: Routledge, 1991.

Lonsway, Kimberly A., and Louise F. Fitzgerald. "Rape Myths in Review." *Psychology of Women Quarterly* 18, no. 2 (1994): 133–64. doi:10.1111/j.1471–6402.1994.tb00448.x.

Lubbers, Marcel, Peer Schneepers, and Maurice Vergeer. "Exposure to Newspapers and Attitudes toward Ethnic Minorities: A Longitudinal Analysis." *Howard Journal of Communications* 11, no. 2 (2000): 127–43. doi:10.1080/106461700246661.

Maruschak, Laura. "Medical Problems of Prisoners." Washington, D.C.: Bureau of Justice Statistics, 2008.

———. *Medical Problems of State and Federal Prisoners and Jail Inmates*. Washington, D.C.: Bureau of Justice Statistics, 2015. Accessed September 17, 2017. http://www.bjs.gov/content/pub/pdf/mpsfpji1112.pdf.

Mason, Paul, ed. *Captured by the Media*. New York: Routledge, 2013.

Mukasey, Michael B., Jeffrey L. Sedgwick, and David W. Hagy. *Strategies to Prevent Prison Rape by Changing the Correctional Culture*. Washington, D.C.: National Institute of Justice, 2008. Accessed September 17, 2017. https://www.ncjrs.gov/pdffiles1/nij/222843.pdf.

O'Sullivan, Sean. "Representations of Prison in Nineties Hollywood Cinema: From *Con Air* to *The Shawshank Redemption*." *Howard Journal of Criminal Justice* 40, no. 4 (2001): 317–34. doi:10.1111/1468–2311.00212.

Routh, Douglas, Gassan Abess, David Makin, Mary K. Stohr, Craig Hemmens, and Jihye Yoo. "Transgender Inmates in Prisons: A Review of Applicable Statutes and Policies." *International Journal of Offender Therapy and Comparative Criminology* 61, no. 6 (2017): 645–66. doi:10.1177/0306624X15603745.

Smith, Anna Marie. "'Orange' Is the Same White: Comments on 'Orange Is the New Black.'" Social Science Research Network, July 2, 2014. doi:10.2139/ssrn.2461799.

Turchik, Jessica A., and Katie M. Edwards. "Myths about Male Rape: A Literature Review." *Psychology of Men & Masculinity* 13, no. 2 (2012): 211–26. doi:10.1037/a0023207.

van Dijk, Teun A. "Critical Discourse Analysis." In *The Handbook of Discourse Analysis*, edited by Deborah Schriffrin, Deborah Tannen, and Heidi E. Hamilton, 352–71. Malden, MA: Blackwell, 2003.

———. "Principles of Critical Discourse Analysis." *Discourse & Society* 4, no. 2 (1993): 249–83. doi:10.1177/0957926593004002006.

van Zoonen, Elizabeth. *Feminist Media Studies*. London: Sage, 1994.

Wilson, David, and Sean O'Sullivan. *Images of Incarceration: Representations of Prison in Film and Television Drama*. Hampshire, UK: Waterside, 2004.

Yousman, Bill. "Inside *Oz*: Hyperviolence, Race and Class Nightmares, and the Engrossing Spectacle of Terror." *Communication and Critical/Cultural Studies* 6, no. 3 (2009): 265–84. doi:10.1080/14791420903049728.

Zola, Irving Kenneth. "Medicine as an Institution of Social Control." *Sociological Review* 20, no. 4 (1972): 487–504.

5. *Prison Wives*: Providing a Voice to the Women behind Incarcerated Men

S. Lenise Wallace

A friend of mine described her first visit to see her spouse behind bars. She explained that she was met by two women in the lobby area who were also there to visit their loved ones. "Honey, it gets easier," said the first woman. "It never gets easier," said the other woman, who had overheard the conversation.

While popular culture frequently depicts life in prison, rarely do the media showcase stories of the family members and loved ones of the incarcerated. The reality is that in the majority of cases in which someone is incarcerated, there is a family that also feels "incarcerated," even though they are not physically locked up. Recently, the reality-based television shows *Prison Wives* (2010), *Mob Wives* (2011), and *Prison Wives Club* (2014) have attempted to provide voices to the underrepresented women who support their incarcerated spouses and loved ones. This chapter examines text, trends, and themes that have emerged throughout a season of *Prison Wives*, a documentary-style program that directly tells the narratives of these women from their own voices, with each episode chronicling the story of a different couple.

Literature Review

According to the U.S. Department of Justice,[1] at the end of 2014, there were approximately 1,561,500 persons under supervision at U.S. prisons. What most people fail to consider are the wives and children who are left to live life with their "new normal" of having incarcerated loved ones. Incarcerated parents in the United States have left behind 1.7 million minor children, who make up 2.3 percent of the population under the age of eighteen.[2]

Scholars have done extensive studies of prison families and the wives who support them. Morris provided a groundbreaking qualitative study of nearly six hundred wives of incarcerated men in the United Kingdom.[3] Fishman examined how prison policies regarding telephone calls affected prison wives and their incarcerated husbands.[4] Black researched how gender roles played a part in the incarceration of male inmates and their supportive wives and girlfriends.[5] In addition, Comfort analyzed the experiences of women who visited men they were in romantic relationships with while the men were incarcerated at San Quentin State Prison.[6]

Many of those who are left behind liken their "new normal" (with its new routines, revised to accommodate their relationships with their imprisoned partners) to doing time along with their incarcerated partner—only theirs is done outside the prison walls. This new normal includes weekly or monthly visits to prison, if possible, while also being subjected to monitored collect phone calls and letters. During these visits some of the women often feel treated as though *they* are also incarcerated. The disrespectful talk of correctional facility staff, a strict wardrobe policy and other rules to adhere to, and a lack of intimacy are some of the prejudices these women can face. Interestingly enough, many of the wives and significant others of the men incarcerated are left to pick up the pieces, which include raising families, paying commissaries and legal fees, and becoming legal advocates for their spouses.[7]

For this "invisible population" of family members, there is a stigma attached to the prison wives and spouses. Even though many of the women confess their true love for their incarcerated loved ones, they are often viewed as weak, crazy, lonely, or desperate.[8] In providing her personal narrative, Judith Brink related that she was a chaplain attached to a secure unit in an upstate New York medical facility where she came in contact with those who were incarcerated. Meeting someone through a mutual friend, she fell in love with "the deepest love" of her life and married him.[9] Her husband was incarcerated. In addition to being chaplain, she was now also a prison wife. However, among many things, she understood that a major issue prison wives face is that of judgment from, well, anyone.

According to Brink,

> Prison families and friends are an invisible group who suffer many of the same punishments as prisoners, only our suffering goes unnoticed. We who love prisoners are often hesitant to reveal our connection to a prisoner because we expect to be judged for it. Often we are lumped into

the same category as they [are]. We are judged guilty by association. By speaking about the relationship, we risk judgment. Think about it. What do you think about my choice of a marriage partner?[10]

Perhaps the judgment many prison wives face is a reason why their stories are rarely told in the media. Who would want to focus on these women? Why should anyone care about their stories? They are supporting criminals after all. In recent years, with the rise of reality television and documentary-style programming, many nontraditional stories are being told through the voices of the marginalized themselves. With nontraditional media outlets such as YouTube, Netflix, and Hulu, not only are people able to create their own stories, but even when the stories are scripted, audiences are able to view the narratives of those who were once marginalized.

Background on Media Coverage

Regarding media representation of wives on reality television, several researchers have covered this particular area of programming. According to Brancato, "By presenting a 'traditional female life narrative,' these shows reproduce traditional roles for female audiences who can vicariously relive important moments such as getting married or giving birth."[11]

Brown quoted reality-show star and executive producer of VH1's *Basketball Wives* Shaunie O'Neal, who explained her vision for the show: "I wanted to show that we do something outside of being a wife—we have goals and dreams. We have businesses, spouses and children—and work hard to balance it all."[12] Jorgenson sought to explore how the media depicted polygamy in the reality show *Sister Wives* "at the family level while simultaneously examining the messages regarding sex roles in the program."[13] Media representations of wives on reality television have also perpetuated negative gendered stereotypes as well, particularly among black women. Samuels wrote, "The mud-slinging makes for watchable TV, but it also highlights an unsettling new formula for the reality TV genre: put two or more headstrong African-American women in the same room, and let the fireworks begin."[14] More specifically, media representation of wives within or affiliated with the criminal justice system and/or prison culture is becoming more prevalent in recent years.

Media representations of the criminal justice system and prison culture are often one of two things: glamorized or androcentric. There are several reality-based programs about the criminal justice system and prison culture such as *First 48*, *Beyond Scared Straight*, and *Cops*. Although these programs do feature true accounts of those associated with the criminal justice system and prison culture, there are few that are told solely from a woman's standpoint, particularly from the women behind the men of organized crime or the Mafia.

The Mafia or organized crime culture is often featured in the media with stories that are either fictionalized or "based on a true story" and are played mainly for their entertainment and dramatic value. According to Rawlinson, "The obscurity, and occasional dramatic displays of violence, as in gangland killings provides a lucrative and attractive hook for the media in their eternal search for 'drama.'"[15] It is well known that the men within this culture are not often seen or heard. However, their presence is clearly known and often respected and feared. The history of the Mafioso, particularly members of the Italian Mafia in the United States, is primarily led by men who are the "voice" of that community. The only representation that many outsiders have of this culture is what they view through the media in films such as *The Godfather* and *Donnie Brasco* and the cable television show *The Sopranos*.[16] These depictions often portray the men of Mafia culture as powerful gangsters who are family oriented despite being criminals. The women of these films and TV shows are very often voiceless and have minimal roles that provide little to no knowledge about them. Thus, these portrayals could cause one to infer that the wives, girlfriends, and daughters behind these men are demure, powerless, weak, and marginalized by the men in their lives. It was not until the reality-based television show on Viacom's cable network VH1 called *Mob Wives* debuted that voyeurs got a front-row seat to the stories of several women filmed for the show. Through this unique and first-time opportunity, onlookers were able to learn about these women's trials, triumphs, families, and support given to the men in their lives—particularly when those men were incarcerated—from their very own perspective. Several of the women featured in *Mob Wives* discuss in detail the challenges of supporting the men in their lives while those men are "away." *Mob Wives* chronicles the stories of several women including Renee Graziano, Drita D'Avanzo, Karen Gravano, and Angela "Big Ang" Raiola. Debuting in April 2011, the show ended with its sixth and final season in 2016.

The *Prison Wives Club* was broadcast in eight episodes on the Lifetime network from October 2014 to April 2015, when the last episode aired. The reality television program followed the stories of four women: Ana, Jhemini, Kate, and LaQuisha. During the filming and airing of the program, all of the women were married to men convicted of felonies and serving lengthy prison sentences. LaQuisha founded the Prison Wives Club as a support system for women married to incarcerated men.

Within the reality television format and similar to *Mob Wives*, *Prison Wives Club* presents another example of the "prison wife" experience. The similarities between *Mob Wives* and *Prison Wives Club* are that both programs feature the wives and loved ones of incarcerated men. They chronicle stories of their daily challenges in being a prison or mob wife. However, unlike *Prison Wives*—a documentary-style series of stand-alone installments featuring one prison wife per episode—in *Mob Wives* and *Prison Wives Club* all of the women are featured every episode and have the opportunity to interact with each other. Having this platform to interact, the women can provide direct support for each other. But this interaction can also have the opposite outcome, namely, altercations leading up to and including violence. This is where the entertainment factor of the latter two programs seems to be evident. Since *Prison Wives* is a documentary-style program, which, again, showcases one wife per episode, the textual analysis of this research focuses on that program.

Study Rationale

The rationale for this study is to provide a better understanding of prison wives and their perceived experiences as women who love and support the incarcerated men in their lives. Due to the minimal media coverage and overall research on this population, this research is essential because it could contribute to scholarship about this underrepresented group of women. Additionally, a main goal of this study is to examine any themes, and their similarities and/or differences, that could emerge.

Feminist Theoretical Framework

This textual analysis examines the stories of "voiceless" women—according to mainstream media. Therefore, it is imperative that it be informed by a feminist theoretical framework. The fact that the media rarely cover the stories of the women behind incarcerated men makes this group underrepresented. According to Spitzack and Carter Spitzack, "Womanless communication research simply leaves women out of its account of human communication. The lives and experiences of women are omitted implicitly."[17] Therefore, one can easily infer that they simply do not exist—or are invisible. Their voices and stories are not being told often; for example, *Prison Wives* and

Prison Wives Club only lasted one season, though *Mob Wives* fared better with six seasons.

Dervin stated that feminist scholarship provides two major outcomes: "One is how to give voice to those who have been silenced; the other is how to give silence and hearing to those who have been voiced."[18] This theoretical position values female experiences, meanings, and perceptions. Such research in this area has the potential to be a foundation for a theoretical framework in feminist scholarship. It is for this reason that it is imperative for all stories to be told, not only those deemed to be important by biased gatekeepers in the media. Steeves stated that "Feminist theories aim to understand the origins and continuing nature of women's nearly universal devaluation in society."[19] Moreover, Stanback added that "Feminist theory is essential to Feminist scholarship because it provides the only explanatory frame that accounts for women's place in the social order, illumines the central social experience of women's lives (i.e., sexism), and assumes a need for a change in women's social position."[20] The Investigation Discovery network's broadcast of *Prison Wives* provided an international outlet for prison wives' stories to be told from their own perspective. As a result, this could usher in the possibility for similar programming in a documentary style to share other women's narratives.

Method

The narratives of prison wives, in general, are quite rare, particularly those captured by the media. In light of this reality, this research sought to answer the following research questions:

RQ1: What, if any, themes emerge in the narratives of the prison wives throughout the season of *Prison Wives*?

RQ2: How, if in any way, do the prison wives use their words and stories to support their husbands?

RQ3: What, if any, similarities and/or differences emerge among the prison wives' stories?

Prison Wives was televised on the Investigation Discovery network from February 14, 2010, to April 21, 2010. It focused on the stories of twelve women and one man married to, or in a serious relationship with, an incarcerated felon serving prison time from a few years up to seventy-one years or life. The prison wives' and husband's spouses were incarcerated for crimes that ranged from drug charges to murder. On the production side, several hours of footage were filmed for each episode and then edited down to a forty-two-minute documentary-style show. The prison wives and husband included Annika Powell, Elli Panitz, LaToya Marion, Jane Bailey, Pam Booker, Tim McDonald, Georgia Benson, Gail Sullivan, Grace Dark Horse, Juli Cummings, Debra Wilmont, Tanya Windham, and Cheryl Engelke. Of the women, eleven were legally married and one was in a serious relationship; however, she considered herself to be married. Many of the women met and/or married their spouses prior to their being incarcerated. However, several of the women and Tim McDonald, the one husband featured, met and married their spouses after they became incarcerated. Each episode followed the prison wives/husband (one per episode) as they conducted their day-to-day activities as a spouse supporting their incarcerated loved one. The series featured the prison wives/ husband taking care of family responsibilities, working at their places of employment, and visiting the prison. On some occasions, viewers were able to witness actual visits inside the prison, but not all of the prisons allowed cameras inside. The prison wives/husband also discussed challenges such as finances, loneliness, and working with attorneys to free their loved ones. In addition, *Prison Wives* chronicled their individual intimate accounts with their partners, including their phone conversations and talks of conjugal visits.

The focus of this research was the stories of the wives, but it is important to note that some of the wives had children and families. Exactly half of the women were mothers, with three of them having minor children. The series did feature segments with some of the children and other family members displaying either their support or lack of support for the prison wives. This research focused only on the twelve women's narratives (husband Tim McDonald was not included in the analysis).

Although all of the prison wives' ages were not revealed, nine of the twelve whose ages were revealed ranged from thirty-two to sixty-three years old. The women who did not reveal their ages appeared to be in their thirties or forties. The wives lived in California, Florida, New Mexico, New York, Oregon, Texas, and Washington State. The racial backgrounds of the prison wives appeared to be ten Caucasian and two African American women. Several of the wives were employed in counseling and social-services work. However, several of the women worked in menial positions, such as being a waitress or cleaning houses. Of all the women, two appeared to know each other and attend the same prison wives support group.

Each episode was viewed and partially transcribed by the author. Textual analysis was used to examine the women's words and stories. In this method, used by communication researchers, the researcher analyzes and interprets the characteristics of written, audio, or visual messages and describes the content, organization, purpose, and themes contained in the text. Communication scholars have used textual analysis to examine all forms of texts, ranging from horoscopes to Christian films to rap song lyrics.[21] The goal of textual analysis is to describe the content, organization, purpose, and themes contained in a text.[22] Specifically, rhetorical criticism was conducted on the text. According to Sonja Foss, rhetorical criticism "is designed for the systematic investigation and explanation of symbolic acts and artifacts for the purpose of understanding rhetorical processes."[23] The rhetorical criticism approach to textual analysis has five functions. These functions include highlighting the purposes of a persuasive message; assisting with comprehending cultural, historical, and social contexts; utilizing the findings as a form of social criticism to examine society; contributing to theoretical frameworks; and serving a pedagogical function regarding effective persuasion.[24]

Findings

In the "Cheryl Engelke" episode, prison wife Cheryl Engelke states, "I don't have time to be angry, I don't have time to sit there and be sad, you know? Tears are a luxury. If we were buried together, what would our epitaph be? Here lies love, the forever kind—that's what it would say."[25] The findings of this research revealed that Cheryl shared a common sentiment that many of the prison wives would agree with, having a "forever kind of love" that served as the foundation for continuing to live the life of a prison wife. Several of the women featured in *Prison Wives* felt marginalized and degraded just like their loved ones who were incarcerated. Not surprisingly, Cheryl felt invisible: "When you're a prison wife it's like you're invisible, you're forgotten, you're completely ignored."

The prison wives' narratives were all unique within each episode; however, there were similarities. The prison wives were mothers and daughters who held employment, and there was even one actual mob wife. Several of the women had strong opinions on how they were perceived by others. In the "Georgia Benson" episode, Georgia knew that there were people who believed she was less than smart to be married to a man in prison: "I know people hear my story and think, 'my God she's an idiot'—I'm not."[26] Evident in each episode was a woman who appeared to love her incarcerated spouse.

Three of the prison wives had their own criminal pasts and could identify with what their spouses were experiencing on the inside. Several of the
women did not have their family's support for their decision to become
involved with an incarcerated man. However, they often benefited from the
support of other prison wives while attending or creating support groups. Of
the twelve women featured, only one prison wife, Georgia Benson, saw her
husband released by the time the program aired. Four main themes emerged
from this research: financial hardship, legal advocacy, sexual intimacy and
loneliness, and faith and hope for freedom.

Financial Hardship

In each episode, the main theme was financial hardship. Several of the wives
discussed not being able to make ends meet due to costs of daily living (a
home, car maintenance, children, etc.), legal fees, and low-paying jobs. In
many cases the prison wives were the sole breadwinner taking on the responsibilities for their household. In the "Gail Sullivan" episode, Gail stated
a sentiment that nearly all the wives shared with regard to money and the
prison culture: "It's very costly if you want to make life comfortable in a prison
setting for your spouse."[27] According to Hattery and Smith, "Incarceration
is extremely resource intensive for spouses on the outside who must travel
long distances for visits, pay hefty fees for telephone calls, and support and
care for the family alone."[28] Some of the aforementioned financial reasons,
and the loss of their spouses to the prison system, had forced many of the
prison wives on the show to rely on public assistance.[29]

In the "Annika Powell" episode, prison wife Annika is on public assistance.
On one occasion she is shown at the supermarket with $30.00 left on her EBT
card (electronic benefit transfer) and buys $16.00 worth of groceries. "[My]
money situation is tight, it's a never ending stress," she explains. "I stress a
lot because my kids want stuff and they deserve to have them and they're
good kids."[30] While Annika stressed over how she and her children would
make ends meet, there are several other financial issues prison wives had to
deal with. On certain occasions, the financial burden was devastating and
forced wives to rely on family members to avoid homelessness. In the "Jane
Bailey" episode, Jane's financial situation was dire. She had lost her house
and car and was forced to file for bankruptcy due her expenses: bills, collect
calls from her husband, and lawyer's fees. As a result, Jane moved back in
with her parents temporarily. However, she perceived that her marriage and
the love she received from her husband was a reasonable exchange for the

unfortunate circumstances she endured. Jane claimed, "I feel like I'm getting so much in return by the sacrifices that I had to make. I don't really think of the sacrifice as a bad thing."[31] Subsequently, in the "Grace Dark Horse" episode, Grace stated that her financial burdens could lead to the loss of her home: "There's a lot of pressure for me to bring home money because if I lose this job, I'm one paycheck away from being on the street . . . from being homeless."[32]

To make ends meet, *Prison Wives* conveys that the wives must work several jobs, often low-paying menial jobs, to care for themselves and their families. In the "Juli Cummings" episode, Juli is seen wearing headphones playing a tape-recorded telephone conversation between her and her beloved Ric while cleaning a home for one of her clients. "I have to go with what I know is going to bring in some income right now so that I can take care of both of us," she says.[33] In the "Cheryl Engelke" episode, Cheryl is shown at her restaurant job tending to customers for $2.13 an hour: "In this situation, unless I win the lottery, money's always gonna be tight."[34] Another wife turned to creative works to secure an income. In the "Tanya Windham" episode, Tanya "TJ" Windham explained that she wrote, directed, and starred in a play about her story as a prison wife. TJ is shown directing cast members during rehearsal for the play: "I chose to write the play—that's my way of making some money to get John an attorney. I couldn't do it with what I was making . . . right now I'm funding everything."[35] Expenses can indeed add up for a prison wife, and often the families must have several sources of employment. In the "LaToya Marion" episode, prison wife LaToya's solution was several means of income: "It's very expensive being a prison wife. I have one full-time job and two part-time jobs on call to save up money for attorneys."[36] Interestingly enough, research shows that LaToya's story of having multiple jobs is not a typical solution for prison wives.

Contrary to prison wives taking on additional jobs, Arditti, Lambert-Shute, and Joest, in a study of the caregivers of incarcerated family members during visiting hours at a prison facility, found that employment rates declined 25 percent (from 89 percent to 64 percent) for the nearly two-thirds of the women who were working at the time their spouses were incarcerated and then afterward became unemployed. In addition, over half of the women in their study were on public assistance, and 70 percent of those began receiving assistance once their spouse was incarcerated. Lastly, nearly half of the women received "other financial help," with amounts and sources not revealed.[37]

Legal Advocacy

Legal advocacy is a significant component to the prison wives' experiences on the show. Many of the incarcerated spouses are serving life in prison, so nearly all of the women were interested in the legalities of their spouse's cases in hopes for exoneration. Several of the women took on the role of a "lawyer," becoming the primary advocate for their spouses. After Ric received a seventy-one-year sentence for a first-time drug offense, his wife Juli found herself doing significant research.[38] TJ mentioned that above and beyond anyone else, she would be the most qualified person to advocate for her husband: "If I was a lawyer, I definitely should be the one to represent him, can't nobody fight for him the way I can."[39] Cheryl shared similar sentiments, noting that prior to her husband's incarceration she had no interest in the law; however, she now felt the need to understand it: "I've never set out to be a lawyer not saying that I am one now, but you have to read 'x, y, z' to get 'b.' It's hard to understand sometimes."[40] Many of the women were shown meeting with attorneys in law libraries or advocating over the phone for their husbands. It was clear that the women were deeply invested in the release of their spouses, with several working tirelessly to try to overturn sentences or advocate for new trials.

In Annika's story line, she proposes to petition the Department of Corrections to urge the State of Oregon to consider allowing conjugal visits and more family time for inmates with wives and families. Annika explains, "In all I need to collect at least 3,000 signatures—that way if the D.O.C. still says we're not going to do this, then I can take it to the legislation level."[41] Annika is shown knocking on the doors of members of her community to explain her petition and ask for their signatures. As determined as Annika and other prison wives were to assist with their spouses' imprisonment and legal situations, there were wives who felt otherwise.

Prison wife Gail, for instance, expresses no desire to challenge her husband's sentence. She never advocates for his release from prison. Her husband, Joe Sullivan, was sentenced to three life sentences, and Gail had accepted it. She reasons, "He was a hit-man for the mob . . . there was never a time that I fought to get Joe out of jail, there were too many convictions.[42] Her acknowledgment of his crime, conviction, and sentence was something she had to live with, including the thought that he would never return home alive: "He's 70 years old now, so he'll die in jail, which is a by-thought."[43] Although Joe will serve the rest of his life in prison, he is in a state prison in New York, one of the only states that has family extended visits that last a weekend. Unlike the majority of the prison wives featured, Gail shows pictures of her family during extended-stay family visits. Overall, *Prison Wives* presented a clear dichotomy between the wives who were determined legal advocates for their husbands and the wives who accepted their spouses' fate and were not.

Sexual Intimacy and Loneliness

One of the most common themes was the intimate bonding between prison wives and their spouses. During every episode, each wife visited her husband. Family extended-stay visits (lasting more than one day) or conjugal visits were desired by the majority of the prison wives. Preparation for the family extended-stay visits could take weeks; however, it is conveyed as worth the trouble. In the "Pam Booker" episode, Pam is shown preparing for an up-coming Family Reunion Program (FRP) visit with her husband. She takes his food shopping requests over the phone and later packs: "The process of preparing for our FRPs is a several week process. The night before is usually the most intense. I'm packing and prepping myself doing all those womanly things we like to do for our husbands."[44] The viewers also see Pam up before dawn getting into a taxicab with her luggage for her long-awaited visit to see her husband. Cameras were not allowed to film the FRP visit; however, viewers see Pam before and after her visit was complete.

Of the twelve prison wives, two had conjugal or family extended-stay visits. The visits took place on the prison grounds in a trailer with living facilities such as a bed, kitchen, and bathroom. For Pam the six visits allotted per year were what she would look forward to: "Our FRPs are so precious to us—just be able to do the simplest everyday activities—even to do nothing at all is truly precious."[45]

The majority of the prison wives who lived near the prisons relied on the weekly or quarterly visits for some sort of intimacy. If visiting was not possible, letters and collect phone calls had to suffice. Annika would set aside a special time to be intimate over the phone with her spouse: "I am a very sexual person and so is Anthony and for us to be sexually frustrated is not a good combination. We have our quiet times where I will go to the bedroom and there's no bills talked about, there's no kids talked about; that is our time as adults."[46] Juli cherished her daily morning telephone call from her significant other Ric, but she realized that they were not alone: "We still tease each other sexually . . . nothing is private, nothing, so it's like your sex life is public, what you have."[47]

It is important to note that some of the prison wives who met and married their husbands after the men were incarcerated have never been sexually (physically) intimate with their husbands. For some of the wives, physical intimacy, albeit difficult to go without, is not "everything." Grace realized the importance of sexual intimacy; however, she accepted that was not her reality: "Sex is a part of a relationship but it's not everything—sure it's nice to have that intimacy, but we don't have that."[48]

On the "Georgia Benson" episode, days before her husband was set to be released, Georgia was anxious. She reveals, "we've never been together, is he going to find me attractive? Is he going to want me? You know, those things? I'm scared to death."[49] In the "Elli Panitz" episode, prison wife Elli would have loved the option of this type of intimacy: "It's hard to keep the intimacy going when you can't be physically intimate with your husband. You're only allowed one kiss at the beginning and one kiss at the end. What would really really be nice is if Florida DM would allow conjugal visits—I would love to have a whole weekend with my husband."[50]

Another issue that surfaced with a prison wife was trying to conceive without having conjugal visits. Jane desired to conceive with her husband— against the advisement of her doctor and lawyer. She researched reproductive rights for inmates. "He's a good man and we want to be a family," she says.[51]

As of 2015, only four states offer the FRP type of program: California, Connecticut, New York, and Washington—federal prisons do not offer them at all.[52] Many of the family extended-stay visits or conjugal visits programs were discontinued in the United States for a variety of reasons, including expensive costs to support the programs and children being conceived and raised by single parents.[53]

Infidelity was another topic that arose with one of the prison wives on the show. John and TJ met in Sacramento, where there was a large amount of gang activity. John was a gang member who was convicted of a felony and sentenced to fifteen years to life. Although TJ knew John prior to him being in prison, she married him while he was an inmate. During the first three years of marriage, John and TJ had conjugal visits, until their state ended that program for inmates in prison for life. Due to a lack of sexual intimacy from her husband, TJ was unfaithful: "In the past, I would go and have sex, then come on back home and wait another 5 or 6 months and then go and have sex then come back home. I mean that was wrong, but that's how I used to deal with it."[54] Subsequently, during a mutual separation, TJ became pregnant by another man. "John was really hurt when I got pregnant," she explains, "but he knew it would change me and I would straighten everything up."[55] TJ later ended the relationship with her son's father and reconciled with John. Although TJ was the only prison wife to admit to an extramarital affair, infidelity is common among some women who are unhappy in their marriage, no matter the circumstances. Nelson described an extramarital affair as "'a can opener' for women unable to articulate for themselves why they're unhappy in their marriages, much less empower themselves to leave or begin an honest conversation with their husbands about what they feel is wrong."[56] The stresses of being a prison wife alone, in addition to the loneliness that could set in, may cause some wives like TJ to have an affair. Fortunately, she was able to confront her indiscretion and reconcile with her husband.

Faith and Hope for Freedom

Prison Wives repeatedly conveyed that the wives had hope for their husbands' releases. In the "Debra Wilmont" episode, Debra had complete faith in her husband and their relationship: "I love him and that's what I want, so I believe it's gonna work. I have no doubt. I have 100 percent plus faith in him."[57] Likewise, Elli remained determined always to advocate for her husband's release from prison: "I will never stop fighting to get him justice and I'll never stop fighting to see him a free man."[58] LaToya had spent over a decade working with her husband's lawyers and researching ways to exonerate him: "I'm 100 percent sure my husband is innocent and I will stop at nothing until he is completely exonerated."[59]

Many of the wives lean on their faith to help explicate their situation. Juli was very spiritual, and that helped her cope with Ric's incarceration. Shown burning candles at her home, Juli was preparing for a spiritual ritual: "I burn candles at an altar that I have in my garden and I pray for Ric's freedom."[60] Jane wanted to remind the audience that all people have iniquities of some sort, and she did not want to be judgmental: "We've all committed some pretty grave sins in our lives, I'm sure, and I don't wanna put a label on if one person's crime is more than another."[61] TJ leaned on her faith and what the Bible said about marriage: "God said some strong things in the Bible about marriage, death do you part . . . through Christ anything is possible, that's a cup that's halfway full."[62] These women were very clear about how important a role faith in their spouses and in their spiritual/religious beliefs played in their being a supportive prison wife. It was also evident that the prison wives were truly in love with their spouses and, although in a trying situation, remained positive. Remaining positive appeared to be their only option.

On the contrary, some wives knew that their husbands would never be released from prison. Annika (whose husband was convicted of murder) was very well aware that she would never reunite with her husband outside the prison walls: "My husband is a lifer without parole, the only way he is coming home is in a box. He will remain in prison for the rest of his life—till he dies."[63] As the only wife on the series whose husband was released, Georgia was relieved: "I am not a prison wife anymore. All I am is Mrs. Don Benson. I am a normal everyday run of the mill, nothing special wife and that's better than anything else."[64] Georgia did not take her privileged experience for granted either; she knew that there were many wives who would never be in her position and so expressed her sincere gratitude.

Discussion

This research examined the narratives of women featured in the documentary-style show *Prison Wives*. Although each prison wife's story was unique to her personal situation, shared themes included financial hardship, legal advocacy, sexual intimacy and loneliness, and faith and hope for freedom. As stated earlier, several scholars have found that women who support their incarcerated spouses have similar though not identical experiences to those of the prison wives featured on the show. Those shared experiences and challenges also include financial constraints, the stress of single parenting, and loneliness.

All of the wives admitted to having significant financial burdens, which included some having to collect public assistance and some having to work low-paying and menial jobs to fund newfound expenses like lawyer fees and daily prison phone calls. A common denominator was that being a prison wife was expensive. As of January 2014, there were nearly 580,000 homeless people in the United States.[65] Sadly, parental incarceration and homelessness for their families has increased dramatically in the last two decades.[66] To avoid homelessness and to attempt to provide for themselves and families, several of the prison wives had some means of employment.

None of the wives had law degrees; however, another major commonality was their role as legal advocate for their spouses. Meeting with lawyers, researching the law, and taking stances to change legislation and attending court dates and hearings were a part of their lives. The viewers were able to witness the prison wives visiting legal libraries, meeting with their husband's lawyers, and taking initiatives to change laws by collecting signatures from their communities. Nearly all of the women worked tirelessly on behalf of their spouses, which was very time consuming.

The lack of sexual intimacy and extreme loneliness was another recurring theme that the prison wives experienced. Of the twelve wives, only two had the privilege of conjugal visits. The other ten women (several of them having never experienced sexual physical intimacy with their husbands due to meeting and marrying their husbands after they were already incarcerated) had to rely on phone calls, letters, and prison visits as their only means to make up for the lack of sexual intimacy and loneliness. During a prison wives support group meeting, LaToya discussed how she never slow danced with her husband, an intimate act that most women take for granted.[67] LaToya spoke for the countless numbers of prison wives whom the world may never get to see.

A number of the prison wives had an undying faith and hope for freedom for their spouses, which was the last common theme. Several of them relied on their faith and spiritual practices. Some of the wives spoke of the Bible and conducted rituals. With the exception of Georgia, the one wife whose husband would be released during the airing of her episode, only Gail was in full acceptance of her husband's fate of serving three life sentences. All of the other wives devoted their lives to trying either to exonerate their spouses or to convince their state to add family extended-stay programs to the prisons.

Feminist theoretical framework guided this research. The women were able to share the trials and tribulations from their own perspective, establishing their own voice. Each and every story shared common themes but was still a woman's unique perspective. Feminist theory suggests that the women should have an equal opportunity to share their stories within the often androcentric media. Investigation Discovery and *Prison Wives* provided the outlet; however, the women had the courage to share their stories, like Pam Booker: "In my wildest dreams I could have never imagined that I would be married to a man who's serving life in prison and I'm here to testify that it can happen to anyone and it can happen in a split second . . . We are a love story, a strange one—but we are a love story."[68]

Throughout the *Prison Wives* series, absent was any discussion of race and/or the effects of racial discrimination in the criminal justice system. There were ten Caucasian wives and two African American wives featured. Perhaps that racial ratio was a reason why race in the criminal justice system was never mentioned, particularly since those commonly affected by racial discrimination in the criminal justice system are people of color. Although not featured in this documentary series, there is a clear issue regarding race and mass incarceration in the United States, which leads all other countries in the world by imprisoning vast percentages of racial or ethnic minorities.[69] With the United States having such a complex history of race and mass incarceration, one could argue that any oversight of race or racial discrimination when covering the criminal justice system in the media could be a deliberate omission. However, on other reality-based programs related to the criminal justice system such as *Beyond Scared Straight* (A&E Television Networks) and *Lockup* (MSNBC), men and women of color are featured, almost exclusively. Yet, conversation on race, racial discrimination, and the criminal justice system is rarely covered. Similar to *Prison Wives*, these programs often feature details of those incarcerated, their families, and their court cases.

Theoretically, gatekeeping may explain why the conversation on race and racial discrimination rarely if ever comes up in this type of programming. Originated by psychologist Kurt Lewin and adapted to the field of communication by Pamela Shoemaker and Tim Voz, "gatekeepers" are those who have control of programming and are responsible for what type of content is created for viewers and what content is not.[70] Their control and influence over programming is crucial because the gatekeepers can create certain narratives, perpetuate stereotypes, and choose not to raise awareness of specific issues—like race and racial discrimination in the criminal justice system.

Conclusion

The *Prison Wives* series provided audiences with a firsthand account of the wives as told from their own perspectives. Although the nature of television programming is primarily to entertain, it is important to note that the prison wives' stories were their own and not exploited or sensationalized by the network. Those viewers who were unfamiliar with prison culture and the criminal justice system were provided a glimpse into the world of these women as captured on camera. Although the series was canceled, research on how the media represent the women behind incarcerated men should be ongoing. There are several avenues to explore for future research on women married to incarcerated men and their narratives. One area to examine further would be social media. Throughout the process of the present research, it was found that social media are another widely used outlet for the wives of incarcerated men to support one another and share their stories. Furthermore, it would be beneficial to conduct textual analyses of an online support group or another program similar to *Prison Wives* that could add to the scholarship in this area.

Notes

1. Carson, "Prisoners in 2014."
2. Glaze and Maruschak, *Parents in Prison.*
3. Morris, *Prisoners and Their Families.*
4. Fishman, "Prisoners and Their Wives."
5. Black, "Doing Gender from Prison."
6. Comfort, *Doing Time Together.*
7. "Cheryl Engelke," *Prison Wives.*
8. Bandele, *Prisoner's Wife.*
9. Brink, "You Don't See Us Doin' Time."
10. Ibid, 394.
11. Brancato, "Domesticating Politics," 49.
12. Brown, "Hoopin' and Hollering," 32.
13. Jorgenson, "Media and Polygamy," 25.
14. Samuels, "Reality TV Trashes Black Women."
15. Rawlinson, "Mafia, Media and Myth," 346.
16. Ibid.
17. Spitzack and Carter, "Women in Communication Studies," 402.
18. Dervin, "Potential Contribution of Feminist Scholarship," 114.
19. Steeves, "Feminist Theories and Media Studies," 96.
20. Stanback, "What Makes Scholarship about Black Women," 28.
21. Tandoc and Ferrucci, "So Says the Stars"; Trammell, "Watching Movies in the Name of the Lord"; Tyree, "Lovin' Momma and Hatin' on Baby Mama."
22. Frey, Botan, and Kreps, *Investigating Communication.*
23. Foss, *Rhetorical Criticism*, 6.
24. Andrews, *Practice of Rhetorical Criticism.*
25. "Cheryl Engelke," *Prison Wives.*
26. "Georgia Benson," *Prison Wives.*
27. "Gail Sullivan," *Prison Wives.*
28. Hattery and Smith, "Families of Incarcerated African American Men," 139.
29. Arditti, Lambert-Shute, and Joest, "Saturday Morning at the Jail."
30. "Annika Powell," *Prison Wives.*
31. "Jane Bailey," *Prison Wives.*
32. "Grace Dark Horse," *Prison Wives.*
33. "Juli Cummings," *Prison Wives.*
34. "Cheryl Engelke," *Prison Wives.*

35. "Tanya Windham," *Prison Wives.*

36. "LaToya Marion," *Prison Wives.*

37. Arditti, Lambert-Shute, and Joest, "Saturday Morning at the Jail."

38. "Juli Cummings," *Prison Wives.*

39. "Tanya Windham," *Prison Wives.*

40. "Cheryl Engelke," *Prison Wives.*

41. "Annika Powell," *Prison Wives.*

42. "Gail Sullivan," *Prison Wives.*

43. Ibid.

44. "Pam Booker," *Prison Wives.*

45. Ibid.

46. "Annika Powell," *Prison Wives.*

47. "Juli Cummings," *Prison Wives.*

48. "Grace Dark Horse," *Prison Wives.*

49. "Georgia Benson," *Prison Wives.*

50. "Elli Panitz," *Prison Wives.*

51. "Jane Bailey," *Prison Wives.*

52. Goldstein, "Conjugal Visits."

53. Sanburn, "Mississippi Ending Conjugal Visits."

54. "Tanya Windham," *Prison Wives.*

55. Ibid.

56. Nelson, "Case Study: Women Who Cheat."

57. "Debra Wilmont," *Prison Wives.*

58. "Elli Panitz," *Prison Wives.*

59. "LaToya Marion," *Prison Wives.*

60. "Juli Cummings," *Prison Wives.*

61. "Jane Bailey," *Prison Wives.*

62. "Tanya Windham," *Prison Wives.*

63. "Annika Powell," *Prison Wives*

64. "Georgia Benson," *Prison Wives.*

65. National Alliance to End Homelessness, *State of Homelessness in America, 2015.*

66. Casey, Shlafer, and Masten, "Parental Incarceration as a Risk Factor for Children."

67. "LaToya Marion," *Prison Wives.*

68. "Pam Booker," *Prison Wives.*

69. Alexander, *New Jim Crow.*

70. Shoemaker and Vos, *Gatekeeping Theory.*

Bibliography

Alexander, Michelle. *The New Jim Crow: Mass Incarceration in the Age of Color-blindness.* New York: New Press, 2010.

Andrews, James R. *The Practice of Rhetorical Criticism.* New York: Macmillan, 1983.

"Annika Powell." *Prison Wives.* Episode 1. Sirens Media for Investigation Discovery, February 14, 2010.

Arditti, Joyce A., Jennifer Lambert-Shute, and Karen Joest. "Saturday Morning at the Jail: Implications of Incarceration for Families and Children." *Family Relations: An Interdisciplinary Journal of Applied Family Studies* 52, no. 3 (2003): 195–204.

Bandele, Asha. *The Prisoner's Wife.* New York: Simon & Schuster, 1999.

Black, Carol. "Doing Gender from Prison: Male Inmates and their Supportive Wives and Girlfriends." *Race, Gender & Class* 17, nos. 3/4 (2010): 255–71.

Bracato, Jim. "Domesticating Politics: The Representation of Wives and Mothers in American Reality Television." *Film & History: An Interdisciplinary Journal of Film and Television Studies* 37, no. 2 (2007): 49–56.

Brink, Judith. "You Don't See Us Doin' Time." *Contemporary Justice Review* 6, no. 4 (2003): 393–96.

Brown, S. Tia. "Hoopin' and Hollering." *Jet*, June 6, 2011, 32–35.

Carson, E. Ann. "Prisoners in 2014." Bureau of Justice Statistics. Accessed January 11, 2016. http://www.bjs.gov/index.cfm?ty=pbdetail&iid=5387.

Casey, Erin C., Rebecca J. Shlafer, and Ann S. Masten. "Parental Incarceration as a Risk Factor for Children in Homeless Families." *Family Relations: An Interdisciplinary Journal of Applied Family Studies* 64, no. 4 (2015): 490–504.

"Cheryl Engelke." *Prison Wives.* Episode 13. Sirens Media for Investigation Discovery, April 24, 2010.

Comfort, Megan. *Doing Time Together: Love and Family in the Shadow of the Prison.* Chicago: University of Chicago Press, 2007.

"Debra Wilmont." *Prison Wives.* Episode 11. Sirens Media for Investigation Discovery, April 7, 2010.

Dervin, Brenda. "The Potential Contribution of Feminist Scholarship to the Field of Communication." *Journal of Communication* 37, no. 4 (1987): 107–20.

"Elli Panitz." *Prison Wives.* Episode 2. Sirens Media for Investigation Discovery, February 14, 2010.

Fishman, Laura, T. "Prisoners and Their Wives: Marital and Domestic Effects of Telephone Contacts and Home Visits." *International Journal of Offender Therapy and Comparative Criminology* 32, no. 1 (1988): 55–66.

Foss, Sonja K. *Rhetorical Criticism: Exploration and Practice*. Long Grove, IL: Waveland, 2009.

Frey, Lawrence R., Carl H. Botan, and Gary L. Kreps. *Investigating Communication: An Introduction to Research Methods*. 2nd ed. Boston: Allyn & Bacon, 1999.

"Gail Sullivan." *Prison Wives*. Episode 8. Sirens Media for Investigation Discovery, March 17, 2010.

"Georgia Benson." *Prison Wives*. Episode 7. Sirens Media for Investigation Discovery, March 3, 2010.

Glaze, Lauren E., and Laura M. Maruschak. *Parents in Prison and Their Minor Children*. Washington, D.C.: Bureau of Justice Statistics, 2008.

Goldstein, Dana. "Conjugal Visits." The Marshall Project. Accessed January 11, 2016. https://www.themarshallproject.org.

"Grace Dark Horse," *Prison Wives*. Episode 9. Sirens Media for Investigation Discovery, March 24, 2010.

Hattery, Angela J., and Earl Smith. "Families of Incarcerated African American Men: The Impact on Mothers and Children." *Journal of Pan African Studies* 7, no. 6 (2014): 128–53.

"Jane Bailey." *Prison Wives*. Episode 4. Sirens Media for Investigation Discovery, February 17, 2010.

Jorgenson, Derek. "Media and Polygamy: A Critical Analysis of Sister Wives." *Communication Studies* 65, no. 1 (2014): 24–38.

"Juli Cummings." *Prison Wives*. Episode 10. Sirens Media for Investigation Discovery, March 31, 2010.

"LaToya Marion." *Prison Wives*. Episode 3. Sirens Media for Investigation Discovery, February 14, 2010.

Morris, Pauline. *Prisoners and Their Families*. New York: Hart, 1965.

National Alliance to End Homelessness. *The State of Homelessness in America, 2015: An Examination of Trends in Homelessness, Homelessness Assistance, and At-Risk Populations at the National and State Level, 2015*. Accessed September 17, 2017. https://endhomelessness.org.

Nelson, Tammy. "Case Study: Women Who Cheat." *Psychotherapy Networker* 37, no. 3 (2013).

"Pam Booker" *Prison Wives*. Episode 5. Sirens Media for Investigation Discovery, February 24, 2010.

Rawlinson, Patricia. "Mafia, Media and Myth: Representations of Russian Organised Crime." *Howard Journal of Criminal Justice* 37, no. 4 (1998): 346–58.

Samuels, Allison. "Reality TV Trashes Black Women." *Newsweek*, May 1, 2011. Accessed September 17, 2017. http://www.newsweek.com.

Sanburn, Josh. "Mississippi Ending Conjugal Visits for Prisoners." *Time*, January 13, 2014. Accessed January 11, 2016. http://nation.time.com.

Shoemaker, Pamela, and Tim Vos. *Gatekeeping Theory*. New York: Routledge, 2009.

Spitzack, Carole, and Kathryn Carter. "Women in Communication Studies: A Typology for Revision." *Quarterly Journal of Speech* 73, no. 4 (1987): 401–23.

Stanback, Marsha Houston. "What Makes Scholarship about Black Women and Communication Feminist Communication Scholarship?" *Women's Studies in Communication* 11, no. 1 (1998): 78–85.

Steeves, H. Leslie. "Feminist Theories and Media Studies." *Critical Studies in Mass Communication* 4, no. 2 (1987): 95–135.

Tandoc, Edson C., and Patrick Ferrucci. "So Says the Stars: A Textual Analysis of *Glamour, Essence* and *Teen Vogue* Horoscopes." *Women's Studies International Forum* 45 (2014): 34–41.

"Tanya Windham." *Prison Wives*. Episode 12. Sirens Media for Investigation Discovery, April 14, 2010.

Trammell, James, Y. "Watching Movies in the Name of the Lord: Thoughts on Analyzing Christian Film Criticism," *Journal of Media and Religion* 11 (2012): 113–26.

Tyree, Tia C. M. "Lovin' Momma and Hatin' on Baby Mama: A Comparison of Misogynistic and Stereotypical Representations in Songs about Rappers' Mothers and Baby Mamas." *Women and Language* 32, no. 2 (2009): 50–58.

6. Dysfunctional Black Men: Representations of Race and Masculinity from the Days of Oz

Adina Schneeweis

You are defending the people who killed the lives you say matter.
—Bill Clinton, 2016

I ain't saying drugs are good. But when your past is past and your present sucks and your future holds nothing but broken promises and dead dreams, the drugs'll kill the pain. Listen up, America, you ain't ever gonna get rid of drugs until you cure pain.
—Augustus Hill, *Oz*, season 1, episode 5, 1997

In my hood, you had to learn to run, before you learned to walk.
—Augustus Hill, *Oz*, season 3, episode 3, 1999

Following the civil rights movement, public attention turned away from the active pursuit of racial equality, though conflicts, racial tensions, and patterns of racial inequality continued.[1] In the late 1980s, some have documented a more subtle type of racism—a "new racism"—taking the form of social and public policies, new immigration laws, and budget cuts for public education, housing, medical care, and other "public services for the poor, who continue to be disproportionately black and Hispanic."[2] In the 1990s, public opinion and political action turned their focus on race from a different angle—that of curbing the crime of "super-predators." In defense of the 1994 Violent Crime Control Act, known as the Crime Bill, then First Lady Hillary Clinton said, "They are not just gangs of kids anymore. They are often the kinds of kids that are called 'super-predators.' No conscience, no empathy, we can talk about why they ended up that way, but first we have to bring them to heel."[3] The Crime Bill is today largely considered a "mistake" that led to overincarceration, tougher policing, and an overall punitive mind-set—instead of encouraging intervention, prevention, or social programs.[4] As Clinton campaigned in spring 2016 during the primaries for the presidential race, an activist confronted her about her comment from the 1990s, which she was "happy to address"—yet did not, as her interlocutor was escorted out of the room for interrupting a campaign event. Her husband, former president Bill Clinton, when asked about the Crime Bill and his wife's comments, in the context of the vibrant activism of the Black Lives Matter (BLM) movement, responded, "You are defending the people who killed the lives you say matter."[5] He tried to rectify his reaction a day later. Undoubtedly, the BLM movement—or rather, #BlackLivesMatter, as the cause best gained momentum via social media, following in the line of #Ferguson, #BBUM, #myNYPD, or #TrayvonMartin[6]—has sparked substantial controversy in recent years. Proponents for and against police intervention, as well as for and against racial reform, recognize that race defines American reality, structuring identities, relations, institutions, and state and civil societies.

This chapter looks back twenty years in the past to examine the representations of black masculinity—at the fore of today's BLM activism—in one television program deemed at the time to include more progressive depictions of racial relations: HBO's hour-long TV drama *Oz*. Constructions of black masculinity continue to sell profitably in American media, at the same time that, in real life, they continue to be feared, and attempts to curb and control whatever "black men" may invoke in white imaginations persevere. In this chapter I revisit the attention masculinity has received in the context of a televised prison drama, with the explicit purpose of connecting its constructions of masculinity—and black masculinity in particular—with the current context of the movement for social justice for African Americans. As I examine how men and black men are constructed in the landmark prison drama *Oz*, I also argue that the show's both spectacular and skewed depictions further fed into the same hegemonic narrative of race it sought to disrupt, with contemporary repercussions.

At a time when the political sphere demanded intervention to curb crime and increased public opinion was marked by fear of a series of issues, including supposed rising crime, drug use, and urban violence,[7] HBO released *Oz* to take on crime and prison life. Broadcast in the United States between 1997 and 2003, the six-season series was HBO's first hour-long drama. Appealing through its cinematic visual style and documentary-like approach (monologue narration is provided by the character of disabled, black Augustus Hill), and heavily relying on the "sex and crime" formula,[8] *Oz* depicts the prison life of Emerald City, a maximum-security prison unit dedicated to prisoner rehabilitation within the fictional Oswald State Penitentiary (or Oz). Despite its purpose, Em City operates in factions, and every group—Aryans, Blacks, Italians, Muslims, or Latinos—is out to get the others, as they "stick close to mutual friends and terrorize mutual enemies."[9] At the time of its broadcast in the United States, it was by far the most violent and sexually graphic television program. *Oz* also gained substantial international attention, being broadcast uncensored or in late-night slots in over twenty countries.

Incarceration, prison drama, the death penalty, corrupt prison guards, sex and violence in prisons, riots, and jailbreaks—all such topics have been dramatized in American popular culture, to the point where representations of prisons and mass incarceration are no longer novel; instead, they are expected and relished. The chapters in this book speak to, and collectively offer a review of, the ongoing fascination that deviance continues to have for popular audiences—where by deviance I mean here an umbrella term covering criminality, torture, public executions, trials, dystopian story lines, and bullying. Such issues have been used for advertising and to serve political agenda, and also, importantly, for sheer entertainment and fascination.[10] Yet in examining popular culture depictions of prison, one must recognize differences in representation and audience alike. In Bill Yousman's words:

> The poor, the working class, and, especially, people of color often experience imprisonment directly or through the experiences of friends and relatives. Simultaneously, wealth and racial privilege provide television's preferred demographic—middle and upper class white Americans—with a buffer from the realities of rampant incarceration. Perhaps partially because prisons and prisoners are mysterious to middle and upper class Americans, and receive so little coverage in the news, they seem to be an on-going Hollywood obsession. When *Oz* debuted it added a new element to a cultural environment devoid of critical analysis of the prison industrial complex yet rife with fictional representations of prisons and prisoners meant to titillate and entertain.[11]

Oz targets HBO's more educated, wealthier audience, to which hyperviolence, and unapologetic and groundbreaking hypersexuality could be pitched. The story lines in the program take on classic *others*—like minority groups but also

Aryan extremists—selling thus a "titillating glimpse of an alien, frightening world."[12] *Oz* offers complex characters, shifting between "good" and "bad," and embodying both extremes, in a sense throwing off genre expectations. The show received, however, substantial criticism for its use of violence. Many have linked, and justified the use of, such representations of violence within the larger popular discourse on crime and punishment, as well as the industrial complex of the justice system that has been shown to discriminate based on class and race.[13] Tom Fontana, the producer of *Oz*, himself argued that much of the brutality and cruelty in the program is based on his research on American prisons.[14] Recent scholarship further confirms how a perceived "dangerous masculinity" is embedded in the structure of prisons today.[15]

Oz seeks to offer a critique of the prison complex, particularly evident in narrator Augustus Hill's statements on the condition of criminality; in the first season, for example, he says, "I ain't saying drugs are good. But when your past is past and your present sucks and your future holds nothing but broken promises and dead dreams, the drugs'll kill the pain. Listen up, America, you ain't ever gonna get rid of drugs until you cure pain." Other overt claims include questioning the impartiality of the justice system (in Schillinger's words, "Yeah, right, like you ever need any evidence" to condemn black men). In the Muslim Said's words in the first season, "[The blacks are] here not for the crimes they committed, but because of the color of their skin, their lack of education, the fact that they are poor . . . It's about the whole judicial system. We don't need more prisons, bigger prisons, better prisons, we need better justice." Yet does the series accomplish its lofty goal? Are the hyperviolent and the spectacular counterhegemonic in the final analysis?

I ground the observations of this chapter in critical and cultural studies, and methodologically I rely on framing analysis. I also rely on the conceptualization of "race" that invokes "social conflicts and interests,"[16] a sociocultural construct that has meaning beyond physical differences.[17] Race is ingrained in a culture's common sense,[18] operating at the level of comprehending, explaining, and motivating interactions in the world. The literature on race representations argues that racism and racial discrimination are among the root causes of much conflict, reliant on inherent hierarchies in societal, institutional, and cultural relations.[19] Such hierarchies include stereotypes, prototypes, and prejudices, but also racial ideologies—of whiteness, of white masculinity, of white power, of racial equality, etc.—and ensuing discriminatory practices.[20]

Overwhelming research suggests that media play a significant role in shaping and reinforcing racial values and attitudes.[21] Despite calls for racial equality and equity, media continue to feature "false images and negative stereotypes of vulnerable individuals or groups of individuals," which "have contributed to the spread of xenophobic and racist sentiments among the public and in some cases have encouraged violence by racist individuals and groups."[22] Even apparently neutral news items have been shown to hold deeply rooted prejudices. The collection of media available popularly "leads"—in a hegemonic sense—by depicting a "symbolic universe,"[23] and by exerting a "total social authority" over representation and the social formation as a whole.[24] Such hegemony of representation is what further motivates critiques of constructions that have become (part of our cultural) common sense. A thoroughly available, recognizable, widespread, repeated, reinforced, consistent, and yet limited repertoire of images becomes translated into tacit and covert relations of power, which are in turn then taken for granted. The continuous reproduction of dominant representations allows oppression to become "structural, rather than individual or incidental."[25] Discourses of race reenact older patterns—both at a macrolevel, transmitted through media or in institutions, and at a microlevel, apparent in everyday talk and interactions—and are also *productive* of race.[26] Many scholars indicate that the United States is the world of a "white male elite," which controls public information and communication.[27]

As I turn to the framing of masculinity in the prison drama, I offer my analysis in conjunction with the literature. This chapter continues with attention to masculinity, followed by my examination of black masculinity. A framing analytical approach proves useful in this exercise, since through framing, media construct definitions, providing an arena where ideologies (about gender and race, for my purpose) are articulated, transformed, and further developed, if only by failure to present alternative interpretations or counterideologies.[28] Frames constitute structures for organizing information, "schemata of interpretation" that, within certain contexts, allow for the perception, promotion, identification, labeling, moral evaluation, and even treatment of issues.[29] From the infinity of details, the principles of selection (what is included and what is excluded), emphasis, and presentation guide the salience of an issue.[30] Over time, the more salient a certain frame (or "package" of information) becomes, the more it solidifies meaning.[31] Devices that point to specific frames include syntactical, thematic, rhetorical (such as metaphors, exemplars, catchphrases, descriptions, and visual images[32]), and script or narrative structures.[33] To illustrate, a thematic structure suggestive of violent masculinity is evident in the first season of *Oz* when the leader of the black gang orders a murder in Em City, which then triggers a chain of violent acts. A script structure that invokes black aggressiveness depicts the story of the white Beecher, forced by the Aryan Schillinger to wear a shirt with the Confederate flag, specifically to infuriate the black gang in Em City—in other words, the script relies on, and assumes, a violent reaction to the reference to racism.

Performative Hypermasculinity and Sexuality in *Oz*

Traditional theorizations of ideal and idealized Western hegemonic masculinity include "authority and dominance over others (women and marginalized men), control (based primarily in violence), heterosexuality, and, at a minimum, a middle-class economic position."[34] The more of these qualities that are embodied in one person, the better, the more respected, the manlier one is and/or is perceived. Differently, hypermasculinity has been defined to emphasize "a subset of the qualities of hegemonic masculinity: Callous sexual attitudes, high levels of violence, and experiencing danger as exciting," in the words of Anna Curtis, who also reminds us that, apart from analyzing military and police representations, the concept has strong limitations in its ignorance of race, class, and the vulnerability embedded in prison contexts.[35] Yet in *Oz*, the inmates (those who survive and lead) constitute the epitome of hypermasculinity. They lead through their sexuality, both in acts (of which rape is the ultimate, most taboo, and yet heavily used) and in language; references to sex and swear words of a sexual nature abound and suffocate the script of the series.

The body is ultimately absolutely central to life, survival, and hierarchy in Em City, sexually and through its violence. In Yousman's assessment, which draws from a cultivation theoretical argument of what "heavy television viewing" constitutes, "despite the very violent nature of prime-time dramatic programming, the frequency of violence on *Oz* is three times greater."[36] Further, the particular flavor of the violence depicted on *Oz* falls into the exceptional category—sadistic, public, spectacular, repeated, calculated, twisted, constant, celebratory, and ultimately "happy violence."[37] Yousman's analysis provides much-needed contextualization for the number and causes of deaths in prison and the proportions of violent versus nonviolent incarcerations as well as prisoner behavior. Men in prison, in other words, are monsters and animals to be feared and without any remorse.

"Masculinity is performative," argue Georges-Claude Guilbert and Valentin Locoge, as they point to inmate hierarchies that are rife with sexual slavery and gang leaders' habitual use of "bitches," who can be raped by anyone in the gang. Rapists are masculinized and empowered by rape acts—and remain heterosexual in their own eyes, no matter how frequent the abuse is. Even the use of "bitch" for the homosexual or heterosexual prisoner treated this way is revealing, as it marks him as weaker and inferior to the more masculine rapists.[38] Oral sex is similarly used in the HBO series to indicate subordination, domination, and virility. Paradoxically, the gay group in Em City is overtly discriminated against. The Muslim Said states his disapproval, as do other inmates ("they ain't guys"). At the same time, rhetorically and narratively, they are also minimally included in the script, as well as depicted stereotypically, with emphasis on theatricality, drag, and flamboyant dancing and manners.[39] Yet *Oz* also challenges hegemonic masculinity in its gaze on the male body. In Joe Wlodarz's words:

> [I]t repeatedly entices viewers with the potential for the visualization of male rape in ways that open up the possibility of actually taking pleasure in that very representation (as in Adebisi's brutal, yet sensationalized, rape of his Italian nemesis Peter Schibetta [Eddie Malavarca] in season two). While clearly demarcated homosexuality often functions as a release valve for those very desires, the more sexually ambiguous space of the prison troubles that disavowal.[40]

Other challenges to established tropes are evident when the Latino Alvarez develops breast cancer, when the same Alvarez is rejected by a new leader for being "too white," in the brutal rape of the Italian Schibetta by the black Adebisi, or in the depiction of the Beecher-Keller danger-laden/romantic relationship. The ambiguity of the latter drew much popular and critical acclaim, and many have argued that *Oz* was innovative, bold, and a trendsetter in its representations of gender and sexuality.[41] As the initially heterosexual Beecher encounters the murderer and gay-bashing Keller, both fall in love with one another, and then they seek to make sense of their new feelings. The show tackles the dyad of love-sex in the context of homosexual relations in the fourth season in particular. The series engages sexuality in conversation with religion, via the Muslim Said (openly against homosexuality) and the Catholic Father Mukada (obscure in his answers to Beecher). Such scenes continue to trouble identity, masculinity, and sexuality, always tying these to the male inmate body.[42] Provocative to some, welcome by others, and troubling and tough to watch in other assessments, "*Oz* destabilizes hegemonic masculinity and forces its viewers to confront the complexities of racial and sexual identity," writes Joe Wlodarz.[43] In *Oz* the tropes of the prison genre—the jail as a machine, with rules and regulations, with punishment and dehumanization as central features, rife with segregated and hierarchical structures, and also with some political critique of an unjust justice and incarceration system[44]—are caricatured and critiqued through the sensationalized depictions of sexuality, nudity, rape, and gender identity. Elements of the soap opera genre—heightened emotions, villainy, victimization, deferred closure—further complicate prison life on TV, and shape "unusual and unsettling" and "queer erotic" scenes and melodrama.[45]

Oz contributes an important point to the social critique of gender roles and identities—it depicts them as permeable, changeable. Whereas television and film tend to rely on well-established archetypes, the series illustrates shifting identities. Although, at first glance, the plot begins in season 1 with expected and familiar characters banded into prison gangs—the black Homeboys and Muslims, the Italian Wiseguys, the Aryan Brotherhood, the Latinos of El Norte, the Irish, the gays, the bikers, the Christians—the setting in Em City proves to be productive for exploring sexual diversity. For example, in the character of the white, middle-class, initially prison-culture-naïve Beecher, audiences see a heterosexual, "normal" white guy who undergoes severe abuse. As Beecher begins to take charge of his imprisonment, he reclaims and rediscovers his own masculinity in his violent outbreak against his archenemy and rapist, the Aryan Schillinger, and continues in the second season to avenge violently the abuses against him (he castrates another Aryan inmate). Beecher's relationship with Keller that blooms in the second season (and moves back and forth, in soap opera style,[46] throughout the rest of the seasons) marks further sexual ambiguity for Beecher, who never claims a gay identity. Yet Beecher becomes unquestionably masculine (and "powerful") as he symbolically deterritorializes both his phallus and his anus, the focal points of his abuse and attempted demasculinization by the Aryans.[47]

Race and Masculinity: Black Men in *Oz*

Research has noted that television programming decisions are made, with few exceptions, toward rather homogeneous audience segments, thus contributing to a racially segregated American culture. It has also consistently documented that racial stereotypes pepper media and culture in general, and are remarkably uniform across genres. African Americans have been depicted as violent, aggressive, lazy, lacking ambition, and typically in subservient positions. Analyses of entertainment television in the United States argue that it reflects "a real-life racial divide."[48] Joe Feagin and Eileen O'Brien found that, "while most no longer see African Americans as biologically inferior, a majority of whites [accept] at least one of the stereotypes about African Americans."[49] Matthew Hughey's ethnographic work confirms such findings that have typically evaluated content, texts, and discourses. As he investigates white nationalists and white activists for racial justice, Hughey identifies three racial discourses. The first he calls dysfunctionalism, indicating hyperviolence and subfunctioning (due to genetics or racism alike)—"making sense of black pathologies in ways that leave white, patriarchal, and North American conceptions of gender and race as pure and normalized."[50] The second discourse refers to the role of white intervention and paternalism in assisting the dysfunctional blacks (by control or education alike), while the third refers to the black body as a sexual threat (to the white female and, in consequence, the need for the white male hero to safeguard her). Hughey concludes that black masculinity has served to help construct and legitimize notions of white masculinity,[51] perpetuating the contested position that black men have occupied in U.S. society. In American popular culture, the lives of O. J. Simpson, Tiger Woods, Michael Jordan, or Kanye West have become spectacles on display (to handpick a few of the celebrated names). A white racial frame—defined by Joe Feagin to encompass "racial ideas, terms, images, emotions and interpretations"—is then used to rationalize, over and over, white privilege and supremacy. The familiarity of the discursive tool of black masculinity in particular has "long functioned as a key metaphor and fundamental referent for white Americans in public discourse," Feagin adds.[52] Likewise, Hughey argues that a hegemonic white racial identity necessarily rests on a process of differentiation of those marked white as being apart from, and superior to, those marked nonwhite.[53]

Black men on *Oz* fall well within the bounds of these discourses. There are no innovations or discursive challenges in *Oz*, I argue, when it comes to black men. The six seasons depict the dysfunctional black, violent and out of control, along with other rigid representations of backwardness, stupidity, manipulability, and laziness. Although all the gangs in prison are portrayed as violent, cruel, and brutal criminals, the black gang in particular is always represented a step below. Examples abound. The black warden, Glynn, and *Oz*'s direct supervisor, the white McManus, are depicted in direct opposition.

While McManus hopes to rehabilitate the prisoners through education, Glynn is aggressive and unforgiving, promoting the use of force and a retributory formula for prison violations.[54] When the Irish O'Reilly plans the murder of an enemy, he hires a black man to do it—instead of asking a killer from a different gang or doing the job himself. The Aryan leader, Schillinger, counts on the black aggressor trope when he hopes the blacks will kill his cell mate, Beecher, if he forces Beecher to wear a shirt displaying a Confederate flag. The fourth season positions a corrupt black man as a unit manager in Em City, who turns out to let the black inmates run amok in drug dealing; although temporarily "punished" in the show's script when he is fired, he is rehired as warden at a different prison and returns to Oz at the end of the sixth season. The depiction of the basketball player Vahue merges and reinforces the stereotypes of the black athlete, the criminal (drug use), and the backward black (Vahue destroys another prisoner's cello as an argument for the supremacy of sports over classical music). The first season shows the case of the black Keane, who fights for his life against two Italians set to murder him under the gaze of bribed guards, who watch the scene from above, filming it, cheering and laughing. The scene recalls ancient gladiator rings and colonial subjugation of natives, as it reduces the black man to mere entertainment for the whites who are in power.

To reiterate the point, black violence is taken to an extreme—even for the standards of *Oz*. During the final episode of the first season, as a riot erupts in Em City, a host of characters go through transformations. In contrast, the black Homeboys give in to their addiction, which subsequently leads to their being eliminated from the inmate council and handcuffed by their own fellows. Not only has society consigned them to prison, but their inmate equals ostracize them as well. The Muslim blacks are portrayed as fundamentally different and separate from the Homeboys, shown in prayer or listening to "the reverend" Said's preaching during almost all camera time given to them. The black leader Adebisi, featured in the first four seasons of the series, is consistently portrayed as an enraged wild animal, assaulting, raping, killing at will, and severely taken over by his drug addiction. Adebisi, played by actor Adewale Akinnuoye-Agbaje, is the epitome of hypermasculinity and hypersexuality in the series. He is a massive black man of African descent, imprisoned for a brutal murder with a machete. Adebisi's portrait is crayoned entirely with violence and cruelty, addictions, laziness (i.e., too slow for kitchen duty), and intellectual inferiority. Adebisi seems to have no life outside prison—while other lead characters are more complexly described, with either fatherly instincts for the Latino Alvarez, family ties for the Aryan Schillinger, a dying wife for the Italian Schibetta, or heart problems for the Muslim Said. Interestingly, in the fourth season it is Said who kills Adebisi—though in self-defense. Perhaps it is the only way a black Muslim can show violence in the series' effort to accustom audiences to a religious *other*. Critics recognize Adebisi's simplistic characterization, while producer Tom Fontana says the brutality was intentional:

> I wanted to keep the audience off balance. It was important to me that the audience *not* sit back in their chair watching the show. That they not feel comfortable, if that makes any sense. If they were gonna experience being in a prison, I felt like they should be constantly going, "Whoa! What's that? What's that?" So that's why, with the characters, I wanted to keep shifting the good and the bad, the good and the bad. Because even Schillinger had this thing with his son. He fucked it up, but he was *trying*. You saw at least he could be a father. He *wanted* to be a father. Adebisi, it was harder, because it was just so much fun to write that character.[55]

This interview with Fontana solidifies the commonsense expectation that a black character—like Adebisi—is "fun" to watch/gaze upon for his out-of-control violence. The working of the hegemonic discourse of race speaks through the script's heavy reliance on familiar race tropes.

Conclusion

In its claims about the justice system, *Oz* appears ultimately to be contradictory. Despite the voices of Hill, McManus, or Said, and

> despite what might appear as the *Oz* series' representation of the reform and rehabilitation discourses of penal modernism as posing some viable counter-hegemony to the discourses of neoliberal penalty that are presently hegemonic in much of the Western world, the *Oz* series reinforces and rearticulates neoliberal representations of prisons as places where only the deserving go, a neoliberal vision of prison as a brutal place where if "we"—the middle-class viewing public—slip, or lose too much of our self control, "we" might deservingly end up.[56]

The series' construction of masculinity is far more complex. Brian Jarvis reminds us of the restructuring of contemporary definitions of masculinities, as men have been "feminized," shown in more flexible roles, with a less-fixed identity depiction.[57] In this context *Oz* offers both a return to the feral and primal masculinity and also a challenge to traditional representations of gaze and sexuality. The construct of masculinity in *Oz* shifts the idealized definition of Western hegemonic masculinity, or simplifies it, to entail authority, dominance, and control. The inmates who survive, and are successful and respected in Em City, are not always heterosexual or of the upper or middle class. In fact, several inmate leaders deploy their bi- or homosexuality to exert their influence—justifying perhaps the critical acclaim for *Oz*'s innovation in sexual representations.

In its racial depictions, however, and particularly in the marriage of race and masculinity in the representation of the black male inmate, I argue that *Oz* fails. It mostly re-creates. It repeats discursive practices in which violence and bodily pain are glorified, whereas bonding and the feminine are "deadly problematic."[58] Despite the cast's ethnic and racial diversity, the frames of black dysfunctionality, hypersexuality, and the ensuing frame of intervention and control continue to legitimize a racist and interventionist justice-system narrative. Beyond HBO's *Oz*, such discourses extend to a popular culture climate that still grapples with the very same issues. Hyperviolence, hypersexuality, and racism continue to be tied to being a man, to being a black man, and to being an appealing character on American television, where audiences continue to be told that incarceration and fierce punishment are the only means to keep *us* safe from *them*, the black monsters and animals.

Notes

1. Schuman, Steeh, Bobo, and Krysan, *Racial Attitudes in America*.

2. Smitherman-Donaldson and van Dijk, "Introduction: Words That Hurt," 13.

3. Gearan and Phillip, "Clinton Regrets 1996 Remark."

4. Johnson, "20 Years Later, Parts of Major Crime Bill."

5. Bradner, "Bill Clinton Spars with Black Lives Matter Protesters."

6. Jackson and Foucault Welles, "#Ferguson Is Everywhere."

7. Yousman, "Inside *Oz*."

8. Kreutzner and Seiter, "Not All 'Soaps' Are Created Equal."

9. As described on the video case of the first season.

10. Sealy, "Hegemony of Neoliberal Penalty Regimes"; Yousman, "Inside *Oz*."

11. Yousman, "Inside *Oz*," 269–70.

12. Ibid., 267.

13. Ibid.

14. Green, "Legacy of *Oz*."

15. Curtis, "You Have to Cut It Off at the Knee."

16. Feagin and O'Brien, *White Men on Race*, 7.

17. Omi and Winant, *Racial Formation in the United States*.

18. Ibid.

19. For instance, see United Nations, *Report of the World Conference against Racism*, 5–7.

20. Feagin and O'Brien, *White Men on Race*; Entman and Rojecki, *Black Image in the White Mind*; Domke, "Journalists, Framing, and Discourse"; Omi and Winant, *Racial Formation in the United States*; Smitherman-Donaldson and van Dijk, "Introduction: Words That Hurt."

21. Domke, "Journalists, Framing, and Discourse"; Hall, "Culture, the Media and Ideological Effect"; Entman, "Framing: Toward Clarification"; Entman and Rojecki, *Black Image in the White Mind*.

22. United Nations, *Report of the World Conference against Racism*, 22.

23. Lears, "Concept of Cultural Hegemony," 573.

24. Hall, "Culture, the Media and Ideological Effect," 332.

25. Smitherman-Donaldson and van Dijk, "Introduction: Words That Hurt," 17.

26. Foucault, *Society Must Be Defended*; see also van Dijk, "Interdisciplinary Study of News as Discourse."

27. van Dijk, "How 'They' Hit the Headlines."

28. Domke, "Press and 'Delusive Theories.'"

29. Entman, "Framing: Toward Clarification"; Pan and Kosicki, "Framing Analysis."

30. Gitlin, *Whole World Is Watching*.

31. Gamson and Modigliani, "Media Discourse and Public Opinion."

32. Ibid., 3.

33. Pan and Kosicki, "Framing Analysis," 59–62.

34. Curtis, "You Have to Cut It Off at the Knee," 121.

35. Ibid., 122.

36. Yousman, "Inside *Oz*," 273.

37. Gerbner, "TV Violence and the Art of Asking the Wrong Question."

38. Guilbert and Locoge, "Just How Queer Is *Oz*?"

39. Ibid.

40. Wlodarz, "Maximum Insecurity," 69.

41. Guilbert and Locoge, "Just How Queer Is *Oz*?"; Wlodarz, "Maximum Insecurity."

42. Guilbert and Locoge, "Just How Queer Is *Oz*?"; Jarvis, "Violence of Images"; Wlodarz, "Maximum Insecurity."

43. Wlodarz, "Maximum Insecurity," 60.
44. Mason, "Prison in Cinema"; Pramaggiore, "Privatization Is the New Black."
45. Wlodarz, "Maximum Insecurity," 62; see also Jarvis, "Violence of Images."
46. Wlodarz, "Maximum Insecurity."
47. Jarvis, "Violence of Images." Beecher first savagely beats Schillinger, then defecates on his face. Beecher later bites the penis of the Aryan who tries to make Beecher perform oral sex on him.
48. Entman and Rojecki, *Black Image in the White Mind*, 149; Smitherman-Donaldson and van Dijk, "Introduction: Words That Hurt," 21.
49. Feagin and O'Brien, *White Men on Race*, 19.
50. Hughey, "Black Guys and White Guise," 107.
51. Ibid.
52. Feagin, *White Racial Frame*, 101.
53. Hughey, "Black Guys and White Guise."
54. Glynn's life is scripted to be put to an end by the close of the program in the sixth season, not McManus's.
55. Green, "Legacy of *Oz*."
56. Sealy, "Hegemony of Neoliberal Penalty Regimes," 45.
57. Jarvis, "Violence of Images"; see also, for instance, Smith, *Daddy Shift*.
58. Jarvis, "Violence of Images," 166.

Bibliography

Bradner, Eric. "Bill Clinton Spars with Black Lives Matter Protesters." CNN, April 8, 2016. Accessed April 10, 2016. http://www.cnn.com.
Curtis, Anna. "'You Have to Cut It Off at the Knee': Dangerous Masculinity and Security Inside a Men's Prison." *Men and Masculinities* 17, no. 2 (2014): 120–46.
Domke, David. "Journalists, Framing, and Discourse about Race Relations." *Journalism and Mass Communication Monographs* 164 (1997): 1–55.
———. "The Press and 'Delusive Theories of Equality and Fraternity' in the Age of Emancipation." *Critical Studies in Mass Communication* 13 (1996): 228–50.
Entman, Robert M. "Framing: Toward Clarification of a Fractured Paradigm." *Journal of Communication* 43 (1993): 51–58.
Entman, Robert M., and Andrew Rojecki. *The Black Image in the White Mind*. Chicago: University of Chicago Press, 2000.
Feagin, Joe R. *The White Racial Frame: Centuries of Racial Framing and Counter-Framing*. New York: Routledge, 2010.

Feagin, Joe, and Eileen O'Brien. *White Men on Race: Power, Privilege, and the Shaping of Cultural Consciousness*. Boston: Beacon, 2003.

Foucault, Michel. *Society Must Be Defended: Lectures at the Collège de France, 1975–1976*. New York: Picador, 2003.

Gamson, William A., and Andre Modigliani. "Media Discourse and Public Opinion on Nuclear Power: A Constructionist Approach." *American Journal of Sociology* 95 (1989): 1–37.

Gearan, Anne, and Abby Phillip. "Clinton Regrets 1996 Remark on 'Super-Predators' after Encounter with Activist." *Washington Post*, February 25, 2016. Accessed April 10, 2016. https://www.washingtonpost.com.

Gerbner, George. "TV Violence and the Art of Asking the Wrong Question." Center for Media Literacy, originally published in July 1994. Accessed April 29, 2016. http://www.medialit.org.

Gitlin, Todd. *The Whole World Is Watching: Mass Media in the Making & Unmaking of the New Left*. Berkeley: University of California Press, 1980.

Green, Elon. "The Legacy of *Oz*: A Chat with Tom Fontana (and a Special Guest)." *The Toast*, August 11, 2015. Accessed on April 30, 2016. http://the-toast.net.

Guilbert, Georges-Claude, and Valentin Locoge. "Just How Queer Is *Oz*? Gender and Sexuality in *Oz*'s Fourth Season." In *Mediated Deviance and Social Otherness: Interrogating Influential Representations*, edited by Kylo-Patrick R. Hart, 53–70. Newcastle, UK: Cambridge Scholars Publishing, 2007.

Hall, Stuart. "Culture, the Media and Ideological Effect." In *Mass Communication and Society*, edited by James Curran, Michael Gurevitch, and Janet Woollacoot, 315–48. Beverly Hills, CA: Sage, 1979.

Hughey, Matthew W. "Black Guys and White Guise: The Discursive Construction of White Masculinity." *Journal of Contemporary Ethnography* 41, no. 1 (2012): 95–124.

Jackson, Sarah J., and Brooke Foucault Welles. "#Ferguson Is Everywhere: Initiators in Emerging Counterpublic Networks." *Information, Communication & Society* 19, no. 3 (2016): 397–418. doi:http://dx.doi.org/10.1080/1369118X.2015.1106571.

Jarvis, Brian. "The Violence of Images: Inside the Prison TV Drama *Oz*." In *Captured by the Media: Prison Discourse in Popular Culture*, edited by Paul Mason, 154–71. New York: Routledge, 2005.

Johnson, Carrie. "20 Years Later, Parts of Major Crime Bill Viewed as Terrible Mistake." NPR, September 12, 2014. Accessed April 10, 2016. http://www.npr.org.

Kreutzner, Gabrielle, and Ellen Seiter. "Not All 'Soaps' Are Created Equal: Toward a Cross-Cultural Criticism of Television Serials." In *To Be Continued... Soap Operas around the World*, edited by Robert C. Allen, 234–55. London and New York: Routledge, 1995.

Lears, T. J. Jackson. "The Concept of Cultural Hegemony: Problems and Possibilities." *American Historical Review* 90, no. 3 (1985): 567–93.

Mason, Paul. "The Prison in Cinema." *Images*, no. 6. Accessed April 26, 2016. http://www.imagesjournal.com.

Omi, Michael, and Howard Winant. *Racial Formation in the United States: From the 1960s to the 1990s*. 2nd ed. New York and London: Routledge, 1994.

Pan, Zhongdang, and Gerald M. Kosicki. "Framing Analysis: An Approach to News Discourse." *Political Communication* 10 (1993): 55–75.

Pramaggiore, Maria. "Privatization Is the New Black: Quality Television and the Re-Fashioning of the U.S. Prison Industrial Complex." In *The Routledge Companion to Global Popular Culture*, edited by Toby Miller, 187–96. New York: Routledge, 2015.

Schuman, Howard, Charlotte Steeh, Lawrence Bobo, and Marya Krysan. *Racial Attitudes in America: Trends and Interpretations*. Cambridge, MA: Harvard University Press, 1997.

Sealy, David. "The Hegemony of Neoliberal Penalty Regimes: A Commentary on the First Seven Minutes of *Oz*." In *Mediated Deviance and Social Otherness: Interrogating Influential Representations*, edited by Kylo-Patrick R. Hart, 44–52. Newcastle, UK: Cambridge Scholars Publishing, 2007.

Smith, Jeremy Adam. *The Daddy Shift: How Stay-at-Home Dads, Breadwinning Moms, and Shared Parenting Are Transforming the American Family*. Boston: Beacon, 2009.

Smitherman-Donaldson, Geneva, and Teun A. van Dijk. "Introduction: Words That Hurt." In *Discourse and Discrimination*, edited by Geneva Smitherman-Donaldson and Teun A. van Dijk, 11–22. Detroit: Wayne State University Press, 1988.

United Nations. *Report of the World Conference against Racism, Racial Discrimination, Xenophobia and Related Intolerance, Durban, 31 August–8 September 2001*. Accessed April 29, 2016. http://www.un.org.

van Dijk, Teun A. "How 'They' Hit the Headlines: Ethnic Minorities in the Press." In *Discourse and Discrimination*, edited by Geneva Smitherman-Donaldson and Teun A. van Dijk, 221–62. Detroit: Wayne State University Press, 1988.

van Dijk, Teun A. "The Interdisciplinary Study of News as Discourse." In *A Handbook of Qualitative Methodologies for Mass Communication Research*, edited by Klaus Bruhn Jensen and Nicholas W. Jankowski, 108–20. New York: Routledge, 1999.

Wlodarz, Joe. "Maximum Insecurity: Genre Trouble and Closet Erotics in and out of HBO's *Oz*." *Camera Obscura* 58, vol. 20, no. 1 (2005): 58–105. Accessed September 17, 2017. http://cameraobscura.dukejournals.org.

Yousman, Bill. "Inside *Oz*: Hyperviolence, Race and Class Nightmares, and the Engrossing Spectacle of Terror." *Communication and Critical/Cultural Studies* 6, no. 3 (2009): 265–84.

SECTION TWO

Connecting Media to Experience

To what extent do media portrayals compare to their real-life counterparts? What are the roles and functions of media in prison? How do inmates perceive the constructed discourses of their stories? In this section, scholars combine textual analysis with ethnography to explore these questions. Through a comparison of written personal correspondence with the portrayal of death row on documentary television, an analysis of inmates making meaning of their experiences and creating community by producing their own media, a survey of women coping with life sentences, and interviews with female inmates reflecting on media's framing of their crimes, this section bridges textual work and ethnography.

7. Stories from Death Row:
Articulations behind the Scenes

Emily Plec

> When one wants to avoid having one's seminar on the death penalty be merely a seminar on the death penalty; when one wants to avoid its being just one more discourse, and a discourse of good conscience to boot, among people who, like us, basically will never be, or believe they never will be, executioners executing a sentence nor legally condemned to death sentences, nor be the lawyers or district attorneys of those who are condemned to death, nor the governors or heads of state having the power of clemency, then, in that case, one must do everything to get as close as possible, in one's own body, to those for whom the death penalty is really the death penalty, in a real, concrete, undeniably and cruelly threatening way, in the absolute imminence of execution.
>
> —Jacques Derrida, "Lecture 6, February 2, 2000"

Gary called tonight. He used to call on Wednesday nights and sometimes still does, when he can. And I occasionally post money so that he can, all the while cursing the system that profits from our monitored communication. I wish he would write. Stamps are cheaper and the labor more valuable for the mental focus it requires, or so I think.[1] He sometimes rambles on the phone; it can feel for me more like a therapy session than a conversation between friends. I try to do several things—be a good listener, be my skeptical self, take his side and take notes. But I fail at most of these most nights. The last part, the note taking, has only been recent, really, and I am reminded of why it is important by our conversation tonight.

He's afraid he's dying. And he may be right. Prison will kill you, and guys on Oregon's death row either volunteer or fade away, with the latter usually being pretty unpleasant—diabetes, dialysis, liver failure, cancer. One of the most famous death row prisoners in the world knows this, too. Writer and death row inmate Mumia Abu-Jamal has been battling the prison system for life-saving medical care that he and other people in prison are often denied.[2] Gary's once-beautiful, enormous body is breaking down. First it was his knee and now a hip. He's got all the all-too-usual ailments of the inside, too, but it's the immobility that makes him feel vulnerable. And the judge just set a new execution date.

I know it rattled him because he didn't even hear the date, couldn't even register what was happening. But there it is again—a date. It looms over us, especially him, and it gives this an urgency that's always been there but that's pushing him now. Will it push him to start writing again? Is it pushing me away?

Origin Stories

The intersections of this chapter and volume were paved, for me, while studying communication at a large public research university on the eve of a new millennium. It was there that I was introduced to the writings of Jacques Derrida and to Michel Foucault's critique of penal systems, to ethnographic methods and the work of Dwight Conquergood; it was there that I refined my capacity to critically analyze media texts; and it was there that I first heard Angela Davis and Sister Helen Prejean speak about the prison-industrial complex and the lives of the people incarcerated within it. A few years after I finished my doctorate and accepted a faculty position in Oregon, I began volunteering with Oregonians for Alternatives to the Death Penalty (OADP) and getting more involved with a group called PCARE (Prison Communication, Activism, Research, and Education).[3] I also began writing to Gary Haugen through OADP's death row correspondence program. Because of my geographic proximity to the state penitentiary, I have visited him many times over the roughly six years we've known each other.

Gary Haugen is a celebrity on Oregon's death row, second only perhaps to Christian Longo, whose notoriety was cemented by a feature film starring James Franco and by news coverage of his efforts to enable condemned inmates to donate their viable organs. Gary is a celebrity because he abandoned his appeals, fought a long and complicated court battle to be determined mentally fit to make the decision to proceed with execution, and was scheduled to be killed by the state when then governor John Kitzhaber intervened. Before dropping his appeals, Gary was a relative newcomer to death row. Sentenced to life with the possibility of parole for a murder committed when he was a teenager, it was almost twenty-two years later that Haugen, along with a codefendant, was accused of stabbing fellow inmate David Polin to death. Haugen turned forty-five years old just prior to being sentenced to death and roughly five years later abandoned his appeals, believing he would either be killed or be a catalyst for the abolition of capital punishment in Oregon.

What has transpired in the legal and political arena since that time is peripheral to this essay, but it is illustrative of the complex, resource-intensive, and emotionally exhausting circus that our system of capital punishment has become, for all parties involved. I am now convinced that it is a system that brings out the worst in prosecutors and judges, irreparably harms jurors and corrections officers, fails to acknowledge the humanity of defendants and their loved ones, is highly fallible and prone to fatal error, and brings less closure and more trauma than victims' loved ones are led to believe it will. For, as a friend recently reminded me, death is only final for the person who dies. The living must constantly deal with the presence of the dead (and for murder victims' family members, with their killers), often in untimely and unpredictable ways.

There are almost three thousand people, mostly men, on death rows across the United States. More than 150 people have been exonerated from death row since 1973. According to the Death Penalty Information Center, in recent years, exonerations from death rows across the United States average roughly five per year.[4] Since 1976, U.S. federal and state governments have killed more than 1400 citizens, and, whether innocent or guilty of their crimes, it is undeniable that their deaths come at an enormous emotional and financial cost. The vast majority of executions are carried out in southern states, with Texas leading all states. At the time of this writing, African Americans constitute as much as 42 percent of the population on death rows in the United States, while less than 2 percent are women. Racist sentencing and judicial practices have been well documented as the cause for the disproportionate representation of people of color in capital cases.[5]

For the most part, support for the death penalty has gradually waned, with the number of sentences steadily declining over the past two decades. The issue has received front-page attention in popular periodicals such as the *Atlantic*'s cover article on execution drugs and *Time*'s "The Last Execution: Why the Era of Capital Punishment Is Ending."[6] In addition, a number of high-profile legal cases, executions, and moratoria have put the lawful practice of intentionally killing civilians in the national spotlight. But it wasn't always this way. For most of my life, death row was not part of a public conversation, even though I was born in the years between *Furman v. Georgia* and *Gregg v. Georgia*, between a national moratorium and its end: the sensational firing-squad death of Gary Gilmore in Utah.

What I knew of capital punishment I learned from mass media, from news stories I ignored and entertainment media I absorbed. I can't remember any detailed examples besides Johnny Cash singing about a woman in a "Long Black Veil" because, until I knew someone on death row, I never really noticed the ubiquity of media representations of the death penalty. But now, whether in cartoons or crime shows, I see executions and references to them *everywhere*. Gallows humor is sometimes actually that: jokes about hangings and electric chairs on *Bugs Bunny*, *The Simpsons*, and *Family Guy*. Or I might stumble across a crime show on a weeknight featuring a couple condemned for a murder that maybe only one of them committed or an investigator who finds out too late that an innocent man was executed for a crime his boss committed. Just last night, catching up on the last episode of a new sitcom about the end of the world, capital punishment was used as a plot device to build intensity around the rescue of two women sentenced to death by an emergency military tribunal. Such references to the death penalty were, for me, for such a long time, something remote, distant, a story from some other world.

The first story about death row that I really *heard* was Sister Helen Prejean's story about coming to know Patrick Sonnier, the story retold in the film *Dead Man Walking*, which had been released about five years earlier. I had come to the small auditorium on the west end of campus quite by accident, en route to the bus or the gym, when a poster caught my eye. I had heard of the Catholic nun and the film, based on her book about her relationship with a death row inmate. The talk was starting in fifteen minutes; I decided to stay. As Sister Prejean talked about her upbringing and experiences after meeting Sonnier, I remember laughing, which I didn't expect to do at a talk like that. And I cried a little, too. I left feeling like there was work I was supposed to be doing and wondering how I would find my way into it. I acknowledged what Walter Fisher calls narrative fidelity[7] when Prejean said that every person is greater, and worth more, than their worst deed. I was interpellated by her appeal to work toward a world in which it is easier for people to be good.[8]

When I later met Gary, the story rang true again. I was at once impressed by his intellect and empathy and appalled by his capacity for brutality. As I came to know him, I began to see how the early chapters of his life resembled sections of a textbook in an introductory psychology or sociology course.

Abuse, mistreatment, abandonment, mental illness, and addiction—the story of Gary's life before the murder for which he was sentenced to prison is all too common.

Analytical Approach

I've thought for a long time about if, and how, I would write about my relationship with Gary. I've started writing generally about the death penalty, which is much easier for a host of reasons, including the increasing media attention given to botched executions, exonerations, and declining public support for capital punishment. Another easy target for a media critic is television, and I'm fascinated by the rhetorical possibilities presented by the CNN series *Death Row Stories*. As I watched the first season, I found myself wondering how the stories of people on death row, and the way they are told in this series, impact audience members. And I wonder if they bear the same sort of narrative fidelity for the men and women on death row as Sister Prejean's story did for me.

Although I have not approached my relationship and correspondence with Gary as an ethnographer, I do believe my relationship with him has fostered what Ruthellen Josselson calls an "empathic stance," enabling me to interpret someone who is engaged in the process of interpreting himself.[9] Due to a host of practical constraints and personal objections, I do not enter the world of the intensive management unit of the state penitentiary to engage in "participant-observation." Rather, I ascribe to what Dwight Conquergood describes as the "rethinking of ethnography as primarily about speaking and listening instead of observing." Elaborating, he writes, "The communicative praxis of speaking and listening, conversation, demands copresence even as it decenters the categories of knower and known. Vulnerability and self-disclosure are enabled through conversations."[10] Indeed, it is through conversation, correspondence, relationship building, and the cultivation of a friendship that Gary Haugen has shared with me his death row story and I have come to know and care about a killer.

Thus my analytical approach, though informed by critical ethnography, is grounded in another methodology that enables me to stitch together the conversational, the representational, and the experiential. "Articulation" is an approach that works at a number of levels; it forges linkages and also enables a politicized utterance, in this case a call for the abolition of capital punishment. Stuart Hall's responses to interviews first published under the title "On Postmodernism and Articulation" indicate a double meaning of articulation both as an uttering or speaking forth and as the conjunctive synthesis that unites seemingly discrete elements, under certain conditions.[11]

Extending this argument, Jennifer Slack considers the epistemological, political, and strategic levels at which articulation works as a way of thinking, exposing power relations, and intervening in particular formations[12] (such as mass incarceration or the death penalty). As a critical practice, articulation "highlights the dynamic nature of social and cultural meanings and the necessary provisionality of methods and strategies of analysis, expression and action."[13] As Barker points out,

> The concept of articulation is also deployed to discuss the relationship between culture and political economy. Thus culture is said to be "articulated" with moments of production but not determined in any "necessary" way by that moment, and vice versa. Consequently, we might explore how the moment of production is inscribed in texts but also how the "economic" is cultural, that is, a meaningful set of practices.[14]

Slack argues that, methodologically, articulation enables us to "engage the concrete in order to change it."[15] This process of "rearticulation" demonstrates how articulation works not only to connect already existing epistemological categories and material practices but also to create new ways of weaving discourses and practices together.

In this analysis, articulation draws a conjunctive synthesis between season 1, episode 8, of CNN's *Death Row Stories*, which features the case of Nathan Dunlap, and the stories Gary Haugen has shared with me about his experience on Oregon's death row. The two stories share much in common: both involve men convicted of committing heinous murders, both involve questions about the thresholds and processes for determining mental illness and the mitigating role it plays in sentencing, and both cases resulted in unusual gubernatorial reprieves that are neither moratoria nor acts of clemency. These articulations reveal economic, political, and social critiques that have the capacity to rearticulate the story we tell our citizens about crime and punishment, and about capital punishment as a failed public policy. In addition, in the places where the mediated and personal stories diverge, we find some of the most pressing questions that trouble the entire prison-industrial complex and the society that feeds it—questions about racism, about the role and rhetorical importance of prior offenses in sentencing, and about the extent to which we really believe, as a society, in rehabilitation.

Analyzing and Articulating Death Row Narratives

A comprehensive introduction to early American death penalty discourse can be found in Stephen Hartnett's two-volume study of the legal, political, and moral arguments about "capital punishment and the making of America," the subtitle to *Executing Democracy*.[16] Hartnett provides a rich and deep historical examination of the topoi and tensions that undergird contemporary capital punishment rhetoric and policy. Similar themes and arguments are taken up in numerous other publications focused on death sentences and executions today, including analyses of representations of people of color and women on death row, which show patterns of negative, dehumanizing, and defeminizing portrayals.[17]

Other studies focus on media representations, framing, and public opinion of capital punishment;[18] particular death row cases that have ignited public controversy;[19] and rhetorical criticism of capital punishment tropes, ideographs, and metaphors.[20] Still another body of literature emerging in the past decade focuses on the role of professionals—chiefly, journalists, attorneys, and jurists—in the formation of attitudes about the death penalty.[21] These works highlight the importance of legal processes and public scrutiny of the justice system, including challenges to limitations placed on journalists' access to imprisoned people and their communication with the outside world. As suggested previously, journalists and news organizations play a crucial role in enabling public deliberation of the death penalty, whether as part of broader policy and public safety conversations or through their ability to amplify voices that would otherwise go unheard. As Angela Davis points out, prisons function "ideologically as an abstract site into which undesirables are deposited, relieving us of the responsibility of thinking about the real issues afflicting those communities from which prisoners are drawn in disproportionate numbers."[22] When media outlets call attention to capital punishment, as some have done in covering the moral and judicial arguments of leaders (such as Pope Francis, former attorney general Eric Holder, and several Supreme Court justices and politicians) or by sensationalizing the "botched execution" of Clayton Lockett and the protests surrounding the execution of Troy Davis, that spotlight has the capacity to introduce, activate, and negate interpretive frames among audience members.

In 2014 CNN began airing a series titled *Death Row Stories*. Narrated by Susan Sarandon and produced by Robert Redford, the series examines the cases of people who have lived on death row; some have been found innocent and exonerated, some are still in prison, and others have been executed in the name of justice. In addition to bringing viewers closer to the stories of death row inmates and the victims of the crimes for which they were sentenced, the series also interrogates the U.S. legal system and the prosecutors who participate in charging innocent people with capital crimes. Currently hoping for renewal for a third season, the program "explores cases that pose hard questions about the U.S. capital punishment system."[23]

Background

I chose to analyze episode 8 of the first season of *Death Row Stories* because of the ways in which Nathan Dunlap's story articulates to Gary Haugen's. Dunlap and Haugen, their crimes, and their victims are, at the same time, also distinguishable in a number of ways. Although it is true that both Dunlap and Haugen committed murder at the age of nineteen, have histories of mental illness and abuse, and may both be seen as having sought revenge for perceived wrongdoing, theirs are also very different stories. Dunlap was convicted of the aggravated murder of four employees of Chuck E. Cheese's and the attempted murder of a fifth; he was sentenced to death in 1996. Haugen was sentenced to life in prison for murdering the mother of his former girlfriend in 1981 and was later sentenced to death after being convicted, along with a codefendant, of the murder of a fellow inmate in 2007. Dunlap is African American; Haugen identifies as white. Dunlap was sentenced to death as a young man; Haugen was forty-five when he received his death sentence. Dunlap committed a quadruple murder at a former place of employment; Haugen murdered a close acquaintance and, many years later, another inmate in what could be described as residential settings. Dunlap used a gun; Haugen did not.

Common Characterizations and Events

Despite these differences, similar characterizations, themes (such as inadequate legal defense and mental illness), and events, including the parallel granting of unprecedented temporary reprieves by Oregon's then governor John Kitzhaber and Colorado's governor John Hickenlooper, tie the two stories together. In fact, as characters in these death row stories, the two governors are alike in more than first name.

Governor Hickenlooper becomes a major character late in the CNN episode, as Dunlap's case did not land on his desk until an appeal for clemency in 2013, with the execution impending. He characterizes his decision to issue a reprieve, which simply defers the issue, as "the hardest decision" because of the criticism from both sides. At the same time, the episode highlights the "swift and vitriolic" reaction from those who favored Dunlap's execution, with audio excerpts of callers saying the governor "basically made a mockery out of the judicial system" and calling him a "ball-less wonder." A clip features the father of one of the murder victims saying, "I just felt like he was driving a tank over us."[24] The extralegal setting for the governor's decision is highlighted, with the district attorney stating, "They found him guilty and sentenced to him to death based on laws that were passed . . . and remain on the books to this day."[25]

The criticisms are similar in Gary Haugen's case. In 2011 John Kitzhaber was governor of Oregon and set the precedent for Hickenlooper's otherwise unprecedented move. No one was more critical of the governor's decision than the family members of Haugen's victims.[26] No one, perhaps, except Gary Haugen, who abandoned his appeals in order to force one of two logical conclusions: he would either be put to death by the state or succeed in challenging the state's death penalty statute. Haugen writes, "Did we make a change? Is this the beginning of an erosion of a system broken? I can't let things just float along. I'm thinking constitutional attorneys, someone with the knowledge to attack this reprieve—does the gov's [sic] reprieve trump my constitutional rights? This is new ground."[27]

Due in part to the timing of our acquaintance, Haugen's frustration has often been directed toward the judicial system and the attorneys with whom he battled over issues of defense strategy and mental competency. In conversations and letters, he also expresses disgust toward some of the other people imprisoned at the penitentiary and on death row (particularly those who have harmed children) and echoes the criticism of other abolitionists that the "worst of the worst" are not always the ones who end up on death row.

As mentioned previously, Haugen's harshest criticism is reserved for the criminal justice system and former governor Kitzhaber, whom he characterizes in ways similar to the media characterizations of Hickenlooper—as self-interested and cowardly. Haugen is angry with Kitzhaber on two counts that are inextricably wound together and beg a question that undergirds too many death penalty cases: Does delay and deferral of death sentences constitute cruel and unusual punishment? Kitzhaber issued a "temporary reprieve in the case of Gary Haugen" and stated that he refused "to be a part of this compromised and inequitable system any longer."[28] The court that issued the death warrant failed to issue a new death warrant before the original warrant expired after the governor abruptly left office, and Haugen remains on Oregon's death row to this day. Kitzhaber's November 2011 statement is still true:

> The death penalty as practiced in Oregon is neither fair nor just; and it is not swift or certain. It is not applied equally to all. It is a perversion of justice that the single best indicator of who will and will not be executed has nothing to do with the circumstances of a crime or the findings of a jury. The only factor that determines whether someone sentenced to death in Oregon is actually executed is that they volunteer. The hard truth is that in the 27 years since Oregonians reinstated the death penalty, it has only been carried out on two volunteers who waived their rights to appeal. In the years since those executions, many judges, district attorneys, legislators, death penalty proponents and opponents, and victims and their families have agreed that Oregon's system is broken.[29]

It is important to note that both governors chose only to defer the issue and absolve themselves of direct complicity in the killing, not to alter the status of the condemned. Prosecutors in both states still seek the death penalty for capital crimes, and death rows continue to be populated at enormous cost to the citizens of these states. Exonerations from life sentences and death row continue to occur in other, mostly southern, states where prosecutorial misconduct, faulty testimony, and inadequate defense trouble the justice system. Thus, it is not only the governors who play similar roles but also trial attorneys who feature prominently in the stories: both Dunlap and Haugen have alleged that their defense counsel was ineffective.

Common Themes
In his capital case Gary Haugen was tried with a codefendant whose appeals have not yet been abandoned. Haugen feels that the nature of the prison environment contributed to his confrontation with his victim but points out that complicating factors were omitted or downplayed in his trial. In one of Gary Haugen's letters, he describes the sudden offers of help that appeared as soon as he abandoned his appeals: "Attorneys claiming they can save your life from the lame duck attorneys who sold you out (though those attorneys called themselves the *dream team*)."[30] Elsewhere he writes about "trying this case as it should have been in the first place"[31] and mentions that he "fought a guy who was armed," stating that he was "scared like nothing in my life ever. The gods smiled on me and I came out alive—the will to survive is a powerful thing!"[32]

In the direct appeal of his sentence, the court notes that a key witness for the prosecution exhibited bias toward the defendant(s) during the cross-examination phase of the trial.[33] The witness also stated that he was a friend of the victim and felt that there were "all kinds of rats in this prison bigger than him. Why not them?" Although these statements do not explain Haugen's assault of fellow inmate David Polin, they are indications of some of the problems that plague the criminal justice and prison system—namely, ineffectual counsel, dangerous environments, and poor mental health management.

In Dunlap's case, the episode of *Death Row Stories* emphasizes the claims about inadequate defense in Dunlap's trial as the primary argument, in addition to his now-managed bipolar disorder, for a reprieve from Governor Hickenlooper. The narrator also sets the stage early in the episode by stating, "At trial, Nathan's lawyers called almost no witnesses, and offered little defense for his actions. It took the jury only three and a half hours to come to a verdict." In light of the overwhelming evidence of Dunlap's guilt, this last fact may not seem surprising, until the episode raises concerns about mitigating circumstances, including mental illness. Later the narrator points out, "During trial, Nathan's attorneys never mentioned his psychiatric evaluations or the idea he may have been suffering from a mental break during the massacre." The theme of mental illness connects the two stories and articulates them to a larger critique of society and the family. Nathan Dunlap's attorneys and supporters claim that his bipolar disorder, left unmanaged, contributed to both his erratic behavior in the courtroom during his trial and to his behavior behind bars, both before and after sentencing. In the CNN episode, Aurora police officer Joe Petrucelli describes Dunlap's behavior: "Nathan lost it. He blew up. He was screaming. . . . When you saw him and you saw the look on his face, he was a different person." Video footage of the trial shows Dunlap turning to his sister in the courtroom, swearing and desperately crying, "I can't do this." The narrator points out that "during the run up to trial, Nathan's behavior became erratic including violent mood swings, signs of depression, and even incidents of spreading feces over his cell and on himself," after which he was "put on suicide watch and moved to a padded cell." His sister Adinea visited him in jail and also suspected "something is not right. His eyes were glassy. And his hair was everywhere. And he was rambling. And I was trying to get him to calm down."

Because Nathan Dunlap's voice is absent from the *Death Row Stories* episode, he is presented to us only in secondhand accounts and archival footage of his trial, which reinforces the theme of mental illness and stresses the callousness of the murders he committed. His only advocate in the episode is his sister, Adinea Dunlap-Ashlock, who describes her brother's mental state at the time as similar to their mother's during a manic episode brought on by bipolar disorder: "His eyes reminded me of seeing my mother when she was in a manic episode. When I saw him, I saw her eyes."

Not long after Dunlap's sentencing, the State of Colorado executed its first prisoner in almost three decades. In the episode former prosecutor Eva Wilson highlights the impact the execution had on Dunlap: "The guards were taunting him that he was next. And that day he had a manic break. He really just started ranting and raving and had to be hospitalized shortly thereafter." Her point is tempered by footage of the district attorney George Brauchler, who asserts that there is "no competent, credible doctors that will tell you his evil conduct was the product of being in a manic state, that his conduct was somehow altered by being bipolar or suffering any other mental illness." Yet, later in the episode, the narrator and Dunlap-Ashlock comment on the change in Nathan's personality and behavior when, in 2006, he was diagnosed as bipolar by prison doctors and put on the powerful drug lithium. Sarandon narrates, "Once medicated, Nathan's behavior on Death Row changed radically. And he became a model prisoner." His sister says, "He was an entirely different person from the young man even that I knew. So it certainly has to be a part of why he did what he did."

Likewise, Gary Haugen's mental illness may very well have contributed to his mental state during the murders for which he was convicted. A 2011 Amnesty International action alert states that he "was diagnosed with mood and seizure disorders" and taken off of the drug Neurontin at the time of the attack, and a psychiatrist testified at his capital trial that he had diagnosed Gary with "intermittent explosive personality disorder and partial complex seizures." The action alert continues,

> A second mental health expert also provided his opinion that it was likely that Gary Haugen suffered from partial complex seizures and had committed an "explosive act" when taken off Neurontin. Prior to the trial, the defence lawyers had sought to have quantitative electroencephalography (QEEG) testing of Gary Haugen to assess the extent of his mental dysfunction, but this type of brain mapping was not available at the time in Oregon.[34]

A neuropsychologist retained by his defense team assessed Haugen as having significant attention deficit disorder and impaired cognitive functioning related to fetal alcohol syndrome and noted that he has sustained repeated head trauma and experiences blackouts. Indeed, the stories of the murders committed by Gary Haugen suggest "explosive acts" that occurred twenty-two years apart and were accompanied by blackouts. Court proceedings indicate that he has a history of mental health issues and heroin abuse.

In a letter Gary wrote shortly after we began our correspondence in 2010, he describes himself to me as a "bipolar con with rejection issues."[35] In the weeks leading up to his execution date, a close friend disappeared into her own grief and anger over his abandonment of his appeals. Gary Haugen expressed his pain at her absence from his life during a critical "end of life" period, writing, "I'm not bullshitting, I'm sick inside—I feel like a piece of me is missing, ole girl got me fucked up. I want to just tear this joint down. Fuck this place—superficial ass world."[36]

Uncommon Representations

Not surprisingly, Dunlap and Haugen and the governors who have halted their executions, for now, are the principal characters in these death row stories. The theme of mental illness as mitigating circumstance is a central feature of both stories and frames the events that have ensued. But there are two other significant and noteworthy representations the stories share in common: sisters and victims' family members. The latter, with few exceptions, want to see the people who murdered their loved ones put to death. It is important that an essay focused so heavily on people who have committed murder acknowledge the justifiable desire for vengeance and closure felt by the loved ones of Dunlap's and Haugen's victims. These death row stories would not be complete if they did not include the anguish and anger of the people affected by the murders committed by Gary Haugen and Nathan Dunlap. Their sisters, however, articulate alternative stories and construct new realities that challenge the conception that criminals are undeserving of compassion, a premise that has been necessary to shore up capital punishment as a public policy.

The stories of Dunlap's and Haugen's sisters are significant precisely because of how they use ethos and pathos to articulate audience members to people who have committed capital murder—through their family ties and the shared trauma of parental violence. It is worth stating again that these stories are not presented as justifications for Dunlap's and Haugen's crimes. Instead, the stories serve to articulate a profile of the capital murderer as someone who fell through the cracks, a story that hints at societal and

166 *Emily Plec*

institutional complicity in the failure to protect children from violence and abuse. In fact, Dunlap's and Haugen's sisters function rhetorically as evidence that people can survive horrific abuse without inflicting it upon others, as they were subjected to sexual, physical, and psychological torment alongside and apart from their brothers. Their presence in the stories is the redemptive possibility to which their brothers' lives are articulated. Moreover, they provide alternative ways of seeing Dunlap and Haugen, as brothers rather than killers. Their relationships are reminders that a person is worth more than his worst deeds, such as when Gary Haugen attempted to donate a portion of his liver to save his eldest sister, Debra, in 2000.

As mentioned previously, Adinea and Nathan Dunlap grew up in a household troubled by untreated mental illness. Carol Dunlap, Adinea and Nathan's mother, suffered from bipolar disorder (as did her father and brother) and would "berate the children, wake them up at night, walk around the house naked." Adinea indicates that their mother had been institutionalized, and she also describes ongoing victimization by their father:

> The abuse and intimidation from my dad started very early with Nathan by grabbing him by the collar, picking him up. It wasn't anything for him to hit him and knock him. . . . My dad did sexually abuse me probably from the time I was about nine until fourteen. And there was a time where Nathan came downstairs when some of this was going on. And my dad thought he saw it. And I think after that, the abuse was really bad. I mean, it was horrible.

Letters from Gary and his half sister, as well as testimony offered by another sister during his first murder trial, tell a similar story of family psychosis and abuse. Their parents would terrorize the children and threaten them with beatings. Clearly suffering from mental illness, their mother would scold her children for being dirty then scrub their little bodies until their skin was raw and bleeding. Later, after their mother split from Gary's father, the boys went into foster homes, and their mother moved and gave birth to a biracial daughter. Gary and his brother were later reunited with their father and stepmother, but his father's alcoholism and abuse continued. He explains that he and his brother "knew deep in our hearts that it wouldn't last, but as [stepmother] helped us pack for a new life in Oregon, little did we know that within a year we would be helping her pack to save her life. My dad almost beat us to death for that one, but better us than [stepmother]. . . . Sitting on the stand was the first time that I saw her since the day me and my little brother helped her pack."[37]

Living with their mother, Gary's half sister was psychologically, sexually, and physically abused throughout her youth by men her mother knew, and then she entered into a string of abusive relationships as a teen and young adult, seeking refuge from her home life. Remarkably, she has endeavored against odds to protect her own children and build a life of security, an ongoing battle that she is committed to winning. Though they had spent time together as children, it was not until he was considering abandoning his appeals that Gary Haugen reunited with his biracial half sister (who is half black), who had reached out to him several times during his incarceration.[38] Her experience of Gary is as a brother, an occasional emotional support system, a world-wise uncle to her already world-weary children, and a part of her family, for better or worse. She does not see the killer the media have depicted, just the damaged brother who still has a lot of good in him and a lot of love to give.

Three of Gary's siblings have already passed away; his half sister is an important part of his life, but her presence is also troubling because it is a reminder that his death will only end his pain; it cannot end hers, mine, or the pain endured by the loved ones of his victims. Nathan Dunlap's sister, Adinea, likewise reminds us that we are more than individuals acting alone, removed from others and from the ripples of our actions. The articulation of these sister stories is significant because it reconnects us to an idea of family, of human obligation and kinship that is fundamentally antithetical to the idea that there are people who deserve to die for the things they have done. Their stories embody the empty promise of closure, for as Hartnett and Larson point out, "Closure is often cast by its supporters as an ending, a sealing off, a walling away of pain; yet it is more accurately described as a passing along, a handing off, a transfer of pain from one class of victims to another class of victims."[39]

And yet it is this last point that continues to trouble me and that articulates Nathan Dunlap's and Gary Haugen's death row stories to so many others. Dunlap and Haugen killed people. The people they killed left behind loved ones who will mourn those senseless murders for the rest of their lives. Most of these people believe that Dunlap and Haugen deserve to die for their crimes. Their executions are supposed to bring closure, to give finality, to provide the retributive justice that vengeful heart's desire. Neither story is capable of completely challenging this presumption. Even the stories of Haugen's and Dunlap's sisters, which humanize and complicate their brothers' lives in ways worth noting, which remind us that murderers too have loved ones who will mourn homicides committed in the name of justice; even these stories are incapable of rearticulating life to justice, of reinvigorating a belief in rehabilitation and redemption.

Instead, we are left with loose ends and questions: Why is it that so many black men sit on Colorado's death row? Nathan Dunlap is one of more than twelve hundred African Americans on death row, who together constitute almost 42 percent of capital convictions. At the same time, Gary Haugen believes that, were he black, his case would receive more public attention. (I counter that, were he black, they would have executed him already). Why is one county (Multnomah, whose seat is Portland) responsible for the vast majority of capital cases in Oregon when heinous murders have been committed all over the state? In the *Death Row Stories* episode, journalist Natasha Gardner says, "In some counties the district attorneys go after a life without parole sentence. In some counties they are known for going after the death penalty. Should your geography really determine your fate?" In both Colorado and Oregon, it appears that it does.

Another loose end: What role do the prior offenses of people like Dunlap and Haugen play in securing capital convictions? *Death Row Stories* articulates this question to a critique of prosecutorial conduct, questioning the tactic of charging and trying a suspect for a lesser crime first, in order to suggest to jurors in the capital case the capacity of the defendant for reoffending if not put to death. And what does our public fear of reoffenders—so much so that we are willing to kill them to suppress it—say about our collective trust in the prison-industrial complex and its capacity to keep us safe from harm? Haugen and Dunlap need not be killed to ensure public safety; they need to be medicated, treated, counseled, and supported. It is likely that the people they have harmed through their criminal actions have similar needs. Neither set of needs is being met by the system we have. But we continue to throw money at it. In Haugen's case, an estimated $1.2 million in five years alone, excluding the costs of maintaining special housing for death row inmates.[40] An estimate cited in the episode of *Death Row Stories* puts the cost of Dunlap's case to the state at $18 million. What are these taxpayer dollars doing? Where does the money go? What interests are served? These are the questions that continue to emerge from these and other death row stories.

As a result of this essay, I become a storyteller in the chain of articulations and find myself thinking about my own death row story. I wonder why I am so willing to reach out to someone on the row and so reluctant to reach out to the people who have lost loved ones to murder. I think of Sister Helen's experience described in *Dead Man Walking* and how she felt when asked why she didn't offer her support to the parents of Patrick Sonnier's victims. I commit to learning more about Murder Victims' Families for Reconciliation and to thanking the penitentiary staff who have done what I do not know how to do, namely, offer support to the families of Gary's victims.

I remember my first letter to Gary, in which I attempted to set the tone for our future interactions. I explained who I was and what I wanted, as well as what I did not want. Striving to strip the introduction of any sexual innuendo, I asked him to think of me like a sister. Sisterhood is a complicated concept for a white, middle-class, antiracist feminist. It has been deftly critiqued by some of the activists and philosophers I most admire, and with good reason. The notion of sisterhood is often deployed by heterosexual, white, middle-class women in ways that obscure or even deny the role of sexuality, class, and race in oppression and inequality. In the context of prisons, sisterhood has been studied as a discourse that enables privileged prison activists on the outside to relate and bridge gaps with poor women and women of color on the inside.[41] One of the ways it does this is by bringing the activists closer to the institutional realities of people who are incarcerated. At its best, *Death Row Stories* attempts to do this as well.

I want to reinvigorate the idea of sisterhood, not as a feminist praxis for relating with other women (though that is important and relevant) but as a critical tool for deconstructing the prison-industrial complex. It is generally a small and often religiously motivated group of people who seek to befriend individuals on death row. The group is enlarged a bit by those stalwart friends and family members who have stuck with those individuals through their sentencing and incarceration. It is further graced by the loved ones of victims who have sought reconciliation by confronting and coming to know the person they've been encouraged to hate through the judicial process. The group is nurtured by those officers and staff of penal institutions who treat their wards with dignity and humanity. Sisterhood is entering that circle of compassion and consideration; it requires story.

So what kind of sister have I been to Gary and, like Adinea Dunlap-Ashlock, what other stories do I have to tell? Stories about advocating for health and medical treatment, stories about the weeks leading up to his first execution date, stories that reveal the jokes and laughs and tears we've shared, stories that juxtapose the cruelty of which he has proven capable with the compassion I have directly observed. To what extent would I compare our friendship to a familial bond? It is nothing like the "brotherhood" he performs behind bars, yet it is also protective, selfish, necessary. How can I help my other friends, family, and the citizens of my state to see in him someone greater than his worst deeds (and extrapolate that vision to all people on death row and in prison)?

Starting with Stories

Gary wrote me that night. Unable to sleep for the grinding pain in his debilitated hip (the worst he's ever felt, he said), he sat up and answered one of the questions I'd posed the last time we talked. I asked him to tell me about the foster homes in which he'd been placed as a child, and, in reply, he described the architecture and interior of a particularly impressive one in detail, even drawing a map of the front of the house and grounds. Giant walnut trees dominate the lawn, and I imagine Gary and his brother climbing them, chucking the large nuts at each other and at their foster brothers.

> Well, you get the picture. Beautiful home, parents had their little quirks, overprotective parents. The sons were weaklings, Tim and I weren't allowed to touch any of their stuff. One day Tim was checking out the telescope looking at the moon. Never seen the moon before. The younger son flipped out, crying, yelling, "Mom he's touching my telescope." They treated us like we were dirty, that they were better than us. The younger son reached out and touched Tim in an attempt to pull him away from his telescope and my brother having never seen the moon before was amazed and turned and pushed the kid just as their mom walked in. The kid hit the floor and his mom snatched Tim up and started spanking wherever she could hit. Tim pushed and pulled away from her. She was aghast. How dare this child that she so graciously brought into her home defy her in such an insolent manner? You get the picture. So it was on. We beat their ass every chance we got and they always went crying to their mom or dad and we would get spanked.
>
> So this went on for a time. The [foster family] owned some apartments next to their home. I remember going with my foster dad to the apartments to do some fixing up. Apparently one of the female tenant's boyfriend kicked the door in and beat her up pretty bad. The bathroom door was damaged and there was holes in the walls. So as I helped him repair the apartment, I asked what had happened and my foster dad was real evasive and told me to just clean up or go back home. I found out later that the lady had died and her boyfriend, or I should say ex-, went O.J. on her.

I remember thinking that we couldn't get away from it, the violence!

Eventually the foster mom got ill and Tim and I were just too much so we were sent to a different home. As bad as things might have been, shit, it was the most stable home Tim and I had ever seen.[42]

Notes

1. I wonder, as I read my own journal, if this isn't an example of what Conquergood critiques as the "hegemony of textualism." See Conquergood, "Performance Studies."

2. For more information about Abu-Jamal's legal efforts to receive treatment for hepatitis C, see "Mumia Abu-Jamal and the Fight," iMIXWHATiLike.

3. PCARE maintains a blog at http://p-care.org/ and published *Working for Justice: A Handbook of Prison Education and Activism* (2013).

4. "Facts about the Death Penalty," Death Penalty Information Center.

5. Statistics taken from the latest "Facts about the Death Penalty," Death Penalty Information Center Fact Sheet; see also Alexander, *New Jim Crow*; Ogletree and Sarat, *From Lynch Mobs to the Killing State*; Dieter, *Death Penalty in Black and White*.

6. Stern, "Cruel and Unusual?"; Von Drehle, "Last Execution."

7. Fisher, *Human Communication as Narration*.

8. Prejean, *Death of Innocents*.

9. Josselson, "Imagining the Real."

10. Conquergood, "Rethinking Ethnography," 183.

11. Hall, "On Postmodernism and Articulation."

12. Slack, "Theory and Method of Articulation."

13. Brooker, *Concise Glossary of Cultural Theory*, 11.

14. Barker, *Cultural Studies*, 9–10.

15. Slack, "Theory and Method of Articulation," 114.

16. Hartnett, *Executing Democracy*, vol. 1; Hartnett, *Executing Democracy*, vol. 2.

17. Dixon and Azocar, "Priming Crime and Activating Blackness"; Farr, "Defeminizing and Dehumanizing Female Murders"; Gado, *Death Row Women*.

18. Till and Vitouch, "Capital Punishment in Films"; Dardis, Baumgartner, Boydstun, De Boef, and Shen, "Media Framing of Capital Punishment"; Diaz and Garza, "Troy Davis Effect"; Ramirez, "Americans' Changing Views."

19. Bock and Araiza, "Facing the Death Penalty"; McCann, "Redemption in the Neoliberal and Radical Imaginations"; Asenas, McCann, Feyh, and Cloud, "Saving Kenneth Foster."

20. Hartnett and Larson, "Tonight Another Man Will Die"; Gavriloš, "Should the Death Penalty be Abolished?"; McCann, "Therapeutic and Material <Victim> hood"; Langford, "Tinkering with the Machinery of Death."

21. Temple, *Last Lawyer*; Culbert, *Dead Certainty*; SunWolf, "Facilitating Death Talk"; Conley, "Living with the Decision That Someone Will Die."

22. Davis, *Are Prisons Obsolete?*, 16.

23. *Death Row Stories*, CNN.

24. Prior to announcing his decision, Hickenlooper met with a victim's family members and was given a book that included crime scene photos and letters from family members, in addition to psychological reports that undermined Dunlap's claims that bipolar disorder had contributed to his crime. The ordering of these events makes Hickenlooper's decision appear somewhat dismissive of the desire by most (but not all) victims' family members to proceed with execution.

25. "Nathan Dunlap: Eye for an Eye," *Death Row Stories*.

26. "Victim's Family Calls Ore. Governor a Coward," King-TV.

27. Gary Haugen, letter to author, December 25, 2011.

28. Kitzhaber, "Statement on Capital Punishment."

29. Ibid.

30. Gary Haugen, letter to author, February 6, 2011.

31. Gary Haugen, letter to author, January 23, 2011.

32. Gary Haugen, letter to author, July 30, 2010.

33. State of Oregon v. Gary Haugen 243 P.3d 31 (Or. 2010). The decision of the Supreme Court of the State of Oregon on Gary Haugen's appeal of his death sentence is available here: http://www.publications.ojd.state.or.us/docs/S054853.htm.

34. Amnesty International "Urgent Action."

35. Gary Haugen, letter to author, September 11, 2010.

36. Gary Haugen, letter to author, December 25, 2011.

37. Gary Haugen, secure email to author, January 5, 2015.

38. Extending the idea of family once he was incarcerated, Gary was mentored by several men who became his "brothers" and entered into the racial politics of a prison system in which whiteness is articulated to a complex cultural identity. As he puts it, in a secure email to me on April 9, 2016:

> Just because someone chooses to preserve their culture and heritage doesn't make them haters. One can't always choose their blood line or family, but it's how they deal with it that reveals the growth, intellect and wisdom of the human being. I'm fortunate to have affiliations/brothers who some may think are knuckle draggers, however we come from a line of knuckle draggers who invented fire.

39. Hartnett and Larson, "Tonight Another Man Will Die," 274.

40. Associated Press, "Tab for Haugen Case: $1.2M."

41. Lawson, "We're All Sisters."

42. Gary Haugen, letter to author, November 18, 2016.

Bibliography

Alexander, Michelle. *The New Jim Crow: Mass Incarceration in the Age of Colorblindness*. New York: New Press, 2012.

Amnesty International. "Urgent Action: First Oregon Execution in 14 Years Looming." Amnesty International, October 20, 2011. Accessed October 4, 2017. https://www.amnesty.se.

Asenas, Jennifer, Bryan J. McCann, Kathleen Feyh, and Dana Cloud. "Saving Kenneth Foster: Speaking with Others in the Belly of the Beast of Capital Punishment." In *Communication Activism*, vol. 3: *Struggling for Social Justice amidst Difference*, edited by Lawrence R. Frey and Kevin M. Carragee, 263–90. Cresskill, NJ: Hampton, 2011.

Associated Press. "Tab for Haugen Case: $1.2M." Updated July 17, 2012. Accessed April 30, 2016. http://www.opb.org/news/article/tab-haugen-case-12m/.

Barker, Chris. *Cultural Studies: Theory and Practice*. Thousand Oaks, CA: Sage, 2000.

Bock, Mary Angela, and José Andrés Araiza. "Facing the Death Penalty While Facing the Cameras." *Journalism Practice* 9, no. 3 (2015): 314–31.

Brooker, Peter. *A Concise Glossary of Cultural Theory*. London: Hodder Education.

Conley, Robin. "Living with the Decision That Someone Will Die: Linguistic Distance and Empathy in Jurors' Death Penalty Decisions." *Language in Society* 42, no. 5 (2013): 503–26.

Conquergood, Dwight. "Performance Studies: Interventions and Radical Research." *Drama Review* 46 (2002): 145–56.

———. "Rethinking Ethnography: Towards a Critical Cultural Politics." *Communication Monographs* 58 (1991): 179–94.

Culbert, Jennifer L. *Dead Certainty: The Death Penalty and the Problem of Judgment*. Stanford, CA: Stanford University Press, 2008.

Dardis, Frank E., Frank R. Baumgartner, Amber E. Boydstun, Suzanna De Boef, and Fuyuan Shen. "Media Framing of Capital Punishment and Its Impact on Individuals' Cognitive Responses." *Mass Communication & Society* 11, no. 2 (2008): 115–40.

Davis, Angela. *Are Prisons Obsolete?* New York: Seven Stories, 2003.

Death Row Stories. Season 1. Produced by Jigsaw Productions and Sundance Productions. Distributed by Cable News Network (CNN), 2014. Accessed February 4, 2016. http://www.cnn.com/shows/death-row-stories.

Derrida, Jacques. "Sixth Session, February 2, 2000." In *The Death Penalty*. Vol. 1, edited by Geoffrey Bennington, Marc Crépon, and Thomas Dutoit. Translated by Peggy Kamuf, 138–65. Chicago: University of Chicago Press, 2014.

Diaz, Stephanie, and Ray Garza. "The Troy Davis Effect: Does Information on Wrongful Convictions Affect Death Penalty Opinions?" *Journal of Ethnicity in Criminal Justice 13* (2015): 111–30.

Dieter, Richard C. *The Death Penalty in Black and White: Who Lives, Who Dies, and Who Decides.* Death Penalty Information Center, 1998. Accessed October 7, 2015. http://www.deathpenaltyinfo.org.

Dixon, Travis L., and Cristina L. Azocar. "Priming Crime and Activating Blackness: Understanding the Psychological Impact of the Overrepresentation of Blacks as Lawbreakers on Television News." *Journal of Communication* 57, no. 2 (2007): 229–53.

"Facts about the Death Penalty." Death Penalty Information Center. Updated November 29, 2017. http://www.deathpenaltyinfo.org/documents/FactSheet.pdf.

Farr, Kathryn Ann. "Defeminizing and Dehumanizing Female Murderers: Depictions of Lesbians on Death Row." *Women & Criminal Justice* 11, no. 1 (2000): 49–66.

Fisher, Walter. *Human Communication as Narration: Toward a Philosophy of Reason, Value, and Action.* Columbia: University of South Carolina Press, 1989.

Gado, Mark. *Death Row Women: Murder, Justice, and the New York Press.* Westport, CT: Praeger, 2008.

Gavrilš, Adina Nicoleta. "Should the Death Penalty Be Abolished? Arguments for and against the Centuries-Old Punishment." *Journal for Communication & Culture* 1, no. 2 (2011): 82–98.

Hall, Stuart. "On Postmodernism and Articulation: An Interview with Stuart Hall." Edited by Lawrence Grossberg. *Journal of Communication Inquiry* 10 (1986): 45–60.

Hartnett, Stephen. *Executing Democracy.* Vol. 1 of *Capital Punishment and the Making of America, 1693–1807.* East Lansing: Michigan State University Press, 2012.

———. *Executing Democracy.* Vol. 2 of *Capital Punishment and the Making of America, 1835–1843.* East Lansing: Michigan State University Press, 2012.

Hartnett, Stephen John, and Daniel Mark Larson. "'Tonight Another Man Will Die': Crime, Violence, and the Master Tropes of Contemporary Arguments about the Death Penalty." *Communication & Critical/Cultural Studies* 3, no. 4 (2006): 263–87.

Josselson, Ruthellen. "Imagining the Real: Empathy, Narrative, and the Dialogic Self." In *Interpreting Experience: The Narrative Study of Lives*, edited by Ruthellen H. Josselson and Amia Lieblich, 27–44. Thousand Oaks, CA: Sage, 1995.

Kitzhaber, John. "Statement on Capital Punishment." November 22, 2011. Accessed October 4, 2017. http://media.oregonlive.com.

Langford, Catherine L. "Tinkering with the Machinery of Death: the Body-as-Gauge in Discourses about Capital Punishment." *Argumentation & Advocacy* 51, no. 3 (2015): 153–70.

Lawson, Jodie Michelle. "'We're All Sisters': Bridging and Legitimacy in the Women's Antiprison Movement." *Gender and Society* 23, no. 5 (2009): 639–64.

McCann, Bryan J. "Redemption in the Neoliberal and Radical Imaginations: The Saga of Stanley 'Tookie' Williams." *Communication, Culture & Critique* 7, no. 1 (2014): 92–111.

———. "Therapeutic and Material <Victim> hood: Ideology and the Struggle for Meaning in the Illinois Death Penalty Controversy." *Communication & Critical/Cultural Studies* 4, no. 4 (2007): 382–401.

"Mumia Abu-Jamal and the Fight over Prisoner Rights and Healthcare." iMIXWHATiLike. Last modified December 24, 2015. Accessed October 4, 2017. https://imixwhatilike.org.

"Nathan Dunlap: Eye for an Eye." *Death Row Stories*. Season 1, episode 8. Distributed by Cable News Network (CNN), July 27, 2014.

Ogletree, Charles, and Austin Sarat. *From Lynch Mobs to the Killing State: Race and the Death Penalty in America*. New York: New York University Press, 2006.

Prejean, Helen. *The Death of Innocents: An Eyewitness Account of Wrongful Executions*. New York: Random House, 2005.

Ramirez, Mark. "Americans' Changing Views on Crime and Capital Punishment." *Public Opinion Quarterly* 77 (2013): 1006–1031.

Slack, Jennifer. "The Theory and Method of Articulation in Cultural Studies." In *Stuart Hall: Critical Dialogues in Cultural Studies*, edited by David Morley and Kuan-Hsing Chen, 112–30. London: Routledge, 1996.

Stern, Jeffery. "Cruel and Unusual? The Botched Execution of Clayton Lockett—and How Capital Punishment Became So Surreal." *Atlantic*, June 2015.

SunWolf. "Facilitating Death Talk." In *Communication Activism, Vol. 1: Communication for Social Change*, edited by Lawrence R. Frey and Kevin M. Carragee, 287–323. Cresskill, NJ: Hampton, 2007.

Temple, John. *The Last Lawyer: The Fight to Save Death Row Inmates.* Jackson: University of Mississippi Press, 2009.

Till, Benedikt, and Peter Vitouch. "Capital Punishment in Films: The Impact of Death Penalty Portrayals on Viewers' Mood and Attitude toward Capital Punishment." *International Journal of Public Opinion Research* 24, no. 3 (2012): 387–99.

"Victim's Family Calls Ore. Governor a Coward over Death Penalty Decision." King-TV, November 30, 2011. Accessed March 6, 2016. http://www.king5 .com/story/news/local/2014/08/02/13039816/.

Von Drehle, David. "The Last Execution: Why the Era of Capital Punishment Is Ending." *Time*, June 8, 2015.

8. Manufacturing Masculinity and Hope through Media Production

Kalen Churcher

We're not in the Dark Ages anymore, where it's chains and balls and stripes. I believe we do more positive things for the prison in this capacity than we can out there in the fields with an axe or a shovel, digging in the dirt. I learned that being with the inmates for so long, they have confidence in us. They have trust in us. We can say one thing to 'em, and you can come say that thing, and when you say it, "Ah phony baloney. But if I tell it to 'em, they'll receive it. So for the people who feel we shouldn't be in these types of jobs, I think they need the grace of God in their lives.

—Donald Spencer, an Angola inmate, on the importance of inmate-produced media

Who is the male prisoner? What does he look like, and perhaps more important for this reading, how does he act? From *Law & Order* to *Oz*, *Prison Break* to *Orange Is the New Black*, television is rife with prison and law-related dramas that answer, intentionally and accurately or not, the aforementioned questions. These programs, and those that came before them, have helped craft a cultural construction of prisoners often rooted in violence, homoeroticism, and intricate power structures. The end result is an extreme Othering of the more than 1.56 million individuals incarcerated in the United States in state or federal prisons.[1]

If one believes that a person's gender identity—in this case masculinity—is continually adapting, often in response to particular events or situations,[2] then surely the high-pressure environment of a prison would serve as an impetus for further adaptation. For at least a small cross section of incarcerated men at the Louisiana State Penitentiary at Angola,[3] through the production of prison media, being a "man" is about more than the hypermasculine stereo-types afforded to them. Masculinity, at least in part, means finding purpose and, in some cases, effectuating change—even if the men themselves are unlikely ever to leave the prison. Men working with the inmate-run media outlets—a magazine, radio station and television station—have the power to be agenda makers and trendsetters for the general prison population. Simul-taneously, the men also manufacture hope, hope that they, and others, may someday continue their lives beyond the confines of a penitentiary. Though inmate-produced media are a rarity both in production and research, their potential are worthy of further study and exploration, with just one prison's media illustrated here.

Prison television and radio stations are still relatively new to the pe-nal system, although the prison press has been around since the 1800 creation of *Forlorn Hope* by William Keteltas in New York's debtors' prison. Despite its presence in almost every U.S. state, as well as its deep historic roots,[4] the prison press has changed dramatically in the last two centuries. Such publications, once akin to mainstream newspapers, have all but vanished from prison systems. Those that have survived have largely transformed into prose journals. Yet even prison journals that have birthed prison poetry[5] have begun slowly to lose their footing in state and local penitentiaries, making historical tracking of them even more pertinent.

This chapter stems from a longitudinal project examining Angola's triad of inmate-produced media.[6] More than 260 hours of direct, on-site obser-vations were conducted in 2007 and 2011, and more than forty in-depth structured and semistructured interviews were held with inmates and prison employees. In addition, more than three decades of the inmate-produced *Angolite* magazine were analyzed for historical context and trends. Inmates were asked, among other questions, why they work in media and what they derive from doing so. This chapter represents a small but telling portion of their answers. Though focused on media employees, this chapter's insights could also apply to other high-profile inmate employment opportunities, including inmate religious or legal counselors. Admittedly, the influence of media and the celebrity status of media "stars" make identity construction for these inmates particularly noteworthy. The end result, though, is sim-ple: for Angola's inmates, the vast majority of whom are destined to die in prison, life in a maximum-security men's prison need not be only violent and oppressive; it can be purposeful.

Situating Angola

Angola is unique. Bordered by the rugged Tunica Hills and the Mississippi River, the penitentiary is roughly the size of Manhattan and, as of 2015, home to more than six thousand men,[7] the majority of whom are serving life or life-equivalent sentences. It is also the site of some of the South's lushest farmland, with new inmates put to work almost immediately harvesting crops that go toward feeding the prison population. It takes only a few moments of looking into the fields to understand why some inmates consider LSP-Angola not the Louisiana State Penitentiary but rather the Last Slave Plantation. Under the hot Louisiana sun, it is easy to spot lines of muscular, (predominantly) black men picking vegetables, their shirts and pants soaked from sweat. With temperatures topping one hundred degrees and work to be done, the men must "man up" and complete their duties. Are there complaints? Yes, but the complaints are more representative of "complaining to complain" than of weakness.

Visually, Angola is still eerily reminiscent of a stereotypic antebellum plantation or chain gang location. However, Angola is not the same penitentiary it once was, even as recently as half a century ago. Today, the administration classifies inmates into levels by their crimes and behavior and then awards privileges accordingly. The levels are more commonly referred to as a prisoner's *trusty* status, a term that shares a name—but little more—with an old organizational management system that used inmate trusties to handle basic daily prison operations, control the prison population, administer punishment, and guard other prisoners.[8] This classic hierarchal structure was marked by violence and utilized hegemonic masculinity to maintain order. In 1974 the U.S. Court of Appeals for the Fifth Circuit upheld a lower court decision to end, among other prison-related practices, this type of trusty guard system. According to the *Gates v. Collier* decision, trusties were instructed to maintain discipline by shooting at inmates who got out of "gun line"; in many cases trusties had received little training in the handling of firearms. In addition to abusing their authority and engaging in loan-sharking, extortion, and other illegal conduct, the trusties shot, maimed, or otherwise physically maltreated scores of inmates subject to their control.[9]

During the time of inmate guards, violence was the norm. As late as 1969, published accounts indicate the penitentiary utilized 239 of the trusty guards.[10] However, by the midseventies, the state followed the *Gates v. Collier* decision and eliminated the trusty system as it had been known,[11] though the inmate classification system that exists today bears a similarity in name. This did not end the perpetration of violence at the penitentiary; it did, however, allow for a framework to be laid for a more rehabilitative institution.

From a historical perspective, modern Angola could serve as an exemplar of transformation regarding constructed masculinity. Once described as America's bloodiest prison, the penitentiary has undergone a religious rebirth, attributed largely to Warden Burl Cain's emphasis on moral rehabilitation. Formerly Angola was a dangerous place:

> At a time in the late sixties when the Louisiana State Penitentiary was at the height of what prison journalists call its "knock 'em down and drag 'em out" days, Angola . . . was considered one of the nation's worst, a brutal world of violence and intrigue, political abuse and racial turmoil, where a staggering one in ten inmates would suffer stab wounds annually and others slept with thick mail-order catelogues [*sic*] taped to the chest to deflect knives in the night.[12]

Modern Angola is very different, however, according to one inmate:

> INMATE 1: When you think that right now we're sitting in a room in the heart of the main prison complex, where there are over two thousand inmates all around you, and most people would say, "Man. This is a dangerous place." Just because of that name "Angola" and the stigmas attached to it from years past . . . being the bloodiest prison in the nation. But you can see the change in that people would say, "Wait a minute. I think we can do this. I think we can have a radio station. I think we can have a television station. I think we can have an *Angolite*. I think we can allow the inmates to voice themselves through those medias, because there's something different about these men. They're a changed group of men."

But how have the men changed? To say that no violence, machismo, or other egocentric behaviors exist within the prison would be naïve. Yet one cannot ignore that a number of the men do not represent the one-dimensionality typically ascribed to prison behavior.

The Media

The men working with Angola's media are few in number, about a dozen men working for the magazine and television station, with the radio station employing more. Interest in a media-related job does not ensure employment. The administration and prison employees carefully vet each man working with the media, and existing staff members may also weigh in on a candidate's fit. The men's high-profile positions with the media force them to eschew violence and become model prisoners for the other inmates. Consequently they must also walk a very narrow line between the administration and their peers and carefully construct—or perform—their identities in what is traditionally considered a hypermasculine and combative environment. At times this means they may present themselves differently depending on their situation and/or company.

Though the men working with the media have their own opinions regarding autonomy, privilege, and working with the administration, they agree, when asked, on the most important attribute of a fellow worker: good character. Prior media experience is not expected; skills, according to the men, can be taught and practiced. Character cannot. The small percentage of men—less than 1 percent—working with the media know they have their own adversaries to deal with, both inside and outside prison. When interviewed, the men, acutely aware that they are under much higher scrutiny than the general inmate population, speak diplomatically when addressing free-world concerns. They have witnessed inmates throughout the prison lose their jobs for minor infractions that would not be an issue beyond the prison grounds. Furthermore, they recognize that one incident, perhaps not even involving them, could force the administration to modify its overall structure and exclude projects like the media. Those working with the media must have stellar prison records. Because the nature of their jobs requires them to move about the prison, often not directly supervised, they hold the highest classification status in the prison, meaning they have already proven themselves to be adapted to the penitentiary and to the administration's rules and expectations. Inmates with recent disciplinary infractions are not likely to find themselves in such an influential and self-directed position. Similarly, those men who break the rules while working with one of the media may find themselves suspended or fired from their position.

Although the men are bound by—and to—the administration and its rules, that does not mean they do not criticize both. The *Angolite*, the penitentiary's award-winning bimonthly magazine, addressed homosexuality, prison rape, and disease in a widely discussed 1979 feature titled "The Sexual Jungle," written by Wilbert Rideau. The piece won a George Polk Award in 1980 and was reprinted in the 1992 book *Life Sentences: Rage and Survival behind Bars.*[13] In "The Sexual Jungle," Rideau wrote about inmates—those at Angola and elsewhere—being *turned out,* "a nonsexual description that reveals the nonsexual ritualistic nature of what is really an act of conquest and emasculation, stripping the male victim of his status as a 'man.'"[14] In a 2011 interview, he discussed how prison administrators dealt with the crime of prison rape:

> Back then prison authorities nationwide did not speak of sexual violence in their prisons. They presented it to the public as something being done by homosexuals, gays, freaks. . . . But the reality of it was it was pretty prevalent and it wasn't isolated—it wasn't done by gays and homosexuals, the rape and enslavement was done by heterosexuals, and it was done with the tacit approval of prison authorities. It was part of the internal power structure and overall inmate economy.[15]

Admittedly, the *Angolite* today is not as critical of Angola as it had been in the past, preferring instead to address broader issues in the Louisiana and U.S. criminal justice systems. The reason why this is so depends on whom you ask. Some of those working with the media, particularly the *Angolite,* which is considered more journalistic than the television or radio stations, argue that Angola has changed considerably in the past fifty years. Story topics addressed then are no longer (or not as) prevalent now, they claim. Yet other inmates, those not directly involved with the media, state simply that the *Angolite* has become a tool for the administration and has lost its critical edge.

At more than eighteen thousand acres, the penitentiary's size makes communication crucial. Thus Cain, the penitentiary's longtime warden, seemed surprised that someone might question why the prison would have a trio of inmate-produced media at the facility. Angola's media serve multiple roles, not least of which involves helping to establish a sense of normalcy in the penitentiary. Normalcy benefits the state by helping to create order and set social norms and expectations. For the inmates it helps them maintain sanity and a sense of self-worth. The realization that these media are *prison* media is not lost on the men, however. Though the *Angolite* is often touted as uncensored, it is reviewed by a warden before it is printed, making its publication schedule sometimes a year or more behind. The television station deals primarily in recorded (as opposed to live) broadcasting, with all material viewed by an Angola employee; and while the radio deejays are live on-air, their broadcasts are typically focused on Christian music and fellowship.

Deviating from the prescribed format could mean losing one's job or being subjected to disciplinary measures and/or punishment.

Hegemonic Masculinity

Butler explains that gender[16] is not a "stable identity" but is instead "an identity tenuously constituted in time . . . instituted through the stylization of the body and, hence, must be understood as the mundane way in which bodily gestures, movements, and enactments of various kinds constitute the illusion of an abiding gendered self."[17] From a feminist perspective, individuals engage over time in certain behaviors or acts that align with societal views of what is masculine or feminine. In a prison, these behaviors are presumed (often correctly) to play more important roles, with individual survival potentially predicated on displaying and honoring those norms.[18] Hegemony, on the other hand, deals with the establishment and maintenance of power.[19] Power can be taken by force, given up willingly or without challenge, or obtained through a combination of both. Thus, hegemonic masculinity sits atop the well-established prison hierarchy, or chain of command.

Considering that the oppression of women and "heterosexuality and homophobia are the bedrock of hegemonic masculinity,"[20] one may question how such a hierarchy exists in an all-male penitentiary. The process is more simplistic than it may seem. As prisons serve as "microcosm(s)" of society,[21] social hierarchies evolve almost organically within them, akin to how they form in the free world. Those who are physically weaker or without social capital are likely to appear at the bottom of the lot, as are pedophiles and snitches.[22] Those with higher social capital or the more "professional criminals"[23] are placed at the top. Yet, while some prisoners opt to create a harder, more hypermasculine façade upon entering prison, others attempt to reassert their masculinity by making up for what they were not prior to entering the criminal justice system[24] or, in some cases, by maintaining pieces of their socially acceptable personae in order to maintain a sense of normalcy and self-worth.

> KERRY MYERS: It keeps me sane. I feel like I contribute something. I don't want to be [at Angola]; I continue to fight to not be here, but if I'm going to have any purpose at all, then this is what I feel is my voice. To have a voice? Look where I am? I'm in Angola. But I have a voice that's reaching. . . . All these guys have a voice that's reaching potentially hundreds and thousands and maybe more, as it gets shared.

As editor of the award-winning *Angolite*, Kerry Myers wears a myriad of hats. Having already served fifteen years of his life sentence when we meet, he is one of the few inmates interviewed who maintains his innocence. However, he does not use the magazine to advocate his particular case. That would fly against his—and journalistic—integrity, he explains. Staff members are given one chance when they are first introduced to speak personally about themselves to *Angolite* readers. As editor, Kerry passes on these values to new staffers and serves as teacher and mentor, journalist and page designer, and the intermediary between the staff and the administration. "We have very open communication, and they don't abuse that. That's unusual," said Sheryl Ranatza, who in 2007 was deputy warden of operations and had the final say over the *Angolite.* Using the *Angolite*'s phone sitting on his desk, Kerry can contact the warden's office with ease. That any inmate staffer may have access to a telephone, restricted line or not, is another normalcy factor afforded to *Angolite* employees. Something as seemingly trivial as answering a ringing phone or reading a fresh newspaper adds to a free-world connection.[25]

Manufacturing Masculinity

The men working with Angola's inmate-produced media try to dispel some of the stereotypes associated with the criminal justice system and those caught up in it. Media like the *Angolite* are more direct in addressing archaic laws or sentencing guidelines and in featuring inmate success stories, while the radio and television stations focus more on entertainment and chronicling the day-to-day activities within the prison. And while the men working with the media are not the only exemplars of socially acceptable masculinity, they are some of the prison's most noticeable ones. Their access to the administration, outsiders, and other parts of the prison complex make them some of the more visible of the penitentiary's inhabitants. But the simpler things about their positions may be what some of the other inmates find more attractive: air-conditioned work spaces, bathrooms with more privacy, and an office with a door.

Ugelvik argues that the "deprivation of liberty, of goods and services, of heterosexual relationships, of autonomy, and of security" challenges the expected masculinity of men in prison.[26] Masculinity—or being a man—is not simply about violence and power but about maintaining strong character values and having integrity. Similarly, the men say they are not out to prove anything, but rather they want to contribute to the greater society, even if they are behind bars.

KERRY MYERS: If I didn't think these guys had the integrity and the character, personal integrity and character that they have, I wouldn't, we wouldn't be around each other. You cannot work in these conditions under the scrutiny that we work. We work under intense scrutiny. Every security [guard] knows who we are. Every administrator knows who we are, and every time we're doing something, we're scrutinized. And if you can't work under that scrutiny, then you don't need to be here.

We're held to a higher standard. We don't live in mortal fear of doing that, but that's because, I believe, and this may sound self-centered, but I believe that's because of who we are. We don't live in mortal fear, because we're the same people we would be. We're not pretending to do this.

Angolite journalist John Corley attributes some free-world misconceptions of prison to blatant ignorance. He views the magazine as an opportunity to educate the public, recognizing that *Angolite* readers outside the penitentiary have a greater opportunity to influence prison reform.

JOHN CORLEY: I think probably only a fool would think prison is just a place, some dark place where you throw your incorrigibles and forget about them, some place that you're immune from, because no one's immune from it. . . . And I think if more people were aware that this is not just a place for people, for the wicked, for the bad, for the terrible people who probably deserve, or need, rather, to be separated from society, I think if more people were aware that they, too, are actually facing the same thing, then maybe, maybe again some changes would be made. . . . I think a lot of times society is not really aware of that or doesn't want to care, so it's important that they be made aware of that and that's another thing we try to do with our magazine.

Corley is not alone in his thoughts. Lane Nelson, an Angola inmate in 2011 and coauthor and editor of the book *Death Watch: A Death Penalty Anthology*,[27] also sees mainstream media as contributing directly to the perpetuation of prison stereotyping and an uneducated, misinformed public. He calls on journalists to challenge information they are given and fact-check even that which is provided by so-called expert sources. His argument speaks to the concept of the criminal as a commodity. Just as advertisers know that sex sells, a criminal and the sordid details of his or her crime are worth more than a rehabilitated person.

> LANE NELSON: [Media] want to sensationalize everything, so they're going to concentrate on the serial killer or whatever, and portray it like all prisoners are that way. They don't try to distinguish. They write about prison and they hardly know anything about it, particularly Angola. They don't know anything about Angola. They don't come here enough to know what it's like, and they don't care.

Visitors traveling the twenty-mile stretch of state Route 66 that leads to Angola's front gate can actually hear the sprawling prison before they see it. The 100-watt KSLP- 91.7 FM, touted as the only radio station licensed by the Federal Communications Commission to operate from within a prison, reaches several miles beyond the penitentiary grounds, offering guests and some scattered nearby residents a taste of Southern gospel and preaching. Nevertheless, there is no doubt that KLSP's audience is the inmates. While other stations' formats may be soft rock or country, Angola's in-house station is all rehabilitation all the time. Still, there is something cool about Angola's deejays. With live broadcasts throughout the day, the men could easily use the station for their own purposes, but they do not. Instead, they echo sentiments similar to *Angolite* staffers.

> DONALD SPENCER: [O]ur record backs us up. You know, we don't have a hundred write-ups, violence and all this type of stuff. We're basically, I guess you could call, the model prisoners. . . . We're not in the wild life. There's another side of prison beside this, and that other side, I'm not involved in.
>
> CARLWYN TURNER: [Y]ou really have to prove yourself that you're worthy of this type of job. You have to strive for that. Show good character. You have to refrain from disciplinary actions, bad behavior. . . . There are some who believe that we don't change, so we deserve to be, maybe, in the fields, doin' the hard stuff. There's change.
>
> KEITH ALEXANDER: I know that I am [under scrutiny] because of the liberty we have here at the radio station. We don't have security over us. We're very much self-governed. . . . The more I'm watched, the more good things they'll see. It's a testimony that a guy in prison can turn his life around, do the right thing consistently, not be putting on a show.

True, Louisiana's life-sentencing laws mean that few men will ever leave the massive penitentiary. However, that does not stop some of them from hanging on to the possibility of a sentence commutation, and should the commutation be granted, the men must be able to support themselves and (in some cases) their families. Pressed about the likelihood of being released, more than one of the men remarked that inmates often cling to the smallest of chances because that is what gets them through each day. "Maybe I can learn enough in here that maybe I can use these broadcasting skills outside the walls of Angola," one of the deejays said. "During my incarceration, one of my goals is to learn as much as I can . . ." Does this particular deejay have a life sentence? "Yes ma'am. I was found guilty of second-degree murder. That's a mandatory life sentence, but that's what man says, not what God says."

Numerous inmate employment opportunities exist at Angola, teaching the men a trade, skill, or new domain of knowledge and affording them a chance to "be a man" and "make a difference." Simply being able to send money to a relative increases an inmate's masculinity, as it feeds into the stereotype of men as breadwinner.[28] The media positions carry a certain celebrity status, as well, because the men serve as agenda setters and information conveyors to the rest of the inmate population. The positions also represent opportunities that are more "white collar" than jobs of manual labor. Because the inmates' character and behavior must stay above reproach if they are to remain in these highly visible positions, any thoughts of violence or deviance are weighed against possible consequences. There are no second chances, a statement supported by observation on a 2011 visit, when obvious staff changes to the prison's television station had been made.

> JONATHAN: This particular job [at the television station], not just this one, but the *Angolite* along with the radio station, you have to be of a certain character because you're around a lot of the upper echelon of the prison—from Warden Cain on down. So you don't want to come over here with the prison mindset. . . . As you well know, inmates in prison have a certain stigma attached to them, people expect you to behave in a certain manner, and when they recognize that you don't, they start extending privileges to you, and it's a very good feeling. It humanizes you again, 'cause prison is a dehumanizing embarrassment. It humanizes you and makes you feel as if you have some type of purpose.

Conclusion

It is cruel that the hypermasculine behavior that allows some men to thrive while incarcerated is what can prevent them from succeeding outside prison. Similarly, the behavior that can help them to flourish (such as sharing emotions and seeking support or assistance) is often frowned on in prison,[29] thereby encouraging recidivist behavior should the individual not be able to toggle between those expectations. As mentioned earlier, the Louisiana State Penitentiary is unique. The emphasis on moral rehabilitation and almost religious indoctrination that occurs at Angola make most hypermasculine behaviors intolerable. Yet hypermasculinity is considered a necessity in prison, with some going so far as to call it "a learned response to the imperatives of inmate culture."[30] Does that mean there is no violence within the prison or that the men do not engage in oppressive behavior or thought processes? Of course not, and the administration reports nominal breaches despite the institution's massive size and population. Similarly, it is possible to have a hypermasculine mind-set yet not act out aggressively. Maintaining a certain bravado by "talking the talk" may be all that is needed to establish and maintain a desired degree of street credibility.[31] It is also possible that some behaviors go uncaught or unreported.

What can be determined from the Angola inmates and their media is that a number of the men have committed themselves to performing masculinity in a way that does not glorify the aggression and violence that is synonymous with the hyper- or hegemonic masculinity portrayed through mainstream media. Does this mean that the men are not, or are no longer, violent? Not necessarily. The motivation to behave according to state requirements may simply outweigh the benefits of aggression. The actual sincerity of behavior is impossible to judge. What can also be determined from studying Angola and its media is that the media help maintain an alternative reality or new normalcy that perpetuates the manufacture of hope.

Haas situates alternative media,[32] to which I would argue inmate-produced media belong, as part of the public sphere and questions whether they should be considered to create an alternative one. Indeed, in the case of inmate-produced media, not only is an alternative public sphere created, but also the power afforded to prisoners' aids in the construction of an alternative reality,[33] one that is built on manufacturing hope. Even the most trivial communication applicable to the inmates helps foster a sense of community.[34] Similarly, inmate media producers illustrate what can happen when Angola's men not only obey, but also serve to model, the administration's ideals. Thus, the media, in addition to the inmate-media producers, have the authority to offer alternatives to hegemonic masculinity and the ability to reconstruct what it means to be a "real man."

Notes

1. Bureau of Justice Statistics, "U.S. Prison Population Declined One Percent in 2014."

2. Messerschmidt, "Masculinities, Crime, and Prison."

3. Data for this chapter stem from close readings of decades of the Louisiana State Penitentiary's award-winning *Angolite* magazine, as well as IRB-approved ethnographic research conducted in 2007 and 2011. This research is part of a longitudinal project examining inmate-produced media at LSP-Angola.

4. Baird, *Penal Press.*

5. In contrast to prison journalism, which has received little recognition throughout its history, prison poetry is a fairly popular form of creative writing, often published in volumes readily available to the public.

6. IRB approval was granted for this project, including approval to use the actual names of the inmates if consent was provided and approved by penitentiary officials. The final project, including additional on-site research, is forthcoming.

7. Goldberg, "End of the Line."

8. McWhorter, "Inmate Identification in an Institutional Setting."

9. Gates v. Collier, 501 F.2d 1291 (5th Cir. 1974).

10. Carleton, *Politics and Punishment*, chapter "Unpredictable Future: 1956–1968."

11. *The Angola Story*, compiled by the Office of the Deputy Warden/Operations.

12. Butler, A., Introduction to *Angola*, 2.

13. Rideau, "Sexual Jungle."

14. Ibid., 75.

15. Lee, "Wilbert Rideau."

16. Gender ought not to be confused with the term *sex*, which instead refers to a person's biological makeup.

17. Butler, J., "Performative Acts and Gender Constitution," 519.

18. Gordon, Hawes, Perez-Cabello, Brabham-Hollis, Lanza, and Dyson, "Examining Masculine Norms and Peer Support."

19. Gramsci, *Selections from the Prison Notebooks.*

20. Donaldson, "What Is Hegemonic Masculinity?," 645; see also Gordon, Hawes, Perez-Cabello, Brabham-Hollis, Lanza, and Dyson, "Examining Masculine Norms and Peer Support."

21. Jewkes, "Mesosphere of Culture," 132.

22. Ugelvik, "Be a Man."

23. Jewkes, "Men behind Bars," 52.

24. Ibid., 44–63.

25. Although inmates may make collect calls from the prison, the telephones they use are carefully monitored, and incoming calls to inmates are not allowed.

26. Ugelvik, "Be a Man," 57.

27. Nelson and Foster, *Death Watch*.

28. Ugelvik, "Be a Man."

29. Gordon, Hawes, Perez-Cabello, Brabham-Hollis, Lanza, and Dyson, "Examining Masculine Norms and Peer Support."

30. Jewkes, "Men behind Bars," 44–45.

31. Ibid.

32. Haas, "Alternative Media, Public Journalism."

33. Foucault, *Discipline and Punish*.

34. Novek, "Heaven, Hell, and Here."

Bibliography

Baird, Russell N. *The Penal Press*. Evanston, IL: Northwestern University Press, 1967.

Bureau of Justice Statistics. "U.S. Prison Population Declined One Percent in 2014." Bureau of Justice Statistics, September 17, 2015. Accessed September 23, 2017. http://www.bjs.gov/content/pub/press/p14pr.cfm.

Butler, Anne. Introduction to *Angola: Louisiana State Penitentiary, a Half-Century of Rage and Reform*, edited by Anne Butler and C. Murray Henderson. Lafayette: Center for Louisiana Studies, University of Southwestern Louisiana, 1990.

Butler, Judith. "Performative Acts and Gender Construction: An Essay in Phenomenology and Feminist Theory." *Theatre Journal* 40, no. 4 (1988): 519–31.

Carleton, Mark T. *Politics and Punishment: The History of the Louisiana State Penal System*. Baton Rouge: Louisiana State University Press, 1971.

Donaldson, Mike. "What Is Hegemonic Masculinity?" Special issue: Masculinities, *Theory and Society* 22, no. 5 (1993): 643–57.

Foucault, Michel. *Discipline and Punish: The Birth of the Prison*. Translated by Alan Sheridan. New York: Vintage Books, 1995. First published 1975.

Goldberg, Jeffrey. "The End of the Line: Rehabilitation and Reform in Angola Penitentiary." *Atlantic*, September 9, 2015. Accessed September 23, 2017. http://www.theatlantic.com.

Gordon, Derrick M., Samuel W. Hawes, M. Arturo Perez-Cabello, Tamika Brabham-Hollis, Stephen, A. Lanza, and William J. Dyson. "Examining Masculine Norms and Peer Support within a Sample of Incarcerated African American Males." *Psychology of Men & Masculinity* 14, no. 1 (2013): 59–64.

Gramsci, Antonio. *Selections from the Prison Notebooks.* New York: International Publishers, 1971.

Haas, Tanni. "Alternative Media, Public Journalism and the Pursuit of Democratization." *Journalism Studies* 5, no. 1 (2004): 115–21.

Jewkes, Yvonne. "Men behind Bars: 'Doing' Masculinity as an Adaptation to Imprisonment." *Men & Masculinities* 8, no. 1 (2005): 44–63.

———. "The Mesosphere of Culture, Interaction and Hyper-Masculinity." Chap. 5 in *Captive Audience: Media, Masculinity and Power*, 131–60. Portland, OR: Willan, 2002.

Lee, Trymaine. "Wilbert Rideau, Former Angola Prisoner, Receives Polk Award." *Huffington Post*, April 16, 2011. Accessed September 23, 2017. http://www.huffingtonpost.com.

McWhorter, William L. "Inmate Identification in an Institutional Setting." *Criminal Justice Review* 1, no. 2 (1976): 81–92.

Messerschmidt, James W. "Masculinities, Crime, and Prison." In *Prison Masculinities*, edited by Don Sabo, Terry A. Kupers, and Willie London, 67–72. Philadelphia: Temple University Press, 2001.

Nelson, Lane, and Burk Foster. *Death Watch: A Death Penalty Anthology.* Upper Saddle River, NJ: Prentice Hall, 2001.

Novek, Eleanor. "'Heaven, Hell, and Here': Understanding the Impact of Incarceration through a Prison Newspaper." *Critical Studies in Media Communication* 22, no. 4 (2005): 281–301.

Office of Deputy Warden/Operations, Louisiana State Penitentiary. *The Angola Story.* Last revised March 2006. Pamphlet.

Rideau, Wilbert. "The Sexual Jungle." In *Life Sentences: Rage and Survival behind Bars*, edited by Wilbert Rideau and Ron Wikberg, 73–107. New York: Times Books, 1992.

Ugelvik, Thomas. "'Be a Man. Not a Bitch.' Snitching, the Inmate Code and the Narrative Reconstruction of Masculinity in a Norwegian Prison." In *Men, Masculinities and the Criminological Field*, edited by Ingrid Lander, Signe Ravn, and Nina Jon, 57–70. Farnham, UK: Ashgate, 2014.

9. "In Here and Out There": The Lived Experiences of Women Lifers

Meredith Huey Dye

Public understandings of the lives and experiences of incarcerated women are shaped by media depictions, which portray women offenders as violent "monsters" or women driven by love who "snapped."[1] Given these commonly accepted, rarely challenged depictions, it is unfortunate but not surprising that citizens and public officials hold a "throw-away-the-key" mentality when it comes to these women's lives—even though the vast majority of incarcerated women will be released from prison.[2] Despite this mind-set, the public is fascinated by what goes on behind bars. However, *Orange Is the New Black* and other depictions of women's incarceration experiences are stereotypical and distorted in their presentation of violence, manipulation, lesbian relationships, and bad mothering. These portrayals are not typical of most women in prison. As a result, the actual lives of incarcerated women remain invisible and their voices silenced.[3] All of this is especially true for women serving life sentences.[4]

The purpose of this chapter is to give voice to women lifers and provide a portrait of their lives both before and during incarceration. This portrait refutes many popular preconceived ideas about women in prison held by the public (and even by those who work in the criminal justice and corrections fields) and supported by media (mis)representations. These ideas include the ways women in prison are portrayed as the "worst of the worst," the way they do "hard time" in prison, and the reasons why women serving life sentences elicit our "throw-away-the-key" mentality. Using qualitative and quantitative data derived from surveys of 214 women lifers in a U.S. southern state system, I describe these women's preincarceration backgrounds including their experiences as victims of violence, incarceration/criminal history, physical and mental health, and family relationships. I then describe the everyday incarceration experiences of the women—their activities, family connections, and prison adjustments. I conclude by discussing the inevitable problems of reentry and reintegration that women lifers face. Throughout the chapter I include quotes provided by the women in their responses to open-ended survey questions, which give voice to their own lived experiences with incarceration and bring to life the summary of their characteristics.

Background

The number of women in U.S. prisons has increased dramatically since the 1980s, with a rate of increase outpacing that of men's incarceration.[5] These trends hold true for the imposition of life sentences as well, which saw a fourfold increase from 1984 to 2012.[6] While the vast majority of all lifers are men, over 5,300 women are currently serving life or life without parole.[7] Despite these numbers, incarcerated women, and women lifers specifically, represent a relatively small percentage of the overall correctional and lifer populations (about 4 percent). As such, women's invisibility is obvious—it is easy to overlook and discount such a small group.

This invisibility is evident not only in allocations of money, time, and attention within the criminal justice system but also within research literature and media depictions. With the exception of a few research articles[8] and a recent ethnography,[9] much of the existing literature on female lifers is dated (from the 1990s) and consists of small samples from prisons in California,[10] Ohio,[11] the United Kingdom,[12] and Canada.[13] Differences in samples and locations, as well as in research methodologies, preclude generalizing from these studies to the overall population of women lifers. However, women serving life sentences tend to be older women (average age of forty), with children, and serving a sentence for a violent offense (primarily murder) perpetrated against a known victim (who may also be a domestic abuser). The vast majority of women lifers have no prior prison history but have extensive histories of physical and sexual victimization.[14]

Although crime and criminal justice are popular subjects for the media, prisons are the least covered[15] and female prisoners, by far, the least "newsworthy."[16] Instead, individual, not-so-typical cases are sensationalized by news media, and stereotypical images of women offenders and prisoners go unchecked. As highlighted in the chapters of section one of this book and in other research, media depictions of women in prison follow a few different formulas depending on the type of media (news, crime dramas, or films). In news media, racialized images of women (and men) committing violent crimes are evident, whereas sexualized and brutal images of women are presented in Hollywood-style films.[17] Documentaries and true-to-TV depictions of women's crime and prisons are not exempt from stereotypical, dramatized portrayals of violence, sexuality, and (bad) mothering.

Within each medium and genre, depictions of women and prison life are sometimes contradictory. In some instances, women offenders/inmates are portrayed as dark and dangerous, as well as "lower-class, vulgar, amoral, mentally deficient, promiscuous, and sexually voracious."[18] In other depictions, women are portrayed as heroines, which usually equates to (attractive) white women who commit homicide for reasons that require lengthy explanations and justifications, or who are viewed as innocent. Cecil's media analysis of four popular crime dramas found white women overrepresented as violent offenders, as accomplices, and as deadly mothers.[19] In a separate study, Cecil analyzed 195 news media articles on Martha Stewart's incarceration in an Alderson, West Virginia, prison camp.[20] She found the clear and dominant portrayal of prison life in these articles to be normal and easy, with relaxing prison routines, menial jobs, accessibility for visits, and postprison success. Cecil's findings and conclusions provide a clear message about media depictions of women in prison: what is left out of the coverage/story is vastly more informative about the more typical experiences. Rarely do media accounts refute normalized depictions by presenting data on or accounts of women's incarceration experiences as "hard time." In the end, the movement toward penal harm is further supported,[21] while researchers, the public, and the media remain misinformed.

Methods

The very invisibility that allows much of the public and media to ignore and stereotype also hinders our ability to understand the lived experiences of women in prison, thus making them even more invisible. Gaining entry to conduct research in prisons is difficult. And once access is gained, gathering data also proves challenging. Among the women serving life, some do not like talking about the fact they are "lifers." As one woman told us, "Everyone handles doing this time differently. I haven't had the opportunity to sit and talk with other lifers because most of the ladies surviving a life sentence do not like talking about the fact that they are lifers. Serving a life sentence is very, very difficult and extremely sensitive subject that is usually never discussed." I take seriously the task of sharing these women's stories so that their voices are heard and their lived experiences become visible.

To do so, my colleague and I collected survey data using a convenience sample from three women's prisons in a southern state. Our methods of data collection included standard procedures for conducting research in prisons, including obtaining permission from the university's institutional review board and the state's department of corrections. On the days of data collection, prison staff brought participants to cafeterias or visitation settings. After describing the nature of the research, we provided consent forms and questionnaires to willing respondents. Some inmates chose not to participate for personal reasons, and some were unable to participate due to work conflicts or administrative reasons (disciplinary and/or mental health reasons, for instance). Of the 303 women serving life sentences in this southern state, 214 participated in the survey (71 percent). Questionnaires consisted of closed and open-ended questions on demographics, prison history, and abuse history; a variety of items related to physical and mental health conditions; prison adjustment, activities, and support; and family contact and satisfaction with family relationships. We assisted inmates with literacy or visual barriers.

In analyzing the open-ended responses and the numerical survey data, we identified several themes in the women's lived experiences both "in here and out there" that contrast with media misrepresentations of women in prison: notions that women lifers are the "worst of the worst," assumptions about how they are "doing hard time," and our throw-away-the-key mentality toward those incarcerated. Our findings, substantiated with prior research, question each of these ideas and work to refute public and media stereotypes of women in prison.

Lived Experiences of Women Lifers

Worst of the Worst or the Most Vulnerable?

An assumption about women in prison, and specifically lifers, is that "these women" are vastly different from law-abiding women. In some ways, this is true: 84 percent of the women in this study reported histories of some type of past abuse—physical, sexual, and/or emotional. Among these women, abuse began as early as 2 years of age or as late as 52 years, with an average age of 19 when the abuse began (standard deviation [SD] = 9 years). Like much of the criminal justice system, the sample of women lifers was disproportionately nonwhite (>50 percent). In these ways, women sentenced to life in prison are some of the most marginalized and vulnerable members of society.

In other ways, lifers do not resemble the larger population of women in prison,[22] and they are similar in demographics and criminal history to nonincarcerated women.[23] As seen in table 1, within the study sample, lifers were relatively older, with ages ranging from 19 to 78 years and an average age of 41. On average, the women entered prison at 30 years of age (range 12–70 years) and had served approximately 12 years of their life sentence at the time of the survey (range <1–35 years). Whether achieved before prison or while incarcerated, over a quarter of the women (26 percent) had at least some college, and another 11 percent held a college degree. Over 70 percent were mothers, and 35 percent were grandmothers.

Table 1. Profile of Women Lifers (n = 214)

	Mean (SD) or Percentage	Minimum	Maximum
Age (y)	41.33 (11.90)	19	78
Age when first incarcerated (y)	29.28 (11.32)	12	70
Prior prison history (1 = yes)	5.2%		
Abuse history (as adult or child)			
Sexual abuse	61.8%		
Physical abuse	63.7%		
Emotional abuse	74.9%		
Any abuse	83.7%		
Age when abuse began (y)	18.73 (8.70)	2	52
Abuse a factor in incarceration (1 = yes)	62.0%		
Race (1 = nonwhite)	53.0%		
Education			
Less than high school (reference category)	25.5%		
High school degree / Equivalent	37.0%		
Some college	26.4%		
College degree or higher	11.1%		
Marital status (1 = ever married)	56.7%		

Table 1, *continued*

	Mean (SD) or Percentage	Minimum	Maximum
Children (1 = yes)	70.6%		
Grandchildren (1 = yes)	34.9%		
Time served (y)	12.00 (6.66)	<1	35
Ever treated for mental health problem (1 = yes)	64.29%		
Depression scale	11.99 (5.24)	0	26
Anxiety scale	7.67 (4.15)	0	19
Interpersonal sensitivity scale	11.00 (4.91)	0	25
Somatization scale	12.08 (6.78)	0	32
Self-reported mental health			
Excellent	20.2%		
Good	46.2%		
Fair	28.4%		
Poor	5.3%		
Suicide ideation prior to prison (1 = yes)	45.5%		
Suicide attempt prior to prison (1 = yes)	43.9%		
Current ideation (thoughts of ending life)			
Never	62.4%		
Rarely	13.3%		
Sometimes	16.2%		
Often	2.9%		
Very often	5.2%		
Self-reported physical health			
Excellent	23.5%		
Good	43.2%		
Fair	26.3%		
Poor	7.0%		
Number of chronic health problems	2.47 (2.24)	0	11

While most of the women (93 percent) were convicted of murder charges, the vast majority had no prior history of criminal offense, especially for violent crime. Neither of these characteristics is typical of most incarcerated women. As noted already, the women lifers reported a high prevalence of victimization. Among women with abusive pasts, 62 percent reported that abuse was a factor in their crime/incarceration, as vividly described in this account: "a man was trying to kill me and told me he was going to. I fought for my life. I wanted to live, not die. I was beat and a gun was held to my head. I think any other person would have done the same thing." Another woman agreed: "we have almost walked the same journey, being abused and/or manipulated, faced with a situation that we either felt trapped in or done so in the name of love."

Other than various degrees of murder, some of the women in this state prison system, specifically, were sentenced to life in prison for being "a party to the crime of [murder, robbery, kidnapping, or rape]." And, in addition to murder, this state considers a second offense of any of the "seven deadly sins" to make one eligible for a life sentence (offenses such as kidnapping, armed robbery, rape, aggravated sodomy, aggravated sexual battery, and aggravated child molestation).[24] Because of this "two strikes" policy, the remaining women were serving life for one or more of these offenses as well as drug-related felonies.

However, for 95 percent of the women, this life sentence was their first time being incarcerated. As such, many of the women expressed thoughts of shock and surprise at first receiving their life sentence. For example, one woman responded, "my life was over at 46. I lost everything—job of 22 years, house, brand-new car. How I would live without my children and how they'd live without me. It was devastating. I'm a good person so this can happen to anyone." Of her initial adjustment, another woman described it as "very difficult. I had never been in trouble before and this environment was scary."

Women lifers reported mental health problems, including depression and anxiety related to histories of abuse, as well as to their current first-time prison experiences. While over 64 percent of the women had been treated for a mental health problem at some point in their lives, 5 percent of the women rated their current mental health as "poor" and others as "fair" (28 percent) or "good" (46 percent). Just 20 percent rated their mental health as "excellent." About half of the women reported, at least sometimes, "being afraid of going crazy" in prison, while about 40 percent were worried, at least sometimes, about becoming institutionalized (psychiatrically). Put into words, one woman stated, "When I wake up in the morning, sometimes I can't believe that I am still here. I wanna go crazy and just lay in my bed and die."

As measured by seven summed Likert-type items from the Hopkins Symptom Checklist,[25] current levels of depression resulted in an average score of 11.99 (range 0–26, with higher scores indicating greater depression). Among these items, 32 percent of women reported feeling lonely or blue often; over 50 percent reported feeling hopeless about the future at least sometimes; and about 30 percent reported feeling low in energy or slowed down often. Similar measures of anxiety, interpersonal sensitivity, and somatization (reporting physical symptoms with no identified organic cause) had scores of 7.67 (range 0–19), 11.0 (range 0–25) and 12.08 (range 0–32), respectively.

As further evidence of mental health and abuse trauma, women also reported past experiences with suicide ideation (46 percent) and attempts (44 percent) prior to prison. These thoughts continued into prison for some of the women and developed after incarceration for others.[26] A little over 16 percent reported current suicide ideation "sometimes" while 8 percent reported ideation "often" or "very often."

Other anxieties about death or dying in prison were also reported. Most women (79 percent) indicated that they were afraid of getting deathly sick in prison and often thought about how short life really is (83 percent). Women were also worried about the possibility of family members dying. Many women faced life and death in prison through a religious/spiritual lens. This may explain why a relatively small percentage (less than 20 percent) reported being afraid to die or troubled by the subject of life after death. In contrast, women who were extremely troubled by receiving a life sentence felt their lives were over and wanted to die.

In addition to indicators of mental health, and given the age/aging of women lifers, not surprisingly women reported a variety of physical health problems and needs. Seven percent rated their health as "poor" and 26 percent as "fair." On average, woman reported 2.5 chronic health conditions including diabetes, hypertension, heart conditions, and digestive disorders (e.g., ulcers). Eleven percent indicated they could not walk independently, and this was visually evident upon visiting the women, as many came to meet with us in wheelchairs or on walkers.

In sum, although women sentenced to life in prison are viewed as "less than" and the worst of society, these women are arguably some of the most vulnerable of society and the least likely to remain in the revolving door of the corrections system in the United States. The vast majority have no prior prison or criminal history but do have extensive experiences with physical, sexual, and emotional abuse, and with mental health issues and suicide ideation.

Doing My Hard Time

Depending on one's worldview, a common assumption about prison is that is it "too easy." According to the penal harm movement, a prison sentence itself is not punishment enough; the experience of life in prison must be characterized by additional punishment, from deprivations to degradations. The message: doing time in prison should not be easy; instead it should be "hard time." For women serving life sentences, the ways they "do time" include dealing with their worries and concerns about living in prison (i.e., adjusting), losing their freedom, and leaving families and friendships. These provide important contradictions to the assumption that prison is easy. As some of the women reported:

> I still have not adjusted. I probably never totally will. I can't get used to this lifestyle. I'm very, very uncomfortable. The adjustment has not changed with time as of yet, even after almost 7 years of incarceration.

> Now that the initial adjustment is over, the rest of my life stretches out with appalling length.

> I'm still not so adjusted to prison. These past 2 years have been hard not just on me but my kids as well as my family.

Worries about family topped the list of adjustment problems for women lifers (table 2). Nearly all the women surveyed (98 percent) were bothered by being separated from family members and worried that family members had forgotten them (85 percent). Women discussed these concerns at length:

> Being taken from my family 10 years ago (son 13, daughter 10) almost killed me and I worried how it'd affect my kid's lives.

> Not being able to see my children was indescribably painful.

> My main worry is that the love my son expresses for me now will dwindle as the years go by and that he won't respect my input as his mother.

> I no longer feel part of a family or have a right to anything due to my circumstances.

> Prison has totally cut my life out of my family's lives. I don't have a significant relationship with my mom, dad, brother, sister, and especially my only child, my son, at all. It's like I've died. . . . My worries I have

Table 2. Indicators of Prison Adjustment (percentage; n = 214)

How often are you bothered by . . . ?	Never	Rarely	Sometimes	Often	Always
Relationship with prison staff	19.9	30.3	38.4	7.1	4.3
Getting along with other inmates	19.8	33.5	37.7	6.6	2.4
Performing job assigned to you	53.4	30.3	12.0	2.4	1.9
Abiding by prison policies and rules	45.7	33.2	17.8	2.9	0.5
Family members who have forgotten you	7.3	9.3	26.8	22.4	34.1
Dealing with your loss of freedom	1.4	2.9	18.3	22.1	55.3
Feeling comfortable in your prison quarters	10.0	21.0	34.3	16.7	18.1
Wishing you had more privacy and quiet	6.2	8.6	27.6	18.1	39.5
Being separated from family members	1.0	1.4	4.8	13.8	79.0
Not knowing where you stand with parole	3.8	5.2	12.8	18.0	60.2
Missing friends and outside social life	7.7	6.2	14.8	20.1	51.2
Worried of getting sick in here	3.3	10.5	19.0	23.3	43.8
Not fitting in with other inmates	45.0	28.4	15.2	6.6	4.7
Being bored, lots of idle time	13.3	23.8	24.8	16.7	21.4
Not feeling physically safe	26.9	25.5	24.0	7.7	15.9
Feeling out of touch with the world	6.8	6.3	26.6	24.2	36.2
Getting annoyed or irritated	6.2	20.1	46.9	15.8	11.0
Being afraid of going crazy	33.7	16.3	20.2	12.5	17.3
Worried about becoming institutionalized	45.0	16.6	17.5	10.0	10.9
Having no goals and ambitions	35.1	17.6	21.5	10.2	15.6
Staff not listening to grievances	15.6	9.0	22.6	21.2	31.6

Source: questions adapted from Zamble and Porporino, *Coping, Behavior, and Adaption in Prison Inmates*, 196–97.

about my family are that I never wanted to be forgotten or not loved and that's what happened. I have been forgotten and I'm not loved by my family anymore. . . . I was harshly sentenced to more than just life.

To cope with these losses, over 85 percent of the women continued to encourage family visits, although nearly one-quarter never received visits from family members or other relatives; over 20 percent never received phone calls. Barriers to visits (distance, financial problems, health, and prison security policies) and phone contact (high costs of phone calls) explain the limited contact with family members. For example, one woman explained, "There are always transportation issues and money is tight. There are always planned visits but something always comes up. Life just seems to go on out there and you become forgotten about."

Women lifers are much more likely to receive letters weekly (22 percent) and fairly often (39 percent) from family members. Mothers especially use letters and phone calls to stay connected and involved with decision making and mothering from the inside. As one woman stated, "I have to continue to be a mother no matter where I am. I write letters and call my family at least once a week. I am involved in all decision making when it comes to my daughter."

Despite feeling disconnected from family, most women lifers do adjust and cope with the deprivations of prison in ways that are not emphasized in media depictions (which tend to focus on violence, fighting, toughness, and sexual relationships). In fact, women's families provide support that helps them survive incarceration: "Some don't have no one. At least I can truly count on my family. Had it not been for them, I could not have made it this far: 11 and a half years."

Other women adjust to prison, eventually, by getting involved in programs, work detail, or other activities. Activity can become a priority for some:

> It took me three years to adjust to where I could reasonably function. It was like I had entered the Twilight Zone. Now I'm involved with as much as possible. I try not to spend more than five minutes a day without occupying my mind with something.

> After I realized and it sunk in that I was going to be in here a while I started to do things like education and trades to better myself and to see and stay positive.

As shown in table 3, over 60 percent of the women pass the time by engaging in work assignments and spiritual/religious activities. Women are equally likely to engage in conversations with others or pass the time by "just being alone." Other solitary activities include reading (86 percent), listening to music (77 percent), and writing letters (72 percent). A much smaller percentage of women lifers pass the time with educational, vocational, or therapy programs. These programs are important for reentry and reintegration purposes, to halt the revolving door to prison and to help address past abuse, trauma, and addiction. As such, these programs are typically reserved for women serving much shorter sentences. According to prison policies, women with long sentences, including lifers, are not eligible for these programs until two years or less remains of their sentence. Thus, lifers' options for meaningful and productive programming, including outlets to address past abuse, are limited. Instead, women lifers rely on the importance of spiritual and religious engagement to cope with a life sentence in prison and the accompanying depression, anxiety, and past trauma.[27] One woman responded with a sentiment shared by many: "Jesus is helping me do the time."

Table 3. Involvement in Prison Programs
and Activities (n = 214)

	Percentage Who Engage in . . .
Cards/other games	46.3
Arts/crafts/gardening	31.3
Work assignment	61.7
Listening to music	76.6
Educational programs	34.6
Reading	86.4
Writing letters	71.5
Helping others	56.5
Watching TV	54.7
Therapy programs	13.1
Just being alone	59.8
Talking/conversation	52.8
Spiritual/religious activities	60.7
Walking/fitness or recreational activities	38.3
Vocational programs	22.9

Although family support, prison activities, and religious meaning are important, lifers rely on support from fellow inmates and staff, and they develop supportive relationships with similar others. Table 4 indicates how important these relationships are to women lifers: 76 percent are satisfied with prison friendships; 85 percent indicate prison friendships are very important to them; and 60 percent are satisfied with their relationships with prison staff. Upwards of 60 to 70 percent of the women surveyed could "depend on fellow inmates," "confide in fellow inmates," and/or "talk about day-to-day problems." Over 85 percent find that fellow inmates share interests and concerns, and enjoy similar social activities. In addition, women are less often bothered with problems of getting along with other inmates or fitting in with other inmates compared to other adjustment issues (see table 2). These lived experiences stand in contrast to media representations of violence in prisons and to accounts that underestimate the varied types of prison friendships that provide support for doing hard time. As one woman answered: "I was happy to be around people sentenced to time like me. . . . The ones doing good are an example to me that I can make it."

Throw Away the Key?

A final assumption about women serving life sentences in prison is that we can and should forget about them because their days left on earth will all be spent behind prison walls. In essence, they are of no concern and make no contribution to society. While for some U.S. states "life means life," most lifers have sentences that allow for the possibility of parole. And, while some women would prefer a death sentence or are resigned to dying inside prison—as one women stated, "I hate it still and strongly believe that we should have a choice of death when given a life sentence"; and another, "I accepted the fact that I will most likely die here"—most are not resigned to die in prison. Instead the women maintain a hope for release and a return to a better life "out there." Consistent with many women's hopes, one women stated, "When I first came, I felt as though I would die in prison but now I feel hope of going home one day."

While they await that day, the possibility of parole is a source of worry for women lifers, who reported that not knowing where they stood with parole sometimes (13 percent), often (18 percent), or always (60 percent) bothered them. As one woman described it, "we are all struggling with the same issues. Mentally we try to grasp the concept that our [lives] are in five people's hands [the parole board] that don't know us at all. They read papers

Table 4. Indicators of Prison Supports and Friendships (n = 214)

	Percentage Yes
I have fellow inmates here whom I can depend on whenever I need them	74.6
I have fellow inmates that I confide in about my personal problems	72.3
Relationships with fellow inmates provide me with a sense of well-being	64.6
Always someone I can talk to about my day-to-day problems	69.0
Enough people here that I feel close to	42.7
Many people that I can count on completely	24.6
Frequently rely on fellow inmates to provide me with assistance	28.2
Plenty of people I can lean on in case of trouble	36.8
Call on friends whenever I need them	57.9
Fellow inmates here who enjoy similar social activities as I do	85.2
Fellow inmates here who share my interest and concerns	85.6
Friends I have made here are very important to me	84.8
Overall, I am very satisfied with the friendships I have made here	75.5
Fellow inmates I feel closest to are near my own age	56.9
Overall, I am satisfied with my relationships with the prison staff	60.1

in a file and don't meet with us or talk with us at all." However, even after decades of imprisonment and numerous parole hearings, a release on parole for one lifer gives others hope for the same: "It's been 20 years but I thank God I'm on my way home."

The hopes for "going home" are also mixed with anxieties. Reintegration for women lifers is more complex than for other women with shorter sentences.[28] In all reality, after living 20 to 30 years of a life in prison, the women inside and the world outside have changed. What then does reentry mean for women who have aged in prison, who lack employment skills and the luxury of retirement planning?[29] Who may have outlived all immediate and supportive family members?[30] Will women go from prison to nursing homes? How will they support themselves financially? Are women after serving decades in prison mentally ready for life "out there"?

The throw-away-the-key mentality toward women in prison is then both a truth and a fiction. It is a truth in that women lifers are forgotten by family, friends, and the larger society. They are denied opportunities for mental health / trauma counseling and treatment; lose opportunities for meaningful education and vocational skills training; and struggle to maintain connections to children, grandchildren, and remaining relatives precisely because "they are lifers" who are thought either not to deserve these opportunities or not to need them given their lengthy sentences. This is unfortunate since most lifers will be paroled, albeit not after their first hearing, and then only after serving 20 to 30 years of their sentence. What then will be left for them "out there" is uncertain, because for many, their chances for (re)integration into society were thrown away with the receipt of their life sentence.

Conclusion

Media depictions of women offenders/inmates are often stereotypical and dramatized to represent the worst of the worst crimes and offenders. If not to conclusions explicitly made, these images lead us to important but inaccurate conclusions about women serving life sentences. The goal of this chapter was to share the voices and lived experiences of women lifers and to describe the ways they do not resemble our common assumptions about women in prison. The overall project was not intended to study the way media depictions are inconsistent with the lived experiences of women in prison, but the findings did provide clear contrasts to our common, media-informed assumptions. Women lifers in many ways are not "the worst of the worst"; they do serve "hard time," but most will return to society despite our having "thrown away the key."

Taking into account media needs and purposes is important, but often these are used to justify, excuse, or minimize inaccurate, stereotypical, and sensationalized images of offenders and inmates. While these types of depictions may not be possible to change—some may not want them to change because they enjoy a "good" crime show or whodunit—by bringing misconceptions to light, more typical and more accurate descriptions of offenders and inmates may be known. Regardless, the outcome of informing the public and policy makers could be the creation of more effective criminal *justice* policies.

Further, the study design relied on a convenience sample of women serving life sentences in one southern state. Given this methodological approach, the findings may not hold true for women who did not participate in the survey or for women in other prisons in the United States. Nevertheless, the sample is drawn from a state with a relatively large population of inmates including those with life sentences. In fact, this project contains the largest known sample of women lifers. When compared with the lifer characteristics in a nationally representative sample of inmates in state correctional facilities,[31] the demographics, criminal records, and mental health histories are consistent. Thus, the findings discussed in this chapter may be consistent with women lifers elsewhere.

Future research on release from prison and reentry/reintegration among women lifers is urgently needed. The throw-away-the-key mentality toward lifers as well as the historically low numbers of lifers eligible for release has made research on reentry among this population almost nil. However, women lifers in this sample and elsewhere are now eligible, and in greater numbers, for parole and release from prison after twenty and thirty years lived in prison. We know very little about the experiences of women lifers that might prove to be barriers or benefits for reentry. What we do know from hearing and listening to the voices of women serving life sentences is that they "want something better from life. Both in here and out there."

Notes

1. Cecil, "Doing Time in 'Camp Cupcake'"; Morash and Schram, *Prison Experience*.

2. Nellis, "Throw Away the Key"; Nellis and King, *No Exit*.

3. Belknap, *Invisible Woman*.

4. Leigey, "For the Longest Time"; Leigey and Reed, "Woman's Life before Serving Life."

5. Sentencing Project, *Incarcerated Women and Girls*.

6. Nellis, "Throw Away the Key."

7. Ibid.

8. Dye and Aday, "I Just Wanted to Die"; Leigey and Reed, "Woman's Life before Serving Life."

9. George, *Woman Doing Life*.

10. Owen, *In the Mix*.

11. Roscher, "Development of Coping Strategies."

12. Gender and Players, "Women Lifers."

13. Jose-Kamper, "Coming to Terms with Existential Death."

14. Leigey and Reed, "Woman's Life before Serving Life."

15. Surette, *Media, Crime, and Criminal Justice*; Sussman, "Media on Prisons."

16. Cecil, "Doing Time in 'Camp Cupcake,'" 142.

17. Ibid., 142–44.

18. Morash and Schram, *Prison Experience*, 21.

19. Cecil, "Dramatic Portrayals of Violent Women."

20. Cecil, "Doing Time in 'Camp Cupcake.'"

21. Cullen, "Assessing the Penal Harm Movement."

22. Handtke, Bretschneider, Elger, and Wangmo, "Easily Forgotten."

23. Demographic data for the U.S. population are available at http://www.census.gov.

24. Carr, "'Truth in Sentencing' in Georgia."

25. Derogatis, Lipman, Rickels, Uhlenhuth, and Covi, "Hopkins Symptom Checklist."

26. Dye and Aday, "I Just Wanted to Die."

27. Dye, Aday, and Farney, "Rock I Cling To."

28. Dodge and Pogrebin, "Collateral Costs of Imprisonment for Women."

29. Aday and Krabill, *Women Aging in Prison*.

30. George, *Woman Doing Life*, 120.

31. U.S. Department of Justice, *Survey of Inmates*.

Bibliography

Aday, Ron, and Jennifer Krabill. *Women Aging in Prison: A Neglected Population in the Corrections System*. Boulder, CO: Lynne Rienner, 2011.

Belknap, Joanne. *The Invisible Woman: Gender, Crime, and Justice*. 4th ed. Stamford, CT: Cengage, 2015.

Carr, Timothy. "'Truth in Sentencing' in Georgia." Georgia Department of Corrections, 2008. Accessed September 23, 2017. http://www.dcor.state.ga.us.

Cecil, Dawn. "Doing Time in 'Camp Cupcake': Lessons Learned from Newspaper Accounts of Martha Stewart's Incarceration." *Journal of Criminal Justice and Popular Culture* 14, no. 2 (2007): 142–60.

———. "Dramatic Portrayals of Violent Women: Female Offenders on Prime Time Crime Dramas." *Journal of Criminal Justice and Popular Culture* 14, no. 3 (2007): 243–58.

Cullen, Francis. "Assessing the Penal Harm Movement." *Journal of Research in Crime and Delinquency* 32 (1995): 338–58.

Derogatis, Leonard R., Ronald S. Lipman, Karl Rickels, E. H. Uhlenhuth, and Lino Covi. "The Hopkins Symptom Checklist (HSCL): A Self-Report Symptom Inventory." In *Psychological Measurements in Psychopharmacology*, edited by P. Pichot and R. Olivier-Martin, 70–110. New York: S. Karger, 1974.

Dodge, Mary, and Mark R. Pogrebin. "Collateral Costs of Imprisonment for Women: Complications of Reintegration." *Prison Journal* 81, no. 1 (2001): 42–54.

Dye, Meredith, and Ron Aday. "'I Just Wanted to Die': Pre-prison and Current Suicide Ideation among Women Serving Life Sentences." *Criminal Justice and Behavior* 40, no. 8 (2013): 832–49.

Dye, Meredith, Ron Aday, and Lori Farney. "'The Rock I Cling To': Religious Engagement in the Lives of Life-Sentenced Women." *Prison Journal* 98, no. 3 (2014): 388–408.

Gender, Elam, and Elaine Players. "Women Lifers: Assessing the Experience." *Prison Journal* 70 (1990): 46–57.

George, Erin. *A Woman Doing Life: Notes from a Prison for Women*. 2nd ed. New York: Oxford University Press, 2015.

Handtke, Violet, Wiebke Bretschneider, Bernice Elger, and Tenzin Wangmo. "Easily Forgotten: Elderly Female Prisoners." *Journal of Aging Studies* 32 (2015): 1–11.

Jose-Kamper, Christina. "Coming to Terms with Existential Death: An Analysis of Women's Adaption to Life in Prison." *Social Justice* 17, no. 2 (1990): 110–25.

Leigey, Margaret. "For the Longest Time: The Adjustment of Inmates to a Sentence of Life without Parole." *Prison Journal* 90, no. 3 (2010): 247–68.

Leigey, Margaret, and Katie Reed. "A Woman's Life before Serving Life: Examining the Negative Pre-incarceration Life Events of Female Life-Sentenced Inmates." *Women and Criminal Justice* 20 (2010): 302–22.

Morash, Merry, and Pamela J. Schram. *Prison Experience: Special Issues of Women in Prison*. Long Grove, IL: Waveland, 2002.

Nellis, Ashley. "Throw Away the Key: The Expansion of Life without Parole Sentences in the United States." *Federal Sentencing Reporter*, 23, no. 1 (2010): 27–32.

Nellis, Ashley, and Ryan S. King. *No Exit: The Expanding Use of Life Sentences in America*. Washington, D.C.: The Sentencing Project, July 2009. Accessed September 23, 2017. http://www.sentencingproject.org.

Owen, Barbara. *In the Mix: Struggle and Survival in a Women's Prison*. Albany, NY: Springer, 1998.

Roscher, Sherri. "The Development of Coping Strategies in Female Inmates with Life Sentences." PhD diss., Wright State University, 2005.

The Sentencing Project. *Incarcerated Women and Girls*. Updated November 2015. Accessed September 23, 2017. http://www.sentencingproject.org/publications/incarcerated-women-and-girls/.

Surette, Ray. *Media, Crime, and Criminal Justice: Images and Realities*. 5th ed. Stamford, CT: Cengage, 2015.

Sussman, Peter Y. "Media on Prisons: Censorship and Stereotypes." In *Invisible Punishment: The Collateral Consequences of Mass Imprisonment*, edited by Mark Mauer and Meda Chesney-Lind, 258–78. New York: New Press, 2002.

U.S. Department of Justice. *Survey of Inmates in State and Federal Adult Correctional Facilities, 2004*. Bureau of Justice Statistics, 2004. Accessed September 23, 2017. https://www.bjs.gov/index.cfm?ty=dcdetail&iid=275.

Zamble, Edward, and Frank J. Porporino, *Coping, Behavior, and Adaptation in Prison Inmates*. New York: Springer, 1988.

10. "I Am More Than a Crime": Interviews with Women Who Kill

Kathryn M. Whiteley

Society has long struggled to accept the phenomenon of a woman who kills. Since men in Western nations perpetrate nearly 90 percent of all homicides, little effort has focused on the study of women who kill. Among the 10 percent of total homicides perpetrated by women in the United States, fewer than 10 percent of the offenders receive convictions of murder, which assumes intent and premeditation.[1] In the last fifteen years, feminist criminologists have increasingly inquired into the phenomenon of women who kill. Among the most prolific voices have been those of Wendy Chan and Belinda Morrissey.[2] In their analysis of the existing understandings, they determined that women kill primarily from within the throes of three scenarios: victimization, mental illness, or out of an evil or wicked nature. As these understandings gained momentum in the literature, a slightly revised and abbreviated explanation became common: a woman kills because she is a victim, mad, or bad.

With the introduction of Lenore Walker's seminal work defining the battered woman syndrome, seeing the woman who kills as a victim gained wide acceptance.[3] During the 1980s, psychological theory introduced conditions such as postpartum depression and personality disorders to explain the "mad" understanding. The "bad" was reserved for the seemingly unexplainable acts. As Morris and Wilcyznski concurred, the use of this label is demonstrated in the comments of a judge at the sentencing of a mother who starved her child to death.[4] In casting her as a bad mother, the judge argued, "When one thinks of the extraordinary maternal sacrifice and care shown by lower animals, one has to wonder at her apparent selfishness."[5] The mother is inhuman or even less than an animal.

There were feminist criminologists, however, who argued that we further victimize women when we label them as victims, crazy, or evil and wicked. Kappeler, Kruttschnitt, and Carbone-Lopez did not deny that women kill because of abusive relationships or frank mental illness, yet sometimes, they contended, women kill like men do, out of jealousy, greed, or revenge.[6] The latter came to be referred to as agency, simply implying that women sometimes make a conscious choice to take a life or lives.

The media have also engaged in defining and labeling the killing done by women. In my research with women incarcerated for murder, some have had books written about them or television programs that reenacted their crime, or even a film produced about one inmate. The act of a woman who perpetrates murder seems to attract more press coverage, again, largely because of our societal and conscientious conflict with this aberrant act and its rarity. Media depictions of the crime and the woman further reflect our societal ambivalence.

Having briefly acknowledged criminological notions of the women who kill and introduced the media's draw to the phenomenon, this chapter now takes as its focus the perspective from the woman who kills. In my past and ongoing interviews with women incarcerated for murder convictions in maximum-security prisons in Australia and the United States, several recurring themes have emerged from the narratives collectively. The women consistently convey that the media failed to capture their larger lives; they contend that more coverage went to the crime itself as well as the victim(s), with little attention paid to their larger personhood. Most of the women express feelings of being demonized by the media. Adjectives used to depict their act were less painful to them than how they were framed as a person. A majority of the women are mothers, and each of these believes to some degree that her identity as a mother was assaulted. Beyond the seeming character assassinations, the women identify what they perceive as a fatal flaw in the media coverage. These are not women whose violent offending is, to some degree, understood through battered woman syndrome or frank mental illness; rather, their offense lies outside understandable explanations. Keep in mind, the women I interviewed were convicted for murder and incarcerated, not exonerated. These are women for which society argued there was no excuse for what they did.

As Wahidin argued, a challenge to our understanding of women incarcerated for murder lies in the fact that they are a hard to reach population.[7] Well established in criminological research is what Patenaude referred to as gatekeeping practices. As an example, prison inmates are a protected population for the purposes of research. Patenaude asserted that prison administration also erect barriers to keep the inquisitive at bay.[8] In my experience as a criminologist, it required over two years of diligent pursuit for me to gain access to a women's maximum-security prison in Australia, after the first prison denied my request. It required nearly as much time in the United States for my research to be approved. Once entry is gained, a prison's regimented schedules tax the most flexible of researchers. These obstacles have consequently discouraged researchers and journalists from doing the arduous work required to navigate the prison system.

Research Background

In 2008 I became a Pennsylvania Prison Society: Official Prison Visitor. In this role I visit inmates within Pennsylvania's State Correctional Institutions as a representative of the Prison Society. I chose to connect with the Women's State Correctional Institution in Muncy, Pennsylvania (SCI Muncy). This is the larger of Pennsylvania's two women's facilities and a maximum-security prison. As a representative of the Pennsylvania Prison Society, I can receive women's concerns and needs and communicate these to Prison Society administrators. In addition to my visits with the women, I maintain an active letter-writing exchange. In 2014 I was approved to conduct research at SCI Muncy. I should note that this research is *not* an effort of the Prison Society but rather a fulfillment of my research requirement as a criminology professor.

To the best of my knowledge, there is no research available to date where *only* extensive face-to-face individual interviews were conducted with women who had been convicted of murder and were serving sentences of life without parole in the United States. No group interviews were conducted. No surveys were presented for the women to complete. No third party was present in the room when the women were being interviewed for my research in Australia and the United States. I interviewed each woman using a tape recorder and handwriting notes on paper. I am the sole researcher, transcriber, and writer for both studies. Rather than answer specific research questions, I sought to gain an understanding of the larger life of women who killed.

I was prompted in part for this pursuit by an incarcerated woman I interviewed in Australia who was convicted of murder. She was articulate and insightful. She chose the pseudonym of Bella. Bella, in my estimation, acknowledged her offense and in our hours of dialogue never sought to rationalize her behavior. What she did frequently was call my attention to what she believed was a shortsighted and unfair representation of her. She called out the media and the court. Bella argued, "I am more than a crime, Kate." In reflecting on her courtroom experience and her personal reading of the media, she methodically conveyed how little of her larger life was depicted.

Of the seven women convicted of murder whom I interviewed in Australia, only one had a previous criminal charge, and it was not a crime of violence. The other women voiced a similar grievance that the media were hungry for crime details and motive and were largely uninterested in knowing more about their larger lives. One of the Australian women, whom I call Jean, commented, "They totally forgot the first 32 years of my life." Jean's point about herself applied to the others: they were not career criminals or repeat offenders.

The statement from Bella—"I'm more than a crime"—has lingered with me for several years and served to guide my research efforts in the United States. As mentioned previously, in 2014 I received approval to conduct research with women at SCI Muncy in Pennsylvania. Again, I did not have specific research questions for the women but sought instead to present open-ended questions that coursed throughout the women's lives as conveyed to me during several hours of face-to-face dialogue. In being true to Bella's declaration, I wanted to capture the larger lives of the women and so intentionally avoided exchanges specific to their offending. Subsequently, in the summer of 2014, I rented a room at a bed and breakfast near the prison. Over the summer, I entered the prison daily and met with the women. I interviewed fifty-four women, all of whom were convicted of violent crimes, with a majority of those crimes being murder. Many of the women who had been convicted for murder were serving a sentence of life without parole.

A Researcher's Personal Reflections

I possess a few hundred hours of recorded one-on-one conversations with the women, which I have personally transcribed into several hundred pages. Given my interest in media portrayals of women *and* the women's perceptions of those portrayals, I included some open-ended questions along this line. The following pages will communicate some thoughts that the women related about their media coverage that document its "felt impact" on them.

However, now I briefly share what it was like to enter both prisons and converse with the women. I am frequently asked some version of the following: What are they like, were you ever scared, do you think they are guilty, and how could you do this? As someone who was first a volunteer working with and visiting female offenders in Australia and now does so in the United States, the notion of ever feeling threatened or scared has rarely, if ever, surfaced. I approach each woman as a *human being*, a woman who wants someone to talk to, not to judge but just to listen. I err on the side of caution and would recommend the same to anyone researching women incarcerated for violent crimes. I have learnt it is best to build a *sincere rapport* slowly through volunteering, letter writing, and/or visiting. I do not come at this with a journalistic background. I approach my research as a woman who "attempts" to uncover the layering of another woman's personal complexities on her pathway to criminality. Then, I further explore the impact of such a journey on her and society as a whole.

To begin, as requested by the Pennsylvania Department of Corrections in the United States and the Department of Corrective Services in Queensland, Australia, the names of the women represented in this chapter are pseudonyms. Questions I posed to the women included ones like "Can you recall what was said and written about you following your offending?" and "Do you think it was a fair representation?" I should say that several women I spoke to at SCI Muncy had been incarcerated for more than twenty years. These women had offended prior to the rapid rise and spread of the internet and social media.

Women's Narratives

One middle-aged woman, Sherri, was a single mom, never completed tenth grade, and came from a low socioeconomic environment. In her words, "Growing up, my father was abusive and my mother was a drunk . . . someone had to look after the family." She mentioned that the father of her children abandoned her during the early stages of her last pregnancy. About her coverage in the news, Sherri commented:

> I didn't expect kind words . . . given what I did . . . it was just wrong, but they went all negative on me. Nothing was mentioned about me . . . raising my brothers and sisters and staying in school. I was a single mom with two jobs, but all you saw were these ugly photos of me . . . and it was like they were reading right off my rap sheet.

A woman called Kira, a single mom who had worked on the streets to "survive," killed her young child. She commented:

> What I did get, was the worst news coverage. It's like nothing I lived through or did in my life got mentioned, like my life just started when I did what I did. They have all these experts and reporters writing and talking and all they know is what someone else told them.

Megan, a middle-aged single woman, who had a college degree and what she described as a "good career and a good life" with "lots of friends," killed her boyfriend. She said:

> It got so bad with the media that my family and friends had to stop listening and reading it. They weren't excusing what I did and neither am I, but it just made me a crime figure and nothing else.

In all fairness to the media, they did not have the luxury of face-to-face extensive interviews and the opportunity to learn of the women's larger lives. When I communicated this to the women, some countered this assertion.

Janie, a woman who claimed that she had been sexually abused most of her childhood by her father, and that her mother did not believe in her, ran away and lived on the streets at the age of fifteen. Now decades later, she spoke about the media:

> If they really wanted to, they could dig and find out much more about us and maybe a few positives. If their son or daughter killed someone, and they could you know, you bet they would see that their kid's whole story would be told.

Layla, a woman in her fifties who participated in the killing of a stranger, reacted strongly to the adjectives chosen to describe her. She argued:

> The . . . writer or journalist shouldn't be able to call us names, unless they could sit down . . . across from us . . . hell, like we are doing now . . . and let us defend ourselves . . . tell me how did they come up with me being a prostitute. I never got into prostitution, now I am stuck with this label. This is part of my identity.

Consistently, the women argued that it was the job of reporters to research and tell the complete story about them. However, what appears to dominate media coverage is a story about *a woman convicted as a murderer*, with limited or no space given to information about the woman beyond the criminal act. For most of those found guilty of murder, there is no space in the media for positives.

Jessica, a well-educated woman raised in an affluent white family who was convicted of killing her female partner, raised concerns about the sources from which the media garnered information. She said she found out through her family that some of her old friends, with whom she had had a falling out, were contacted and interviewed by the media. She argued that their continued animosity toward her was reflected in their accounts through half-truths and "trumped-up stories."

One woman's concern was her past substance abuse and how her addiction had been a centerpiece in her media coverage. Myra was a recovering addict when she took a person's life. She had been in and out of treatment since a teenager, and most of her prior offending was drug related. Myra said:

> You know, I finally got the drug addiction thing right . . . under control and I was clean for over a year, but I got no credit for that. All the stories . . . referred to me as a drug addict. I was this murderer and drug addict. Have they missed that drug addiction is a disease, yeah, and that some of us can recover?
>
> You see . . . if I was this rich and famous person with a drug problem . . . and happened to kill someone, it would hardly be mentioned, right? Or it would be used as an excuse for them, in self-defense. I bet they would play it down and give some kind of pity. Yeah, I think there is a double standard for sure. It sells papers, doesn't it? They got the drug addict right . . . but just happened to leave out my struggles to get clean and . . . what about my recovery . . . they don't mention that . . . do they?

One could argue that the most heart-rending and painful written and spoken commentary came from personal attacks on their motherhood. Several of the women questioned why their children had to become a focal point of storytelling. Carla, a mother of three children, contended, "What does my mothering, me being a mom, have to do with my crime?" She continued to argue that the media coverage focused on her bad parenting, her being a bad mother:

> All they could say was what I did was selfish . . . [be]cause, according to them, I left my kids to fend for themselves and like . . . how could any mother do this . . . and forget about her kids. It's like the headlines have to read something about a single mother who has all these kids and she deserts them. Why not talk more about the woman who killed someone . . . not focus on me as a mom.

Anna, an African American woman and a single parent, expressed her view:

> You see for me . . . as a mom, what the media did, over and over again, they talked about my kids and how they had different fathers. What does that have to do with what I did? I'll tell you why . . . it's nothing more than a personal attack on me . . . I guess that's what they expect from a single Black woman.

It was Vickie who presented a different take on her victim. According to her, she killed her violent male partner, who had children with other women. Vickie added:

> It's like they praised this violent man, who had a criminal record . . . as being a good father. They questioned how could I, as a mother do this, this crime . . . only to leave his kids fatherless. I'll tell you, I was far a better mother to my kids than he was a father to his. The news . . . the news story, they made it all about me. Me, as this terrible mother who left her kids motherless and his fatherless. The truth is, I never left my kids and he never lived with his.

As several of the women pointed out, their perceptions were not intended to position themselves as victims of some evil media conspiracy to defame them. In fact, the women in this study largely rejected the victim status. Their responses are better understood through their utter disrespect for the tantalizing narratives the media spin simply to gain an audience. Some of the women laughed at headlines shown to them as they revisited stories written about their case. Between the headlines and photos, obvious to most was the insensitivity and bias of the media. Beth, a woman from a small rural town, commented on how coverage of her case monopolized the papers for months as it unfolded: "I think I got more coverage than O. J. Simpson." Marge recalled asking her friends and family to pay attention to the magazines at the grocery checkout and let her know if she ever made the cover.

I asked the women to explain the overall impact that the media coverage had on them. In reply, Carol, a woman from an affluent suburb, asserted, "Their insensitivity served to traumatize my children." Carol took the life of a man with whom she was having an affair. She framed the affair and her offending as inexcusable and expressed deep remorse for them. Carol, however, also shared that she was devastated by the continued coverage of the affair and her passionate slaying of her lover. She discussed how it greatly affected her children at school, as their classmates were hearing and reading about her and the crime. She recalled her children being taunted at school and on the playground. She mentioned there was even vandalism to the outside of their home. Carol questioned the necessity of such prolonged coverage. She pointed out:

> An acquaintance . . . or you could say, just someone I knew from my hometown, was driving under the influence . . . they had a few drinks, apparently. They got behind the wheel and collided with another car and killed a woman. That case, after a few weeks . . . the story just disappeared, no more was said. However, in my situation, the stories kept going on for months. What the media wrote about me, I can share with you, was far more revealing about my personal life, and it was not positive.

Carol concluded:

> It would have been so much easier for my family and me, if a story read that I was really, deeply distressed and saddened about my actions. If they had said that prior to my crime . . . I did have a good life, I did lead a good life . . . no crimes, never in trouble . . . nothing, which is true. In their eyes, outside of here, I will remain this selfish and jealous woman . . . who had an affair and ended up violently killing her lover. This is how I will be remembered and little about who I really was back then . . . and now, who I am today.

Other women expressed concerns with media reports and their instant accessibility on the internet. Gracie tearfully conveyed her lingering fear:

> It is bad enough my kids will be reminded of what I did . . . and I am afraid my grandkids will one day read about it too. You can read anything out there today. They shouldn't be punished . . . you know, reminded about what I did. Probably years from now, they will still be reminded. It saddens me a lot.

Another angle was presented by Amy, who questioned society's seeming insatiable appetite for violent stories. She spoke of the preponderance of television and documentary cop shows and murder investigation programs:

> It's like people are longing for it . . . they can't get enough of it . . . you know, to watch shows that have violence, things about violence, to hear about people and violent crimes. You have these television shows now . . . about women . . . they commit violent crimes. Then these detective

programs . . . you see where the cops are always chasing the bad guys . . . and some of these, they can be really violent. It's crazy, but people can't seem to get enough of them.

Amy concluded:

Media and all the reporting on women like us . . . feeds the hunger for people out there, at our expense, you know . . . and the expense of our families. It's like they have to punish our families, too.

Claire also explained:

If they could only understand . . . think about it, all that was written about me out there, some fact, some not at all . . . and it's written to entice them . . . and it gets you in. I don't believe my kids can ever be free of what I did, it will always find them. This hurts me deeply. My kids are not protected, not at all protected . . . because of the media and the internet.

The last question I asked the women about their coverage in the media was a hypothetical one:

If a group of journalists and or editors from a variety of media organizations were here today, and I asked you to address the group on their media coverage, based on your experience, what would you communicate to them?

I quipped to them that this would be their letter to the editor in response to their news coverage. The initial reaction I got from the women told me they had not anticipated this question, so I asked them to think carefully about their answer. I reminded them that their answers may reach media organizations through my forthcoming publications.

Women's Challenges to the Media

As previously established, the women cited in this chapter are serving sentences without the chance of parole. As such, they stand to gain nothing from garnering the favor of the media. The women I quote all conveyed their guilt and acceptance of their punishment. With this in mind, they were able to approach this question with some level of objectivity based on their personal experience with the media and the media experiences as conveyed by their peers. Most concurred that, after many years of confinement, "You have to release your anger or it will eat away at you like a cancer." They agreed that they would not approach the media "angrily" but seek rather to add their perceptions and educate the media. Many women acknowledged that they understood journalists and editors have a job to do. However, they were less sympathetic to the other role of the media: that of selling the women's stories and gaining an audience at their expense.

Erin was a college graduate who had lived a comfortable suburban lifestyle prior to her offending. Erin challenged the media representatives on a personal level, arguing:

> If your colleague or a friend, say, did the unthinkable, as I admit I did, would you first of all . . . even write the story? Let's assume you had to, would it have the same tone and intent as mine? Do you step back and consider the impact of your writing on the innocents . . . innocent people . . . keep in mind that the innocents of the victim are not the only innocents, but the offender's innocents as well. What is written, sticks!

Marcia, a middle-aged woman who had engaged in a robbery in which the victim was killed, had a graduate degree and often wrote to fill time while incarcerated. She felt compelled to ask about the quality of media reporting. Marcia said she would ask reporters, "Is your writing about good investigative journalism or are you writing to please the crowds?" She spoke about some of the media's coverage of her offending:

> I read newspaper stories about me, which really, really, belonged in the supermarket tabloids. Therefore, I would like to ask them . . . when they write a story, are they guided by the quality and accuracy of their story or only driven by their desire for making headlines and making sales . . . selling papers. I would ask them about their professional code of ethics . . . of conduct. Then, get them to explain to me the guidelines . . . for what makes good journalism. I would ask them to explain this to me.

In the course of our discussions, some women revisited the point that, when a woman kills, it is considered far more newsworthy than when a man kills. Emma shared:

> What I would like to ask them, if a woman kills on Monday and a man in the same town kills that day, why is so much more attention given to the woman and her crime? That's what I would like to know. I don't understand why the focus always seems on us.

It was Rosie who reflected on the adjectives used to describe her and other women, which seem worse in comparison to the media coverage of men who kill. Rosie, a woman from the inner city who killed a close family member, shared her concerns:

> You know, men kill all the time, right? They call them evil and bad . . . for what they did. But I tell you . . . I do the same crime and I am called inhuman, despicable and evil, she's got to be evil! Then they go on and trash me. I am this horrible mom. They said I am an unfit parent . . . and lots of other things about me as a mom.
>
> I made the front page news when they arrested me. Think about men who kill someone. Do they think if a man kills, he's not worth being sensationalized? Because that's what they do to women like me. What makes us . . . a woman like me different? We both committed a murder.

Of paramount concern to the women appeared to be a desire to stress the complexity of a life and to situate their own life as "more than a crime," as Bella from Australia asserted. Another woman serving time for murder in Australia (Jennifer) discussed how she tried to process her life and offending. She was Egyptian by birth and was brought to Australia for an arranged marriage. She shared that she was forced into a foreign culture with no under-standing of the language and no family or social support. In her frustration to reconcile her life with her offending over many years of incarceration, she concluded, "My life, my story . . . it's complex." Jennifer commented on how the media need to recognize the complexities of a person's life. She argued:

> Without examining deeply into someone's life . . . you present a limited understanding of our life as daughters, as mothers, as women and our offending . . . this victimizes us, as well as our loved ones and our families.

Summary and Analysis

As was established in the introduction, women perpetrate approximately 10 percent of all homicides in Western nations (Australia, Canada, and England). As a consequence to this rarity, there is a scarcity of research on women who kill. Instead, research on homicide has been dominated by the study of men who kill. The theories that attempt to understand the phenomenon tend to explain a woman's killing as a result of her abuse or mental pathology. A later explanation was expounded in Kappeler's book *The Will to Violence*, in which she was among the first to contend that women make a conscious choice to kill, which resonates as true for the women in this study.[9] While explanations like Kappeler's do exist, there is no readily agreed-on theory that explains killing by a woman.

When society lacks an understanding of a phenomenon, particularly one that startles us, there is an inherent risk of demonizing or exploiting. Arguably, this has been the case with a woman who kills. Critical to this analysis is to clarify that a conviction of murder implies premeditation and intent. The women engaged in this study, per their sentences, chose to kill and as such were not ascribed a victim status. They exercised agency or choice in killing, which collides with the prevailing discourse of normative femininity. Normative femininity depicts women as the gentler and nurturing gender. The capacity to offend violently is in the nature of men but not so in women. The narratives of the women cited in this chapter reflect this lack of understanding and burden of the dominant discourse.

Schur asserted that feminist criminological research has long argued that framing oneself as a good mother is a master identity for women.[10] As supported by Chan and Jensen's research, the majority of the women in this study were mothers, which holds true across all female homicide offenders.[11] Nicolson claimed that motherhood is assumed to be instinctual in the provision of love and nurturing to children.[12] Subsequently, women whose behaviors fall outside the ideals of motherhood become a media focus. In Loue's analysis, journalists may contrast a good mother as a consummate nurturer with a bad mother as an accomplished destroyer.[13]

According to Roberts, race and class are two major variables used to define motherhood in Western culture. Roberts noted that white middle-class women are often stereotyped as good mothers, whereas women of color are depicted as an out-group or bad mothers.[14] In one of the most frequently cited articles in this area, Huckerby compared and contrasted two cases of infanticide that received significant media coverage. One of the women was a married white nurse and the other a single Asian mother. Huckerby concluded that the two mothers shared many similarities. Both were treated for depression. The white woman was framed as a good mother with an illness or as a victim of her depression, whereas the Asian mother was deemed bad and without extenuating circumstances. Her promiscuity was exploited and her depression overlooked.[15]

No one among the women I interviewed for this study endured more assaults on their identity as a mother than the women who had killed their children. Two women communicated what seemed to be relentless attacks on them as mothers. The media would call attention to their histories of addiction, criminality, and sexual promiscuity, and the "how could she?" question seemed to loom over their heads. Their media depictions mirrored what Meyer and Oberman found when exploring explanations and portrayals of mothers who killed their children: "Women characterized as bad are depicted as cold, callous, evil mothers who have often been neglectful of their children and domestic responsibilities. These mothers are often betrayed as sexually promiscuous, non-remorseful, and even non-feminine."[16]

Finally, Edwards wrote about the killing of a child as so at odds with motherhood that such women can only be understood as immutably unnatural.[17] Arguably, women who kill their children are the least understood among the women who kill and are subjected to the harshest depictions.

Personal Experience and Media Coverage

The narratives of the women I interviewed largely confirm the conclusions of research that has analyzed media coverage of women who perpetrate murder. The women are framed as evil, wicked, bad, and engaged in the unthinkable, killing just like men. The research further suggests that women who kill their children receive the most damning media coverage. Also well established is that women of color tend to be depicted more harshly.

A woman who kills is largely misunderstood. As was cited in the introduction, the universal explanation for such killing, as espoused by Morrissey, frames the woman as victimized, mad, or bad.[18] The victim explanation applies largely to victimization through abuse such as domestic violence and child abuse. The mad pertains to understandings couched in mental illness or psychopathology. The bad, however, implies that a woman has stepped outside the boundaries of normative femininity and domesticity and has therefore engaged in the unnatural.

What the narratives of the women from my research in the United States and Australia agree on is that the media ignore the larger lives of these women. If they could communicate one criticism to the media, this would be their message. Toward understanding murder committed by women, Leonard was among the first to challenge the universal explanations of victimization and mental illness. She argued that they were shortsighted and failed to account for the larger context of the woman's life as well as her offending.[19] In support of Leonard's contention, Jensen argued that universal explanations yield an incomplete understanding of the phenomenon of a woman who kills.[20] Without having read the research literature, these women arrived at the same conclusion, the significance of incorporating their *larger life* into the equation. This is what the women wanted the media to know.

I would maintain that the women presented in this study lie outside the universal explanations and, as such, defy our understanding. It is, as Easteal posed, problematic to shift the prevailing paradigm with the male as the aggressor and the female as the victim.[21] Many women who commit homicide are exonerated or convicted of lesser charges than murder based on their victimization from abuse and mental illness. The women engaged in this study all received murder convictions for which intent and premeditation were established. The universal explanations of victimhood and madness were not applicable, so the explanation of badness was applied by the media.

In conclusion, the women's hypothetical letters to the editor, formed in response to my question, acknowledged that their acts of murder are front-page news. They would caution, though, not to demonize women and their behavior, of which little is known. Most women expressed how upsetting the demoralizing adjectives were and would ask if this is "necessary" for good reporting. The women who cited published assaults on their identity as mothers were particularly offended. They asked, What value or purpose does this accomplish? Last and most important, writers for the media should move beyond the crime and its victims to consider the *larger life* of the woman. Anything less renders an incomplete understanding of the woman's life and offending.

Final Thoughts

I have been graced for years to meet and visit with a large, almost forgotten and often misunderstood, subgroup of incarcerated women. Similar to my research experience in Australia with women incarcerated for murder, I find the women of SCI Muncy eager for an opportunity to share information about their lives, not only their crimes. The women identified in this research volunteered to be interviewed. No woman received any money or gifts for their participation. These women argue, through their accounts of their lives, that most existing research, and society as well, sticks to the universal explanations and remains entrapped in notions of normative femininity and domesticity.

I would not wish to offend my fellow researchers or the media. I understand that women incarcerated for murder are extremely challenging to reach and that this accounts for the dearth of research and multidimensional reporting on them. However, there is much to be learned in dialogue with these women, and I would therefore encourage the endeavor.

Notes

1. Morrissey, *When Women Kill.*
2. Chan, *Women, Murder and Justice*; Morrissey, *When Women Kill.*
3. Walker, *Battered Woman Syndrome.*
4. Morris and Wilcyznski, "Rocking the Cradle."
5. Ibid., 213.
6. Kappeler, *Will to Violence*; Kruttschnitt and Carbone-Lopez, "Moving beyond the Stereotypes."
7. Wahidin, *Older Women in the Criminal Justice System.*
8. Patenaude, "No Promises, but I Am Willing to Listen."
9. Kappeler, *Will to Violence.*
10. Schur, *Labeling Women Deviant.*
11. Chan, *Women, Murder and Justice*; Jensen, *Why Women Kill.*
12. Nicolson, "Telling Tales."
13. Loue, *Intimate Partner Violence.*
14. Roberts, "Motherhood and Crime."
15. Huckerby, "Women Who Kill Their Children."
16. Meyer and Oberman, *Mothers Who Kill Their Children*, 70.
17. Edwards, *Women on Trial.*
18. Morrissey, *When Women Kill.*
19. Leonard, *Women, Crime and Society.*
20. Jensen, *Why Women Kill.*
21. Easteal, *Balancing the Scales.*

Bibliography

Chan, Wendy. *Women, Murder and Justice.* Hampshire, UK: Palgrave Macmillan, 2001.

Easteal, Patricia. *Balancing the Scales: Rape, Law Reform, and Australian Culture.* Sydney: Federation Press, 1998.

Edwards, Susan. *Women on Trial: A Study of the Female Suspect, Defendant and Offender in the Criminal Law and Criminal Justice System.* Manchester: Manchester University Press, 1984.

Huckerby, Jayne. "Women Who Kill Their Children: Case Study and Conclusions concerning the Differences in the Fall from Material Grace by Khoua

Her and Andrea Yates." *Duke Journal of Gender Law & Policy* 10 (2003): 149–72.

Jensen, Vickie. *Why Women Kill: Homicide and Gender Equality.* London: Lynne Reiner, 2001.

Kappeler, Susanne. *The Will to Violence: The Politics of Personal Violence.* Cambridge: Polity, 1995.

Kruttschnitt, Candace, and Kristin Carbone-Lopez. "Moving beyond the Stereotypes: Women's Subjective Accounts of Their Violent Crime." *Criminology* 44, no. 2 (2006): 321–51.

Leonard, Eileen. *Women, Crime and Society: A Critique of Theoretical Criminology.* White Plains, NY: Longman, 1982.

Loue, Sana. *Intimate Partner Violence: Societal, Medical, Legal, and Individual Responses.* New York: Kluwer Academic/Plenum, 2001.

Meyer, Cheryl, and Michelle Oberman. *Mothers Who Kill Their Children: Understanding the Acts of Moms from Susan Smith to the "Prom Mom."* New York: New York University Press, 2001.

Morris, Allison, and Ania Wilcyznski. "Rocking the Cradle: Mothers Who Kill Their Children." In *Moving Targets: Women, Murder and Representation,* edited by Helen Birch, 198–217. London: Virago, 1993.

Morrissey, Belinda. *When Women Kill: Questions of Agency and Subjectivity.* New York: Routledge, 2003.

Nicolson, Donald. "Telling Tales: Gender Discrimination, Gender Construction and Battered Women Who Kill." *Feminist Legal Studies* 3, no. 2 (1995): 185–206.

Patenaude, Allan. "No Promises, but I Am Willing to Listen and Tell What I Hear: Conducting Qualitative Research among Inmates and Staff." *Prison Journal,* no. 84 (2004): 69S–91S.

Roberts, Dorothy. "Motherhood and Crime." *Iowa Law Review* 79 (1993): 95–141.

Schur, Edwin. *Labeling Women Deviant: Gender, Stigma, and Social Control.* New York: Random House, 1984.

Wahidin, Azrini. *Older Women in the Criminal Justice System: Running Out of Time.* London: Jessica Kingsley, 2004.

Walker, Lenore. *The Battered Woman Syndrome.* New York: Springer, 1984.

SECTION THREE

Forgotten Voices in Media

We know that media depictions offer a limited set of experiences, typically those of the protagonist, with one-dimensional characters rounding out the cast. While contemporary representations expand on these perspectives, they still leave out a diversity of issues and voices from the prison population. This section offers perspectives from some of the forgotten groups through an analysis of breastfeeding in prison as an extension of motherhood, the challenges of being transgender in a men's prison, black masculinity as conceived by former inmates, and a scholar's experience of volunteering in prison.

11. Breastfeeding in Prison

Amanda Barnes Cook

For a convicted mother, a sentence has profound effects on her relationship with her children and on her maternity itself. For a pregnant or breast-feeding mother, incarceration amounts to a loss of the ability to decide to breastfeed and a loss of access to her children.[1] In this chapter I consider the case of incarcerated mothers in the United States and theorize, from the standpoint of feminist political theory, how state policies should treat women offenders to preserve their rights and equitable treatment under the law. Just treatment of women offenders, I argue, does not always mean treatment that is the same as the treatment of men offenders. Gender-neutral incarceration policies are a disservice to women offenders, especially in the face of sex-specific issues like lactation.

The Problems Facing Incarcerated Mothers and Pregnant Women

The number of women under correctional control has increased dramatically in the past few decades; even as women's criminality has remained stable, the number of women in prison increased by 646 percent between 1980 and 2010.[2] This increase is due, in large part, to the war on drugs. Most women offenders are arrested and incarcerated for property and drug crimes; violent crime among women has decreased. Female prisoners often come from traumatic backgrounds, as more than 40 percent of women offenders have been victims of physical or sexual abuse, and "a total of 22.3 percent of women in jail have been diagnosed with PTSD."[3] Addiction and mental illness frequently affect this population, with 80 percent having substance-abuse problems[4] and one in four having been

231

diagnosed with a mental illness. Furthermore, of those with mental illness, 75 percent have a co-occurring substance-abuse disorder. In addition to these obstacles, most of the women under correctional control—70 percent—are mothers of minor children.[5] Most incarcerated mothers were, prior to conviction, single mothers with sole custody of, on average, two children. Further, it is estimated that 4–9 percent of women offenders are pregnant at the time of incarceration.[6] Around ten thousand babies are born in prison each year in the United States. Nearly a quarter of children with an incarcerated parent are age four or younger.[7] As such, separation from children is a primary concern of incarcerated women. Barbara Bloom argued, "Separation from children is considered to be among the most damaging aspects of imprisonment for women. The difficulties of separation are exacerbated by a lack of contact. In some cases, the forced separation between parent and child results in permanent termination of the parent-child relationship."[8] More than half of mothers are never visited by their children during their period of incarceration, mostly because of logistical difficulties and the long distances to women's prisons.[9] Moreover, incarcerated mothers face the constant worry of losing their children permanently. For children in the foster care system, the Adoption and Safe Families Act of 1997 provides for termination of parental rights once a child has been in foster care for fifteen or more of the past twenty-two months. Incarcerated mothers serve an average sentence of eighteen months.[10] Even mothers with children under the care of family members (usually the maternal grandmother) must face legal requirements for reunification—housing, economic support, medical services, and more—that are nearly impossible to meet.[11]

Evidence shows, too, that some judges attempt to protect fetal health by incarcerating pregnant substance abusers who would not otherwise serve time in prison, in effect doling out harsher penalties than average for pregnant women.[12] Surveys of judges indicate that they may give these harsher sentences precisely because there are so few community-based substance-abuse treatment options.[13] This practice, however, is not legally or medically sound. From the legal side, it infringes on the constitutional rights of the mothers: "Constitutional principles of equal protection and due process, privacy and bodily integrity, as well as Eighth Amendment issues, restrict a judge's options when faced with a pregnant, drug-using criminal defendant."[14] Medically, it is not indicated because women often get better treatment in the community and because increased criminalization has the unintended consequence of keeping substance-abusing pregnant women who are not incarcerated from seeking necessary medical treatment.[15] These punitive sentences for pregnant women have lasting implications for a mother's access to her child after giving birth and for the possibility of a mother being able to decide to breastfeed (methadone treatment does not contraindicate breastfeeding).[16]

Institutional support for breastfeeding is, moreover, urgently needed in local jails. Jails have a higher proportion of pregnant offenders, and most have specific regulations for pregnancy-related medical issues.[17] Micaela Cadena, the policy director for Young Women United, argued, "Pregnant or lactating women should be in their communities, not in jail awaiting their plea bargains or hearings."[18] Being held in jail is even more troubling for breastfeeding mothers. As Cadena explained, "One of the concerns that we have is if somebody's locked up for a few days, takes a couple days to post bail or bond and may be a breastfeeding mother, in that time span her milk may have dried up, and she may have lost her milk supply."[19] Jails have the burden of dealing with mothers who are under correctional control for short periods and for whom that time is critical in maintaining their milk supply.

The situation, then, for mothers under correctional control is that they are systematically deprived of access to their children, their families are torn apart, and they are not allowed to breastfeed. These mothers may also be struggling with drug addiction, poverty, and past abuse. What these women and children need is not incarceration but comprehensive support in all facets of life to prevent their coming under correctional control:

> We need to create a community response to the issues that impact women's lives and increase their risk of incarceration. Basic needs that, if unmet, put women at risk for criminal justice involvement: housing, physical and psychological safety, education, job training and opportunities, community-based substance-abuse treatment, economic support, positive female role models, and a community response to violence against women. The greatest needs are for multifaceted drug abuse and trauma recovery treatment and for education and training in job and parenting skills.[20]

Instead of getting the treatment and opportunities they need—particularly job training and drug-abuse and trauma-recovery treatment—they are robbed of access to and relationships with their children, making them ever more vulnerable to continued criminality and drug abuse. Bloom stated, "Research demonstrates that both male and female offenders who maintain ties to their families and communities during incarceration are less likely to recidivate."[21] The correctional treatment of incarcerated mothers continues a cycle of victimization of vulnerable women.

So if these mothers pose no threat to their communities, and if the logical place for them is in drug-abuse and trauma-recovery treatment, why are we separating these mothers from their children, in many cases terminating their parental rights? One explanation is that regulation of maternal separation has historically been driven by normative ideas of "proper" motherhood. There is a notion that we cannot give a break to "bad mothers." People assume that children should be separated from a parent who has engaged in criminal activity, particularly drug use. An official from the New Mexico Breastfeeding Task Force, in an interview with the author, reported that the group advocating for breast pumps in New Mexico prisons passed up the opportunity for media coverage because of a concern that it "would attract community pushback for providing some sort of leniency for women criminals." But Myrna Raeder, a legal scholar who advocated for criminal justice reform for women offenders, argued that "a parent who commits a criminal act may still have a substantial and responsible relationship with a child."[22] Raeder noted that "obviously, mothers who are substance abusers make unreliable parents, but even then children are not usually benefitted by their mother's incarceration if she is suitable for supervision and drug treatment in the community."[23] Elsewhere, she explained:

> There is a Pollyanna view that children have better alternatives than being with their "bad" parent. But neither adoption nor foster care is a panacea. It would be naive to think that being shuttled among strangers is always preferable to remaining with their family. Numerous surveys reveal astoundingly high incidences of abuse or neglect within foster care. In addition, multiple placements and failure to adequately provide for the child's needs are widespread problems in the foster care system. Exposure to physical and sexual abuse may put children in greater jeopardy than staying with a parent who is obtaining supervised treatment.[24]

It is imperative, then, that we question the logic behind claims of what is in the "best interest" of incarcerated families. Women offenders who are mothers necessarily defy norms of "good motherhood." But defying norms of good motherhood is not in itself justification for separating those women from their children. Decisions to separate mothers from their children must be based on something more.

Furthermore, if a given case raises concerns about the ability of a mother to provide good care to her children, we must ask why, rather than end the conversation with incarceration. Is it because she does not have access to good drug rehabilitation services or because she is unable to get a job? We must work to provide the services that will allow her to succeed, to mother. Otherwise, women are being asked to navigate impossible situations—and when they, unsurprisingly, fail, they are told it is an individual failing of a "bad" mother and are separated from their children. This system, with its lack of support for vulnerable mothers, criminalization of drug use, minimal rehabilitation services, and incarceration and separation from children, does not respect each individual in a way that honors her rights.

So how can society give a woman offender, who is most likely dealing with a history of drug addiction, mental health disorders, and physical or sexual abuse, what Martha Nussbaum called "the preconditions of a life worthy of human dignity?"[25] The answer, almost universally advocated by those who study gender and the criminal justice system, is alternative sentencing, or community-based corrections. These programs provide close supervision for the mother and child in a community-based residential setting, saving money and reducing recidivism. As was mentioned earlier, most women's crimes are drug or property related, so many of these women are good candidates for community-based corrections programs: "Female offenders are frequently good candidates for community-based corrections. The least restrictive alternative to incarceration should be considered for the female offender."[26] The American College of Obstetricians and Gynecologists committee opinion asserted,

> It is important to avoid separating the mother from the infant. Prison nurseries or alternative sentencing of women to community-based noninstitutional settings should be considered for women during the postpartum period. . . . Given the benefits of breastfeeding to both the mother and the infant, . . . accommodations should be made for freezing, storing, and transporting the milk. This can be difficult to facilitate and is another argument for prison nurseries or alternative sentencing of women to community-based noninstitutional settings.[27]

But community-based corrections programs are not the only model for accommodating incarcerated mothers and their young children. In the next section I explore three possibilities for meeting the needs of breastfeeding incarcerated mothers and their children: prison nursery programs, in-prison pumping programs, and community-based corrections programs.

Accommodations for Breastfeeding Inmates

Breastfeeding is generally impossible for women under correctional control, even though the World Health Organization, the American Academy of Pediatrics, the U.S. surgeon general, and health authorities around the world agree that the optimal feeding option for infants is exclusive breastfeeding for the first six months of life, followed by breastfeeding with complementary foods until at least twelve months, with continued breastfeeding for as long as mutually desired by mother and child.[28] These recommendations come from a scientific consensus that breastfeeding is the healthiest choice for both mother and child.[29] Furthermore, mothers can provide breast milk for their children by using an electric breast pump, with a mother expressing her milk as often as her baby needs to eat.

Theoretically, lactation is compatible with incarceration in a few different ways.[30] Under the current correctional model, some women might give birth shortly before they are due for release, in which case they may be interested in maintaining lactation through a pumping regimen (possibly discarding the milk) so that they can breastfeed their child upon release. Other women might be interested in pumping milk for transport to their babies, which would require a prison infrastructure to support the safe storage and transportation of milk. Other women might be interested in keeping lactation going so as to feed their baby during visitation. To accommodate breastfeeding inmates, prisons need to have clear policies on how breast pumps are to be treated: Are manual pumps classified differently from electric ones? Would pumps have to be kept in a secure area? How are the logistics of milk storage to be addressed? For prison nurseries, the prison must have clear policies on how the babies are cared for and how women are to mother their children in a prison. For community-based corrections, policies must be clear about the conditions under which women offenders can remain with their children and what sort of infractions would make them ineligible for community-based programs or for remaining with their children.

In fact, the vast majority of incarcerated women do not have any of these options; in most prisons breast pumps are regarded as "security violations" and are confiscated, even for mothers who are only trying to maintain lactation through pumping and discarding their milk.[31]

Prison Nursery Programs

It is possible to maintain maternal access to young children through prison nursery programs. Prison nursery programs are not new; historical records of American prison nurseries date back at least to the early nineteenth century.[32] They were often unregulated; babies stayed with their mothers as a matter of course. Prison records from Maryland, Massachusetts, New York, and Pennsylvania in the period of 1800–1840 indicate that children were present in the facilities.[33] Extremely poor treatment of pregnant women and newborns, and consequently high levels of infant mortality, led reformers to advocate in the 1870s for separate correctional facilities for male and female inmates.[34] As a result, many American women—especially white and middle-class women—were sent to reformatories instead of prisons; in most reformatories, children born during the period of incarceration were able to stay with their mothers until two years of age.[35] During this historical period, some reformatories built homelike cottages with kitchens for women and children; the inmates received lessons in homemaking and domesticity.

The Great Depression and World War II era saw the closing of many reformatories, as female inmates were expected to join the war effort rather than mother their children. Until this time, most prisons and reformatories allowed mothers to keep their babies with them for at least a short time period, while two states had a two-year limit and three states had no age limit at all. But by the 1950s, the trend was toward facilities allowing children to stay with their mothers for less and less time. Social workers from the Department of Health, Education, and Welfare and judges alike became concerned about the welfare of the children in prison nurseries, declaring that prison was "no place for children."[36] By the 1960s, "the era of nurseries in prisons came to an end."[37]

With more restrictive age limits on mother-child programs, mothers were often severely distressed when their babies reached the maximum age for the program and were removed. In 1963 Elizabeth Gurley Flynn, a labor organizer and communist who served time in a federal prison, observed:

> The parting of a mother and child, especially if she faced a long sentence, was heartrending. The grief and worry of these poor women affected their health and spirits, sometimes to the point of collapse. Certainly, in these cases there should be some special provisions, especially for first time offenders, to keep the mother and baby together.[38]

Over time, though, the number of prison nursery programs decreased. Child advocates worried about incarcerating children: in-prison programs "generally maintain the traditional structure of incarceration . . . [and] effectively imprison the children."[39] In a desire not to submit infants to institutional-ization, most mothers and children, instead, were separated.

Nevertheless, some prison nursery programs survived this era. Currently, ten states have some sort of prison nursery program. Bedford Hills in New York is probably the most famous example. Bedford Hills opened a mother-child program in 1901 that has been running continually since that time. At Bedford Hills mothers may keep their babies with them until they are between twelve to eighteen months old. Mothers and babies live in the same room; mothers participate in parenting classes and bring their babies to pediatricians who come to the prison. The program also provides vocational training for moth-ers and a visiting program for the older children of incarcerated mothers.[40] In 1994 the Nebraska Correctional Center for Women opened its prison nursery; infants are allowed to reside with their mother if her release date will come before the child turns eighteen months old, and parenting classes are mandatory.[41] A nursery opened at Washington Corrections Center for Women in 1999, offering an inmate, with a sentence of less than three years after the birth of her child, the option to keep her child in the nursery until the child turns eighteen months old, at which point mother and child move to a prerelease center for the next eighteen months.[42] These programs have worked well and have not faced major issues, as is evidenced by the more than one-hundred-year history of the program at Bedford Hills.

Evidence gathered from existing and historical prison nurseries suggests no ill effects on children as a result of their stay in prison. In fact, one study determined that the majority of prison nursery infants tested as "securely attached" to their mother.[43] Mary Byrne, a nurse who studies prison nursery documents, found that "infant development was threatened by infant insecure behaviors if transitioned to alternate caregiver in the community. DOCS [department of corrections] initiated separations from mother produced setbacks in infant self-regulatory behaviors"; however, infants of all ages in prison nursery programs met developmental, mental, and motor milestones.[44] Nevertheless some critics of prison nursery programs note that prisons are prisons first and child-care facilities second, so the quality of care for the children is not guaranteed. Moreover, they worry that access to medical care for the children might be difficult to secure (though existing prison nursery programs do provide access to pediatric care).[45]

Retaining access to children is also beneficial to the flourishing of the mother. Evidence shows that "stress associated with limited contact with children was related to higher levels of anxiety, depression, and somatization

. . . as well as increased institutional misconduct. Incarcerated women experience considerable distress related to parenting, manifest in psychological and behavioral adjustment."[46] Moreover, mothers who participated in prison nursery programs had lower rates of recidivism after release.[47]

In-Prison Pumping Programs

Under the current scheme in most prisons, incarcerated women who give birth are generally allowed to remain with the newborn until released from the hospital, at which point the baby is released to its guardian and the mother returns to prison. Prison administrators voice concerns over inmate lactation. They are concerned that the prison would be held liable in cases of mastitis, a potentially serious breast infection. They worry that the prison would be responsible for the safety and sanitation of the milk and that ethical issues would arise over the storage of milk and on the sale of unused milk. They worry that there would be a contraband market for breast milk, especially for milk from those mothers who were being weaned from methadone, an opioid that is used to treat withdrawal symptoms in people, including breastfeeding mothers, addicted to narcotic drugs like heroin. Administrators are concerned that there is a lack of privacy for pumping and that any special privileges granted to lactating inmates (such as a private room or breaks for pumping) could been seen as coercing inmates to breastfeed. They also wonder how to deal with a situation in which the family caring for the child may not permit contact with the mother or condone the ongoing breastfeeding relationship. Prison administrators even worry that nonlactating inmates would use the pump for sexual gratification.[48] These concerns are (mostly) logistical, but they point to a prison system that was designed for male inmates and then applied, after the fact, to women offenders. The fact that female inmates have a different set of needs, life circumstances, biology, and family responsibilities is seen by prisons as irrelevant.

Some programs, like the Breastfeeding Behind Bars program supported by the New Mexico Breastfeeding Task Force, are fighting difficult battles to secure access to breast pumping and milk storage for incarcerated mothers.[49] The group has been working for years to secure access to pumping for incarcerated mothers at the Metropolitan Detention Center in Albuquerque. The group has, in consultation with prison officials, drafted a policy for the program, called the Breast Milk Expression and Storage Policy. The group has secured $2,500 in funding to purchase a freezer, locks, transportation coolers, and other supplies. They have received donations from local hospitals and from the state WIC (Women, Infants, and Children) office, including a hospital-grade pump and milk collection bags. But despite the lengths that the task force has gone to address the logistical difficulties of a prison pumping program, the program has yet to go into effect because officials remain concerned about liability.

According to planned policy, the program will integrate with a program for incarcerated pregnant women with substance-abuse problems, the Milagro Program at the University of New Mexico Hospital. Nurses in the Milagro Program and lactation nurses at the hospital will provide pregnant inmates with information about the pumping program. When a new mother returns to the jail after her hospital birth, she can either stay in the medical wing for two weeks with access to a hospital-grade electric pump or she can opt to return to her cell with a manual pump. The medical wing, however, is sometimes perceived as a privilege and sometimes as a punishment, so the program administrators do not expect all inmates to be interested in taking advantage of a medical wing stay. When a program participant returns to her regular cell, she can pump as often as she likes (and is encouraged by the program administrators to pump at least eight times per day) with a manual pump donated by the university hospital. The milk will be placed in locking freezers and picked up by a nonprofit community organization that serves families of inmates, Wings for Life International. The milk will be stored in the Wings for Life offices, where the infants' caregivers can pick up the milk. As part of the program plan, a pumping circle would be provided for the mothers, offering them education and information, as well as a chance to use the hospital-grade pump. Eligibility for the program will be limited to women in the Milagro Program who have complied with the rules and who screen drug free every six weeks for the duration of their pumping. Women in the program who are on medications like methadone are eligible. As the policy is written, there are no time limits for continued eligibility in the pumping program.

Still, even after years of fighting, negotiating, and gathering support, the program was not yet in effect as of March 2016. The experience of the pumping program at the Metropolitan Detention Center in New Mexico highlights that prisons are highly bureaucratic and were not designed to meet the diverse and varying needs of women, like lactation. Meeting the needs of breastfeeding inmates requires changing the institutions, a process that is often resisted by prison administrations. It is logistically difficult to accommodate lactation within an existing institutional incarceration scheme.

Community-Based Correctional Programs

Most criminal justice reformers today advocate for community-based corrections for mothers and babies, rather than prison nursery programs or in-prison pumping programs. These programs provide close supervision for the mother and child in a community-based residential setting, saving money and reducing recidivism. Community-based alternatives are in a better position to offer women offenders the wraparound services that they require: trauma-informed programs addressing poverty, abuse, and drug addiction.[50] These programs are especially valuable to offenders who are mothers because most community-based alternatives let mothers remain with their small children, allowing them to breastfeed and parent their children.

A new program in Delaware, called New Expectations, serves as an alternative sentencing option for pregnant female offenders with a history of drug abuse. "The goal here is long-term recovery," said the director of reentry services. "We hope with preparation and support that she'll stay out of prison the rest of her life."[51] One pregnant woman enrolled in the program reported:

> They were going to give me Level 3 probation, but I knew if I did that I'd just mess up again. When you're on drugs it's really hard to know your priorities. This will be a new start away from the people that I was with before, and a chance to be around other girls who also want to be clean.[52]

New Expectations explicitly allows women to breastfeed, if they decide to do so. They counsel the women on breastfeeding safely, noting that breastfeeding is safe for a mother on methadone treatment. The program is available to women until their child is six months old. A similar program in North Carolina, Horizons, provides residential substance-abuse treatment to pregnant women and mothers. Run by the Department of Obstetrics and Gynecology at University of North Carolina Hospitals, the program differs from New Expectations only in that it does not serve as an alternative to correctional control (even though all women in Horizons have broken the law). At Horizons the women get education, gain employment, and learn parenting and life skills, all while receiving free child care at a five-star facility.[53]

Some contend that alternative sentencing like community-based corrections amounts to reverse gender discrimination: unequal and preferential treatment of female prisoners. But real gender differences necessitate gender-responsive sentencing and programs. The goal of the criminal justice system, Myrna Raeder argued, "should not merely be to mete out equal sentences to females [and to male offenders], but rather to guarantee that they receive just sentences which reflect their dissimilar patterns of criminality and family responsibilities."[54] Indeed, many counter that the current system is, in fact, gender responsive—only that it is gender responsive in favor of male offenders: "It is ironic that while women have traditionally been placed in a prison system based on a male model for facilities, programs, and services, providing them with gender-responsive programming is viewed by some as inappropriate from an equal protection perspective."[55] Care must be taken to avoid perpetuating gendered stereotypes, but that care can coexist with a prison system that considers the realities of women offenders' lives.

Community-based corrections allows offending women to maintain contact with their families, to breastfeed their babies, and to receive substance-abuse and trauma-recovery treatment, as well as provides training in parenting and life-skills classes that will allow them to succeed during reintegration. Community-based corrections, however, is not appropriate for all offenders; in most existing programs, women are ineligible if they have a history of violent crime or crime against children. Programs designed specifically for pregnant women and new mothers sometimes have age limits: women can live in the supervised home with their child until the child turns one or two years old. Community corrections is, importantly, a reasonable choice for battered women who are convicted survivors. Convicted survivors, including those who are homicide offenders, are the least likely of all felons to repeat their crimes and are generally viewed as model prisoners.[56]

The Law, Judges, and Policy

We have seen the importance of community-based corrections (or other alternatives) for women offenders and, especially, for mothers. But "to date, most mother-child facilities have few beds and short-term placements."[57] So what policy changes are necessary to give women offenders the "preconditions of a life worthy of human dignity," to allow all eligible women to receive alternative sentencing instead of incarceration and separation from their children? Funding expansions for community-based corrections, particularly for facilities that integrate substance-abuse treatment, trauma-recovery services, and parenting and life-skills classes, should be a priority. Funding these alternatives is politically viable, as it can be framed as saving taxpayer dollars while reducing recidivism. A bipartisan Criminal Justice Reform Subcommittee in the New Mexico state legislature has been pursuing these reforms with some success. Eligibility criteria for these programs should be as broad as possible, and the programs should be considered especially appropriate for mothers with substance-abuse problems.

Legislation to protect new mothers who are incarcerated is also necessary. Laws like New York Correction Law section 611—which allows a breastfeeding infant to accompany its mother committed to a correctional facility and which also allows an infant born to a committed mother to live in the correctional facility until one year of age if the mother is capable of caring for it—should protect women in all fifty states.[58] This New York law has been in place with minimal revision since 1929, so it should be emphasized that it is practicable.[59] New Mexico Senate Bill 363, or the Expectant and Postpartum Prisoners Act, was proposed in January 2015 and attempted to create a "presumption . . . in favor of release for a woman who is pregnant or lactating, unless there is good cause to keep the woman in a correctional setting" until determination of release or bond, or in the computation of earned meritorious deductions.[60] Senate Bill 363, furthermore, would have allowed lactating prisoners to pump, store, and transfer milk, as well as have visits to breastfeed their baby in person. The bill gained bipartisan support but died at the end of the legislative session. In Massachusetts a group of formerly incarcerated women is spearheading an effort to pass House Bill 1382, which would create a presumption of a community-based sentence for parents of minor children. The bill reads as follows: "If the court determines that a person convicted of a non-violent offense is a primary caretaker of a dependent child, the court shall impose an individually assessed sentence, without imprisonment, based on community rehabilitation, with a focus on parent-child unity and support."[61] Legal protections like these are necessary to change the current correctional culture.

Sentencing that considers a convict's family ties as a mitigating factor is also appropriate for pregnant or lactating offenders. Federal sentencing guidelines set out a uniform policy of expected sentences for different crimes; judges are required to consider the guidelines during sentencing but are not required (since *United States v. Booker*) to hand down sentences within the guidelines.[62] Family connections and responsibilities are one of the legitimate categories dictated by the guidelines for which a judge can issue a sentence milder than the federal uniform penalty (an action known in criminal law as a *downward departure*). That is, family ties and responsibilities can be used as a reason to give an offender a lower sentence. While parity in sentencing is an admirable goal, sentencing that is blind to the context of offenders' lives is not intelligent sentencing:

Maybe the dawning of a new millennium will make us wiser and more willing to question whether a rule that denigrates offenders' relationships with their children in order to stamp out sentencing disparity makes sense from a criminal justice or community-oriented perspective. The guidelines beckon judges to ignore the risk that lengthy imprisonment of nonviolent single parents will cause an increase in intergenerational crime, precipitate the rise of an orphan class of children, and fail to rehabilitate offenders who in an earlier era would have been supervised in the community.[63]

It would be appropriate for the guidelines to advise judges that lactation deserves consideration as grounds for a downward departure.

Legal protections should also be sought for mothers who are being held in local jails. These short-term periods are often the most devastating for breastfeeding mothers because they face the prospect of losing their supply and developing clogged milk ducts or mastitis before a sentence is even given. Questions about lactation status should be added at all levels of correctional control, particularly upon the arrest of a woman and at local jails where women may be awaiting bail or bond.[64]

Observations and Conclusions

For women who must remain under institutional control, whether because they do not qualify for community-based corrections or because it is not available to them, protections should be put in place for lactation in prison. It should be noted at the outset, though, that provision for lactation within prison should be pursued only as a secondary resort, as this option does not preserve maternal access to children; community-based corrections or prison nursery programs are preferable from the standpoint of lactation capability, mother and infant well-being, and long-term health and reduced recidivism. It should also be noted that accommodating breastfeeding within prison walls is much more difficult than accommodating breastfeeding under alternative sentencing options. State regulation of prison policies should be structured like proposed New Mexico Senate Bill 363, guaranteeing prisoners the ability to pump, store, and transfer milk, as well as the opportunity of visits to breastfeed the baby directly. Lactation support should be available, including medical counseling about the safety of milk expression. Prisons can implement these policies as they see fit (by providing a special place for women to pump or by allowing them to pump and turn in the milk at regular checks). It may be appropriate for community partners to be involved in the transfer of milk from the prison to the infants. As successful programs become established, we will gain more evidence about the most effective structure and logistics.

It is also important to note that alternatives to incarceration must not constitute a veiled attempt to impose standards of "good" mothering on women offenders. Haney noted that, for some community-based correctional facilities, "the gendered message was clear: women were primarily, even solely, responsible for caretaking. Yet there was also very little attention to how this burden affected women. Many inmates had real ambivalence about their roles as mothers."[65] Tabbush and Gentile pointed out that in some Argentine jails, "half of the incarcerated women with children under age four opted not to take their sons and daughters with them into prison."[66] It is imperative, therefore, that the safeguards to protect women who desire to breastfeed and stay with their children are not, in turn, used to limit the choices of other women. While it is important that women offenders be able to breastfeed, it is also important that the correctional system not use its power to foist breastfeeding on all inmates who deliver babies. Similarly, even though women should be able to retain access to their babies, it would not be a satisfactory alternative to force all incarcerated mothers to bring their young children with them into a correctional facility. We must ensure that presumptive norms of good motherhood are not imposed on mothers; the political goal is the *ability* of mothers to choose to breastfeed and to have access to their children, not to achieve a 100 percent breastfeeding rate. The goal of access cannot preclude the possibility of maternally chosen separation.

For any of these options, whether community-based corrections, prison nurseries, or pumping programs, child age limits should be employed as sparsely as possible. Ideally, community-based corrections or a prison nursery program could treat women and children until the mother is ready to reintegrate into society. It is not desirable to tear mothers away from their breastfeeding children when a child reaches an arbitrary age (past and current programs have had limits of three months, six months, twelve months, or three years). And as I have argued, "offenders who maintain ties to their families and communities during incarceration are less likely to recidivate."[67] There should be a presumption toward a family-ties downward departure for a mother to serve her sentence in community-based corrections or in a facility with a prison nursery program with a maximal age allowance for children. If restrictive policies must be written because of budget constraints, or because a mother has a particularly long sentence, care should be taken to allow the transition to happen in a way that respects the mother-child relationship. Prison pumping programs should have no end date—that is, mothers should be allowed to pump for as long as they continue to have an interest in pumping.

But for any approach to work, law and policy makers must retain empathy toward women offenders. As Lillian Hewko, an attorney with the Incarcerated Parents Project, stated, "No law, however good, will be implemented fully if people do not believe people in prison deserve to parent and that prison doesn't need to be the primary form of holding people accountable."[68] But if we can look past our preconceived notions about criminals and "bad" mothers, the path forward is clear. A comprehensive approach that takes into account the context of female criminality, the gendered pathways to crime, the special needs of trauma survivors and addicts, and the difficulty of community reintegration and economic viability for offenders will have the best outcome for mothers and their children, breastfed or not.

Notes

1. In my argument I am not considering cases in which the mother has engaged in abuse of her children of the sort that would result in her children being taken into the custody of child protective services.

2. Bloom, *Gendered Justice*, 3.

3. Ibid., 16.

4. Bloom, Owen, and Covington, *Gender-Responsive Strategies*, vii.

5. Ibid., vi.

6. Ibid., 68.

7. Greene and Allard, "Alleviating the Impact of Parental Incarceration," 2.

8. Bloom, *Gendered Justice*, 11.

9. Bloom, Owen, and Covington, *Gender-Responsive Strategies*, 17.

10. Ibid., 77.

11. Bloom and Steinhart, *Why Punish the Children?*

12. Hora and Becker, "Judicial Considerations When Sentencing Pregnant Substance Abusers."

13. Ibid., 4.

14. Ibid., 8.

15. Ibid., 50.

16. LactMed, "Methadone." It is also worth nothing in this context that some states are in the process of specifically criminalizing drug use during pregnancy even though experts agree that this is bad public health policy because it will

discourage drug-abusing pregnant women from seeking prenatal care and medical treatment. (For example, see Tennessee S.B. 1391, 108th Congress, 2014.)

17. Markham, "Options for Pregnant Inmates."

18. Demarco, "Local Advocates Fight for Incarcerated New Mothers."

19. Ibid.

20. Bloom, *Gendered Justice*, 13–14.

21. Bloom, Owen, and Covington, *Gender-Responsive Strategies*, 69.

22. Raeder, "Remember the Family," 253.

23. Ibid., 253.

24. Raeder, "Gendered Implications of Sentencing and Correctional Practices," 185.

25. Nussbaum, *Creating Capabilities*, 73.

26. Bloom, *Gendered Justice*, 17.

27. American College of Obstetricians and Gynecologists, "Committee Opinion."

28. World Health Organization, *Planning Guide for National Implementation*; American Academy of Pediatrics, "Policy Statement"; U.S. Department of Health and Human Services, *Surgeon General's Call*.

29. Researchers have shown, for example, that breastfed infants experience reduced incidence and severity of diarrhea, lower-respiratory infection, lymphoma, otitis media, and chronic digestive diseases, as well as reductions in mortality (Ruhm, "Parental Leave and Child Health," 935). Research has also shown improved health outcomes for mothers who breastfeed, including improved postpartum health, weight loss, and blood pressure, and a lower incidence of breast, uterine, and cervical cancer, as well as of osteoporosis (Weissinger, West, and Pitman for La Leche League International, *Womanly Art of Breastfeeding*).

30. It is probable that as more women give birth in Baby-Friendly Hospitals (a designation overseen by the World Health Organization and the United Nations Children's Fund), the number of female inmates interested in breastfeeding will increase.

31. ACLU of Nevada, "ACLU of Nevada Sues NDOC."

32. Craig, "Historical Review of Mother and Child Programs."

33. Ibid., 36S.

34. Ibid., 40S.

35. Ibid., 41S.

36. Ibid., 43S–44S.

37. Ibid., 45S.

38. Flynn, *Alderson Story*, 89.

39. Harvard Law Review Association, "Developments in the Law," 1932.

40. Pishko, "Rise of Prison Nurseries."

41. Nebraska Department of Correctional Services, "Nebraska Correctional Center for Women."

42. Women's Prison Association, *Mothers, Infants, and Imprisonment.*

43. Byrne, "Maternal and Child Outcomes."

44. Ibid.

45. For an overview of arguments against prison nurseries, see Dwyer, "Jailing Black Babies"; Legal Services for Prisoners with Children, "California's Mother–Infant Prison Programs."

46. Houck and Loper, "Relationship of Parenting Stress to Adjustment," 548.

47. Goshin, Byrne, and Henninger, "Recidivism after Release."

48. These concerns of prison administrators are compiled from personal interviews with advocates who have discussed with prison administrators the possibility of breastfeeding support for inmates: Maria Munoz (obstetrician) in discussion with the author, September 2014; Lissa Knudsen (New Mexico Breastfeeding Task Force) in discussion with the author, January 2015; Stephanie Andrews (RN/IBCLC) in discussion with the author, February 2015.

49. Ellis and Knudsen, "Breastfeeding behind Bars"; Stephanie Andrews (RN/IBCLC) in discussion with the author, February 2015; Lissa Knudsen in discussion with the author, March 2015.

50. Bloom, *Gendered Justice,* 17.

51. Burke and Rini, "New Home Gives Hope to Pregnant Offenders."

52. Ibid.

53. Horizons, "Horizons Residential Programs."

54. Raeder, "Gendered Implications," 189.

55. Ibid., 196.

56. Leonard, "Stages of Gendered Disadvantage," 131. Gendered pathways to criminality render supposedly "gender-neutral" guidelines to assessing offender risk (in terms of risk to community and risk of recidivism) incorrect when applied to female populations. See Reisig, Holtfreter, and Morash, "Assessing Recidivism Risk"; Hannah-Moffat and Shaw, "Meaning of 'Risk' in Women's Prisons."

57. Raeder, "Gendered Implications," 188.

58. 2009 N.Y. Laws, Chap. 411; SB 1290.

59. Craig, "A Historical Review of Mother and Child Programs," 42S.

60. Expectant and Postpartum Prisoners Act of 2015, S.B. 363, 57th Legislature, State of New Mexico. Senate Bill 363 passed the New Mexico State Senate Judiciary Committee, the Senate, and the House Judiciary Committee unanimously before dying at the end of the legislative session without being heard in the House.

61. Massachusetts House, Providing Community-Based Sentencing Alternatives for Primary Caretakers of Dependent Children Convicted of Non-violent Crimes, 189th General Court of the Commonwealth of Massachusetts, H.B. 1382, 2016.

62. United States v. Booker, 543 U.S. 220 (2005).

63. Raeder, "Remember the Family," 251.

64. See International Association of Chiefs of Police, *Safeguarding Children of Arrested Parents*.

65. Haney, "Motherhood as Punishment," 119.

66. Tabbush and Gentile, "Emotions behind Bars," 137.

67. Bloom, Owen, and Covington, *Gender-Responsive Strategies*, 69. See also American College of Obstetricians and Gynecologists, "Committee Opinion."

68. Law, "Formerly Incarcerated Moms Fight for Reforms."

Bibliography

ACLU of Nevada. "ACLU of Nevada Sues NDOC for Ankle Shackling Woman during Childbirth." American Civil Liberties Union of Nevada, June 20, 2012. Accessed December 20, 2013. http://www.aclunv.org.

American Academy of Pediatrics. "Policy Statement: Breastfeeding and the Use of Human Milk." *Pediatrics* 115, no. 2 (2005): 496–506.

American College of Obstetricians and Gynecologists. "Committee Opinion: Health Care for Pregnant and Postpartum Incarcerated Women and Adolescent Females." 2013. Accessed November 12, 2014. http://www.acog.org.

Bloom, Barbara E., ed. *Gendered Justice: Addressing Female Offenders*. Durham, NC: Carolina Academic Press, 2003.

Bloom, Barbara, Barbara Owen, and Stephanie Covington. *Gender-Responsive Strategies: Research, Practice, and Guiding Principles for Women Offenders*. National Institute of Corrections, June 2003. Accessed March 3, 2015. https://s3.amazonaws.com/static.nicic.gov/Library/018017.pdf.

Bloom, Barbara, and David Steinhart. *Why Punish the Children? A Reappraisal of the Children of Incarcerated Mothers in America*. San Francisco: National Council on Crime and Delinquency, 1993.

Burke, Melissa Nann, and Jen Rini. "New Home Gives Hope to Pregnant Offenders." *Delaware Online: The News Journal*, January 29, 2015. Accessed February 1, 2015. http://www.delawareonline.com.

Byrne, Mary W. "Maternal and Child Outcomes of a Prison Nursery Program: Key Findings." 2014. Accessed November 12, 2014. http://www.nursing.columbia.edu/byrne/prison_nursery.html (material no longer available on the website).

Craig, Susan C. "A Historical Review of Mother and Child Programs for Incarcerated Women." *Prison Journal* 89, no. 1 (2009): 35S–53S.

Demarco, Marisa. "Local Advocates Fight for Incarcerated New Mothers." *KUNM*, June 2, 2014. Accessed January 29, 2015. http://kunm.org/post/local-advocates-fight-incarcerated-new-mothers.

Dwyer, James G. "Jailing Black Babies." Faculty publications, paper 1715 (2014). William and Mary Law School Scholarship Repository. Accessed March 19, 2016. http://scholarship.law.wm.edu/facpubs/1715.

Ellis, Jessica, and Lissa Knudsen. "Breastfeeding behind Bars: A Community-Based Project to Support Breastfeeding and Breast Pumping for Incarcerated Women." Presented at the 9th Breastfeeding and Feminism International Conference, Chapel Hill, NC, March 21, 2014.

Flynn, Elizabeth Gurley. *The Alderson Story: My Life as a Political Prisoner*. New York: International Publishers, 1963.

Goshin, Lorie S., Mary W. Byrne, and Alana M. Henninger. "Recidivism after Release from a Prison Nursery Program." *Public Health Nursing* 31, no. 2 (2014): 109–17.

Greene, Judith, and Patricia E. Allard. "Alleviating the Impact of Parental Incarceration on Indigenous, African-American and Latino Children." Shadow Report of Justice Strategies to the International Convention on the Elimination of All Forms of Racial Discrimination, July 2014. Accessed September 24, 2017. http://www.ushrnetwork.org/sites/ushrnetwork.org/files/justice_strategies.cerd_submission.2014.pa_.pdf.

Haney, Lynne. "Motherhood as Punishment: The Case of Parenting in Prison." *Signs* 39, no. 1 (2013): 105–30.

Hannah-Moffat, Kelly, and Margaret Shaw. "The Meaning of 'Risk' in Women's Prisons: A Critique." In *Gendered Justice: Addressing Female Offenders*, edited by Barbara E. Bloom, 45–68. Durham, NC: Carolina Academic Press, 2003.

Harvard Law Review Association. "Developments in the Law: Alternatives to Incarceration." *Harvard Law Review* 111, no. 7 (1998): 1863–990.

Hora, Peggy, and Barrie Becker. "Judicial Considerations When Sentencing Pregnant Substance Users." *Judges Journal* 35, no. 3 (1996): 3–53.

Horizons. "Horizons Residential Programs." 2015. Accessed September 24, 2017. https://www.med.unc.edu/obgyn/Patient_Care/unc-horizons-program.

Houck, Katherine D. F., and Ann Booker Loper. "The Relationship of Parenting Stress to Adjustment among Mothers in Prison." *American Journal of Orthopsychiatry* 72, no. 4 (2002): 548–58.

International Association of Chiefs of Police. *Safeguarding Children of Arrested Parents*. Bureau of Justice Assistance, U.S. Department of Justice, 2014. Accessed November 12, 2014. https://www.bja.gov/Publications/IACP -SafeguardingChildren.pdf.

LactMed. "Methadone." National Institutes of Health, Toxicology Data Network. Accessed February 5, 2015. http://toxnet.nlm.nih.gov.

Law, Victoria. "Formerly Incarcerated Moms Fight for Reforms to Save Families." *Yes Magazine*, March 11, 2016. Accessed March 19, 2016. http://www .yesmagazine.org.

Legal Services for Prisoners with Children. *California's Mother–Infant Prison Programs: An Investigation*. November 2010. Accessed March 19, 2016. http://www.prisonerswithchildren.org.

Leonard, Elizabeth Dermody. "Stages of Gendered Disadvantage in the Lives of Convicted Battered Women." In *Gendered Justice: Addressing Female Offenders*, edited by Barbara E. Bloom, 97–140. Durham, NC: Carolina Academic Press, 2003.

Markham, Jamie. "Options for Pregnant Inmates." *North Carolina Criminal Law: A UNC School of Government Blog*, June 15, 2011. Accessed February 1, 2015. http://nccriminallaw.sog.unc.edu/options-for-pregnant-inmates/.

Nebraska Department of Correctional Services. "Nebraska Correctional Center for Women." Accessed March 19, 2016. http://www.corrections.nebraska.gov /nccw.html.

Nussbaum, Martha C. *Creating Capabilities: The Human Development Approach*. Cambridge, MA: Belknap Press of Harvard University Press, 2011.

Pishko, Jessica. "The Rise of Prison Nurseries." *Pacific Standard*, February 18, 2015. Accessed March 19, 2016. http://www.psmag.com.

Raeder, Myrna S. "Remember the Family: Seven Myths about Single Parenting Departures." *Federal Sentencing Reporter* 13, no. 5 (2001): 251–57.

———. "Gendered Implications of Sentencing and Correctional Practices: A Legal Perspective." In *Gendered Justice: Addressing Female Offenders*, edited by Barbara E. Bloom, 173–208. Durham, NC: Carolina Academic Press, 2003.

Reisig, Michael D., Kristy Holtfreter, and Merry Morash. "Assessing Recidivism Risk across Female Pathways to Crime." *Justice Quarterly* 23, no. 3 (2006): 384–405.

Ruhm, Christopher. "Parental Leave and Child Health." *Journal of Health Economics* 19, no. 6 (2000): 931–60.

Tabbush, Constanza, and María Florencia Gentile. "Emotions behind Bars: The Regulation of Mothering in Argentine Jails." *Signs* 39, no. 1 (2013): 131–49.

U.S. Department of Health and Human Services. *The Surgeon General's Call to Action to Support Breastfeeding.* Washington, D.C.: U.S. Department of Health and Human Services, Office of the Surgeon General, 2011. http://www.surgeongeneral.gov/topics/breastfeeding /calltoactiontosupportbreastfeeding.pdf.

Weissinger, Diane, Diana West, and Teresa Pitman for La Leche League International. *The Womanly Art of Breastfeeding.* 8th ed. New York: Ballantine Books, 2010.

Women's Prison Association. *Mothers, Infants, and Imprisonment: A National Look at Prison Nurseries and Community-Based Alternatives.* May 2009. Accessed March 19, 2016. https://www.prisonlegalnews.org.

World Health Organization. *Planning Guide for National Implementation of the Global Strategy for Infant and Young Child Feeding.* 2007. Accessed February 15, 2016. http://whqlibdoc.who.int/publications/2007/9789241595193 _eng.pdf.

12. Agnes Goes to Prison: Gender Authenticity, Transgender Inmates in Prisons for Men, and Pursuit of the "Real Deal"

Valerie Jenness and Sarah Fenstermaker

In 2009 Raewyn Connell published a thoughtful consideration of Harold Garfinkel's story of "Agnes," a young woman who identified herself to the UCLA Neuropsychiatric Clinic researchers and clinicians studying gender identity disorders and who was seeking a surgical "correction" for the "mistake" that was her penis.[1] Agnes became what Garfinkel referred to as a "practical methodologist" who deliberately sought acceptance as an unassailably "normal, natural" female deserving of surgical attention.[2] Agnes's project was to convince Garfinkel and others that she was "naturally" a female whose "inner" female was adequately reflected in her outward appearance, comportment, and point of view as a woman. From this West and Zimmerman concluded in 1987 that "[Agnes's] problem was to produce configurations of behavior that would be by others seen as normative gender behavior."[3] Garfinkel's chronicle of this "production" provided what Zimmerman referred to as "an unusually clear vision": to wit, the empirical means to decouple the initial outcome of sex assignment from the interactional accomplishment of gender.[4]

The discovery that Agnes was not intersex, as she was asserting, but instead was taking hormones to enhance her feminine appearance drew attention to the fact that Agnes was passing—conventionally understood as successfully making efforts to hide a stigmatizing secret. Connell argued that this "preoccupation" with Agnes's efforts to pass avoided "important issues of contradictory embodiment."[5] Without denying the central role of accountability, Connell suggested an alternative: that Agnes was not so much hiding a secret about herself as she was seeking affirmation and an identity within a particular community that sex category might deliver.

Connell reminds us that Agnes's problem was not only one of interaction in the abstract but of *embodied* interaction in the here and now. It requires concerted effort, specific actions, and constant evaluation to ensure that the embodied comportment adequately reflects the ultimate purpose of achieving recognition. Connell has advanced a consideration of the implications of "contradictory embodiment"—embodiment that is at once unnatural, unpredictable, and unacceptable—as understood through an empirical examination of transsexuality in all its complexity.[6] She calls for a turn away from a preoccupation with matters of individual identity toward the realities of practice and process in the interactional achievement of gender in specific contexts. Referring to transgender as "intransigent" (that is, demanding recognition), Connell argues that the "contradiction has to be handled, and it has to be handled at the level of the body, since it arises in the process of embodiment."[7]

The compulsory character and the everyday challenges of such embodied recognition provide a theoretical point of departure for our analysis of transgender women in men's prisons. As an exemplar of Connell's "contradictory embodiment," Agnes—our imagined Agnes—cannot pass in a prison for men. In prison, Agnes and her transgender sisters reside in a setting where "everyone knows" they are biologically male but where they nevertheless are motivated to seek continuous affirmation of their "natural" female and womanly characters. Under the sometimes brutal, and always difficult, conditions of a prison, transgender prisoners engage in a competitive pursuit of a femininity that does not constitute passing but that does involve accountability to a normative standard and a "ladylike" ideal. Such practices require an intense preoccupation with bodily adornment and appearance as well as a deferent demeanor and a studied comportment. The result is the achievement of a *recognition* from others that one is close enough to a "real girl" to be deserving of a kind of privilege.

The unique and often predatory environment of prison is defined by deprivation, including both loss of freedom and markers of individuality typically used on the outside. In this context transgender prisoners are distinct from their counterparts on the outside who seek to pass, and often do pass, as women. Precisely because transgender prisoners' lives are so radically unconventional, we use this chapter as an occasion to give voice to the pursuit of femininity in a men's prison and to reaffirm the value of a theoretical and empirical focus on the actual practices that constitute our gendered lives. To do so, we first turn to the theoretical stakes that motivated our empirical inquiry, and then we describe the original data employed to understand the lives of transgender prisoners. Thereafter, we offer an empirical analysis of how transgender prisoners orient to and accomplish gender in prisons for men. We conclude with a discussion of the complicated relationship between embodiment and accountability in a context in which doing gender is problematized in consequential ways.

Theoretical Considerations

In their 1987 classic work "Doing Gender," West and Zimmerman made problematic the prevailing perspective that the sex categories of female and male are (a) naturally defined and spring from mutually exclusive reproductive functions rooted in an unchanging biological nature; (b) clearly reflected in the myriad differences commonly observed between girls and boys, men and women; and (c) foundational to social inequalities that are commonsensically and adequately rationalized via these apparently intractable differences between males and females.[8]

At the heart of the "doing gender" approach is the idea that individuals and their conduct—in virtually any course of action—can be evaluated in relation to a womanly or manly nature and character. The powerful gender ideals and norms that dominate in popular culture, advertising, and the media serve as cultural resources to guide a normative understanding of a gendered world. However, the doing of gender is far more than stylized performance or a regimented, scripted interaction. Owing to sex category assignment, women and men operate as if they are "naturally" different and navigate a world that instantiates those differences. This is a cultural constant; how and in what ways those differences are created, granted meaning, and rendered consequential, however, vary by the particulars of, for example, social setting and historical period.

This is akin to what Connell refers to as the ontoformative character of gender: "Practice starts from structure, but does not repetitively cite its starting point. Rather social practice continuously brings social reality into being, and that social reality becomes the ground of new practice through time."[9] Founded on this very idea, "doing gender" attends to the social mechanisms by which people preoccupy themselves with the gendering of social life, organize their expressions of themselves as competently feminine or masculine, and reaffirm the social structure that lends social life meaning and consequence. Seen in these terms, what animates the sex category / gender system is crucial to understanding both the unshakeable salience of sex category and the workings of gender in social life. For that, we turn briefly to the concept of "accountability."

In a recent reexamination of the concept of accountability as it applies to gender, Jocelyn Hollander provides a road map to disentangling three distinct aspects of accountability: *orientation* to sex category, evaluative *assessment* of oneself and others in relevant accountable conduct, and interactional *enforcement* of expectations associated with categorical membership, with a vast range of consequences for violation.[10] In her discussion of each aspect, Hollander reaffirms what West and Zimmerman argued over a quarter of a century ago: orientation to sex category is ubiquitous—and probably inevitable—but what is wholly dependent on context and can change markedly over time is the particular focus of assessment, enforcement, and that which constitutes accountable conduct.[11]

West and Zimmerman did not concern themselves with the myriad ways in which social life is gendered; they theorized *how* we as members of social worlds make them meaningfully gendered.[12] They did not show us the consequences of a gendered world; they identified and theorized an interactional route to those consequences. Likewise, they did not merely argue that gendered social structures produce inequality; they theorized the mechanisms behind the production of that inequality. By interrogating these mechanisms, they gave us a way to think about social order *and* social change. As Connell explained, "If the situated accomplishment of gender creates the illusion of a hierarchical natural order, this same situated accomplishment is a site where hierarchy can be contested."[13]

Gender scholars are turning to the experiences of transgender people to reinterrogate the workings of gender in social life.[14] These treatments underscore the situated character of gender, resist the impositions of the binary, and raise possibilities for structural disruption and social change. As Susan Stryker explained with regard to transgender studies writ large, a focus on transgender people and their experiences in specific institutional contexts brings to the fore "myriad specific subcultural expressions of gender atypicality."[15] Also breaking new ground, Schilt and Westbrook examined the interactions of so-called "gender normals" and transgender people.[16] They found that the demands of doing gender appropriately varied not only by situation but by how sexualized those situations were. In addition, they found that the policing of gender to identify failures to fulfill gender expectations was itself gendered (see also Catherine Connell's analysis of the experiences of nineteen transgendered people[17]). More recently, Connell directed analytic attention to how a changed embodied position in gender relations grounds new practices. She reminds us that "a transsexual woman must generate a practice" and asks, "What is to be done?"[18] Taking this call seriously, we turn to the unique data for revealing gender practices that are found within the dual realities of incarceration and contradictory embodiment.

Research Methods and Data

California, home to one of the largest correctional systems in the Western world, is an ideal site for collecting data on transgender prisoners.[19] When data collection began in 2008, approximately 160,000 adult prisoners were incarcerated in California's thirty-three prisons. Well over 90 percent of California state prisoners are housed in thirty prisons for adult men. Among these prisoners, there are over three hundred transgender inmates in prisons for men.[20] Assuming Brown and McDuffie's estimate that there are approximately 750 transgender prisoners in the United States is correct, California is home to nearly half of all those prisoners.[21] Because lengthy descriptions of the data collection for the larger project can be found elsewhere,[22] here we provide a brief overview of how the transgender prison population in California prisons was delineated and offer a description of the protocols that drove original and secondary data collection.

David Valentine argues that the term *transgender* emerged in the early 1990s and came to be understood as "a collective category of identity which incorporates a diverse array of male- and female-bodied gender variant people who had previously been understood as distinct kinds of persons."[23] It is not surprising that there is little agreement on what being transgender means in the context of a men's prison and by what criteria an inmate could be— and should be—classified as transgender. In one of the most illuminating publications on the topic, Donaldson found distinctions among a "jocker," "punk," "queen," "booty-bandit," "Daddy," and "Man." He describes confinement institutions as "the most sexist (as well as racist) environments in the country, bar none" and explains that within this institutional environment "the prison subculture fuses sexual and social roles and assigns all prisoners accordingly."[24] Likewise, prison officials do not have an agreed-on definition of transgender that is used to identify and classify inmates, and they often conflate transgender with homosexual prisoners.[25]

Recognizing that distinct types of gender-variant people may or may not identify as transgender, for this work transgender prisoners were identified by deploying four specific criteria. A transgender inmate is a prisoner in a men's prison who (a) self-identifies as transgender (or something comparable); (b) presents as female, transgender, or feminine in prison or outside prison; (c) receives any kind of medical treatment (physical or mental) for something related to how she presents herself or thinks about herself in terms of gender, including taking hormones to initiate and sustain the development of secondary sex characteristics to enhance femininity; or (d) participates in groups for transgender inmates. Meeting any one of these criteria qualified an inmate for inclusion in the larger study from which this chapter derives.[26] These criteria sidestep grander debates about who is and is not transgender and worked well for the diverse types of prisoners in California prisons who were identified by others as transgender and identified themselves as transgender. Even when transgender prisoners might prefer a different term, they nonetheless generally identified with "transgender," too, and referred to themselves as "transgenders," "tgs," "trannies," and "transwomen."

Inmates in California prisons who met the eligibility criteria described were invited to participate in the study. Field data collection began in late April 2008 and ended in late June 2008. During this time a trained interview team of eight interviewers traveled to twenty-seven California prisons for adult men, met face to face with over five hundred inmates identified by the California Department of Corrections and Rehabilitation (CDCR) as potentially transgender, and completed interviews with 315 transgender inmates. The interview schedule employed for the larger project from which the data are drawn was designed to capture a wealth of information on inmates' lives inside and outside prison. The mean duration for interviews was slightly less than one hour, with total interview time approaching three hundred hours, and the response rate was 95 percent. The final step in data collection involved concatenating existing official data retrieved from the CDCR's database on inmates—the Offender Based Information System—to the original self-report data (for more details[27]).

Transgender Prisoners in California

The transgender population in California prisons for men is paradoxically visible and invisible.[28] Prison officials and prisoners alike distinguish transgender prisoners as a special population of inmates in prisons for men. Transgender inmates constitute a highly visible population because their gender displays—for example, the shape of their eyebrows—often mark them as a distinct type of prisoner in an alpha male environment. Because transgender prisoners do not conform to the dictates of an extremely heteronormative and masculinist environment, corrections officials perceive transgender prisoners as a potential source of in-prison disorder and attendant management problems. Corrections officials and prisoners alike share an understanding of transgender prisoners as prisoners failing to "man up" in prisons for men.[29] In contrast, from the point of view of systematic, empirical social science, they are—or more accurately, *were*—what Tewksbury and Potter dubbed "a forgotten group" of prisoners.[30]

In addition to being incarcerated, transgender prisoners are drastically and disproportionately marginalized along other dimensions of social status and health and welfare. When examined along the lines of employment, marital status, mental health, substance abuse, HIV status, homelessness, sex work, and victimization, the transgender prisoners in this study are more precariously situated than nonincarcerated and/or incarcerated nontransgender populations.[31] For example, transgender prisoners are *thirteen times* more likely than their nontransgender counterparts to be sexually assaulted in prison.[32]

Reported at length elsewhere, transgender prisoners are diverse in terms of self and identity.[33] The vast majority (76.1 percent) identify as female when asked about their gender identity, with considerably fewer identifying as "male and female" (14 percent). A third (33.3 percent) identify as "homosexual," while 19.4 percent identify their sexual orientation as "transgender," 18.1 percent identify as heterosexual, 11.3 percent identify as bisexual, and the remaining 17.8 percent identify as something else. The vast majority reported that they are sexually attracted to men in prison (81.9 percent), but a small minority indicated being attracted to both men and women in prison (15.6 percent), and a majority (75.8 percent) reported being attracted to men both outside and inside prison. The picture that emerges includes considerable same-sex attraction as transgender women make their way through differentially gendered social landscapes and engage in contextualized identity projects associated with being in prison.[34] More recently, Sexton and Jenness found that, despite competing centrifugal forces, there is an empirically discernable collective identity among transgender prisoners.[35]

Distinguished from the prison population and reporting a diverse repertoire of identities, sensibilities, and desires, transgender prisoners bring a plethora of understandings that are manifested in their daily embodied gender practices; their bodies are, quite literally, locked up. In this institutional context, transgender prisoners face very different interactional challenges from those faced by their counterparts on the outside. These challenges reveal a great deal about the situated character of gender as well as how gender practices unfold in the context of contradictory embodiment.

Pursuit of the "Real Deal"

One of the basic underlying assumptions of prison operations is that there are two types of people—males and females—and that fact looms large. Until the latter part of the twentieth century, sex segregation in prison was arguably the least contested prison policy/practice across geographical region, local government, prison level, and inmate population.[36] In short, the institutional manifestation of the prison culture's sex/gender binary is taken for granted and defines prison existence in virtually every aspect.

It is within this context that we focus on the pursuit of the "real deal" to refer to the complicated dynamic whereby transgender prisoners claim and assert their femininity in prison—a hegemonically defined hypermasculine and heteronormative environment with an abundance of alpha males, sexism, and violence. By their own account, transgender prisoners assert themselves with well-understood motivations, patterned manifestations, and an understanding of very real consequences for themselves and others. To quote them, they are "the girls among men." For these inmates, their very presence in a men's prison establishes their sex categorization as male; subsequent and ongoing interaction, however, offers the chance to vie for an "authentic" femininity.

We use the term *gender authenticity* to refer to the pursuit of full recognition, or what some transgender prisoners refer to as the "real deal" or being a "real girl." This pursuit begins with an orientation to, and acknowledgment of, the self as male (at least in the first instance) and an awareness of the fact that, as prisoners in a men's prison, transgender prisoners are immediately understood as male.[37] The manifest desire to be taken as feminine, and thus female, prompts and sustains a commitment to "act like a lady." The commitment to, and everyday practice of, acting like a lady sets the stage for a playful *and* serious competition among transgender prisoners for the attention and affection of "real men" in prison. The attention and adoration of "real men," in turn, is taken to be an important measure of gender status among transgender prisoners. These features of the competitive pursuit of gender authenticity are crucial to the social organization of gender in prison.[38] The effort to be recognized as a lady is not something one finally achieves but rather pursues as an ongoing proposition. The status of lady—as authentically female—is a provisional one deployed in a context in which transgender prisoners are "clocked," a subject to which we now turn.

Being Known as Male: "I'm in Here and I'm Already Clocked"
Transgender prisoners often used the word *clocked* as a way of indicating that their ability to pass as women is effectively denied in a prison built for and inhabited exclusively by males. The institutional context in which they reside determines to which side of the sex categorical binary they are thought to belong. Being clocked, therefore, is not about attempting to pass and being "discovered" such that some are privy to the "truth" and others are not. A sex-segregated prison for men is a unique environment where there is no other truth possible: all prisoners are male, no matter how they look or act. It is here where the institutionalization of sex category membership interacts so critically with gender practice. Being clocked sets the terms and conditions for doing gender in prison precisely because it precludes passing as it is conventionally understood.

A white transgender prisoner,[39] who was in her midtwenties, reported taking hormones when she was fifteen and coming to prison when she was eighteen for "an armed robbery and carjacking I did with my boyfriend" (ID #35).[40] She explained, "I was stupid, just stupid. But, I've learned the hard way. Twenty-four years of my life! That's the hard way." Comparing her life outside prison to her life in prison, she said, "I lived as a girl in high school, passed on the streets. Now [in prison], everyone knows, so who cares?" She explained that now that she is in prison, there is no passing "because I'm in here and I'm already clocked." Elaborating, she described how outside prison she didn't wear shorts because she has "manly legs," but she contrasted this to life in prison: "now I'll wear shorts, too, even though I have manly legs." She went on to say, "my legs are not manly in a good way—not like Tina Turner's." In this case, even as "clocking" makes one vulnerable to certain dangers, it can also be liberating to be relieved of the need to pass.

Likewise, an African American transgender prisoner in her midthirties, who identified herself as a "pre-op transsexual" with "some facial surgery (chin, cheeks, and nose)," reported, "I've never been clocked on the streets" (ID #32). However, later in the interview she explained that, while in prison, she is treated by CDCR personnel and other inmates alike as male. When asked how correctional officers treat her, she reported being harassed routinely: "Most of the time, actually. Just today an officer said, 'Your jaw is wired shut, you're out of service.' C'mon, how rude is that? They also call me 'sissy boy.'

That gets old."[41] Later in the interview she made it clear how correctional officers and other prisoners reveal their thoughts about her: "they think I'm gay or a gay boy."[42]

Other transgender prisoners made explicit connections between being clocked and the many challenges they face being transgender in prison, including the ongoing management of the threat and reality of violence. A biracial transgender prisoner serving time for fraud reported that she came to California from a state in the Midwest because she assumed California would be more tolerant of alternative lifestyles. She described the nature of being transgender in a men's prison this way: "Everyone in prison knows I'm transgender. But outside they don't" (ID #34). Later in the interview she lamented, "Yes, but most people don't know. They think, 'You like men, you're gay.' Most people don't get it—that I'm transgender, not gay." An African American transgender prisoner, who lived as a woman on the streets in Los Angeles and worked as a prostitute for over twenty years, proclaimed, "I know I'm not a girl; I was born a boy. But I have tendencies as a girl" (ID #1).

Other transgender prisoners cited anatomical realities (as they existed at the time of the interview) as evidence of their non-normative status as women, referencing their maleness along the way. An African American transgender inmate who reported removing her own male genitals and being on hormones to enhance her feminine appearance since her teen years made it clear that she has not forgotten how she was born (as a male). She complicated the picture by describing her attributes compared to those of other transgender prisoners:

> I'm 40D. Not many like that in here. And, I have a big ass, we call it "booty." I don't mind being on a yard with other transgenders because they can't match this. And, the hormones shrink your dick and I don't have any testicles. I had them cut off when I was a teenager. . . . When you're in prison, everyone knows who you are—a man. It's not a big secret. Or, at least they think they know who you are. I'm a man. I'm not confused. I'm not a woman. I know I don't bleed, I can't produce children, I don't have a pussy, I have breasts because I grew them with hormones. It's not like you. I just assume your breasts are natural. Anyone who says, "I'm just like you" is full of shit. C'mon. We're women, but not like you. You know the difference, I know the difference, and they know the difference.

Here we see differing theories reflected in inmate accounts for why, if they are embodied males, they are transgender. The prisoner just quoted alludes to "tendencies," suggesting misplacement in sex category. Others bow to the primacy of embodiment and the naturalness of sex category when they say, as they often did, "I'm not like you" (to a female interviewer) or "I'm a woman, but not a female."

Transgender prisoners made reference to women who are "biologics" as compared to themselves, who are not. Consider the description provided by an outspoken white transgender prisoner who self-identifies as "the transgender ring leader" and who "takes care of the girls around here" while serving a life sentence and maintaining a "marriage-like" relationship with another prisoner. During an interview she asked the lead author, "Val, you're a biologic, right?"[43] After receiving an affirmative response, she went on to say:

> I figured. We have the utmost respect for biologics. You are perfection. I am Memorex. You are what I can never attain. But, like all good Memorexes, I try to get close. Always a copy. Never the real deal. But a damn good copy. People can't tell the difference between the real deal and a damn good copy. You're real. I'll never be the same. Do you know Lt. Commander Data [on *Star Trek*] looks human and acts human, but will never be human. He's an android, not a human. It's kind of the same. (ID #40)

The distinction between a biologic and another type of woman is illustrated with reference to anatomy and biological functioning. When a transgender prisoner who proudly revealed she has legal documentation that identifies her as female was asked whether she would prefer to be housed in a men's prison or a women's prison, she immediately replied, "Men's." She added, "That's a hard one. I don't want to be with women because they are vicious. They are worse than men. Their hormones are going all the time. Imagine being around 60 women and two are on their period at the same time! God. Imagine how bad that would be?" (ID #34). Likewise, an Asian transgender prisoner, who was born outside the United States and expressed concerns about her immigration status, reported that she had been transgender since high school, began taking hormones at fourteen, and earned a good living as a hairdresser before coming to prison. Noting that her family accepts her transgender status, she said, "Before I got into drugs I had a good life. I got into meth—the monster. Everything went downhill" (ID #39). She went on to compare herself to other transgender prisoners, as well as other (real) women:

People on the outside are way different. I came here transgender, but I call them broken souls. A lot of them find themselves here, transition in here. I think it is for affection, the attention, the loneliness. You could be anything in here. You can still find yourself a man. They are gay boys, but men. I came in transgender. I'm different. I knew I was transgender, not a gay boy who became transgender. I would give my soul to be a woman. Who wouldn't want to be nurturant, to be loving, to be kind? Women bring peace to the world. They unite people. A mother is everything.

She made a distinction between "fat men titties" and the breasts of women and lamented that she can never give birth like other women.

Regardless of whether one believes one is inherently female, the biologic remains a crucial reference point, as transgender prisoners expressed enthusiasm for being as close to the real deal as possible. A Hispanic transgender prisoner with a long history of engaging in sex work, struggling with drug addiction, and enduring imprisonment explained, "They [respect me because they] see that I'm all the way out—that I'm the real deal. I'm going all the way. I'm hoping to have surgery. I'm not a transgender, I'm a woman. I have my breasts from hormones. I'm the real deal. I want Marcy Bowers to do the surgery" (ID #4).[44] Expressions such as these are often accompanied by self-assessments regarding how close to the goal—the real deal—one is, and is becoming.

What we might call the "problem of approximation" is an ever-present normative benchmark to separate the biologic from both the real woman and the failed pretender, even when intentions to seek sex reassignment surgery are in play. Therefore, existing theories of passing as a sociological process are inapplicable, and accountability to membership in one's sex category is no longer at issue. However, orienting accountability to a locally defined authenticity puts a premium on the process of pursuing a convincingly feminine appearance and demeanor. The context renders sensible and recognizable the ongoing effort (and its consequence) that seeks to move beyond the (known) biological truth to approach the real deal, even if it is inevitably a "Memorex." Accordingly, passing is less about biological and anatomical secrets to be managed and more about making gender commitments visible.

The prison environment sets the stage for embodiment to be understood as unforgiving ("Everyone knows") *and* eminently *deniable* ("Who cares?"). Through the pursuit of the real deal, however, gender expectations remain and demand that the transgender prisoner's behavior reflects an inherent femininity—*as if* one were really and truly female. To do this requires participation in an additional dynamic—acting like a lady in prison—which, as we describe in the next section, reveals the distinct ways in which gender is embedded in individual selves, cultural rules, social interaction, and organizational and institutional arrangements.[45]

The Importance of Acting like a Lady: "It's Being Proper"

To enhance one's feminine appearance and approach the real deal, transgender prisoners emphasized the importance of "acting like a lady." As they did so, particular constructs of classed normative understandings were employed to establish a valued femininity as a route to respect, as revealed in the following exchange:

INTERVIEWER: How do transgender inmates get respect?
PRISONER: Act like a lady.
INTERVIEWER: Why does acting like a lady in a men's prison get you respect?
PRISONER: If a man is a gentleman and they see a queen act that way, it's important for him to trust you because you're showing self-confidence in an environment that is crazy. That's why queens don't get hurt. You being a lady is like a gold credit card.

The dynamic nexus between being transgender in a sex-segregated environment and the centrality of earning respect as a lady is anchored in the embrace of a feminine ideal akin to the iconic Victorian-era normative construct first described by Barbara Welter in "The Cult of True Womanhood, 1820–1860."[46]

When asked, "What does a 'lady' act like?," transgender prisoners provided illuminating answers. A Mexican transgender prisoner explained that acting like a lady entailed "staying in the women's spot. Don't talk bad. Don't make comments about things that don't concern you. Being a woman is about staying in line" (ID #12). Another transgender prisoner, who attributed many problems throughout her adult life to methamphetamine use that led to prostitution, went further:

INTERVIEWER: What does a lady act like?
PRISONER: No sleeping with everyone. No going out on the yard with just a sports bra on. C'mon, you know what a lady acts like. It's being proper. (ID #35)

Many transgender prisoners were quick to talk about other transgender prisoners as "skanks," a clear reference to sexual promiscuity with connotations of disapproval in a context in which the values of social and sexual restraint are privileged. Jennifer Sumner explained the transgender code of conduct: "Transgender inmates who are seen to be 'messing' with another's man or 'messing' with too many men are labeled as 'slutty' and considered to be 'whores' or 'skanks.'"[47]

For transgender prisoners in men's prisons, a commitment to acting like a lady often was revealed in response to questions designed to solicit respondents' sense of what gets them—and other transgender prisoners—respect in prison. When asked, "Does appearing more feminine get you respect from other (nontransgender) inmates?," the majority of the respondents (64.3 percent) said yes. When asked why, a transgender prisoner in her midthirties serving her third term explained the benefits of acting like a lady in prison this way:

> PRISONER: They [other prisoners] give me a different pardon. If I'm going in line to chow, it's likely someone will let me go first.
> INTERVIEWER: What exactly is a different pardon?
> PRISONER: A pardon is a special consideration. That's what makes me feel respected. It's tasteful, especially if it comes from a regular guy. That's him telling me that I'm carrying myself like a lady. It's about being treated like a lady and made to feel like a lady. That's a special pardon. The more you get special pardons, the more you are being treated like a lady. (ID #32)

In a more dramatic illustration, a middle-aged African American transgender prisoner, who introduced herself by using a famous model's name and later in the interview called herself a "crack whore," invited the interviewer to see the poster above the toilet in her cell and said, "I act like a lady and I have a poster that says so above the toilet in my cell" (ID #3). She explained that she sits when she pees, and because cells are shared and visible to other prisoners in the cell block, everyone can see that she sits when she pees. For her, this is a sign for all to see that she acts like a lady and pees accordingly.

Life for transgender prisoners is nothing if not variable and marked by contradictions, and here is where the multiplicities of gender are evident. Transgender prisoners reported circumstances in which the luxury of "acting like a lady" necessarily gave way to expressions of violence. Almost half (44.7 percent) of the transgender prisoners in this study reported being involved in violence while living in their current housing unit, and on average, they had been in their current housing unit only about a year. Moreover, well over half (89.2 percent) of the transgender prisoners in this study reported being involved in violence while incarcerated in a California prison, with an average sentence in California prisons of 10.9 years.

For some, engagement in physical violence was not at odds with acting like a lady insofar as any woman in a situation that requires violence would behave similarly. A middle-aged African American transgender prisoner convicted of a second strike for "great bodily injury" explained how she initiated a violent confrontation with a group of four men on the yard after they refused to cease making pejorative comments about her husband (who was also her cell mate for over three years) because he was openly involved with her. She approached the men on the yard, confronted them about their harassment, asked them if there was a problem, told them to "cut the comments," and advised them that, if the comments continued, she would have to "get busy" with them:

> INTERVIEWER: What do you mean by "get busy"?
> PRISONER: You know, put the cheese on the crackers and make it happen.
> INTERVIEWER: And what does that—"put the cheese on the crackers"—mean?
> PRISONER: Fight. (ID #105)

In response to being asked, "Does fighting feel at odds with being a woman?," she said:

> Oh, girl, you just don't understand. Let's review. Take a transgender. Take any female. A Black woman. A Latina woman. A Asian woman. *Any* woman. There is no way a woman with a strong will and self-respect is going to let themselves be mistreated. You'd be surprised what women can do. Women will cut you. Women will stab you. Violence is violence. There's no such thing as transgender violence and other women's violence. It's all the same. People do what they have to do to take care of themselves. The difference with us is, well, violence is ugly. We don't want to be violent. We want to be beautiful. We're on hormones, girl. But hit me or disrespect me and I'll knock you out. I will. You would knock someone out, too. You'd be surprised what you would do if you had to; you just haven't had to—have you?

Others described situations in which they had to "man up," "put on my shoes," and "put down my purse and fight." In many cases transgender prisoners reported taking a "time out" or a "stop pattern" to acting like a lady, and engaging in physical altercations with other prisoners as a way to protect or marshal respect. An older white transgender prisoner explained, "If you don't respect yourself, no one will. You don't have to be tough. I can fight and lose and get respect. I can run from a fight and get no respect. I'd be a coward. So, it's not about being tough, it's about standing your ground" (ID #6). The use of violence for transgender inmates to gain respect is comparable to Nikki Jones's vivid descriptions of West Philadelphia high school girls crafting a femininity that accommodates periodic violent defense of one's self-respect.[48]

In more dramatic terms, when asked if there were situations in prison in which violence between inmates is necessary, an HIV-positive transgender prisoner said:

> PRISONER: Yes. Gang bangers come in here and say something—like, "Hey, half dead!" [to HIVs] or "You're dying anyway." With me, if it becomes too much I put my purse down and fight. I'll let that part of me come out.
> INTERVIEWER: What part is that?
> PRISONER: The non-ladylike. The ugly side of me. (ID #8)

Here the dual status of clocked as male and feminine like a lady exist in social proximity. The situatedness of gender in this context allows us to see this dynamic as far more than a choice between absolutes—*either* femininity *or* masculinity. The violence engaged in may draw its content from forms of expression typically understood as masculine, but such forms are undertaken in the context of a *suspended* ladylike ideal or an extension of what a woman has to do to demand, secure, and demonstrate respect. In other words, violence represents an "ugly side" of a lady and not the lady herself. As a consequence, the accomplishment of gender that invokes a normative *feminine* standard rests next to the accomplishment of gender that invokes a normative *masculine* standard. In the context of a prison, there is perhaps no better example of the situated character of gender than when one pees "like a lady" in one moment and "stands her ground" in the next.

For transgender prisoners, however, violence can carry consequences for the successful pursuit of the real deal. Being clocked as male means that any deployment of the "ugly side" constitutes a counteraffirmation of a "natural" status as male. Thus transgender prisoners are motivated to find ways to avoid physical violence. A white transgender prisoner with long flowing hair, who had been doing time off and on since the late 1980s and was now in her midforties, explained this dilemma:

PRISONER: I am a man, but I choose to look like a woman and I want to be treated like a woman. That's what makes me transgender. I recently had an argument with my cellie and he told me to put my shoes on, which means to fight. I wouldn't put them on. I wouldn't fight.

INTERVIEWER: So women don't fight?

PRISONER: Right.

INTERVIEWER: What else makes you feel treated like a woman?

PRISONER: All the courtesies a man would afford a woman, like my trays are cleared by my cellie—he takes my tray in chow line. (ID #26)

Whether transgender women actually fight or not—and the data suggest they do—is not the point; it is the fact that they render fighting sensible through a gendered lens.

Competition among the Ladies: "Fun, Dangerous, and Real"

Ample self-report evidence reveals friendly competition among ladies. For example, when asked, "Would you prefer more transgender inmates in your housing unit?," quite often transgender prisoners expressed ambivalence, one born of wanting more "girls" in their living environments in hopes of importing understanding and support, but at the same time, of not wanting to invite increased competition for social status into the prison order. An African American transgender prisoner said, "It's hard. I want the company of men, but I feel safe around the transgenders, but I like women friends" (ID #1). When asked the same question, a Hispanic transgender prisoner replied:

We call them [other transgender inmates] bitches, but with affection. Because the straights will try to hit on them as much. It's odd. You want friends, but you don't want the hassle, the drama that comes with them. I'm torn. I want them around, but I don't want them around. It's good and bad. (ID #2)

Similarly, an HIV-positive transgender prisoner, who reported recently breaking up with her cell mate and institutional husband, and having "a gentleman on the street who is waiting for me," described her relationship with other transgender prisoners:

Yes, they flirt, but it's not pressure. That's just play. They know what kind of person I am—monogamous. I don't behave like a slut. Most of the other girls do, but I don't. I respect myself too much. [I] don't want to live with other transgenders—it's like too many women in the kitchen. It sounds so selfish, but less transgender inmates is better; like I said, too many women in the kitchen. Too much promiscuity. I want a relationship that is monogamous. Some of the girls, I don't respect. They are more promiscuous. They are nasty. Skanky. They are. I'm not like that. (ID #5)

When asked, "Does appearing more feminine get you respect from other transgender inmates?," a white transgender prisoner living among many other transgender prisoners explained, "It tends to get negative. They get jealous. Because I look and act like a woman; they have to try harder [than I do]. They feel threatened by how natural it is for me" (ID #8). Similarly, a white transgender prisoner who has served almost twenty years of a life sentence in more than ten different prisons said, "I'm not sure. Sometimes it's jealousy, competition. If people compete with me that means they respect me enough to treat me as a girl—and they do compete" (ID #9). An older, more subdued white transgender inmate, who explained that she "didn't become transgender until I hit [current housing unit]" and whose "morals have come a long way [since being in prison]," commented on the complexities of femininity and respect:

Some respect you a lot; some are angered because you do better than they—you look better; some are angry because you're not normal. Lots goes on when you're trying to be fem. It's fun, dangerous, and it's real. All girls learn from other girls. Transgenders learn from other transgenders. It's a way of learning to do things better, to be better women. (ID #6)

Finally, a young Hispanic transgender inmate said, "No, they're jealous. It's like a beauty pageant. You're all here and seemingly getting along. But not really. Really, it's a competition. They smile to your face, but not sincerely. There's only one winner and maybe runner-up" (ID #35).

This "pageant" requires other prisoners—the men—to be judges socially positioned to bestow status on transgender prisoners. The accomplishment of gender by transgender prisoners must draw crucial meaning from their primary audience. In various ways transgender prisoners reported the centrality of securing attention from men (the nontransgender prisoners). An older white transgender prisoner described it playfully:

I was going into chow and a couple of other inmates grabbed my ass and told me how sweet it is. They are males who are here and want sex. It's like a guy who goes to the strip club. I'm the entertainment and the meat. I wasn't offended. Those kinds of comments and gropes—I find it complimentary at my age. I'm [over 50]. I'm glad I can still draw the attention. (ID #6)

Moving beyond stories of (seemingly) superficial pleasure, transgender prisoners told touching stories of caretaking they received from other non-transgender prisoners with whom they formed intimate relationships. In an emotional interview, a very ill transgender prisoner who reported struggling with addiction most of her adult life, living on the streets before coming to prison, engaging in prostitution for many years, and being HIV-positive explained how important her prison husband is to her ability to manage in prison:

> PRISONER: We [my husband in prison and I] clicked and we have a lot in common. He's very supportive of me. Because I'm on an HIV regime he does nice things for me.
> INTERVIEWER: Like what?
> PRISONER: Well, like hold my hair when I vomit in the cell and not get mad at me. (ID #8)

This simple consideration took on significant meaning to her because it came at the hands of a man (and a husband, no less) and is easily seen by her as an affirmation of her status as female (that is, a woman worthy of being cared for and taken care of like a wife). Throughout the interviews, transgender prisoners expressed appreciation for caring interactions with real men that served to recognize them as women. These simple, but much desired, interactions included being walked across the yard, given cuts in the chow line, and having an umbrella held over your head in the rain.

From the point of view of many transgender prisoners, the nontransgender prisoners are seen as protectors as well as providers. When asked, "What is the best way for transgender inmates to avoid being victimized?," a white transgender prisoner who worked as a marketing researcher before coming to prison described a familiar gendered reciprocity: "Get someone to protect you. He'll take you under his wing. He'll become protective of you—like men do with women" (ID #10). She went on to explain her own relationship situation:

> We're involved, but it's not sexual yet. It's been a month. It's good for us to be in a marriage. We can and we can't fend for ourselves. He's our protector—just like on the streets. If someone did something to you,

he would take care of them. If someone were to put his hands on me or degrade me, he would go and tell him, "Don't disrespect her. If you're disrespecting her, you're disrespecting me." See, I can get some respect through him.

She paused and added, "One of the things I have to do as a transgender is to deal with men who always want sex. So, I've found that the best thing to do is to make them give me something. I make them give me things—like take me to the mini canteen. It's like going on a date." She then described the similarities in terms of "give and take" in which "I give them a little flirt—it doesn't take much" and concluded, "It's like petting a dog, only the dog pays you. I've found that men need women to be vulnerable. They want to take care of you—almost like a pet. I like it."

When asked about the best way to avoid victimization in prison, another transgender prisoner said, "I've been lucky to have guys who look at me as female and then they want to take care of me. They have that natural instinct—to protect me as a woman—from other men. That's how men are" (ID #8). Here, the bargain that results in a borrowing of respect depends on accepting an accomplishment of gender indicating a "natural" state, whether that be the male instinct to protect a woman or the essential female qualities exhibited by transgender prisoners. According to transgender prisoners, nontransgender prisoners may be moved to chivalry, exhibiting solicitous or protective behavior toward them as "ladies" who call forth a "natural" response from the men. For some, respect is the precursor to love. An African American transgender prisoner said, "It just means getting to be nice, getting to be taken care of, and getting to be, you know, understood and loved" (ID #1).

The pursuit of femininity within this particular context illuminates the body's uncanny ability to override the biological convictions that are being imposed on it through institutional conditions. The absence of biologics within the men's prison system does not undermine gender, nor does the obvious lack of the real deal suspend the pursuit of femininity inside this alpha male space. A Latina transgender woman in her twenties, self-described as a "gay boy" who had been "doing drag outside [prison]," reported first taking hormones in prison and showcased her breasts during the interview by lifting them and talking about their growing size. She said, "A lot of guys get fed the illusion. I give good illusion. My hair. My ass. The hormones help. I create the package. They buy it—sometimes, anyway" (ID #21). She continued, "I'm still male. I know that. I know I'm not a woman. I'm transgender. Everything about me is female. But, my anatomy is male . . . See, I know I'm an illusion." However, it is not a capricious or arbitrary illusion. As a transgender prisoner explained, "It's not something I just made up" (ID #27).

Within the institutional context of sex-segregated carceral environments, the "fragile fictions" of personhood[49] and the interactional dynamics we report are informed by a binary logic that supports the "natural" gendering of bodies and, at the same time, serves as a catalyst for a radical rupture of that logic. In the context of prisons for men (and only men), it is not the commitment to biological differences that dictates the gender dynamics among members but rather the *commitment of bodies* to act like, and be received as, "ladies" and "men." Though biological considerations are readily available, they are systematically rendered incompatible with the business of upholding categorical distinctions between women and men. In their capacity to engage in social practice, transgender people and bodies triumphantly make use of "natural categories" despite institutional evidence that claims otherwise.[50] The dynamics reported in this analysis reveal that transgender women in men's prisons are simultaneously positioned as a source of cultural affirmation, intervention, and critique.

Discussion and Conclusion

The empirical analysis we present in this chapter suggests that, under the harsh conditions of men's prisons, transgender prisoners engage in a set of activities that together constitute what we refer to as a pursuit of gender authenticity, or what they call the real deal. These activities begin with an orientation to sex category, which acknowledges that the prisoners are institutionally understood as male. Transgender prisoners express a desire to secure standing as a "real girl" or the "best girl" that is possible in a men's prison. This desire translates into expressions of situated gendered practices that embrace male dominance, heteronormativity, classed and raced gender ideals, and a daily acceptance of inequality. To succeed in being "close enough" to the real deal requires a particular type of participation in a male-dominated system that can, under the right conditions, dole out a modicum of privilege and respect.

We argue that orientation to sex category is crucial to understanding the content of specific gender practices that make reference to a "natural" female and that are informed by expectations of what it means to be a "real lady." The playful yet serious competition among transgender prisoners for the attention and affection of "real men" allows the community of prisoners—transgender and nontransgender alike—to participate in a gendered existence that orders everyday expectations and behaviors, as well as the allocation of resources, symbolic and material. The experiences of transgender inmates illustrate that whatever femininity is undertaken, in whatever way and for whatever ends, it is not done to pass—to mask a secret that, if revealed, could be discrediting.[51] In prison the pursuit of femininity involves accountability to a set of normative standards, informed by cultural constructions of a ladylike ideal, even when sometimes transgender prisoners engage in a "stop pattern" and allow the "ugly side" to be revealed. What is sought is accountability to a putative sex category: if, through the accomplishment of gender in this setting, one can appear to embody the imagined biologic real deal, then one is close enough—and good enough—to be deserving of some privilege and respect. All gendered practices are undertaken within the context of a powerfully heteronormative masculine environment that privileges males and denigrates females. One pursues a femininity that achieves the real deal in order to manage the inevitable disrespect and violence heaped upon the feminine.

In her recent article, Raewyn Connell wrote eloquently of the "multiple narratives of embodiment,"[52] such that we cannot speak meaningfully of *the* transgender or *the* transsexual experience. This should come as no surprise to gender theorists, which is likely why Connell calls for greater empirical and analytical attention to the multiplicities of transsexual lives. Those social scientists who study gender are less likely to be seduced by a unitary construction of transgender or a new binary composed of "us" and "transgender." Attention to both the complexities of transgender and its situated character reveals the myriad ways in which social change is—and is not—made. Transgender women in prisons for men are, to borrow the words of Connell one last time, "neither enemies of change nor heralds of a new world."[53]

Transgender prisoners assessed themselves and other transgender inmates according to a set of normative expectations deftly designed with a sex categorical world in mind. We learn from the Agneses in prison that the accomplishment of gender through the pursuit of the real deal certainly *affirms* one's *elective* place in the binary and *justifies* behavior as if springing "naturally" from it. Moreover, it directs us not only to the agentic power of embodiment that Connell asserts but also to the likewise powerfully constructed and situated nature of both sex *and* gender.[54] Together they are adapted to and are made meaningful in a real world, including the harsh world of prisons for men.

Transgender inmates exemplify a will to present and live one's "real" self, even under impossible—and sometimes impossibly dangerous—conditions. Future research that includes not only the "real girls" but also the "real men" would be able to contribute to the picture we paint here of how masculinity and femininity are accomplished by transgender prisoners. What are, after all, "real girls" *without* "real men" and vice versa?

We conclude where we began: in the UCLA clinic long ago when Agnes's behavior was interpreted only as passing. The Agneses in prison do not hide and they cannot deceive. Their gendered behavior in prison can be understood as part of an ongoing, cooperative collusion where their selves are revealed and their relationships with nontransgender prisoners likewise reaffirm an unequal, often violent and always hegemonically male, community. The search for the real deal is fundamentally a pursuit of recognition, respect, and belonging.

Acknowledgments

This project was funded by the California Department of Corrections and Rehabilitation and the School of Social Ecology at the University of California, Irvine, and supported by the University of California, Santa Barbara's Institute for Social, Behavioral and Economic Research and the University of Michigan's Institute for Research on Women and Gender. We thank the following contributors for assistance with data collection and interpretation: the CDCR's Offender Information Services Branch and the CDCR's Office of Research, as well as key CDCR personnel, especially Wendy Still; the wardens who made their prisons available for data collection and their staff, who ensured access to hundreds of transgender inmates; academic colleagues who commented on analyses presented in this chapter, including Catherine Bolzendahl, Patricia Cline Cohen, Joycelyn Hollander, and Jodi O'Brien; and a team of hardworking and talented research assistants, including Akhila Ananth, Alyse Bertenthal, Lyndsay Boggess, Joan Budesa, Tim Goddard, Philip Goodman, Kristy Matsuda, Randy Myers, Gabriela Noriega, Lynn Pazzani, Lotus Seeley, and Sylvia Valenzuela. We especially thank Lori Sexton and Jennifer Sumner, who were integral to the larger project from which this chapter derives, and, most importantly, hundreds of transgender inmates in California prisons who agreed to be interviewed. Direct all correspondence to Valerie Jenness, Department of Criminology, Law and Society, University of California, Irvine 92697-7080. Email: jenness@uci.edu.

Notes

1. Connell, R., "Accountable Conduct"; Garfinkel, *Studies in Ethnomethodology*.

2. Garfinkel, *Studies in Ethnomethodology*, chap. 5.

3. Connell, R., "Accountable Conduct," 134; Zimmerman, "They Were All Doing Gender."

4. Zimmerman, "They Were All Doing Gender," 197.

5. Connell, R., "Accountable Conduct," 107.

6. Connell, R., "Transsexual Women and Feminist Thought."

7. Ibid., 868.

8. West and Zimmerman, "Doing Gender."

9. Connell, R., "Transsexual Women and Feminist Thought," 866; Butler, *Bodies That Matter*.

10. Hollander, "I Demand More of People."

11. Sex category is not the only categorical membership around which we order social life (see West and Fenstermaker, "Doing Gender," for a discussion of "doing" race, class, and gender).

12. West and Zimmerman, "Doing Gender."

13. Connell, R., "Accountable Conduct," 109.

14. Gagné, Tewksbury, and McGaughey, "Coming Out and Crossing Over"; Halberstam, *In a Queer Time and Place*.

15. Stryker, "(De)Subjugated Knowledges," 3.

16. Schilt and Westbrook, "Doing Gender, Doing Heteronormativity."

17. Connell, C., "Doing, Undoing, or Redoing Gender?"

18. Connell, R., "Transsexual Women and Feminist Thought," 868.

19. Petersilia, "California's Correctional Paradox."

20. Jenness, Sexton, and Sumner, "Transgender Inmates in California Prisons."

21. Brown and McDuffie, "Health Care Policies Addressing Transgender Inmates."

22. Jenness, Maxson, Sumner, and Matsuda, "Accomplishing the Difficult but Not Impossible"; Jenness, "Getting to Know 'the Girls'"; Jenness, Sexton, and Sumner, "Transgender Inmates in California Prisons."

23. Valentine, *Imagining Transgender*, 4.

24. Donaldson, "Million Jockers, Punks, and Queens," 118.

25. Ibid.; Sumner and Jenness, "Gender Integration in Sex-Segregated U.S. Prisons."

26. Jenness, "From Policy to Prisoners to People"; Jenness, Sexton, and Sumner, "Transgender Inmates in California Prisons."

27. Jenness, "From Policy to Prisoners to People"; Jenness, Sexton, and Sumner, "Transgender Inmates in California Prisons."

28. Jenness, "Pesticides, Prisoners, and Policy"; Tewksbury and Potter, "Transgender Prisoners—a Forgotten Group."

29. Jenness, "From Policy to Prisoners to People"; Jenness, "Getting to Know 'the Girls.'"

30. Tewksbury and Potter, "Transgender Prisoners—a Forgotten Group."

31. Sexton, Jenness, and Sumner, "Where the Margins Meet."

32. Jenness, Maxson, Sumner, and Matsuda, "Accomplishing the Difficult but Not Impossible"; Jenness, Sexton, and Sumner, "Transgender Inmates in California Prisons."

33. Jenness, Sexton, and Sumner, "Transgender Inmates in California Prisons"; Jenness, Sumner, Sexton, and Alamillo-Luchese, "Cinderella, Wilma Flintstone, and Xena the Warrior Princess"; Jenness, "Pesticides, Prisoners, and Policy."

34. Jenness, Sexton, and Sumner, "Transgender Inmates in California Prisons."

35. Sexton and Jenness, "We're Like Community."

36. Sumner and Jenness, "Gender Integration in Sex-Segregated U.S. Prisons."

37. Jenness, "From Policy to Prisoners to People"; Sumner and Jenness, "Gender Integration in Sex-Segregated U.S. Prisons."

38. Not every transgender prisoner was engaged in the quest for "gender authenticity" as we describe it, and therefore any interpretation of the analysis as a unitary one is misplaced. Nevertheless, the transgender prisoners who participated in this study revealed a preponderance of evidence that both the expectations and the practices we describe are an important aspect of daily existence and a salient feature of prison culture.

39. Designations of the race/ethnicity of these prisoners are presented to render visible the diversity of the transgender prisoner population. These designations are based on their self-identification, if given during an interview, or on official institutional data. These two sources of designations may differ in interesting ways (Calavita and Jenness, "Inside the Pyramid of Disputes"), and different classification categories are a function of the fluid and contingent nature of racial identification and the larger processes of racialization in a prison context (Saperstein and Penner, "Race of a Criminal Record").

40. The use of interviewee numbers allows us to maintain confidentiality and allows the reader to track particular study participants throughout the chapter as well as to attribute multiple quotes to the same prisoner. We considered using pseudonyms selected by study participants, but in the interest of not imposing

gendered identities on them, we chose the neutrality of interviewee numbers. According to prisoners with whom we have consulted, this practice is not offensive or dehumanizing; some prefer it to the assignment of a false name insofar as that practice seems misleading and falsely intimate. Fortunately, the use of ID numbers is an accepted convention in sociology journals (e.g., Calavita and Jenness, "Inside the Pyramid of Disputes").

41. This person had just been discharged from the infirmary after sustaining injuries in a physical altercation with another prisoner. Her jaw was wired shut, but she was able to do the interview, which she wanted to do.

42. Transgender prisoners often distinguish themselves from what they and other prisoners call "gay boys."

43. Being a "biologic" means being born biologically female.

44. Marcy Bowers is a well-known male-to-female transgender surgeon seen on television.

45. Lorber, *Paradoxes of Gender.*

46. Welter, "Cult of True Womanhood."

47. Sumner, "Keeping House," 190.

48. Jones, *Between Good and Ghetto; Miller, Getting Played.*

49. Snorton, "New Hope."

50. Fenstermaker and Budesa, "Contradictory Embodiment."

51. Goffman, *Stigma*; Connell, R., "Transsexual Women and Feminist Thought"; Snorton, "New Hope."

52. Connell, R., "Transsexual Women and Feminist Thought," 867.

53. Ibid., 872.

54. Ibid.

Bibliography

Brown, George R., and Everett McDuffie. "Health Care Policies Addressing Transgender Inmates in Prison Systems in the United States." *Journal of Correctional Health Care* 15, no. 4 (2009): 280–91. doi:10.1177/1078345809340423.

Butler, Judith. *Bodies That Matter.* New York: Routledge, 1993.

Calavita, Kitty, and Valerie Jenness. "Inside the Pyramid of Disputes: Naming Problems and Filing Grievances in California Prisons." *Social Problems* 60, no. 1 (2013): 50–80.

Connell, Catherine. "Doing, Undoing, or Redoing Gender? Learning from the Workplace Experiences of Transpeople." *Gender & Society* 24, no. 1 (2010): 31–55. doi:10.1177/0891243209356429.

Connell, Raewyn. "Accountable Conduct: 'Doing Gender' in Transsexual and Political Retrospect." *Gender & Society* 23, no. 1 (2009): 104–11.

———. "Transsexual Women and Feminist Thought: Toward New Understanding and New Politics." *Signs* 37, no. 4 (2012): 857–81. doi:10.1086/664478.

Donaldson, Stephen "Donny." "A Million Jockers, Punks, and Queens." In *Prison Masculinities*, edited by Don Sabo, Terry A. Kupers, and Willie London, 118–26. Philadelphia: Temple University Press, 2001.

Fenstermaker, Sarah, and Joan Budesa. "Contradictory Embodiment." Unpublished manuscript, 2013.

Gagné, Patricia, Richard Tewksbury, and Deanna McGaughey. "Coming Out and Crossing Over: Identity Formation and Proclamation in a Transgender Community." *Gender & Society* 11, no. 4 (1997): 478–508. doi:10.1177/089124397011004006.

Garfinkel, Harold. *Studies in Ethnomethodology*. Englewood Cliffs, NJ: Prentice Hall, 1967.

Goffman, Erving. *Stigma*. New York: Simon & Schuster, 1963.

Halberstam, Judith. *In a Queer Time and Place*. New York: New York University, 2005.

Hollander, Jocelyn A. "'I Demand More of People' Accountability, Interaction, and Gender Change." *Gender & Society* 27, no. 1 (2013): 5–29. doi:10.1177/0891243212464301.

Jenness, Valerie. "From Policy to Prisoners to People: A 'Soft Mixed Methods' Approach to Studying Transgender Prisoners." *Journal of Contemporary Ethnography* 39, no. 5 (2010): 517–53. doi:10.1177/0891241610375823.

———. "Getting to Know 'the Girls' in an 'Alpha-Male Community.'" In *Sociologists Backstage*, edited by Sarah Fenstermaker and Nikki Jones, 139–62. New York: Routledge, 2011.

———. "Pesticides, Prisoners, and Policy: Complexity and Praxis in Research on Transgender Prisoners and Beyond." *Sociological Perspectives* 57, no. 1 (2014): 6–26. doi:10.1177/0731121413516609.

Jenness, Valerie, Cheryl L. Maxson, Jennifer Macy Sumner, and Kristy N. Matsuda. "Accomplishing the Difficult but Not Impossible: Collecting Self-Report Data on Inmate-on-Inmate Sexual Assault in Prison." *Criminal Justice Policy Review* 21, no. 1 (2010): 3–30. doi:10.1177/0887403409341451.

Jenness, Valerie, Lori Sexton, and Jennifer Sumner. "Transgender Inmates in California Prisons. Report to the California Department of Corrections and Rehabilitation." Unpublished manuscript, University of California, Irvine, 2011.

Jenness, Valerie, Jennifer Sumner, Lori Sexton, and Nikkas Alamillo-Luchese. "Cinderella, Wilma Flintstone, and Xena the Warrior Princess: Capturing Diversity among Transgender Women in Men's Prisons" In *Understanding Diversity*, edited by Claire Renzetti, Daniel Curran, and Raquel Kennedy-Bergen. Upper Saddle River, NJ: Allyn & Beacon Press, 2007.

Jones, Nikki. *Between Good and Ghetto*. New Brunswick, NJ: Rutgers University Press, 2009.

Lorber, Judith. *Paradoxes of Gender*. New Haven, CT: Yale University Press, 1994.

Miller, Jody. *Getting Played: African American Girls, Urban Inequality, and Gendered Violence*. New York: New York University Press, 2008.

Petersilia, Joan. "California's Correctional Paradox of Excess and Deprivation." *Crime and Justice: A Review of Research* 37, no. 1 (2008): 207–78.

Saperstein, Aliya, and Andrew M. Penner. "The Race of a Criminal Record: How Incarceration Colors Racial Perception." *Social Problems* 57 (2010): 92–113.

Schilt, Kristen, and Laurel Westbrook. "Doing Gender, Doing Heteronormativity: 'Gender Normals,' Transgender People, and the Social Maintenance of Heterosexuality." *Gender & Society* 23, no. 4 (2009): 440–64. doi:10.1177/0891243209340034.

Sexton, Lori, and Valerie Jenness. "'We're Like Community': Collective Identity and Collective Efficacy among Transgender Women in Prisons for Men." *Punishment & Society* 18, no. 5 (2016): 544–77.

Sexton, Lori, Valerie Jenness, and Jennifer Macy Sumner. "Where the Margins Meet: A Demographic Assessment of Transgender Inmates in Men's Prisons." *Justice Quarterly* 27, no. 6 (2010): 835–66. doi:10.1080/07418820903419010.

Snorton, C. Riley. "'A New Hope': The Psychic Life of Passing." *Hypatia* 24, no. 3 (2009): 77–92. doi:10.1111/j.1527–2001.2009.01046.x.

Stryker, Susan. "(De)Subjugated Knowledges." Introduction to *The Transgender Studies Reader*. Vol. 1, edited by Susan Stryker and Stephen Whittle. New York: Routledge, 2006.

Sumner, Jennifer. "Keeping House: Understanding the Transgender Inmate Code of Conduct through Prison Policies, Environments, and Culture." PhD diss., University of California, Irvine, 2009.

Sumner, Jennifer, and Valerie Jenness. Gender Integration in Sex-Segregated U.S. Prisons: The Paradox of Transgender Correctional Policy. In *Handbook of LGBT Communities, Crime, and Justice*, edited by Dana Peterson and Vanessa R. Panfil, 229–59. New York: Springer, 2014.

Tewksbury, Richard, and Roberto H. Potter. "Transgender Prisoners—a Forgotten Group." In *Managing Special Populations in Jails and Prisons*, edited by Stan Stojkovic. New York: Civic Research Institute, 2005.

Valentine, David. *Imagining Transgender*. Durham, NC: Duke University Press, 2007.

Welter, Barbara. "The Cult of True Womanhood: 1820–1860." *American Quarterly* 18, no. 2 (1966): 151–74. doi:10.2307/2711179.

West, Candace, and Sarah Fenstermaker. "Doing Difference." *Gender & Society* 9, no. 1 (1995): 8–37.

West, Candace, and Don H. Zimmerman. "Doing Gender." *Gender & Society* 1, no. 2 (1987): 125–51. doi:10.1177/0891243287001002002.

Zimmerman, Don H. "They Were All Doing Gender, but They Weren't All Passing." *Gender & Society* 6, no. 2 (1992): 192–98.

13. Vagrant Masculinity: A Process of Masculine Self-Conceptualization in Formerly Incarcerated Black Men

Le'Brian A. Patrick

There is a direct relationship among media organizations, media content, and the everyday world. It follows that those in power are the ones who control what is displayed in the media, which is in turn absorbed, unquestioned by consumers, and implemented in everyday life. However, media portrayals of the incarcerated population (what I term *prison media*) tend to be skewed toward sensational images of inmates as simply savages whom we should fear.[1] Such imagery has pushed us to create conservative, aggressive criminal justice policies that serve the interests of the powerful, thus creating huge impediments to change in the lives of former inmates as they reenter communities.[2]

As a major source of information, the media play a vital role in shaping beliefs and human interactions, especially when it comes to people "foreign" to us. Specifically, prison media are problematic in that they distort the lives of former inmates, presenting them all as dangerous career criminals with no desire ever to become productive members of society and always working in opposition to law enforcement.[3] Such limited exposure to former inmates encourages us to define them by their criminality, and if they are lucky enough to have a person actually speak to them, then possibly they are defined only by their crime. It is rare to find media focused on humanizing the formerly incarcerated or their reentry process. This writing explores this highly important but overlooked area in prison media studies.

It's All about the "Men"

So, why focus on gender and sex? James Messerschmidt argues that masculinity is the key to explaining criminality.[4] Accounting for differences among men, he argues that middle-class White men can use power structures, such as education and respectable careers, to establish their masculinity and provide for themselves and their families. However, for lower-class White males and men of color, fewer legitimate options are available to them, and thus they are more likely to use crime and delinquency to prove their masculinity. Moreover, once gender differences are accounted for, Messerschmidt claims that it is far more important for men than for women to show power in order to prove their masculinity. This need to prove one's masculinity is partially due to accountability.[5]

Accountability allows people to conduct their activities in relation to their circumstances. In essence, we "do" gender, race, and class differently—depending on the social situation and circumstances. In this view, gender, race, and class are accomplished systematically, not imposed on people or settled beforehand, and are never static or finished products. Rather, people participate in self-regulating conduct whereby they monitor their own and others' social actions. Even though Black* men's concepts of masculinity may provide them with limited options outside crime, Messerschmidt's work highlights room for their agency to play a part in changing gendered interactions and focusing on crime as a viable option only in certain social situations. My research problematizes gender in that I emphasize transitions in gender conceptualizations postincarceration, specifically focusing on the impact of incarceration on masculinity during reentry.

Outside Insiders

There is a unique historical context for thinking about Black masculinity today. Patrick reviewed major historical eras that have had significant impacts on Black masculinity, such as slavery, emancipation, Reconstruction, Jim Crow, the civil rights movement, and the contemporary war on drugs.[6] He

---

* *Black*, like *White*, is a broad description of skin color/complexion. Both should be capitalized because they are used as references to one's ethnicity in the same way that Asian, Hispanic, Arab, and other designations are, despite the fact that these are all proper names describing not the person but the geographic or ethnic origin or ancestry of that person. Not to capitalize *Black* in this work would further minimize the importance of this group of people rather than uplift them as a worthy category. Besides, just as people might describe themselves as "Japanese" or "Chicano" rather than "Asian" or "Hispanic," people who are Black or White are just as likely to describe themselves as "African American" or "Caucasian."

examined how each era was laced with various ways of legally denying Black men (and women) the ability to obtain employment, housing, and public benefits. Moreover, his work highlighted significant factors that structure Black men's lives today—family, work, and prison.

The experience of being Black and male in America often means unemployment, school failure, and violence and crime.[7] Living lives shaped by racism, discrimination, and poverty, compounded by incarceration, these men literally move into the status of noncitizen, losing basic American constitutional rights. In fact, it is estimated that one in three Black men, compared to one in seventeen White men and one in nine of all men in the United States, will be imprisoned at some point in their lifetime, according to the Bureau of Justice Statistics.[8] For these reasons, it has become critical to understand how social and structural constraints, primarily incarceration stigma, gendered expectations, racism, and economic inequality, influence self-concepts of masculinity and desistance (cessation of lawbreaking) post-incarceration for Black males.

Theoretical Orientation

I have employed multiple theoretical perspectives to investigate how formerly incarcerated Black men (FIBM) construct, negotiate, perform, and sometimes redefine masculinity in my desire to provide a different, multidimensional, nonfictional image of "ex-cons" that has been missing from the media.

Theorizing Gender

Gender theorists have revealed a number of ways through which gender is (re)produced. At the individual level, gender is produced through social learning.[9] At the interactionist level, gender is an omnirelevant, situated accomplishment. So, people "do gender" together in specific contexts that are grounded in shared cultural and interactional expectations.[10] And, at the structural level, social structures, organizations, and institutional forces are active in shaping gender. Simply put, social institutions are not "out there" but are inside and around us, illuminating how gendered practices, power dynamics, and norms will and do vary within the contexts of various social institutions.[11]

This research is nestled in the interplay of human agency and social structure, between individual action and structural and institutional traditions, and in moral and legal codes that constrain the choices of FIBM. Because we are speaking about men with limited upward social mobility postincarceration, it is important to note that, like gender, the accomplishment of race and class is also unavoidable.

Conceptual Lens: Masculinities

Since the 1980s, gender theorists have argued that gender is structured relationally and hierarchically, and it consists of multiple masculinities and femininities for men.[12] To speak of *femininities* and *masculinities* indicates that genders are not homogenous entities; rather they are multiple, shifting, and constantly constructed and negotiated in daily interactions. Media representations of inmates and the prison culture, however, tend to show a monolithic vision of a hyperviolent, hypermasculine environment behind bars that is naturally ingrained in, and becomes further embedded in, the ex-con after serving a prison sentence. The present study presents alternative forms of masculinity in FIBM, which put these men in an active position to engage in altering habitual and normative social relations.

Because masculinity is viewed as constantly shifting, FIBM construct their understandings of masculinity through relationships with themselves, the media, other Black men, other former inmates, and their social environments. Beyond the prison walls, the reactions of "law-abiding" citizens intersect with prior incarceration experiences to create a new perception of the masculine "self" postincarceration.

Methodology

The goal of this project is not to estimate the distribution of similar or dissimilar attitudes toward masculinity postimprisonment but rather to explore the worlds of these men with respect to negotiating gender norms during reentry, a major life-course event for inmates that is overlooked or sensationalized in the media.

It is paramount to know who is included when discussing the process of reintegration into society, otherwise denoted as "reentry." Reentry can be vast in its scope, including the entire volume of persons who have spent time in prison (both those under supervision and not), or small, involving only those recently released.[13] If the prior group is considered, then the scope of reentry includes the several million living people who have spent time in prison. Even considering only the latter, a large number of persons in the U.S. population belong to that group. In fact, in October 2013, U.S. federal prisons released over six thousand inmates, the largest release in American history, to reduce overcrowding.[14] For this work, I spoke only with men whose time since reentry exceeded five to six months.

I employed a number of sampling strategies because, if there is one thing that I have learned about qualitative sampling, there is no one "best" sampling strategy to follow, since which strategy is best will depend on the context in which one is working, the nature of one's research objective(s), and, ultimately, what it is one wants to know.[15] My sampling techniques included criterion, convenience, snowball, and theoretical sampling for reasons of the sensitive subject matter, the state of Louisiana's high incarceration rate, the stigma associated with incarceration, and the analytical methods employed.

My analysis draws on twenty semistructured, audiotaped, in-depth, information-rich interviews with a sample of seventeen formerly incarcerated African American men in Louisiana (see the table for a detailed subsample description).[16] Interview questions were open ended and enabled me to gather in-depth information regarding the men's thoughts, beliefs, knowledge, reasoning, motivations, sentiments, and negotiations about their self-concepts and life postincarceration. The interview questions were designed and evolved from themes in the literature, theoretical frameworks, the responses of participants, and my personal experiences and observations.

I employed an active interviewing approach because interviews are "unavoidably collaborative and interpretively active"—involving the agency of both the interviewer and the respondent in the meaning-making process.[17] In this approach, the participant is not a passive vessel of knowledge but instead "consults repertoires of experience and orientations, linking fragments into patterns, and offering theoretically coherent descriptions, accounts, and explorations," all of which make the participant somewhat of a researcher in his or her own right.[18]

Analysis

By taking a constructionist approach to this project, I employed *grounded theory* techniques, which consist of systematic yet flexible guidelines for collecting and analyzing qualitative data used in theory construction.[19] Such a method of analysis is especially useful because it is comprehendible to laypersons, researchers, and policy makers. Because a grounded theoretical method looks at explanatory conceptual categories generated from the everyday social world and because the categories generated reflect the experiences

Formerly Incarcerated Black Men Interviewed for the Study

Name	Age (y)	Education	Occupation	Current Relationship	Kids	Sentence (y)
Fred	25	Dropped out	Grocery store	Married	Yes	3
Steven	29	N/A	Unemployed	Separated	No	2
Jarred	33	High school	Unemployed	Girlfriend	No	12
Shane	37	Dropped out	Store	Single	No	20
Kris	41	High school	Warehouse manager	Girlfriend	Yes	2
Randall	48	Dropped out	Grocery store	Married	Yes	16
Andre	48	High school	Store	Single	Yes	10
Jacob	51	High school	Warehouse	Married	Yes	8
Justin	59	High school	Unemployed	Single	Yes	15
Anthony	60	Some college	Organizer	Married	Yes	27
Carlito	66	Some college	Manager	Single	N/A	20
Nicholas	66	High school	Unemployed	Married	Yes	7
Marcus	68	High school	N/A	Widowed	No	5
Renzo	69	High school	N/A	Widowed	Yes	10
Michael	77	Master's	N/A	Single	N/A	3

of the participants under investigation, it is serves well here as a process of data collection and analysis.

While I am not attempting to produce a complete grounded theory, I aim to create a conceptual framework that accounts for various ways that FIBM construct and negotiate masculine self-concepts and behaviors postincarceration other than the monolithic view presented in prison media. I use this framework to understand the impact of social structure on successful reentry or recidivism. I urge readers to understand that grounded theory is a perspective-based methodology and to remember that people's perspectives vary. Using the multiple perspectives of my participants, I attempt to raise these perspectives to the abstract level of conceptualization, hoping to see an underlying or latent pattern, which is another perspective. According to Charmaz, "constructivism assumes the relativism of multiple social realities, recognizes the mutual creation of knowledge by the viewer and the viewed, and aims toward interpretive understanding of subjects' meanings."[20] Constructivism points out that it is impossible for a researcher to tell the whole story, for a whole story exceeds anyone's knowledge; however this mutually interpretive process allows a researcher to uncover a particular story.[21] Using the perspectives of my participants, I tell *our* story in the following pages.

Turning Point: A Brief Discussion of Life Prior to Reentry

The process of becoming a man is influenced by many experiences. My participants' negotiations with socially constructed norms of masculinity had led each of them to incarceration at some point in their lives, which, in turn, has shaped the way they understand and embody manhood today. The irony of Black masculinity is that it is not far removed from mainstream cultural definitions of masculinity. However, Black male images have become an exaggerated mirror of American macho.[22] I find that the issue is not that Black men are depicted as physical manifestations of American hypermasculinity, but rather it is not seeing the implications of embodying this image that is troublesome for many African American men. Ross argues that, on the one hand, the imagery of Black supermanliness is inspiring because of African American historical survival; but, on the other hand, it enhances the tendency to cast Black men as self-destructive, self-castrating, and self-paralyzing.[23] Thus, doing *Black masculinity* can come with great consequences, which was apparent for the men I interviewed.

Due to the vast range of historical and contemporary powerfully negative influences on the development of young Black males, they have learned to cope and resolve problems differently than White middle-class men do. African American men learn to succeed in modern-day culture through the use of violence, impatience, and alienation.[24] For many, masculinity is exhibited through a limited range of emotions like anger and aggression. This is not to say that White men do not use anger and aggression as forms of emotional expression; however, as Kimmel points out, their anger and aggression is something that many times results from a sense of "aggrieved entitlement": a sense that those benefits White men believed were their due have been snatched away from them.[25] Here, I emphasize that African American men have not been supplied with sufficient images of other Black men who express a wide range of emotions to use as role models. With limited options for self-expression, masculinity for the men here, prior to and during incarceration, manifested itself through self-destructive behavior like consuming alcohol and drugs and/or engaging in an overindulgence of sex. Thus, these men found themselves incarcerated for reasons related to the toxic nature of their understandings of masculinity. However, of even greater importance here is what happens after the "welcome" to prison.

One of the greatest challenges anyone can face, whether outside prison walls or in confinement, is a loss of autonomy and freedom. A continued loss of autonomy can have adverse effects on the individual, and for this reason prisons can present negative turning points for inmates. On the one hand, Wheeler has shown that prisoners become more "prisonized" the longer they are incarcerated; that is, inmates are more likely to make decisions on the basis of criminal rather than law-abiding values.[26] On the other hand, according to the environmental / learned helplessness model of personal control, in situations where individuals are unable to exercise autonomy, they develop a "learned helplessness."[27] Helpless individuals react passively to situations because they have learned that attempts to exert outcome control or choice or to obtain predictability are futile. So, inmate reactions to the prison environment can make them either more criminally aggressive or more passive. Either way, both of these can be negative turning points.

This research stands in contrast to my own in that a loss of personal autonomy produced positive cognitive and behavioral changes for the men I interviewed. It prompted them to realize they no longer had complete control over their circumstances. For some of the men, the loss of autonomy became a vehicle for long-term positive changes in their lives. Andre's narrative fragment sheds light on this phenomenon:

> Going into it [prison], I found out I couldn't keep the same attitude that I had before I left the streets. Well, I had a don't give a damn attitude and you not going to tell me anything because I don't want to hear it and I am who I am. I'm gonna be me and if you don't like it get the fuck away from me. Well, in jail you have to adapt and adjust because you're around thousands of different attitudes and if one offender's attitude don't get to you, you best believe an officer's attitude will. And they make an attitude adjustment!

Becker argues that in order to survive in prison, new inmates discover that they must make peace with the criminally oriented social structure—akin to the prisonizing process mentioned above—by adopting more toxic elements of masculinity.[28] As inmates approach release, however, they realize that the world they are returning to is dominated by people who respect the law and that the criminal values, which have served them well in prison, will not work as well beyond the cell walls. Thus, they become more law abiding. Nicholas reflected on the beginning of changing how he responded to challenges:

> In order to know what your reality is going to be like, you have to go through something. So, I believe me going through it led me to be more prosperous and more understanding. Because I had to go through it at first to know how to carry myself at the next institution. So, once I got there I never had big problems again.

For Nicholas this shift began well before his sentence was coming to a close, at a time when he was transferred to another institution.

These men's changes provide empirical support for Seligman's learned helplessness theory or for the notion that individuals are agentic beings who can in fact change their situations. Andre and Nicholas both felt that their behavioral changes helped them survive incarceration.

Of course, change is not always easy, and these men are not just passively experiencing such changes. Andre indicated that change takes a lot of effort and sometimes must start within the individual. He recalled thinking while incarcerated, "Now when I have a problem with an inmate, I could walk away from the inmate, but you can't walk away from the officer. This is where the problem comes in at because that is hard, but I did it." While Andre's response indicates that change may difficult but not impossible, it is also not the same for everyone. In media depictions of former inmates, when they are presented, we miss such changes in character development, which could affect public interactions with former inmates.

Cultural Control: Postincarceration Challenges to Autonomy

The challenge to living freely is not limited to prison; it is a challenge that is omnipresent in the transition from incarceration back into the community. In *Punishment and Inequality in America*, Bruce Western explores lowered human capital in former inmates, pointing out that rehabilitation traditionally included counseling, psychotherapy, drug treatment, education, and vocational training.[29] However, the increase in the prison population has only resulted in more prisons, without additional dollars for rehabilitative resources. Former inmates are at the bottom of the social totem pole, and they are aware of it. According to Randall, "When it comes down to filling out an application, sadly I already know that I have to take the leftovers. I already know that. But I also know that I have to have the job. I'll take the leftovers rather than have no job."

The mark of incarceration makes it difficult to obtain access to resources for survival. Even though Randall did not go into detail about what he brings or does not bring to the labor market, he did speak to the lack of enthusiasm that the labor market has for former inmates. Incarceration can undermine economic prosperity in the labor market on both the supply and the demand sides. Workers may be made less productive by serving time in prison, or employers may be more reluctant to hire job applicants with criminal records.[30] Direct barriers, found in various statutes and occupational code licensing requirements, require that employers exclude applicants with criminal convictions and, in some cases, arrest records.[31] Simply because of a lack of options, there is the possibility that some men feel that prison is a viable alternative to reentry struggles. David, who had been released for about two years, elucidated this point when he said:

> When I come home it was rough not being able to get a job and not having the correct money I need to support what I have [his family]. It's rough and sometimes it drives me to want to go back to jail because I don't have bills there. But at the same time, even though you don't have bills there, you having other issues.

Recidivism rates are extraordinarily high in the American criminal justice system, consistently remaining above 60 percent.[32] Steven, released nearly eight years ago, shared a narrative that sheds experiential light on why recidivism rates are as high as they are:

> The stigma of being on probation, that stuck with me for years. It was hard to get a decent job. The things that you need to move forward in your life and be a member of society. Well I couldn't get a place to live and I couldn't get a job, so how can I be productive. All I can do is go back to the corner and sell drugs or go steal stuff to try and make ends meet. I'm not justifying for those people that do that, but I can understand the stress behind them doing it.

The restricted circumstances that former inmates encounter when they reenter communities can be excruciating. Consistent with research, my participants experienced reduced access to resources and diminished citizenship upon reentry. However, social support can be a mitigating factor in the lives of inmates,[33] a theme lacking in prison media.

The men I interviewed demonstrated that, despite the lack of rehabilitative resources, incarceration can change inmates, but this is not a visual we get in prison media. Upon initial entry into prison, they found that prior ways of behaving were not sufficient for survival in prison. Incarceration can potentially increase the toxicity of those behaviors that got them arrested in the first place. However, it is important to remember that change is possible. Although minimally discussed here, inmates experience various losses, both institutional and personal ones, other than autonomy alone, both during and after incarceration. As Anthony summed things up: "man, I had given away so much for so little in return; losing this time with my family." I now show how it is precisely the weight of these significant losses that began to bring change to the lives of my interviewees.

A "New" Masculinity

The impact of incarceration and media on gender ideologies is hardly an area that we can afford to ignore, as it has shaped the way these men and the larger society understand and enact masculinity today. Using a subset of my interview data, I focus on how masculinity is actually performed differently in changing social contexts, providing support for understanding the multiplicity of masculinities. Specifically, the findings presented here focus on a major area missing from prison media studies: transitioning postincarceration or reentry, specifically shifts in the masculine self-concept.

Possible Selves

Over their life course, people construct and strive to implement normative projections of themselves and their future. Normativity is relative, and for young Black males, the image of the hypersexual, hyperaggressive, sexist tough guy may be *normative*. However, for the men here, incarceration shifted their perceptions of their selves and motivated them to transform their life trajectories.

Possible selves are defined as conceptions of ourselves in the future.[34] Miller argues that there is a projective element to agency in which thought processes and patterns of behavior may be significantly reconfigured in relation to one's hopes, fears, and desires for the future.[35] Possible selves provide "a bridge of self-representations between one's current state and one's desired or hoped for state."[36] Much of the research related to possible selves and incarceration focuses on fatherhood possibilities for inmates. Meek suggests that parenthood is a key component of present and future representations of fathers in prison.[37] One participant, Justin, a fifty-nine-year-old grandfather, spoke about the consequences of missing a lot of time with his children while incarcerated:

> Due to me missing my kids, my biological kids. That's why I'm so respectful to my grandkids. My wife's grandkids. You know, that's why I want to raise them so bad. I want to tell them the stories that I went through. I want to tell them the right and the wrong way to go because I feel in my heart that I don't want them without some strong person behind them letting them know the right thing to do.

Justin's change was prompted by infrequent and inconsistent contact with his own children. He realized the detriment that his absence was causing in the lives of his children, which made him to want to be a better father in the future. Because his children are adults now, he is using himself as a positive role model for his grandchildren and helping to break the cycle of incarceration that troubles African American communities. His actions show that FIBM can use their experiences as lessons to prevent crime and delinquency in minority youth communities. With media's limited production of shows, like the *Scared Straight* and *Beyond Scared Straight* series, that use inmates as a method of crime/delinquency intervention, the public may miss this side of inmates. Even in documentaries and shows that use inmates in this manner, the inmates or the accused are still presented as deviant persons or the ever-present hyperaggressive criminal.

For some men, possible selves function as goals, with an incentive power that pulls them toward a desired end state, and are sometimes helped by an undesired negative possible self to be avoided. The concept of possible selves has been further enriched by the emphasis on its function in motivation.[38] However, Oyserman and Markus argue that a negative possible self is not in itself motivating except in the role of balancing and boosting a positive possible self.[39] When asked about events that made him want to change for the better, Jarred responded:

> In prison I done seen people get killed, people raped. I done seen young men 17, 18 get life sentences; ain't coming out. I'm talking about life sentences, ain't no way! When they say life without the eligibility of parole, ain't nothing can bring you out, but death. You can come out in a box and that's it. Not gonna be me!

Visualizations of negative possible selves have been shown to be important tools for behavior control.[40] Motivated by the hope of freedom and the fear of a life sentence, Jarred realized change was necessary. Erikson cautions that hopes and fears are not necessarily possible selves; however, they can give rise to possible selves.[41] The distinguishing factor is that possible selves include experiences of what it could and would be like if a situation becomes a reality, making them more than abstract notions of future states. Possible selves are the link between cognition and motivation, as they function as incentives for future behavior, or they create drives to manifest fantasies of future selves as authentic beings. As opposed to generalized shapeless goals and fears, possible selves are personalized representations that give meaning and form to these broader conceptions.[42] I argue that by his emphasizing, "Not gonna be me," Jarred's fears and hopes created images of himself in those future positions as he evaluated where his life was headed and shifted his behavior to take him in the direction he wanted to go.

Future-oriented expectations, fears, and strategies are constrained by feedback from one's sociocultural context, suggesting a relationship between support in one's immediate context and the development of strategies for achieving desired future selves. Feedback that guides an individual's possible self is likely to come from several potential sources, with the media being one but not the only one. Others include social and religious institutions, significant others, and the individual's own interpretation of environmental feedback and past experiences.[43] Randall felt that he needed just one person's support—his wife. He elaborated:

> She gave me something that at my age that I know it had to be God because out of all the people in the world, they couldn't give it to me. She showed me the care and the love, even though I was incarcerated. She wrote me every day. And I had a choice when I got out. I could've ran this way or that way, but she trusted me. She believed in me enough to change my life and all I ever wanted in my whole born life was for somebody to believe in me. Somebody to say, "Well I trust you."

For Randall, his wife and religion worked together to help him see himself differently and transform. Furthermore, by acknowledging the need for trust and support, he highlights other ways that the media can intervene to minimize recidivism by presenting supportive imagery to consumers.

In brief, possible selves are not covered as positive life trajectories in prison media. These cognitive processes are valuable tools for desistance that can be used in prison media. In thinking about their current identities, these men remember thinking of people that they wanted to be there for and the support received from significant others, as well as people that they did not want to become. It is these images of who they want to be, how they see their futures, and how others see their futures that have had a significant impact on how they conceptualize themselves today.

"Redefining" Masculinity

Because gender is so taken for granted, it is rare that men consciously think about what it means to be a man. As Paechter argues, "It is only when we find ourselves performing, or attempting a masculinity that for some reason fails to 'fit' a particular social situation that [the] performative aspect is recognized as we subtly, or not so subtly, change our behavior."[44] For my participants, preincarcerated masculinity was not "fitting" their lives because it contributed to their troubles prior to, and possibly during, incarceration. During and following their incarceration experience, participants gained a new perspective on their lives and decided to reorient their definitions of masculinity in an effort to alter their life trajectories. What is missing in prison media are depictions of inmates, both current and former, redefining masculinity to encompass positive elements.

As Patrick discussed, the concept of Black masculine identity was fashioned and codified during and after the formal collapse of slavery.[45] Thus, Black masculine identity is a product of narrowly defined understandings of White maleness. Understanding the interaction of incarceration with current conceptions of Black masculine identity is important because of the high incarceration rate of Black men in contemporary society.

I listened as participants revealed new orientations to masculinity and what it meant for them to "be a man" that developed after incarceration. For example, Anthony, a sixty-year-old former inmate of twenty-seven years, said, "I tell people all the time that prison, for me, was a bad experience with good results. I don't think I could chart a better course, than the one I have been on." Anthony's sentiments summarize the outlook of many of my participants, wherein they turned poor circumstances into positive results. These men transformed their lives through learning from their incarceration histories and redefined how they constructed and performed masculinity in their own lives.

Masculinity is a personal and social matter. How people choose to define it and whether they align with conventional conceptions depend on their

individual and cultural upbringing.⁴⁶ For example, when asked what it meant
to be masculine and to be a man, Shane, who grew up in a single-parent
home, explained:

> They are different. Being a man is being in control of your responsibilities,
> not only for yourself, but also for the people that you are surrounded by.
> That's not just kids, a wife, and family or something like that, but you
> kind of like have to be responsible for your entire surroundings, whether
> it be on the job, at the house or wherever you are. And masculinity is
> totally different because in my opinion and in my definition a woman
> can be a man. You don't have to be masculine to be a man. Hey, I could
> be wrong, but that's how I see it because we have so many single mothers
> out here playing momma and daddy. And for that reason alone being a
> man is not described by being a male. That's how I look at it.

Shane sees masculinity and manhood as distinct, albeit related, entities.
His narrative exposes the ways that masculinity is neither uniform nor unchanging. The cultural and demographic shifts that contribute to the absence
of so many African American men in homes had led Shane to distinguish
masculinity from manhood. He recognizes that one is not a necessity for
the other, and he has revealed his reverence for women who take on what
would have previously been qualities and responsibilities reserved for men.
Yet, in his definition, he still incorporates control, a core element of hegemonic masculinity and one that distinguishes hegemonic masculinity from
other masculinities—that is, control over one's time, over women, and for
very few men, control over other men, etc.⁴⁷ For Shane that sense of control
comes in a form that would allow him to have control over his own responsibilities, not necessarily only for himself but for the good of his family. He
has challenged what it means to be a man by expanding who has access to
manhood. He disconnects masculinity from male bodies.

A major similarity that binds the transformations experienced by these men
is their affiliation with organizations that work with formerly incarcerated
people. Focusing on reentry programs has definitely been missed in prison
media. These men have all been exposed to institutional scripts that they
use to construct their narrative selves. For the men in my study, they have
begun to see themselves as "new" men who have turned imprisonment into
a positive turning point—a distinct institutional narrative of these support
groups. Gubrium and Holstein define "institutional selves" as patterns
that emerge when an image of a type of self is discursively created by an

organization.[48] The pattern of institutional selves has been documented in battered women support groups,[49] codependents,[50] as well as dysfunctional families.[51] Miller finds that they can also emerge from individuals engaged in therapeutic sessions.[52] I urge media producers to highlight in their works how the institutionalized support received postincarceration is important for leading former inmates to see their prison experiences as positive turning points, shifting the way they see themselves as men and changing how they conceptualize and embody masculinity.

Messner argues there are significant shifts in the cultural and personal styles of hegemonic masculinity;[53] however, such shifts do not undermine conventional structures of men's power. In other words, "softer" and more "sensitive" styles of masculinity are developing in contemporary times, but these styles do not necessarily negate traditional hegemonic masculinity. For example, the way Edward, a thirty-eight-year-old former inmate of five years, sees it, "A man is a provider, a support system; a man is a person that would take his last just to see his family happy. That's what I think a man is." Edward's description is multifaceted and incorporates new aspects that did not surface in preincarcerated definitions of masculinity. Although he still conceptualizes man as the provider—a throwback to traditional masculinity—the fact that he peppers this with a support system is also characteristic of a softer masculinity.

Moreover, these men have not just constructed a singular version, but rather they are envisioning multidimensional and dynamic masculinities in which there is room for variation among men. Anthony discussed some of the complexities of men: "The man is also the guy who can think himself out of the same situations that sometimes will result in physical altercations. The man is also the person who is responsible to his family, especially if you got kids. And he is able to absorb responsibility. I think that the man is all of this in one."

Similarly, Justin explains:

Sometimes when we see people, we get pieces of them. You don't get that whole person. You get the person who is this guy for a reason. The guy who tries to take care of his family is also a man. He may not be as strong as this other man. And then you get the intellectual guy over here, who is not as physically strong or courageous, he's not weak, he don't take care of his family, but the intellectual, this guy knows how to do the things that need to get done. He can do the right thing. He is a man. You don't have to be the guy who goes and puts on a coat of metal and slang iron to say I'm a man. Yeah, you a man, but you're a damn fool!

My participants invoked tropes of hegemonic masculinity in their narratives of what it means for them to be men; for example, they discussed the importance of being the economic provider, being physically strong, and having control. Yet, alternative and multidimensional definitions of masculinity, like that of emotion, were strategically woven into their narratives as well. Ultimately, their narratives are consistent with the more current, pluralist interpretation of multiple masculinities.

These findings highlight the extent to which incarceration, or more specifically the institutionalized support that these former inmates received upon reentry, can be positive cognitive and behavioral turning points in the lives of FIBM. Unifying their positions on incarceration is their connection to reentry programs that build hope in their lives and reorient their focus away from the negatives of incarcerated pasts. Binswanger and colleagues advise that we reach out to former inmates.[54] Thus, it is best for prison media to highlight the positive along with the negatives of incarceration or, as my participants put it, show incarceration as "a bad experience, with good results"! Moreover, these men open masculinity to variation among men and expose phallocentric fallacies about what it means to be a man.

Discussion

It is true that prisons are hypermasculine environments that can be extremely dangerous and have the potential to create violence in the character of inmates and former inmates, but this is not necessarily the case for all former inmates. Just as deviance varies in the law-abiding population, so does it among the formerly incarcerated population; however, more humane images are lacking in prison media. Moreover, structural barriers to reentry are rare topics of discussion and are not readily displayed in the media. With the growth of the prison industry and the incarceration population, it is time to see inmates as persons with variations in who they are or can be, images that will help us heal the disconnect between "criminals" and the social structure.

By presenting more humane images of FIBM, I aim to remove a little of the incarceration stigma that has been sensationalized in media representations of criminals. I stress how these FIBM have reconstructed and negotiated their ideals of masculinity during reentry, an image of their masculinity that, although needed, rarely appears in media. Despite living in the "borderlands" of mainstream acceptance and support, these men have developed a new set of masculine principles. Whereas for many law-abiding persons, these principles may seem axiomatic; because former inmates are limited in their access to resources for doing gender, these reorientations to masculinity are interesting and important to understand. Moreover, media representations of such reconceptualizations have the potential to repair relationships between the former inmate and societal attitudes towards "ex-cons."

Sociological Implications
My participants have shifted the way they conceptualize masculinity in efforts to improve their circumstances. What sets these men apart from other former inmates is that these men recognize the necessity for taking action if change is going to occur, which highlights the dynamic nature of masculinity.

Masculinity is constantly constructed and maintained through our everyday social patterns and institutions. According to Connell,[55] one of the ways masculinity is constructed is through the structure of organized sports; it is these competitions, ordered so that an athlete either wins or loses, that create a form of aggressive masculinity. In this view, prisons can be seen as arenas for the development of aggressive masculinity. The very organization of prisons requires a masculine presence from inmates—at the very least for protection, as my respondents pointed out. Moreover, prison staff and administration also contribute to this hypermasculine atmosphere, even in women's institutions.[56] Such a necessity is recognized by these men; however, they also acknowledge there is a time to change and that change is possible. Their stories call for media to present former inmates in more than a two-dimensional manner in an effort to help close the social distance between former inmates and the general population.

While gender inequality remains a constant struggle, intersections of race, ethnicity, class, and citizenship matter as well. FIBM, more than other groups of men, must continue to confront these challenges to economic survival. Social forces have placed Black men lowest on the masculinity hierarchy.[57] And the former inmate is even lower on this totem pole.

Policy Implications
There has been a strong push for law enforcement agencies, policy makers, social support groups, and individuals alike to aid in the prevention and reduction of crime and recidivism. However, strategies need revision as we are not seeing any reduction in the inmate population, especially for Black males. It may be that the public equates rehabilitation with softness, but one does not have to be soft on crime to believe in rehabilitation. It

may be that public perceptions are slow to change, but the lack of positive images of inmates, both present and former, is not helping to speed up the process.

An area not focused on is reentry agencies that work to provide services to the formerly incarcerated population. Highlighting these agencies in media could help the public understand the lack of resources available to help these men become "productive" citizens postincarceration. Moreover, knowing that many of these organizations are founded and run by FIBM, and that their goals are to help these men learn from their experiences and use what they have learned to help others, may increase public efforts to support these agencies, as well as votes for more rehabilitative, rather than punitive, strategies for inmates. The media are one such outlet to increase awareness and advocacy for former inmates and the organizations that work with them.

These men, along with others who support and believe in them, are creating new ways and resources for doing masculinity and seeing themselves as real and capable men, but this imagery is missing in much of the prison media. Implementing similar programs in prisons and increasing the resources for postimprisonment programs would help greatly reduce recidivism. Furthermore, by funding these programs, the government would be participating in a movement of social change, one that would combat issues behind bars by reorienting these men prior to release, which would help programs outside prisons as well as help to reduce recidivism. Movies, television shows, and news reports are excellent ways to kick-start such efforts by showing the human side of the inmate. The media's role in furthering this is not just timely, but unarguable.

Limitations and Future Research

Like any study, my findings and contributions should be viewed in light of their limitations. For example, one should be cautioned to avoid using them as generalizable to the larger population of FIBM both locally and nationally. The objective here was to present a more humane, positive image of FIBM and the social processes they experience postincarceration (reorientations in masculinity, reentry, and recidivism), which has been lacking in prison media; however, some may view my relatively small sample as perhaps the most glaring limitation. This serves as an introductory exploration of the ways gender can be reoriented in beneficial ways to aid in reentry. Future research should include larger confirmatory studies that will increase the evidence for supporting reentry programs.

Despite the homogeneity of my participants, they represent a large portion Louisiana's inmate and former inmate population with their significantly difficult social realities. Nonetheless, future research should consider the experiences of White men, as their experiences will provide a look into a group who are, by physical appearance, quicker to benefit from hegemonic masculinity. Moreover, incorporating various types of men would provide a more holistic view for prison media projects on the issues that various groups face during reentry.

Concluding Thoughts: Reimagining Black Masculinity in the Context of Mass Incarceration

As the number of Black males who are released from prison continues to rise, access to resources for survival will demand attention in prison media, especially if we continue to hold these men to the same standards of masculinity that we do all other groups. It is time for media projects to draw attention to the numerous legal restrictions we place on former inmates and to the resources for doing masculinity (or lack thereof).

I hope to have explored several aspects of life that show a more humane image of former inmates now missing from prison media. First, under current circumstances, FIBM must reconstruct how they negotiate dominant standards of masculinity in their interactions with former inmates and law-abiding persons during reentry. Second, incarceration can potentially activate an image of a possible self that is capable of a positive masculinity. A reorientation from toxic to positive aspects of masculinity can possibly arise out of incarceration experiences, when there is a desire to change and reestablish oneself as a man. As cultural shifts in ideas around race/ethnicity and gender continue to occur, the media are a prime vehicle to drive such shifts by informing the public of the structural, institutional, and cultural barriers that limit the life choices of our former inmate population. Racial stereotypes, combined with a general mistrust of criminals, create obstacles to doing positive masculinity, and this has been exaggerated by prison media. With limited access to citizenship, these men are viewed as deficient and unworthy, an assumption that also penetrates much of the research and media images of FIBM.

The existence of often-negative images of Black males is undeniable, with various forms of media attending to, contextualizing, or simply highlighting the litany of problems associated with and attributed to Black males.

Notwithstanding an exceptional few who become media superstars and highly
visible public figures, it is important to see how men at the low end of the
social spectrum are able to create positive senses of self and lead productive
lives. In taking on the task of reimagining Black masculine identity, I have
made a vessel for these men to provide alternative ways of seeing formerly
incarcerated persons, Black men in particular, which are missing from prison
media today.

Notes

1. Krajicek, *Scooped!*; Altheide, *Creating Fear.*
2. Altheide, *Creating Fear.*
3. Chermak, "Police, Courts, and Corrections in the Media"; Levenson, "Inside Information."
4. Messerschmidt, *Masculinities and Crime.*
5. Messerschmidt, *Crime as Structured Action.*
6. Patrick, "Outside Insiders."
7. Wilson, *Truly Disadvantaged*; Garibaldi, "Educating Black Male Youth"; Bureau of Justice Statistics, "Prisoners in 1988."
8. Bonczar, "Prevalence of Imprisonment." For some relatively recent statistics collected by the Bureau of Justice Statistics, see Carson, "Prisoners in 2013."
9. Coontz, "Way We Never Were"; West and Fenstermaker, "Doing Difference"; Root-Aulette and Wittner, *Gendered Worlds.*
10. Lorber, "Dismantling Noah's Ark"; West and Zimmerman, "Doing Gender"; West and Fenstermaker, "Doing Difference"; Root-Aulette and Wittner, *Gendered Worlds.*
11. Giddens, *Constitution of Society*; Sandler and Hall, *Campus Climate Revisited.*
12. Carrigan, Connell, and Lee, "Toward a New Sociology of Masculinity"; Connell, *Gender and Power*; Connell, *Masculinities*; Connell, *Gender*; Connell and Messerschmidt, "Hegemonic Masculinity."
13. Lynch and Sabol, *Prisoner Reentry in Perspective.*
14. Schmidt, "U.S. to Release 6,000 Inmates from Prisons."
15. Marshall, "Sampling for Qualitative Research"; Johnson and Christensen, *Educational Research*; Biernacki and Waldorf, "Snowball Sampling"; Glaser, *Theoretical Sensitivity.*
16. Two of the participants featured in this chapter, David and Edward, were men I encountered impromptu at a meeting. We were able to discuss what I was researching, and I acquired their consent to talk about their experiences. We spoke briefly, but I was unable to catch up with them later for a more detailed

discussion of their current situations. I did not collect enough information to list them in my summary table of participants, but I learned enough from them to include them in the chapter.

17. Holstein and Gubrium, *Active Interview.*

18. Ibid.

19. Charmaz, *Constructing Grounded Theory.*

20. Ibid., 210.

21. Stake, "Qualitative Case Studies."

22. Ross, *Success Factors of Young African-American Males.*

23. Ibid.

24. Majors, "Cool Pose"; Majors and Billson, *Cool Pose.*

25. Kimmel, *Angry White Men.*

26. Wheeler, "Socialization in Correctional Communities."

27. Seligman, *Helplessness.*

28. Becker, *Human Capital.*

29. Western, *Punishment and Inequality in America.*

30. Holzer, Raphael, and Stoll, "Will Employers Hire Ex-offenders?"

31. Harris and Keller, "Ex-offenders Need Not Apply."

32. This statement is based on examining U.S. Department of Justice statistics over a period of recent years.

33. Carlson and Cervera, "Incarceration, Coping, and Support"; Clear, Rose, and Ryder, "Incarceration and the Community."

34. Erikson, "Meaning of the Future."

35. Miller, "Changing the Subject."

36. Markus and Ruvolo, "Possible Selves," 211.

37. Meek, "Experiences of a Young Gypsy-Traveller."

38. Erikson, "Meaning of the Future."

39. Oyserman and Markus, "Possible Selves and Delinquency."

40. Oyserman, Gant, and Ager, "Socially Contextualized Model of African-American Identity."

41. Erikson, "Meaning of the Future."

42. Markus and Nurius, "Possible Selves."

43. Ibid.

44. Paechter, "Masculinities and Femininities as Communities of Practice," 69.

45. Patrick, "Outside Insiders."

46. Wetherell and Edley, "Gender Practices."

47. Donaldson, "What Is Hegemonic Masculinity?"

48. Gubrium and Holstein, *Institutional Selves.*

49. Loseke, "Lived Realities and Formula Stories of 'Battered Women.'"
50. Irvine, *Codependent Forevermore.*
51. Gubrium, *Out of Control.*
52. Miller, "Changing the Subject."
53. Messner, "'Changing Men' and Feminist Politics."
54. Binswanger, Stern, Deyo, Heagerty, Cheadle, Elmore, and Koepsell, "Release from Prison"; Binswanger, Blatchford, Lindsay, and Stern, "Risk Factors for All."
55. Connell, *Masculinities,* 4.
56. Denborough, *Family Therapy*; Zimmer, "How Women Reshape the Prison Guard Role."
57. Staples, "Masculinity and Race."

Bibliography

Altheide, David L. *Creating Fear: News and the Construction of Crisis.* New York: Aldine de Gruyter, 2002.

Becker, Gordon. *Human Capital: A Theoretical and Empirical Analysis, with Special Reference to Education.* New York: Columbia University Press for the National Bureau of Economic Research, 1964.

Biernacki, Patrick, and Dan Waldorf. "Snowball Sampling: Problems and Techniques of Chain Referral Sampling." *Sociological Methods and Research* 10, no. 2 (1981): 141–63.

Binswanger, Ingrid, Patrick Blatchford, Rebecca Lindsay, and Marc Stern. "Risk Factors for All—Cause, Overdose, and Early Deaths after Release from Prison in Washington State." *Drug and Alcohol Dependency* 117, no. 1 (2011): 1–6.

Binswanger, Ingrid, Marc Stern, Richard Deyo, Patrick Heagerty, Allen Cheadle, Joann Elmore, and Thomas Koepsell. "Release from Prison: A High Risk of Death for Former Inmates." *New England Journal of Medicine* 356 (2011): 157–65.

Bonczar, Thomas. "Prevalence of Imprisonment in the U.S. Population, 1974–2001." Bureau of Justice Statistics, 2003. Accessed September 24, 2017. https://www.bjs.gov.

Bureau of Justice Statistics. "Prisoners in 1988." Washington, D.C.: U.S. Department of Justice, 1988. Accessed September 24, 2017. https://www.bjs .gov/content/pub/pdf/p88.pdf.

Carlson, Bonnie E., and Neil Cervera. "Incarceration, Coping, and Support." *Social Work* 36, no. 4 (1991): 279–85.

Carrigan, Tim, Robert Connell, and John Lee. "Toward a New Sociology of Masculinity." *Theory and Society* 14, no. 5 (1985): 551–604.

Carson, E. Ann. "Prisoners in 2013." Bureau of Justice Statistics, 2014. Accessed September 24, 2017. https://www.bjs.gov.

Charmaz, Kathy. *Constructing Grounded Theory: A Practical Guide through Qualitative Analysis*. London: Sage, 2006.

Chermak, Steven. "Police, Courts, and Corrections in the Media." In *Popular Culture, Crime, and Justice*, edited by Frankie Y. Bailey and Donna C. Hale, 87–99. Belmont, CA: Wadsworth, 1998.

Clear, Todd, Dina Rose, and Judith Ryder. "Incarceration and the Community: The Problem of Removing and Returning Offenders." *Crime & Delinquency* 47, no. 3 (2001): 335–51.

Connell, Robert. *Gender*. Cambridge: Polity, 2002.

———. *Gender and Power*. Sydney: Allen and Unwin, 1987.

———. *Masculinities*. Cambridge: Polity, 1995.

———. "Masculinities and Globalization." *Men and Masculinities* 1, no. 1 (1998): 3–23.

Connell, Robert, and James Messerschmidt. "Hegemonic Masculinity: Rethinking the Concept." *Gender & Society* 19, no. 6 (2005): 829–59.

Coontz, Stephanie. "The Way We Never Were." In *A Companion to Post-1945 America*, edited by Jean-Christophe Agnew and Roy Rosenzweig, chap. 30. New York: Basic Books, 1992.

Denborough, David, ed. *Family Therapy: Exploring the Field's Past, Present and Possible Futures*. Adelaide, Australia: Dulwich Centre, 2001.

Donaldson, Mike. "What Is Hegemonic Masculinity?" *Theory and Society* 22, no. 5 (1993): 643–57.

Erikson, Martin. "The Meaning of the Future: Toward a More Specific Definition of Possible Selves." *Review of General Psychology* 11, no. 4 (2007): 348–58.

Garibaldi, Antoine M. "Educating Black Male Youth: A Moral and Civil Imperative." New Orleans: Committee to Study the Status of the Black Male in the New Orleans Public Schools, 1988.

Giddens, Anthony. *The Constitution of Society: Outline of the Theory of Structuration*. Berkeley: University of California Press, 1984.

Glaser, Barney. *Theoretical Sensitivity*. Mills Valley, CA: Sociology Press, 1978.

Gubrium, Jaber. *Out of Control: Family Therapy and Domestic Disorder*. Newbury Park, CA: Sage, 1992.

Gubrium, Jaber, and James Holstein, eds. *Institutional Selves: Troubled Identities in a Postmodern World*. New York: Oxford University Press, 2001.

Harris, Patricia, and Kimberly Keller. "Ex-offenders Need Not Apply: The Criminal Background Check in Hiring Decisions." *Journal of Contemporary Criminal Justice* 21, no. 1 (2005): 6–30.

Holstein, James, and Jaber Gubrium. *The Active Interview*. Thousand Oaks, CA: Sage, 1995.

Holzer, Harry J., Steven Raphael, and Michael A. Stoll. "Will Employers Hire Ex-offenders? Employer Perceptions, Background Checks, and Their Determinants." In *The Imprisoning America: The Social Effects of Mass Incarceration*, edited by Mary Pattillo, David Weiman, and Bruce Western, 205–46. New York: Russell Sage Foundation, 2003.

Irvine, Leslie. *Codependent Forevermore: The Invention of Self in a Twelve Step Group* Chicago: University of Chicago Press, 1999.

Johnson, Burke, and Larry Christensen. *Educational Research: Quantitative, Qualitative, and Mixed Approaches*. Boston: Allyn & Bacon, 2004.

Kimmel, Michael. *Angry White Men: American Masculinity at the End of an Era*. New York: Nation Books, 2013.

Krajicek, David J. *Scooped! Media Miss Real Story on Crime While Chasing Sex, Sleaze, and Celebrities*. New York: Columbia University Press, 1998.

Levenson, Joe. "Inside Information: Prisons and the Media." *Criminal Justice Matters* 43 (2001): 14–15.

Lorber, Judith. "Dismantling Noah's Ark." *Sex Roles* 14 (1986): 567–80.

Loseke, Donileen. "Lived Realities and Formula Stories of 'Battered Women.'" In *Institutional Selves: Personal Troubles in an Organizational Context*, edited by Jaber F. Gubrium and James A. Holstein, 107–26. New York: Oxford University Press, 2001.

Lynch, James P., and William J. Sabol. *Prisoner Reentry in Perspective*. Crime Policy Report, Volume 3. Washington, D.C.: Urban Institute Justice Policy Center, 2001.

Majors, Richard. "Cool Pose: Black Masculinity and Sports." In *African Americans in Sport: Contemporary Themes*, edited by Gary A. Sailes, chap. 2. New Brunswick, NJ: Transaction Publishers, 1998.

Majors, Richard, and Janet Billson. *Cool Pose: The Dilemmas of Black Manhood in America*. New York: Lexington Books, 1993.

Markus, Hazel, and Paula Nurius. "Possible Selves." *American Psychologist* 41 (1986): 954–69.

Markus, Hazel, and Ann Ruvolo. "Possible Selves: Personalized Representations of Goals." In *Goal Concepts in Personality and Social Psychology*, edited by Lawrence Pervin, 211–41. Hillsdale, NJ: Lawrence Erlbaum Associates, 1989.

Marshall, Martin. "Sampling for Qualitative Research." *Family Practice* 13, no. 6 (1996): 522–26.

Meek, Rosie. "The Experiences of a Young Gypsy-Traveller in the Transition from Custody to Community: An Interpretative Phenomenological Analysis." *Legal and Criminological Psychology* 12, no. 1 (2007): 133–47.

Messerschmidt, James. *Crime as Structured Action: Gender, Race, Class, and Crime in the Making*. Thousand Oaks, CA: Sage, 1997.

———. *Masculinities and Crime: Critique and Reconceptualization of Theory*. Lanham, MD: Rowman & Littlefield, 1993.

Messner, Michael A. "'Changing Men' and Feminist Politics in the United States." *Theory and Society* 22, no. 5 (1993): 723–37.

Miller, Gale. "Changing the Subject: Self-Construction in Grief Therapy." In *Institutional Selves: Troubled Identities in a Postmodern World*, edited by Jaber Gubrium and James Holstein, 64–83. New York: Oxford University Press, 2001.

Oyserman, Daphna, Larry Gant, and Joel Ager. "A Socially Contextualized Model of African-American Identity: Possible Selves and School Persistence." *Journal of Personality and Social Psychology* 69 (1995): 1216–32.

Oyserman, Daphna, and Hazel Markus. "Possible Selves and Delinquency." *Journal of Personality and Social Psychology* 59 (1990): 112–25.

Paechter, Carrie. "Masculinities and Femininities as Communities of Practice." *Women's Studies International Forum* 26, no. 1 (2003): 69–77.

Patrick, Le'Brian. "Outside Insiders: Remember the Time." *Journal of Pan African Studies* 7, no. 6 (2014): 106–27.

Root-Aulette, Judy, and Judith Wittner. *Gendered Worlds*. 2nd ed. New York: Oxford University Press, 2011.

Ross, Marilyn. *Success Factors of Young African-American Males at a Historically Black College*. New York: Praeger, 1998.

Sandler, Bernice, and Roberta M. Hall. *Campus Climate Revisited: Chilly for Women Faculty, Administrators, and Graduate Students*. Washington, D.C.: Association of American Colleges, 1986.

Schmidt, Michael. "U.S. to Release 6,000 Inmates from Prisons." *New York Times*, October 6, 2015. Accessed February 28, 2016. http://www.nytimes.com.

Seligman, Martin. *Helplessness: On Depression, Development, and Death*. San Francisco: W. H. Freeman, 1975.

Stake, Robert. "Qualitative Case Studies." In *The Sage Handbook of Qualitative Research*, edited by Norman Denzin and Yvonna Lincoln, 433–66. Thousand Oaks, CA: Sage, 2005.

Staples, Robert. "Masculinity and Race: The Dual Dilemma of Black Men." *Journal of Social Issues* 34, no. 1 (1978): 169–83.

West, Candace, and Sarah Fenstermaker. "Doing Difference." *Gender & Society* 9, no. 1 (1995): 8–37.

West, Candace, and Don Zimmerman. "Doing Gender." *Gender & Society* 1, no. 2 (1987): 125–51.

Western, Bruce. *Punishment and Inequality in America*. New York: Russell Sage Foundation, 2006.

Wetherell, Candace, and Nigel Edley. "Gender Practices: Steps in the Analysis of Men and Masculinities." In *Standpoints and Differences: Essays in the Practice of Feminist Psychology*, edited by Karen Henwood, Christine Griffin, and Ann Phoenix, 156–73. London: Sage, 1999.

Wheeler, Stanton. "Socialization in Correctional Communities." *American Sociological Review* 26 (1961): 697–712.

Wilson, William. *The Truly Disadvantaged*. Chicago: University of Chicago Press, 1987.

Zimmer, Lynn. "How Women Reshape the Prison Guard Role." *Gender & Society* 1, no. 4 (1987): 415–31.

14. Volunteering behind Bars: Negotiating Roles, Resources, and Relationships

Pauline Matthey

Prisons are meant not only to keep inmates away from the rest of the world but also to keep the rest of the world away from inmates. That is a common view of prison as described by several of the incarcerated men I have had the opportunity to work with, including Eddie, a gentleman in his sixties whom I met at the prison where I currently volunteer. He has been incarcerated for over forty years, sixteen of which were spent in solitary confinement, and he has not received a visit in over six years. Eddie's lack of visitors is not unusual. Duwe and Johnson reported that between 39 and 58 percent of inmates do not receive any visits, and only 2.5 percent had received a visit from a community volunteer, which also demonstrates the rarity of volunteers behind bars.[1]

As a communication studies scholar who is passionate about intercultural and interpersonal communication, I have found my time as a volunteer in prison to be invaluably enriching. Learning about prisoners' speech patterns and vocabulary, as well as their cultural norms and relationship management, has been a fascinating side effect of the volunteer work itself. This chapter centers on volunteer work in prison, comparing the volunteer experience to the socialization process in a new environment. It focuses on my journey as a volunteer educator making my way behind bars, first by looking at the prison experience itself, then by focusing on the three phases of the socialization process, before commenting on the influence of media and its implications.

My Prison Volunteer Experience

Community volunteers inside prisons play a crucial role in bridging the barrier created by prison walls. Duwe and Johnson researched the impact of visits on the recidivism rate,[2] and they found, like many others,[3] that programs do assist in rehabilitating prisoners and in reducing recidivism rates. In a study of the Penitentiary of New Mexico by Colvin, people in prison who had access to "social support activities related to education and other rehabilitation programs"[4] expressed experiencing a sense of hope and a positive change within the prison, "which led to the most significant reductions in levels of violence and escapes in the prison's history."[5] Not only do visits from the community have an impact on the recidivism rate; they are also found to reduce the level of hostility within the prison, as they lowered disciplinary infractions in a Florida facility, for instance.[6] Many of the volunteer programs in correctional facilities are faith based and attract more prisoner participation than other types of opportunities.[7] For example, in Florida, 42 percent of the incarcerated population participates in at least one chaplaincy program.[8]

I became a prison volunteer in 2010, while I was in graduate school, because of how our society uses prison as a source of entertainment yet refuses to look critically at the prison system to reevaluate it. It is as though we consume a somehow romanticized version of life in prison while we refuse to see these people as people. Intrigued by our society's fascination with prison life through various media, despite how ineffective the system seemed to be, I was determined to focus my graduate research on prison life to better understand the correctional institution. In addition to needing institutional review board approval for my research, I also needed to be cleared by the facility where I was going to conduct interviews, and that meant becoming a volunteer. That process involved submitting proposals for the research, and later for the programs, that I wanted to conduct, for which I had to detail my research purpose, anticipated benefits for the facility, logistics, required materials, and the anticipated length and number of visits. Once the proposal was approved, I had to undergo a training session, which outlined the dress code and other rules of the maximum-security men's facility where I was about to start my prison volunteer journey. I learned what bathroom I could use and whether or not I needed to be escorted or could get the keys from an officer, when I could or could not shake hands with the prisoners I would work with, and what equipment I was allowed to bring. There were many rules, but what I learned very quickly is that prison is full of inconsistencies: everything requires a long time to get set up and yet things change in an instant; the rules enforced by some officers are not enforced by others.

My first semester as a volunteer was spent focusing on my thesis research. At the start of my second semester as a volunteer, I began meeting with three incarcerated men to develop my own curriculum: a class on communication theories focused on dialogues about social justice, intercultural awareness, identity issues, and more. We called the class "Talk Back." The name came from the experience of the three men helping me develop the course. They explained that this class was opening up a space for incarcerated people to reclaim their own thinking, and because it was about communication, they decided to call it Talk Back. Since the creation of the class, parts of the class materials have subsequently been taught by the incarcerated men on the curriculum development team, and I am currently teaching the class at another facility.

So far, I have volunteered at two different institutions, one in the Midwest and one in the South. Both times, the process of becoming a volunteer was similar, and yet the experiences were very different. After graduate school, once I had settled into my new job and environment, I was ready to start volunteering in prison again. I wanted to create a theatre group similar to the one for which I had provided assistance while in graduate school, and I also wanted to carry on with my newly developed curriculum. Unfortunately, it was extremely difficult to reach anyone about getting involved. In the South, my emails and phone messages seemed never to reach the people in charge of programming. When they did, I would initially be told that they did not need anyone at the moment. Disappointed but not defeated, I waited and tried again for nearly a year until I was able to reach a facility. I finally connected with the chaplain in charge of volunteer programming at a prison that housed violent offenders with long sentences. Seeming to be cautiously enthusiastic, the chaplain asked me to email him a brief description of what I would like to do at the prison. After he looked at both of my programming ideas, the one for a theatre group and the one for Talk Back, he gave his approval for me to get started.

The chaplain approved my programs, and I went through an orientation phase, a less formal one than what I had experienced before, with no structured and rigorous training. Instead I met with the chaplain, who casually discussed some safety concerns with me. Most of the discussion focused on his worries about my presence as a young woman in a facility housing about one thousand male "offenders," as the chaplain referred to the people at the facility. That conversation was an uncomfortable one as I felt singled out for my gender and age, but I stayed motivated by the prospect of the work I would be able to do. Once my background check was cleared, I became an official volunteer. Unlike what I had previously grown accustomed to in the Midwest, where I had to request meeting times weekly, I now have an assigned weekly time slot for which I am expected to report.

My experiences with the incarcerated population in the South, thus far, look very similar to the ones I had before in the Midwest. My students are eager to learn and always extremely grateful for my time, thanking me after each visit and reinforcing how much they appreciate the opportunity to engage. Negotiating my relations with the staff, the administration, and the prisoners is a work in constant progress, but it is a rewarding experience through which I try to bridge the community and the prison world. With the theatre group, the plan is to record our upcoming performance and have a showing at my campus. The writers in the theatre group are free to explore any topic they choose, but almost exclusively they choose to write about their prison-related experiences. Similarly, the students in Talk Back are working on projects that will be displayed on the university campus where I work.

Willis defines culture as "the very material of our daily lives, the bricks and mortar of our most commonplace of understandings."[9] As such, the definition can be interpreted as positive in that it provides a solid foundation, but it is also a constraining one, as it allows for little to no fluidity.[10] From my conversations with two administrations, I have come to see prison volunteers acting as a link between prisoners and the outside world.

Prison administrations hold a lot of power, not only in deciding what programs are offered, but in shaping how volunteers run their curricula. The developing and teaching of programs is telling of the expectations that society and the incarcerated population have of each other. The next section explores the roles that facilities, prisoners, and volunteers play in achieving one another's goals, providing insight into the discrepancy between prison representations and prison experiences.

Socialization Phases and Their Impact on the Volunteering Process

In the field of communication studies, the process of becoming familiar with a new workplace is called the socialization process,[11] and it is divided into three phases: the anticipatory stage, the encounter stage, and the metamorphosis stage.[12] The socialization process helps to explain how newcomers start making sense of their environment and determine and define their role in that new environment. Using the socialization process as a framework for discussing the dialectical tensions experienced by volunteer educators, this chapter applies these stages to the learning of the new culture, the prison culture, with which I became acquainted.

Stage One—Anticipatory Phase

The anticipatory phase consists of the knowledge one acquires about a workplace environment prior to entering it and becoming a member of that culture. Before going behind bars for the first time, the volunteer will already have been exposed, directly or indirectly, to much information about the environment.

The information gathered during the anticipatory phase is what might drive someone to volunteer her time in prison. It can sprout from a wide range of personal or professional experiences, social activism responsibilities, or moral calls, but most times, prison educators just fall into those roles "casually" rather than as a premeditated choice.[13] The members of Prison Communication, Activism, Research, and Education (PCARE), a scholarly group affiliated with the National Communication Association, explain the need for communication and cultural scholars to focus their research on the prison-industrial complex. PCARE is "calling upon [its] colleagues to help change the world."[14] The recidivism rate in the United States is extremely high, at 76.6 percent in the first five years after release,[15] suggesting a clear need for change and a shift from a punitive system to one that focuses primarily on rehabilitation, where volunteer programs can help.

Because of the misrepresentations of prison in the media, the anticipatory stage is actually rather misinformed. The media tend to depict prisoners as violent and unworthy of dignity. My decision to start doing work in prison was sparked by my reluctance to accept what the American media were showing me of America's prisoners as accurate and by my desire to make a positive impact on a system that seemed broken. Growing up in Switzerland, where prisons are rarely a part of pop culture, I found myself fascinated by the amount of prison depictions I was seeing in the media, real or fictional, when I first arrived in the United States. I found the system to be barbaric and inefficient and felt compelled to respond to PCARE's call.

Because of the amount of exposure through the media during the anticipatory phase, as a society we believe we know much about prisons, but in fact "most people know little about life in prison."[16] Programs and education in prison are necessary to rehabilitate prisoners and prepare them for life after prison. Education in prison has been proven to reduce the recidivism rate. The odds of recidivism are 43 percent lower with education, and the odds of finding employment after release are 13 percent higher with education.[17] For these reasons, education is crucial to rehabilitation.[18] Volunteers can provide many of the rehabilitative services and necessary skills for prisoners' reentry into society at no cost to the correctional facilities: "volunteers provide a positive role model for inmates, for whom a positive influence often has not been present, bring to the facility a variety of skills, and can assist the offenders in making positive changes."[19] Furthermore, I believe in education as a fundamental human right and in learning for learning's sake. So while a lower recidivism rate is a common way for society to measure success, I also believe volunteer educators have a unique opportunity to contribute to individuals' growth and development for the betterment of the self.

Stage Two—Encounter Phase

The encounter phase of the socialization process takes place when a new member enters the organization.[20] The "point of entry" is pivotal in the socialization process. During this phase the new member "relies on predispositions, past experiences, and the interpretations of others" to start making sense of the new space.[21] For a volunteer entering a prison setting, the encounter phase is when it quickly becomes clear that life behind bars is much different from the hostile and volatile world we see on screens.

The first time I went into a prison, I felt prepared in that I had been researching the topic of prison life in some of my classes and one of my mentors had told me all about her experience. Still, going into the facility felt surreal—exhilarating and full of unknowns. I was physically guided by the series of locked doors and checkpoints, waiting for further instructions or the buzz of an opened door. Going through airport security is the closest experience I could relate it to, but yet it is so far from the prison experience. The most vivid memory I have of that day is the sound of the doors when they opened and then closed behind me. It made me feel so alert. Sometimes I could not see the officers operating the locks behind one-way mirrors, keeping me guessing how long I would have to wait in the small space between doors. I then remember feeling intimidated when I met the men who had signed up to participate in the programs. Not so much because I was afraid but mostly because I was completely unsure of how I, a young white woman from Switzerland not quite in her midtwenties at the time, was going to be able to connect with them so that we could work together. There is also a sense of irony in that situation, in regard to power. As volunteers, we are given the authority to run a program, and just like a teacher in a traditional classroom, we are the ones in charge of the incarcerated participants. That authority seemed completely delusional considering that I was the outsider coming into these men's world, a world I knew virtually nothing about.

Early in the encounter phase, one of the ways we connect with one another is by addressing one another as people. Before I met my students in prison, I was given a list at orientation of who would be attending my programs. The list included the incarcerated students' recorded names and their inmate numbers. I was made aware by the chaplain, who knew the men well, that some of them go by a different name, but I was instructed not to call them by their preferred name and to use their given first or last name instead. The prison administration justifies this rule by suggesting that it shows them more respect than if I were to "reduce" them to a "nickname." However, for transgender individuals or anyone else who identifies strongly with a preferred name that is different from their given name, calling them by their given name is another way to assert control and strip them of any choice, even that of their identity.

Connecting with students is invaluable, but early in the encounter phase, creativity is necessary to establish that connection since the administration prevents any sharing of personal information or fraternizing with the prisoners. Going through the encounter phase, I had to negotiate how to relate with my incarcerated students without breaking any rules. As a volunteer in the Midwest, for example, I was not allowed to let the men touch, in the literal sense, my belongings, including my pencils, for example. In the South, I have to keep a certain physical distance between my seat and the man sitting next to me. I am not allowed to be in contact with my incarcerated students outside our program meetings. I am instructed never to reveal any personal information about my life.

Additionally, connections can be hindered by some of the perceptions our society has pushed on us. Many view prisons as "human dustbins,"[22] which strip prisoners of any dignity or humanity. Yates and Frolander-Ulf state that "most incarcerated persons in the United States are poor [and that] their poverty [is] often compounded by racial and ethnic discrimination."[23] Those ideas, combined, are not innocent. Our system of oppression targets minority groups, and prisons are just one other way for our society to keep power in the hands of those already in power. During the encounter phase, it is my responsibility to work against the challenges that come from these views in order to create a connection with my incarcerated students.

The administrative rules are in place for safety purposes but can feel very limiting at times. In a traditional classroom on a college campus, I introduce myself on the first day, sharing pictures, professional and personal interests, goals, and previous experiences. I tell my students about where I am from and how I spend my leisure time, before I listen to them share about who they are. At both of the penal facilities where I have volunteered, I struggled early on to find ways to re-create a sense of comfort and familiarity in the prison classroom. Altman and Taylor's social penetration theory teaches us that for relationships and trust between people to develop healthily, all parties should disclose information about themselves at a similar pace and with similar depth.[24] Such reciprocity seems unattainable in prison.

Another step in the encounter stage when I had started to volunteer in the Midwest was the orientation session, during which an administrative assistant, who was guiding us new volunteers through our training, insisted on describing the men as potentially violent and always manipulative. More recently, in my orientation at the southern facility, the chaplain in charge of the volunteers shared some of his concerns with me about one of my programs. He was not sure he could find another ten men in the facility "who would be intelligent enough" to attend the next round. He characterized the men's intellect as the equivalent of a seventh grader's. However, in my experience, the men are eager to learn and thirsty for an educational challenge. I have also never been manipulated into any unruly or unethical behavior by any of my incarcerated students.

The men I work with are intelligent, engaged, and also desperately craving any form of connection with the world outside the prison walls. Many prisoners recognize the value of education and welcome opportunities to become involved, because as Frolander-Ulf and Yates state, it helps not only with the long-term rehabilitative goal but is also beneficial in making the everyday lives of the inmates more tolerable.[25]

Volunteers bring something that is otherwise absent from the prison environment, a way to challenge the power inequalities by giving the incarcerated students a voice. Kramarae's muted group theory explains that "people belonging to low-power groups must change their language when communicating publicly, thus, their ideas are often overlooked."[26] Even as early as the encounter phase, working as a volunteer in educational programs in prisons is a way I have brought some agency to a group of people who are isolated and rendered less powerful by a system of continued oppressions. In Talk Back the men explore issues related to social justice or identity and engage in a high level of critical thinking and writing.

Volunteers need the prison administration to support their goals, but paradoxically, the prison administration is also one of the main elements perpetuating a high level of oppression and control over the incarcerated population indirectly through its volunteers. The encounter stage is one of negotiation, during which volunteers need to highlight for the administration the benefits of allowing programs into the facility. It is about positioning oneself as instrumental in showcasing the facility in a positive light for the community and bringing encouraging publicity about the work being done. This negotiation feels like a true embodiment of Burke's dramatistic understanding of communication.[27] Life is a stage, and the speaker must identify with the audience.[28] In other words, the volunteer needs to play into the oppressive system in order to reach the incarcerated students and empower them against that same system of oppression, thereby creating much cognitive dissonance in the process.

Reciprocity in the Encounter Phase, or Lack Thereof

Unlike television would have us believe, prisoners are very apprehensive at the prospect of meeting someone from the outside. The encounter phase is not only experienced by the volunteer but by all parties who start sharing a cultural space. One of my incarcerated students disclosed to me that he had not had any interaction with someone from the outside in over ten years. He said he was very scared to meet me because he did not feel worthy of the opportunity, nor did he feel prepared and was worried I would judge him for being so unequipped to have a conversation with someone from the outside.

Bell hooks believes that, as educators, "our work is not merely to share information but to share in the intellectual and spiritual growth of our students. To teach in a manner that respects and cares for the souls of our students is essential if we are to provide the necessary conditions where learning can most deeply and intimately begin."[29] In the search for this genuine and honest process, much cognitive dissonance is experienced. The prison volunteer experiences a position of power over the incarcerated students,[30] based on the level of access to information, for example.

This imbalance of information was obvious and palpable during the first encounter. By the time I met my incarcerated students for the first time, I had already collected much information about them, voluntarily or not. The prison chaplain in charge of all programming at the facility had shared a lot with me about the men's accomplishments and behaviors. Furthermore, prior to meeting them, I had deliberately chosen to look up online the crimes they had been convicted of, whereas my incarcerated students had only been informed of my name and job title. Some did not even know what my class was about.

Stage Three—Metamorphosis Phase

Something beautiful and invigorating happens in the metamorphosis phase. This stage of the socialization process takes place when an employee embraces the workplace culture. The once newcomer finds her role in the organization and understands, embraces, and embodies the values of the culture.[31] There is a sense of belonging and a sense of comfort that develops at this stage. Because most of the negotiating has been done already, the volunteer is now able to focus on the goals rather than on making sense of the environment. For example, I am receiving a tremendous amount of support from key members of the institution in the South who genuinely believe in my work. Not only is it encouraging, but it also allows me to feel at ease with the process, giving me more time to focus on the class rather than on the creation of a routine.

The support I receive is allowing me to focus on the "important stories" of the people behind bars.[32] It is creating a new level of understanding, perspective, growth, and respect. It is a mutual process during which individuals who are incarcerated can feel humanized and valued in a way they may have never experienced before. Programs in prison are a platform for opportunities to learn from one another. According to a radio show host on NPR, there is so much "we can learn when we listen to people and to places that are almost never heard, listening as an act of generosity and also a path to discovery."[33]

The metamorphosis phase is my favorite because the level of uncertainty is as its lowest. A routine has formed, and it feels comfortable to know what to expect. But mostly it is the most exciting part of the experience because it is when I get to engage with my incarcerated students in the most meaningful ways. By the metamorphosis phase, we have established a level of trust that allows for sharing of experiences such as their relationships with families on the outside or some of their struggles while on the inside.

However, as those relationships with the incarcerated men develop, my sense of alertness heightens. I am always very aware of and sensitive to the way my interactions with them would look to an officer walking by, for example. It is a strange state to be in because, on one hand, I feel a high level of connection to the men with whom I work and yet, on the other hand, I have to be hypervigilant of what I say or do; were my behavior to be interpreted as too friendly, an officer could remove a prisoner from the group and punish him with a write-up or even ask me not to come back. It does not take much for officers to interpret respect as fraternization, so physical space and body movements are always in the back of my mind when I am with my incarcerated students, as I do not wish to jeopardize the opportunities that we have been able to build.

Additionally, during the metamorphosis phase, it is as if the volunteer were a dog who forgets for a moment that she is on a leash. At any point, the administration can pull on that metaphorical leash to remind the volunteer of who is in control, as had happened when the administration decided to cancel a play we had been working on in the institution in the Midwest. As an educator, Scott states that because of the power dynamics, all educators must "choose a side."[34] If a volunteer chooses to become an advocate for her incarcerated students, she will find herself in a dialectically tense relationship with the prison administration.

For example, during the time I visited the midwestern facility, the men in the theatre group led by my mentor wrote two original plays. The administration loved the first one but called a halt to the second one after the first performance, arguing that the play was too fun and its use of humor was inappropriate. Prison, they said, was no laughing matter. The script had been turned in to the administration prior to the performance, and no concern about the tone of the play had been raised. As an assistant for my mentor's theatre group, I wanted to step in and talk to the administration about how the play was an artful form of expression and to explain that in no way was the humor of the play trying to diminish the hardship of the environment, but there was no space for dialogue.

This one incident exemplifies how metamorphosis is not a static stage and how it still requires some negotiating. Because of the instability of the prison environment itself, some level of uncertainty is always present, and therefore the socialization process only partially explains the experience.[35] No matter the level of metamorphosis, I argue that the third level of Schein's model of culture[36] can never fully mesh for all parties sharing the prison environment. Schein's model of organizational culture offers three distinct levels: artifacts, espoused values, and basic assumptions.[37] Levels one and two are attainable, as some of the artifacts are rather easy to observe in the form of office décor and espoused values become clear early on from conversations and other ambient messages. Yet it seems virtually impossible for all individuals in a prison context to hold a shared core of beliefs, or as Schein calls them, basic assumptions about the world and how it works. The role of the volunteer and the goal of the volunteer's work are therefore perceived from greatly divergent points of view by the incarcerated individuals, the administration, and the volunteer.

Beware of the TRAP

As noted above, the administration exerts more or less power over the volunteers at different times. When everything has been running smoothly for
a little while, I tend to anticipate some resistance from the administration
at some point in the near future. For example, I had been volunteering
weekly for almost a year when an officer at the main gate would not let
me in anymore because of my facial piercing. He told me it was against
the rules despite the fact that I had been allowed into the facility without
any issue prior to that day. In the Midwest, the metaphorical leash had also
regularly manifested itself in the form of class meetings being cut short with
no explanation.

The frustration experienced during those times can be explained by
making an addendum to the metamorphosis phase. Instead of viewing
metamorphosis as a static level at which we stay once it has been reached, it
can be better understood as a space within which we experience a variety of
connectivity to the culture with which we have become familiar.[38] Inmates
and volunteers alike can experience disconnect at times. I have described
that space within metamorphosis as the TRAP, a temporary relapse alluding
to the past.[39] For long-term prisoners, that experience might drive them to
revert to "convict" behaviors (running an underground prison store, using
or selling drugs, acquiring a cell phone, etc.) they had left behind once they
started focusing on their education, if they start feeling that all of their efforts
are not paying off. Falling into the TRAP is usually only temporary, but
having this addendum highlights the nonlinear socialization and complex
challenges that continue to occur even after having established a high level
of understanding and appreciation for the culture.

The TRAP acts as a revolving door and helps to account for the fluctua-
tion and sometime inconsistency in prisoners' behavior. Wellford defines the
inmate code as "a series of conduct norms that define the proper behavior
for inmates" as perceived by other inmates.[40] Further, Wellford explains that
the inmate code normalizes and encourages behaviors that are contrary to
the ones deemed acceptable by the administration. As such, the more one
identifies with the inmate code, the more one's behaviors run counter to
societal expectations for a successful reentry.

From interviews and observations, it becomes clear that through direct,
indirect, and ambient messages, incarcerated people pick up on what the
expectations are for their behaviors around others.[41] Once prisoners reach

metamorphosis, they tend to let go of some of the criminal lifestyle they may have led when they first entered the facility. That can include focusing on release rather than on performing the act of a tough guy on the yard. But after some time of modeling good behaviors, incarcerated individuals start losing trust that it is worth it, since they do not see immediate rewards for their positive behaviors. Even though they are following the rules, they are likely still not to be much closer to being released. One incarcerated student told me that "at least, when [he] was running a[n unruly] prison store, [he] had money to buy commissary." Those thoughts become the justification for falling into the TRAP and regressing back to behaviors that align with prisonization more so than with rehabilitation. The TRAP is mostly temporary because the incarcerated men find focus again and recognize that the good behaviors are not just a means to an end but a lifestyle to make the most of their time in prison in preparation for the future.[42]

Not unlike the prisoners, the volunteer can also succumb to the TRAP. Bell hooks explains that many educators are "committed to freedom and justice for all" and that is a noble yet extremely ambitious goal.[43] I often reflect on my work in prison and periodically feel inadequate in pursuit of the goal set out by bell hooks, going so far as to wonder whether I "help create an un-free world" by perpetuating oppressive systems rather than make a positive dent in this ineffective prison-industrial complex.[44] When I feel too restricted and limited by the administration, I sometimes question my drive to continue volunteering at the facility until I can refocus on the reasons I value this kind of volunteer work, my love and appreciation for education.

The administration is not the only cause for my doubts when I am in the TRAP. Sometimes, outside factors are the source for falling into the TRAP. My commitment is tested regularly by the administration every time it reestablishes its power through the metaphorical leash as explained earlier, by a society that often asks me to justify my choice to volunteer behind bars, by the media spreading inaccurate representations of the relationships between inmates and volunteers or staff members, and by the few incarcerated individuals who do seek time cuts to their sentence through the educational process. Fortunately, organizations such as the National Conference on Higher Education in Prison, where faculty, students, professionals, volunteers, program coordinators, and currently and formerly incarcerated people share a space for conversations and ideas, provide the validation necessary to lead me out of the TRAP and put me back on track.

What about Individualization?

My main issue with the current setup is that it feels like a one-sided relationship. The volunteer and the incarcerated students have to learn, adapt, embrace, and perpetuate the current culture while the prison administration remains in total control of the culture itself. The lack of reciprocity in this process is one that I find suffocating at times. Miller explains that the socialization process is where the employee finds a way to "fit" into the organizational culture.[45] But *individualization* happens when the organization adapts to the changes brought by the employee.[46]

As a community volunteer, I wish that I could have a greater impact on shaping the prison culture I visit. But the socialization process feels more like assimilation to a culture than a relational process. Certainly, the prison does adapt to the volunteer to some extent, but the dynamic follows a very linear model in which the feedback loop is not a priority. After the initial negotiation of the relationship, the volunteer has very little flexibility to individualize the prison system. As a result, the exchange is limited, and the impact one can have on the prison and all the people who work and/or live in it is controlled and calculated, with serious constraints and limitations, but it is nonetheless important to expand the boundaries slowly and move the linear model of socialization toward a transactional one.

The Implications of Media's Depiction of Prison

The media like to show and exaggerate a facet of prison life with which I cannot identify with firsthand. In the *Orange Is the New Black* episode "We Have Manners. We're Polite," the fictional correctional officer and counselor Sam Healy organizes a support group called Safe Place for the women at the institution where he works.[47] In an earlier episode, "Little Mustachioed Shit," Doggett, one of the incarcerated women, is seen warning Healy that the rest of the women would not attend: "but you know that ain't nobody gonna do nothing without getting something from it . . . like free donuts, days off work . . . I'm telling you, no one is gonna come on their own."[48] Contrary to what the media depict, incarcerated students are thirsty for knowledge and education[49] and are genuinely interested in the intellectual interaction and stimulation that programs and classes offer; this makes the educational process often more engaging than it is in a regular classroom, where students can sometimes act entitled and not recognize the true opportunity, which is to work on their education. Every Wednesday morning, as class starts, my incarcerated students tell me about their experiences and how they were able to relate to the readings for that day. They are inquisitive during class time and always eager to discuss the material for the week. They show a high level of critical thinking and are not afraid to speak up when they are challenged by the work we do in class. They want to learn for the sake of learning, as opposed to taking classes for the sake of obtaining a degree. Before I leave, every week without fail, they thank me for my time and reiterate how grateful they are for this learning opportunity.

As discussed in the chapters throughout this book, the demand for prison stories is high, and Hollywood and television studios continue to deliver on the promise to keep viewers entertained by depicting the lives of men and women behind bars. The media are exploiting the very real experiences of men and women in prison and feeding them to us. This creates the expectation that prisoners are enraged, caged animals with no fear of consequences, driven by a thirst for violence and a desire to break rules and manipulate others to get what they want, while recounting emotional life histories in an attempt to garner sympathy.[50]

Conrad corrects this misguided information on multiple occasions when he explains that "prisoners are relatively nonviolent, [and that] their rare violent outbursts occur primarily because the prison is an institution that teaches by example that coercion is required if compliance is to be gained."[51] Framing incarcerated people as violent beings serves a purpose of exploitation beyond scapegoating. When we strip prisoners of their human qualities, it makes treating them with little respect or dignity more acceptable, thus giving our society a way to justify its choices when it comes to punition over rehabilitation.

However, all of the somehow romanticized stories we are exposed to, and that we as a public consume for entertainment, are just a caricature of what prison is truly like, a dehumanizing institution meant to keep a portion of our citizens a voiceless, powerless, and forgotten people.[52] Gordon describes prisons as "repositories of society's poorest, most vilified outcasts, as repositories for men and women who live in settings that are notable for their exceptionally high levels of psychic pain, self-loathing, pent-up frustration, hate, gore, fear of rape, desire to rape, proximity to evil, proximity to grace, the ever-present threat of sudden violence, and—above all—despair."[53]

This chapter has explored the tense negotiation of relationships among incarcerated individuals, the prison system, and the volunteer at the different stages of the socialization process. The process is certainly not a linear one, but it is teaching an important lesson: media vastly deform and exaggerate the realities of men and women behind bars, creating false and romanticized expectations of what life in prison is and the illusion that the volunteer has full control over her curriculum. Regardless of what television tries to portray, ultimately the prison administration acts as a gatekeeper by determining what is allowed within the confines of the facility, and with all this power, it has the opportunity to create illusions of what can be accomplished. What is notable is that, in making those decisions, the prison administration mostly affects the lives and experiences of prisoners, keeping them under close scrutiny, with high levels of judgment and oppression. Until the prison-industrial complex recognizes the value of prisoners' interactions with the outside world, not only for their sake but also for our society as a whole, there will not be enough opportunities for growth. A reform of this broken system is needed in order for our society to stop pretending that a portion of its people do not exist while yet continuing to apply an unreasonable amount of pressure and expectations on the same group of people that we, as a society, continue to demean, deprive, and dehumanize.

Notes

1. Duwe and Johnson, "Effects of Prison Visits."

2. Ibid.

3. See Aos, Phipps, Barnoski, and Lieb, "Comparative Costs and Benefits of Programs to Reduce Crime"; Cullen, "Rehabilitation and Treatment Programs"; Gates, Flanagan, Motiuk, and Stewart, "Adult Correctional Treatment"; Lawrence, Mears, Dubin, and Travis, *Practice and Promise of Prison Programming*; MacKenzie and Hickman, *What Works in Corrections?*

4. Colvin, "Applying Differential Coercion and Social Support Theory," 369.

5. Duwe and Johnson, "Effects of Prison Visits," 2.

6. Siennick, Mears, and Bales, "Here and Gone."

7. Duwe and Johnson, "Effects of Prison Visits."

8. Campbell, "Impact of Charity & Volunteerism."

9. Willis, "Shop Floor Culture," 185.

10. Sloop, *Cultural Prison*.

11. Jablin and Krone, "Organizational Assimilation."

12. Miller, *Organizational Communication*.

13. See Geraci, *Teaching on the Inside*; Eggleston, "Correctional Education Professional Development"; Wright, "Going to Teach in Prisons."

14. PCARE, "Fighting the Prison–Industrial Complex," 403.

15. Bureau of Justice Statistics, "Recidivism."

16. Irwin, "'Inside' Story," 513.

17. Davis, Steele, and Bozick, *How Effective Is Correctional Education?*

18. Irwin, "'Inside' Story."

19. Campbell, "Impact of Charity & Volunteerism."

20. Jablin and Krone, "Organizational Assimilation."

21. Louis, "Surprise and Sense Making," quoted in Miller, *Organizational Communication*, 123.

22. Irwin, "'Inside' Story," 512.

23. Yates and Frolander-Ulf, "Teaching in Prison," 115.

24. Griffin, Ledbetter, and Sparks, *First Look at Communication Theory.*

25. Yates and Frolander-Ulf, "Teaching in Prison."

26. Kramarae, *Women and Men Speaking*, 19.

27. Griffin, Ledbetter, and Sparks, *First Look at Communication Theory.*

28. Burke, *Rhetoric of Motives.*

29. hooks, *Teaching to Transgress*, 13.

30. Scott, "Distinguishing Radical Teaching."

31. Miller, *Organizational Communication.*

32. National Public Radio, "Dave Isay."

33. Ibid.

34. Scott, "Distinguishing Radical Teaching," 5.

35. Jablin and Krone, "Organizational Assimilation."

36. Schein, *Organizational Culture and Leadership.*

37. Miller, *Organizational Communication.*

38. Matthey, "Inmate Code."

39. Ibid.

40. Wellford, "Factors Associated with Adoption of the Inmate Code," 2.

41. Matthey, "Inmate Code."

42. Ibid.

43. hooks, *Teaching to Transgress*, 27.

44. Ibid.

45. Miller, *Organizational Communication.*

46. Ibid.

47. Kohan, Kerman, and Heder, *Orange Is the New Black.* "We Have Manners. We're Polite."

48. Kohan, Kerman, Heder, Morelli, and Jones, *Orange Is the New Black.* "Little Mustachioed Shit."

49. Snyder, "Teachers Find Prisoners Their Most Eager Pupils!"

50. Irwin, "'Inside' Story," 513.

51. Conrad, "Prisons and Prison Reform," 115.

52. Scott, "Distinguishing Radical Teaching."

53. Gordon, "My Life as a Prison Teacher," para. 3; see also Gordon, *Funhouse Mirror*.

Bibliography

Aos, Steve, Polly Phipps, Robert Barnoski, and Roxanne Lieb. *The Comparative Costs and Benefits of Programs to Reduce Crime*. Olympia: Washington State Institute for Public Policy, 2001.

Bureau of Justice Statistics. "Recidivism." Accessed September 24, 2017. http://www.bjs.gov/index.cfm?ty=tp&tid=17.

Burke, Kenneth. *A Rhetoric of Motives*. Berkeley: University of California Press, 1969.

Campbell, Terry. "Impact of Charity & Volunteerism at Correctional Facilities." Corrections.com, December 15, 2014. Accessed September 24, 2017. http://www.corrections.com.

Colvin, Marc. "Applying Differential Coercion and Social Support Theory to Prison Organizations: The Case of the Penitentiary of New Mexico." *Prison Journal* 87, no. 3 (2007): 367–87. doi:10.1177/0032885507304774.

Conrad, John P. "Prisons and Prison Reform." *Current History* 53, no. 3 (1967): 88–93.

Cullen, Francis T. "Rehabilitation and Treatment Programs." In *Crime: Public Policies for Crime Control*, edited by James Q. Wilson and Joan Petersilia, 253–91. Oakland, CA: Institute for Contemporary Studies Press, 2002.

Davis, Lois M., Jennifer L. Steele, and Robert Bozick. *How Effective Is Correctional Education, and Where Do We Go from Here? The Results of a Comprehensive Evaluation*. Santa Monica, CA: RAND, 2014.

Duwe, Grant, and Byron R. Johnson. "The Effects of Prison Visits from Community Volunteers on Offender Recidivism." *Prison Journal* 96, no. 2 (2015): 279–303. doi:10.1177/0032885515618468.

Eggleston, Carolyn R. "Correctional Education Professional Development." *Journal of Correctional Education* 42, no. 1 (1991): 16–22.

Gates, Gerald G., Timothy J. Flanagan, Laurence L. Motiuk, and Lynn Stewart. "Adult Correctional Treatment." In *Prisons*, edited by Michael Tonry and Joan Petersilia, chap. 8. Chicago: University of Chicago Press, 1999.

Geraci, Pauline. *Teaching on the Inside: A Survival Handbook for the New Correctional Educator.* Scandia, MN: Greystone Educational Materials, 2002.

Gordon, Robert Ellis. *The Funhouse Mirror: Reflections on Prison.* Pullman: Washington State University Press, 2000.

———. "My Life as a Prison Teacher." *Christian Science Monitor,* March 12, 2001.

Griffin, Em, Andrew M. Ledbetter, and Glenn Sparks. *A First Look at Communication Theory.* 9th ed. New York: McGraw Hill Education, 2014.

hooks, bell. *Teaching to Transgress: Education as the Practice of Freedom.* New York: Routledge, 1994.

Irwin, Tracy. "The 'Inside' Story: Practitioner Perspectives on Teaching in Prison." *Howard Journal of Criminal Justice* 47, no. 5 (2008): 512–28. doi:10.1111/j.1468-2311.2008.00536.x.

Jablin, Frederic, and Kathleen J. Krone. "Organizational Assimilation." In *Handbook of Communication Science,* edited by Charles R. Berger and Steven H. Chaffee, 711–46. Newbury Park, CA: Sage, 1987.

Kohan, Jenji, Piper Kerman, and Sian Heder, writers. *Orange Is the New Black.* "We Have Manners. We're Polite." Season 2, episode 13. Directed by Constantine Makris. New York: Lionsgate, 2014. Netflix.

Kohan, Jenji, Piper Kerman, Sian Heder, Lauren Morelli, and Nick Jones, writers. *Orange Is the New Black.* "Little Mustachioed Shit." Season 2, episode 10. Directed by Jennifer Getzinger. New York: Lionsgate, 2014. Netflix.

Kramarae, Cheris. *Women and Men Speaking: Frameworks for Analysis.* Rowley, MA: Newbury House, 1980.

Lawrence, Sarah, Daniel P. Mears, Glenn Dubin, and Jeremy Travis. *The Practice and Promise of Prison Programming.* Washington, D.C.: Urban Institute, 2002.

Louis, Meryl Reis. "Surprise and Sense Making: What Newcomers Experience in Entering Unfamiliar Organizational Settings." *Administrative Science Quarterly* 25, no. 2 (1980): 226–51. doi:10.2307/2392453.

MacKenzie, Doris, and Laura Hickman. *What Works in Corrections? An Examination of the Effectiveness of the Type of Rehabilitation Programs Offered by Washington State Department of Corrections: Report to the State of Washington Legislature Joint Audit and Review Committee.* College Park: University of Maryland, 1998.

Matthey, Pauline. "The Inmate Code: The Stories Lived and the Stories Told of Men behind Bars." Master's thesis, Eastern Illinois University, 2013.

Miller, Katherine. *Organizational Communication: Approaches and Processes*. 6th ed. Boston: Wadsworth Cengage Learning, 2011.

National Public Radio. "Dave Isay: What Happens When People Are Given a Voice?" TED Radio Hour, June 5, 2015. Accessed September 24, 2017. http://www.npr.org/templates/transcript/transcript.php?storyId=411697565.

PCARE. "Fighting the Prison–Industrial Complex: A Call to Communication and Cultural Studies Scholars to Change the World." *Communication and Critical/Cultural Studies* 4, no. 4 (2007): 402–20. doi:10.1080/14791420701632956.

Schein, Edgar H. *Organizational Culture and Leadership*. 2nd ed. San Francisco: Jossey-Bass, 1992.

Scott, Robert. "Distinguishing Radical Teaching from Merely Having Intense Experiences While Teaching in Prison." *Radical Teacher*, no. 95 (2013): 22–32. doi:10.5406/radicalteacher.95.0022.

Siennick, Sonja E., Daniel P. Mears, and William D. Bales. "Here and Gone: Anticipation and Separation Effects of Prison Visits on Inmate Infractions." *Journal of Research in Crime and Delinquency* 50, no. 3 (2012): 417–44. doi:10.1177/0022427812449470.

Sloop, John M. *The Cultural Prison: Discourse, Prisoners, and Punishment*. Tuscaloosa: University of Alabama Press, 2006.

Snyder, Harry. "Teachers Find Prisoners Their Most Eager Pupils!" *Saturday Evening Post*, October 31, 1959, 10.

Wellford, Charles. "Factors Associated with Adoption of the Inmate Code: A Study of Normative Socialization." *Journal of Criminal Law, Criminology, and Police Science* 58, no. 2 (1967): 197–203. doi:10.2307/1140837.

Willis, Paul. "Shop Floor Culture, Masculinity and the Wage Form." In *Working Class Culture: Studies in History and Theory*, edited by John Clark, Chas Critcher, and Richard Johnson, 185–98. London: Hutchinson, 1979.

Wright, Randall. "Going to Teach in Prisons: Culture Shock." *Journal of Correctional Education* 56, no. 1 (2005): 19–38.

Yates, Michael D., and Monica Frolander-Ulf. "Teaching in Prison." *Monthly Review* 53, no. 3 (2005): 114–27. doi:10.14452/mr-053-03-2001-07_10.

Conclusions and Implications:
Through the Distorted Window;
Connecting Media to Experience

Katherine A. Foss

There's only three ways to spend the taxpayer's hard-earned when it come to prisons. More walls. More bars. More guards.
—Warden Samuel Norton, *The Shawshank Redemption*, 1994

The genius of the current caste system, and what most distinguishes it from its predecessors, is that it appears voluntary. People choose to commit crimes, and that's why they are locked up or locked out, we are told. This feature makes the politics of responsibility particularly tempting, as it appears the system can be avoided with good behavior. But herein lies the trap. All people make mistakes. All of us are sinners. All of us are criminals.
—Michelle Alexander, *The New Jim Crow: Mass Incarceration in the Age of Colorblindness*, 2010

This edited volume has attempted to bridge the vast disparity between public perceptions of incarceration and the contextualized realities of that experience, adding depth and understanding to who inmates are, what prison may be like, and why most media representations play on one-dimensional stereotypes of prisoners, guards, and the system, rather than address broader issues within the prison-industrial complex. As Prison Communication, Activism, Research, and Education (PCARE) stated in its call to action: to implement effective prison reform, we need to have media reform.[1] One means of achieving change is to have a more informed public that understands prison and the prison system beyond the stereotypes, tropes, and myths perpetuated by media.

Unifying Themes

This book centers on the notion that media paint a limited picture of prison, by blaming individuals for their crimes, emphasizing punishment over rehabilitation, and overall by misrepresenting the experience, while ignoring contextual factors that contribute to incarceration. We see many of the same one-dimensional characters and tropes consistently reappear. Bratten's analysis of women-in-prison films in chapter 1 presents archetypes that persist across medium and time—for example, reemerging in *Prison Break* and *Orange Is the New Black* (*OITNB*). Similarly, Whiteley explains how the "women who kill" that she interviewed felt reduced to their crimes, likely due to media's one-dimensional portrayals. Or consider the parallels that Plec articulates in her comparison of personal correspondence with a death row inmate to a similar story of another death row inmate recounted on documentary television.

Throughout the book, we also see how greater constructions of gender, identity, race, and class have shaped public perceptions of prisoners' and inmates' understanding of themselves and have contributed to the gross disparities in prison demographics. Schneeweis links the constructions of black masculinity in *Oz* to contemporary contexts in the #Black Lives Matter movement, and Patrick demonstrates the human cost of this construction, explaining how black masculinity has been defined by aggression and violence. Patrick's interviews with formerly incarcerated African American men support this connection between public perception and personal identity. Parallels also emerge in terms of understandings of femininity, motherhood, and sexuality. Challenges for fictional female characters (as seen in Bratten's presentation of different women-in-prison archetypes, Kern's description of *OITNB*'s characters and their mothers, and Foss's examination of pregnancy story lines) touch on the real-life implications for female inmates. Prison is clearly designed for men, meaning that women's specific needs are overlooked and ignored, as Cook discusses with respect to the lack of lactation support in prison. Furthermore, the prison system is profoundly categorical—prisoners are identified by race and binary sex, thereby amplifying racial segregation[2] and making life extremely difficult for inmates who are transgender, as explored by Jenness and Fenstermaker.

In some ways prison and its portrayals can offer opportunities for agency and/or challenges to hegemonic notions of race, gender, and class. As Kern articulates, *OITNB* has also offered points of resistance to a gendered hegemony by challenging the traditional "gaze" and presenting more in-depth looks at characters from underrepresented groups (particularly class and race). Jenkins and Wolfgang show how religion also functions as an outlet for the characters on that program. Additionally, reality TV can give voice to those usually left out of media representations, as Wallace demonstrates with *Prison Wives*. In real life, the production of media can give some agency to inmates privileged enough to work for a prison magazine, radio station, or television station, as exemplified by Churcher's interviews at the Louisiana State Penitentiary. And as Dye describes, prisoners may also find opportunities for agency in how they choose to spend their time—forming friendships, participating in religion, reading, or other activities. Moreover, with her volunteer experience, Matthey discusses inmates' participation in theatre groups and educational classes as a means of exercising individual choice. While some of these points may seem mundane or minor, they challenge the top-down, rigid prison portrayed in films like *The Shawshank Redemption* and the penitentiaries presented in *Prison Break*.

Differences between the Screen and Experience

Of course, gaps between representations and real life are also highlighted by the work in this book. In chapter 4, Foss notes that prison dramas significantly downplay health concerns by ignoring many of the chronic conditions that especially plague prison populations. In their ethnographic chapters, Plec and Dye refer to the prevalence of significant mental and physical issues in male prisoners on death row and in women serving life sentences. Similarly, health issues associated with pregnancy and childbirth are also minimized on television. Yet, as Cook outlines, given the number of female inmates who are pregnant and/or have small children, the prison system is woefully inadequate when it comes to serving the needs of this population. The daily lives of prisoners also vastly differ between media's depictions and the stories of real-life inmates. In the chapters concerned with media, the authors describe many fictional representations of exciting events—identifying the prison "rat," welcoming the "new fish," romance between inmates or between inmates and guards, horrifying sexual assault, religious "miracles" in the prison cafeteria, riots and violence, and, finally, escape! What is missing is how most real-life inmates spend most of their time: reading and consuming other media, writing letters, making friends, and just living. And, other than the aftermath of the escape on *Prison Break*, life after prison is also largely ignored, an experience that Patrick describes in this volume. Furthermore, the difficulty of accessing prison as a guest is also downplayed in media, as Matthey tells of her own challenges in entering and habituating to prison as a volunteer.

Why Is Prison Misrepresented in Media?

With the disconnect between prison and experience acknowledged, we need to explore why these inaccuracies exist. Several sites offer possible explanation. First, gatekeeping from prison administrators and within media organizations has, at least somewhat, hindered communication between media's producers and those working in prisons. As Sussman discussed,[3] some correctional facility administrators have been reluctant to let reporters in or to let issues behind the walls be covered in depth. Similarly, censored correspondence from within the prison may also discourage such stories. Additionally, the challenges of accessing prisons make ethnographic research on inmates and officers difficult, thus limiting the extent to which those outside the system get to learn about the experience inside.[4]

Since media organizations (at least within the United States) are capitalist opportunists, limited coverage also may be a result of gatekeeping within media production. Would advertisers be less inclined to sponsor programs that praise prison reform and rehabilitation? This question may seem outdated in contemporary times, in which decentralized media and infinite outlets have somewhat changed dependency on sponsors, yet it may explain the roots of prison archetypes and narrow subjects. Additionally, there may be misperceptions that the public is not interested in having stories set in penitentiaries portray rehabilitation or day-to-day life. And yet, the agenda-setting theory suggests that people will likely "care" or discuss such topics *when* media outlets cover the story.[5] For example, the overhyped news stories on child abductions in the 1980s that led to "stranger danger" programs ignored statistical evidence suggesting that abductions by strangers rarely occur.[6]

Of course, with fictional prison narratives, we must consider conventions of storytelling in film and television. Stereotypes and tropes that emerged in early film (as described by Bratten in chapter 1) likely reflect deeply rooted fears of criminals and incarceration. At the same time, these narratives perpetuate fear of criminals, stereotyping them as scary or dangerous.[7] Such messages reinforce harsh consequences for offenders that feature a punitive rather than a rehabilitative framework.[8] These misrepresentations unfortunately shape public perceptions of crime, criminals, the justice system, and prison and, with that, support (or lack thereof) for programs that could reduce crime or help to rehabilitate those who have been incarcerated.

The exaggeration presented in prison narratives is not unique to these popular culture products. Fiction itself is driven by drama, with heightened stakes driving the narratives. What else could explain the musical episode of the prison drama *Oz* or the underground panty operation that fictional Piper runs in *OITNB*? Other genres are similarly exaggerated. For example, most crime scene investigators wait weeks or months for samples to be processed, yet results appear in a jazzy montage on television, with each specimen collected directly contributing to the narrative. Likewise, scrubbing a burned skull of residual flesh only takes minutes for the forensic anthropologist in *Bones*. And we never see TV's beloved docs filling out paperwork—only performing risky life-saving surgery without concern for their own well-being. Therefore, it is not surprising that the constructed prison world is filled with riots, corruption, escape plans, forbidden sexual escapades, and other riveting moments. One could argue that few viewers would tune in to a *CSI* episode in which the investigator spends the hour swabbing a folding chair. Similarly, producers may wonder whether people would watch inmates read their favorite poetry or take a college correspondence course. The result then is the distorted window, with the omission of real-life experience.

Changing Cultural Constructions and Perceptions

Why do misrepresentations and forgotten voices matter? We should not simply write off the hypersexuality in *OITNB* or disparities between the constructed prison wife and real-life families' experiences with loved ones in prison. Nor should we overlook serious issues that inmates face, including lactation and motherhood or life after incarceration. Moreover, the public should know about positive outlets for prisoners doing their time, as demonstrated by the Louisiana inmates' experiences with media in the penitentiary.

Just as important as these missed and misrepresented experiences are the greater implications of the media discourse, particularly in regard to social inequities. Thus while *OITNB* has been praised for its diversity, it is perpetuating stereotypes about people of color as criminals at the same time. Other prison representations ignore racial issues altogether, presenting the whitewashed penal system evident in *Prison Break*. Little do we see media messages that address why certain groups are more at risk for committing crime or the disproportionately harsh sentencing of convicts of color. Such messages could help reduce discrimination against African Americans by police officers, for example. More coverage of successful rehabilitation programs, like educational courses taught in prisons, could reframe the function of prison in the public eye and, in turn, bolster support for policies and programs that reduce recidivism, as opposed to perceiving prison as the end of the line.

So how do we shift from stereotypes and misrepresentations to a more accurate public understanding of prisoners and the criminal justice system? How do we move beyond the penal spectator and turn prison voyeurism into something authentic and reflective of the actual experience? Ross problematized the issue of solely learning about incarceration as a spectator: "Prison voyeurism includes attempts to understand and/or experience corrections without intimately engaging in the subject matter. It is also characterized by superficiality in terms of economic, physical, mental, emotional, and psychological investment in the experience."[9]

Understanding that media distort experience is a first step, along with reading the narratives of the forgotten or overlooked. Ross proposed a ten-step typology of prison engagement to help one understand the spectrum between authenticity and voyeurism. On one end is living as an inmate within a correctional facility. The middle-engagement steps include working or volunteering in correctional facilities, visiting prisons, and learning about them in formal educational settings. On the low-engagement side of the spectrum are situations with less authenticity, like watching nonfiction films or TV programs, touring a prison museum, or staying in a hotel that was converted from a prison.[10] The more that the public can really experience prison, the more that those in power will be able to make policies that change why people go to prison, beyond dismissing individual inmates as "bad apples." As Kappeler, Blumberg, and Potter explained, "Criminals are an easy explanation for deeper social problems that we do not have the will to confront."[11] In other words, the prison-industrial complex is far more complex than the criminal scapegoat because it is shaped by fears of deviance and a lack of understanding about the racial, class, and gender inequities that contribute to this flawed system.

Concluding Thoughts

As stated in PCARE's call to action, media reform is necessary for penal reform.[12] Such measures would include loosening restrictions to media access

within prisons, as well as focusing scholarly attention on the prison-industrial complex itself.[13] The acknowledged inaccuracies of media's depictions
of prison have ramifications beyond those of other types of depictions. As
this conclusion's epigraph from Alexander suggests,[14] people do not become
criminals out of individual choice. Rather, crime and whom we incarcerate
are indications of much larger and more troubling facets of society: poverty,
lack of educational opportunities, access to illicit drugs at a young age, the
impact of having a parent incarcerated, and other factors that significantly
increase the likelihood of later criminal activity.[15] Stigmas about mental illness, which are heavily perpetuated in portrayals of prison, also continue to
put blame on individuals, while ignoring opportunities for societal support
of mental illness treatments and therapies.

Moreover, we have to look at disadvantages and maltreatment of certain
populations within the criminal justice system, by acknowledging that prejudices
regarding skin color, gender, ability or disability, and other factors absolutely
affect how police, attorneys, judges, and juries perceive offenders.[16] At the
macrolevel, policies and legislation regarding sentencing for drug crimes must
be considered, especially the consequences for first-time offenders (specifically
those with children). In other words, these issues are more intertwined with
inequality in society than simply attributing blame to individual bad apples.
Furthermore, we need media coverage and representation of positive actions
within and after prison, such as college correspondence courses in correctional
facilities and successful rehabilitation programs that could reduce recidivism.
The more that media scholars and producers are aware of racial and gender
hegemonies channeled through prison representations and news stories, the
more these texts can be changed so that disparity can be corrected and the
public can finally understand the complexities that pervade the criminal
justice system. While we can still enjoy watching the fictionalized world of
OITNB or singing along to "Folsom Prison Blues," we need more accurate
media discourse to balance such narratives.

Notes

1. PCARE, "Fighting the Prison–Industrial Complex."
2. Goodman, "It's Just Black, White, or Hispanic"; Sumner and Jenness, *Gender
Integration in Sex-Segregated U.S. Prisons.*
3. Sussman, "Media on Prisons."
4. Wacquant, "Curious Eclipse of Prison Ethnography."
5. McCombs and Shaw, "Agenda-Setting Function of Mass Media."

6. Kappeler, Potter, and Blumberg, *Mythology of Crime and Criminal Justice*.

7. Brown, *Culture of Punishment*; Kappeler, Potter, and Blumberg, *Mythology of Crime and Criminal Justice*.

8. Kappeler, Potter, and Blumberg, *Mythology of Crime and Criminal Justice*.

9. Ross, "Varieties of Prison Voyeurism," 400.

10. Ibid.

11. Kappeler, Potter, and Blumberg, *Mythology of Crime and Criminal Justice*, 357.

12. PCARE, "Fighting the Prison–Industrial Complex."

13. Ibid.

14. Alexander, *New Jim Crow*.

15. Sickmund and Puzzanchera, "Juvenile Offenders and Victims."

16. Brunson, "Police Don't Like Black People"; Rojek, Rosenfeld, and Decker, "Policing Race."

Bibliography

Alexander, Michelle. *The New Jim Crow: Mass Incarceration in the Age of Color-blindness*. New York: New Press, 2012.

Brown, Michelle. *The Culture of Punishment: Prison, Society, and Spectacle*. New York: New York University Press, 2009.

Brunson, Rod K. "'Police Don't Like Black People': African-American Young Men's Accumulated Police Experiences." *Criminology & Public Policy* 6, no. 1 (2007): 71–101. doi:10.1111/j.1745-9133.2007.00423.x.

Goodman, Philip. "'It's Just Black, White, or Hispanic': An Observational Study of Racializing Moves in California's Segregated Prison Reception Centers." *Law & Society Review* 42, no. 4 (2008): 735–70. doi:10.1111/j.1540-5893.2008.00357.x.

Kappeler, Victor E., Gary W. Potter, and Mark Blumberg. *The Mythology of Crime and Criminal Justice*. 4th ed. Prospect Heights, IL: Waveland, 2005.

McCombs, Maxwell E., and Donald L. Shaw. "The Agenda-Setting Function of Mass Media." *Public Opinion Quarterly* 36, no. 2 (1972): 176–87.

PCARE. "Fighting the Prison–Industrial Complex: A Call to Communication and Cultural Studies Scholars to Change the World." *Communication and Critical/Cultural Studies* 4, no. 4 (2007): 402–20. doi:10.1080/14791420701632956.

Ross, Jeffrey Ian. "Varieties of Prison Voyeurism: An Analytic/Interpretive Framework." *Prison Journal* 95, no. 3 (2015): 397–417. doi:10.1177/0032885515587473.

The Shawshank Redemption. Directed by Frank Darabont. Burbank, CA: Warner Brothers, 1994. Film.

Sickmund, Melissa, and Charles Puzzanchera. *Juvenile Offenders and Victims: 2014 National Report.* National Center for Juvenile Justice, December 2014. Accessed September 24, 2017. http://www.ojjdp.gov/ojstatbb/nr2014/downloads/NR2014.pdf.

Sumner, Jennifer, and Valerie Jenness. *Gender Integration in Sex-Segregated U.S. Prisons: The Paradox of Transgender Correctional Policy.* New York: Springer, 2014.

Sussman, Peter Y. "Media on Prisons: Censorships and Stereotypes." In *Invisible Punishment: The Collateral Consequences of Mass Imprisonment*, edited by Marc Mauer and Meda Chesney-Lind, 258–78. New York: New Press, 2002.

Wacquant, Loïc. "The Curious Eclipse of Prison Ethnography in the Age of Mass Incarceration." *Ethnography* 3, no. 4 (2002): 371–97. doi:10.1177/1466138102003004012.

Contributors

Index

Contributors

L. Clare Bratten is a professor emerita of electronic media communication. Her scholarly work centers on issues of gender and media forms such as the internet, television, radio, and film documentary. She also taught video and film production and produced and directed several documentary films.

Kalen Churcher is an assistant professor of communication studies at Wilkes University in Wilkes-Barre, Pennsylvania, where she teaches courses in multimedia journalism, media studies, and media law. Her research interests rest at the intersection of journalism and cultural studies, especially in how marginalized groups may use media for empowerment purposes.

Amanda Barnes Cook received her PhD in political science from the University of North Carolina at Chapel Hill in 2015. Her dissertation, "Breastfeeding, Feminism, and Political Theory," explores breastfeeding from the standpoint of a feminist political theorist, interrogating the optimal role of the state in accommodating, promoting, and supporting breastfeeding mothers. Her work has appeared in *Politics and Gender*.

Meredith Huey Dye is an associate professor of sociology at Middle Tennessee State University. Her research focuses on the effects of incarceration, prison suicide, and women in prison. Recent publications have appeared in *Women and Criminal Justice*, *Prison Journal*, *Criminal Justice and Behavior*, and *Deviant Behavior*.

Sarah Fenstermaker is a research professor emerita at the University of California, Santa Barbara, and the former director of the University of Michigan's Institute for Research on Women and Gender. Her research explores the creation of inequality through the accomplishment of race, class, gender, and sexuality. Her publications include *Doing Gender, Doing Difference* (with C. West), *The Gender Factory*, and *Sociologists Backstage* (with N. Jones). With feminist psychologist Abigail Stewart, she is editing a volume titled *Gender, Considered: Feminist Reflections across the Social Sciences*.

Katherine A. Foss is an associate professor in the School of Journalism at Middle Tennessee State University. She is the author of *Breastfeeding and Media: Exploring Conflicting Discourses That Threaten Public Health* and *Television and Health Responsibility in an Age of Individualism*. Her research explores media representations of underrepresented groups.

Joy Jenkins is a postdoctoral research fellow in digital news at the Reuters Institute for the Study of Journalism. Her research focuses on the sociology of news production and critical-cultural and feminist assessments of news content. She has studied the changing roles of editors in newsrooms, the role of local journalism in facilitating community engagement, and magazine journalism.

Valerie Jenness is a professor in the Department of Criminology, Law and Society and in the Department of Sociology at the University of California, Irvine. Her research focuses on the politics of crime control and transformations in corrections and public policy. She is the author of four books including, most recently, *Appealing to Justice: Prisoner Grievances, Rights, and Carceral Logic* (with Kitty Calavita, University of California Press, 2015) and many articles published in sociology, law, and criminology journals.

Rebecca Kern is an associate professor of communication, media studies, and advertising at Manhattan College. Her research interests focus on community and identity discourse and practice, gender studies, critical/cultural studies, and their intersections with television, new media, and advertising formats.

Pauline Matthey is a senior lecturer in the Department of Communication at Clemson University. She serves as a volunteer at a maximum-security men's prison where she teaches communication theories and leads a theatre group that writes and performs its own original work. Her community outreach is a continuation of the research she started as a graduate student at Eastern Illinois University.

Le'Brian A. Patrick is a member of the residential faculty in the Social Sciences Department at Glendale Community College in Glendale, Arizona. His research specializations center on the intersection of crime/deviance, gender, sexuality, and inequality.

Emily Plec is a professor of communication studies at Western Oregon University and a member/blogger of Prison Communication, Activism, Research, and Education. She serves on the advisory board of Oregonians for Alternatives to the Death Penalty and advocates for a national moratorium on executions.

Adina Schneeweis is an associate professor in the Department of Communication and Journalism at Oakland University. She specializes in international communication, with focus on Eastern Europe, ethnicity and race, gender, identity, advocacy, and institutional discourses. Her research examines the Gypsy/Roma communities in the press, within the advocacy movement for Roma rights, and in worldwide popular culture.

S. Lenise Wallace is an associate professor teaching communication courses at CUNY LaGuardia Community College in New York City. Her research interests include public relations and race, gender, and sexuality in mass media.

Kathryn M. Whiteley is a criminologist who teaches in Pennsylvania in the United States. Her primary interests include women who commit murder and women who sexually offend, and their personal experiences as incarcerated women.

J. David Wolfgang is an assistant professor of journalism and media communication at Colorado State University. His research focuses on participatory journalism, media sociology, and critical and cultural studies of media. In particular, he studies the relationship between journalists and online commenters in public discourse.

Index

PERSPECTIVES
ON CRIME AND JUSTICE

Open, inclusive, and broad in focus, the series covers scholarship on a wide range of crime and justice issues, including the exploration of understudied subjects relating to crime, its causes, and attendant social responses. Of particular interest are works that examine emerging topics or shed new light on more richly studied subjects. Volumes in the series explore emerging forms of deviance and crime, critical perspectives on crime and justice, international and transnational considerations of and responses to crime, innovative crime reduction strategies, and alternate forms of response by the community and justice system to disorder, delinquency, and criminality. Both single-authored studies and collections of original edited content are welcome.

Board of Advisers

Beth M. Huebner, University of Missouri–St. Louis
John P. Jarvis, Federal Bureau of Investigation
Natalie Kroovand Hipple, Indiana University
Justin W. Patchin, University of Wisconsin–Eau Claire
Sean P. Varano, Roger Williams University

QUERIES and SUBMISSIONS
Joseph A. Schafer, Series Editor
Department of Criminology and Criminal Justice
Southern Illinois University Carbondale
Carbondale, IL 62901-4504
jschafer@siu.edu
618-453-6376